THE TUDORS BUILT WITH TIMBER

The large forests which covered England in medieval and Tudor times provided a natural building material; that is why so many houses had timber frames, and this illustration shows how little filling in was needed after the timber work was complete.

The stoutest timbers of all were the principal posts (A) at the corners. Tie beams (B) formed the horizontal part of the framework. The beams which supported the upper floor could often be seen projecting with shaped ends, as at C.

The roof itself was a sturdy structure of sloping principal rafters (D) held by purlines (E) which were horizontal, and supported by struts as shown at F. There were also collar beams (G) to give added strength. When completed the roof was covered with tiles or roof plates (H).

The walls were filled with bricks (J) or wattle and daub.

This style of building varied from district to district, but the most decorative wooden types are found in the Midlands, Cheshire and south Lancashire.

The small inset drawing shows the ground plan of the house. The entrance (1) leads to the hall (2). On the left is the eating room (3) while on the right is the main parlour (4). At the rear is the kitchen and pantry (5). The stairs (6) lead to the upper rooms.

TODAY'S HOUSE IS BRIGHT AND OPEN

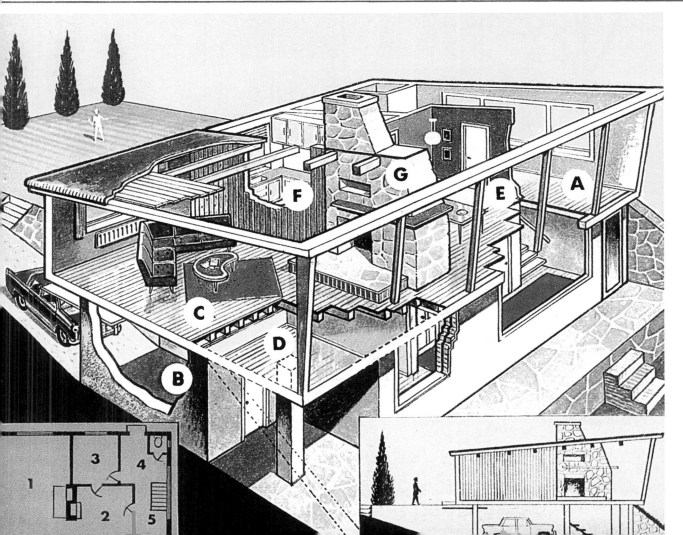

The contemporary house of our own times has no connection at all with what has gone before. Much of its exterior is glass, and warmth is no problem in winter because of central heating.

This one is built on a sloping site and at ground level we have the entrance hall (A) and garage (B).

At the upper level we have the living room (C), the dining room (E) and the kitchen (F). Even with central heating the occupants like to see an open fire, and this is achieved by a double fireplace (G) built of natural stone which serves both living room and dining room.

The bedrooms occupy most of the lower floor between the stairs and the wall marked D.

Wood is seen throughout the house in its natural state and is actually used as a dividing wall in the living room.

In the plan you can see the living room (1), dining room (2), kitchen (3) and upper hall (4), with stairs (5) leading down to the bedrooms and bathroom.

The other small sketch is a section through the house showing the different levels.

THE BUMPER BOOK OF

THE BUMPER BOOK OF

LOOK AND LEARN

Selected and edited by Stephen Pickles

C

CENTURY

Published by Century 2007

2 4 6 8 10 9 7 5 3 1

First published in Great Britain in 2007 by
Century
Random House, 20 Vauxhall Bridge Road,
London SW1V 2SA

www.randomhouse.co.uk

Addresses for companies within The Random House Group Limited can be found at:
www.randomhouse.co.uk/offices.htm

The Random House Group Limited Reg. No. 954009

A CIP catalogue record for this book
is available from the British Library

ISBN 9781846052910

The Random House Group Limited makes every effort to ensure that the papers
used in its books are made from trees that have been legally sourced from well-managed
and credibly certified forests. Our paper procurement policy can be found at:
www.randomhouse.co.uk/paper.htm

Origination by Thomson Digital, India
Printed and bound in China by C&C Offset Printing Co., Ltd

CONTENTS

Frontispiece: Robin Hood

EDITOR'S PREFACE

Look and Learn is fondly remembered by many of us as the source of countless now half-forgotten facts about our island nation and the world at large, about its landscape and its heroes, its history and its hopes for the future. The magazine ran weekly for twenty years from 1962, with a circulation in its early days measured in the hundreds of thousands. However, with the increasing pervasiveness of television, and the general emancipation of children from their more traditional stereotypes of Janet and John, the magazine's popularity waned through the 1970s. It closed in the spring of 1982, and so ended perhaps the most beautiful chapter in mass market children's publishing.

Now, after a quarter of a century, this famous title with its wondrous archive of pictures and words, has been rediscovered and re-imagined for the information age at www.lookandlearn.com. An incomparable picture library of children's illustrations is being constantly expanded, and a blog daily re-publishes articles written at a time when the Personal Computer could only be imagined. Not content with a new presence in cyberspace, *Look and Learn* is also currently publishing, by subscription for a run of 48 issues, a magazine made up of the best of the original.

The present *Bumper Book of Look and Learn* is an extensive tribute to the genius of the magazine's illustrators, and the tremendous range of subjects its editors chose to embrace. Whilst some artists are clearly identified in these pages, several are not, and readers should go to www.lookandlearn.com for a fuller account of the many contributors and their work.

I have looked at some 40,000 pages in order to select material for the present 256-page book, and with so vast an undertaking I determined to be guided by the quality of illustration as I fashioned the story I have chosen to tell. Many marvellous things were regrettably left out, such is an editor's burden; but, as I hope you will agree, much thrilling stuff has been included. I am particularly pleased to reprint one complete story from *The Rise and Fall of the Trigan Empire*, placing episodes at regular intervals throughout the book, by way of conjuring up one of the chief, even cult, pleasures in the original magazine.

So *The Bumper Book of Look and Learn* is neither an annual nor an art book: it is quite simply a colourful and occasionally eccentric narrative, pieced together from those 40,000 pages, and illustrated with some of the finest and loveliest illustrations in the entire field of children's literature. For very many, these pages will rekindle memories of that now distant realm of childhood, but I also believe that these pictures and words still have the magic and power to enchant and engage even the most sophisticated children of today.

Stephen Pickles
2007

Mammoths were not much larger than modern elephants but their tusks were much longer. Their bodies were also covered with long, thick hair.

Animals
Ice

THE Ice Age—the very phrase chills the blood and makes the average person draw his coat more closely around him.

Think for a moment—almost the whole of the northern hemisphere was covered with ice and even the ice at the Antarctic was thicker and more widespread than it is today. Surely no one and nothing could have lived under such conditions!

But, in fact, they could and they did. The animals on these pages lived during the Ice Age and primitive man was their contemporary.

What then, you may ask, were Ice Age animals like?

The answer is that they were nearly all much larger than their descendants of the present day and they were all incredibly strong.

The mammoth is perhaps the exception to one of these rules since it was not very much bigger than a modern elephant. The largest mammoth ever found stood about 13 ft. in height. The interesting thing about the mammoth, however, is that whole specimens have been found in north-eastern Siberia. It is thought that their weight made them sink into the cold mud and that subsequently they froze there.

They were covered all over with long hair and this, in turn, covered thick woolly underfur. Their tusks were extremely long and curled upwards and

Cave Bears were frequently hunted by primitive man. The flesh was good for eating and their fur made warm articles of clothing.

of the Age

outwards. Like modern elephants, they were vegetarians and apparently ate grasses, wild thyme, crowfoot and sedges.

The cave bear, however, in all probability was omniverous—that is to say, it ate vegetables but was also capable of killing and eating quite large animals.

The cave bear itself was a huge animal, being much bigger than even the largest modern bear.

It was undoubtedly hunted quite widely by early man and must have provided both food and clothing for our ancestors.

The Giant Elk or Irish Elk, however, an extinct deer found in Ireland, Great Britain and central and northern Europe, was probably hunted only rarely.

This magnificent creature stood about 6 ft. high at the shoulders and the antlers were of enormous size, those of a really fine specimen measuring in the region of 11 ft. between the tips.

To look at, these Ice Age animals were not really unlike their modern counterparts. They were certainly not monstrous. You might be startled to meet one when walking along a country lane but if you saw one safely behind bars in a zoo, the chances are that you would look, admire and move on.

After all, it is doubtful if any of these animals survived beyond the Ice Age— about a million years ago—so perhaps to them it seemed quite bearable. It was their world and they understood it.

The Giant Elk was a magnificent beast. The antlers of the male were enormous and extremely heavy.

A sabre-tooth tiger was a frightening animal to meet. Its upper teeth were enormous and capable of tearing off great lumps of its victim's flesh.

FIGHT TO SURVIVE

ALL the animals and birds on these pages were alive during the Pleistocene era—that is about the time when primitive man began to rule the Earth.

Man was certainly more intelligent than the other animals inhabiting this planet at the time, but he was very unlike modern man and had only the most simple weapons with which to combat the enemies that must have lurked everywhere. He had perpetually to be on the look-out. Food was scarce for all animals and, on occasion, must have been particularly scarce for man. But although he had to take care that he did not starve, he also had to take care that he did not himself provide a meal for one of the many predators with whom he had to share the earth.

Perhaps the most terrifying of these predators to modern eyes was the sabre-tooth tiger or *Machairodus*. This animal is usually regarded as having been a member of the cat family—*Felidae*—and apart from its lack of stripes certainly resembled the modern tiger in many ways. But the way in which it differed was really its most terrifying aspect—its two enormous sabre-like teeth. These, in fact, were upper canine teeth, and to all intents and purposes were tusks which it used for stabbing and slashing at its prey. To use the teeth in this way, its jaws could not, in fact, have been opened normally, as they would have blocked the gap. But when the animal's mouth was closed, the teeth must have hung down below the jaw line. The alternative is that the lower jaw was dropped completely, so that the whole length of the teeth was exposed.

Teratornis had the largest wingspan of any known flying bird. It is seen here in dispute with two Dire Wolves over the carcase of a Pronghorn Antelope.

There is still some doubt, however, about the exact way in which the sabre teeth were used for attack.

The lower canine teeth were quite small, rather like incisors and presumably were used only to a limited extent.

The largest of the sabre-tooth tigers were from South Africa and were about the size of the modern European bear. The limbs and feet were shorter than those of a modern lion but the claws were much larger. The upper teeth were about one inch wide and about five to six inches long, excluding that part in the socket.

Skeletons of some rather smaller specimens have been found in the asphalt beds of La Brea in California, America.

Sabre-tooth tigers, of course, were carnivorous—that is to say, they were flesh-eating and probably, on occasion, were not averse to eating the odd man or child.

There were, however, some birds that were also flesh-eating. But they contented themselves with eating carrion—dead flesh. One of the most impressive of these birds was the *Teratornis incredibilis*. This bird was probably the largest bird actually to fly that has ever lived. The remains of one of these birds found in Nevada in 1952 had a wingspan of about 16 feet 4 inches and is thought to have weighed about 50 lb.

The teratornis had enormous talons and a huge beak so that it was capable of ripping the flesh from its victims in quite large pieces, and it could therefore fight on equal terms with predators such as wolves, six feet long, known as Dire Wolves.

A more friendly animal of the same period, from the human point of view anyway, was the *Doedicurus* of South America. This animal belonged to an extinct genus related to the armadillos, known as *Glyptodon*.

This strange animal was a mammal and was provided with a shell or carapace all in one piece made up of numerous bony plates all joined together. The animal had teeth—eight on each side of the jaws—and these were divided by vertical grooves, giving them a fluted appearance. Its head, which was protected by a shield of bone, could be pulled back into the shell proper rather in the manner of a modern tortoise. It had three toes on each of its front feet and four on each of its back feet. The tail, which was a most awe-inspiring weapon, ended in a kind of club, armed with a number of horny spikes.

The doedicurus is thought to have been about 12 feet long and was entirely vegetarian.

There are descendants of these animals alive today. They are much modified and their appearance is by no means so terrifying—or maybe usage has removed any element of surprise. But man, too, has changed. The actual structure of his body is different. His skull has a different shape and his arms, at least, are rather shorter.

Perhaps man a million years from now will look with wonder at the remains of animals now living and think that we must have been brave indeed to have accepted them with so little comment.

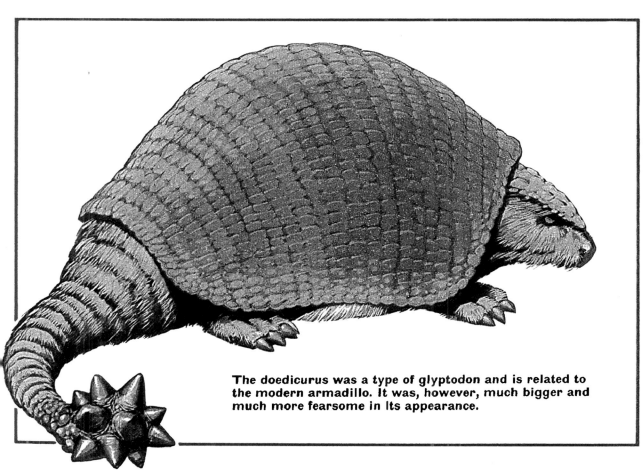

The doedicurus was a type of glyptodon and is related to the modern armadillo. It was, however, much bigger and much more fearsome in its appearance.

PARTNERS UNDER THE SEA

Nature has arranged some strange partnerships for her ocean inhabitants— partnerships which enable defenceless creatures to work unharmed with the killers of the sea

WHEN the long, slender trumpeter-fish (A) meets the colourful parrot-fish (B) on either side of the tropical areas of the Atlantic Ocean the trumpeter-fish will sometimes swim alongside the parrot-fish, using him as a "stalking horse" for food.

The parrot-fish finds his meals among coral reefs and whenever it removes food from the coral it also bites out a chunk of the reef. When this happens the trumpeter-fish swims in for any tit-bits.

Parrot-fish use their sharp, parrot-like beaks to attack coral and their activities cause a good deal of erosion on tropical reefs. They crush the coral and any food adhering to it in their teeth before swallowing.

The trumpeter-fish is about eighteen inches to two feet long and, like chameleons, they have the ability to camouflage themselves when danger threatens.

A number of fishes can produce light while swimming, but Lantern-eyed fish of the *anomalopidae* family (C) are the only ones which have a built-in shutter that permits them to turn the light off or on as they like. The light, switched constantly off and on as they swim, is used as a defence mechanism against attacks of predator fish. Beneath each eye these fish have a series of tubes which provide an anchorage for luminous bacteria.

The squid-like sepiola (D) have a similar organ and it is thought that they spray out their luminous bacteria hosts as a means of defence.

When a big Grouper (E) has had a meal of another fish, smaller creatures swim by and feed on any bits that have become stuck in its mouth or gills, getting a free meal while they help to keep the Grouper clean.

This cleaning operation is practised by a number of

small sea creatures on their larger brothers. Sometimes the little fish swims up to the bigger one and forages along its body; at other times the offer of cleaning and acceptance of the invitation is an elaborate ritual of weaving and darting. The cleaner will often enter the fish's mouth and disappear from sight as it "vacuums" the teeth, jaws and throat of troublesome food particles.

The Melia Tesselata crab (F) is handicapped in life by having two very small claws, a deficiency which it counteracts by carrying in its claws two small sting-

ing anemones. This "baggage" has a dual purpose— it helps to ward off enemies and to capture food.

For the same reason the tropical Hermit crab (G) carries anemones on its shell. And since the anemones are themselves immobile the arrangement helps them, too, to new feeding grounds.

Some anemones, like the Dislosoma anemone (H) prey on small fish, but other fish, called anemone fish, far from being snared by these underwater death-traps, actually use them as a refuge, living on scraps left by them and even sharing their prey.

A curious feature of this partnership is that the anemones have stinging poisonous cells that kill their prey—cells to which the anemone fish are immune. The reason why the anemone fish are able to swim in and out of their hosts' treacherous tentacles is that they secrete a mucus which stops the anemone discharging its poison.

A FORTUNE FROM FANTASY

"Tarzan of the Apes" made its author, Edgar Rice Burroughs, into a millionaire

THE youngster in the uniform of the U.S. 7th Cavalry wiped the sticky dust from his face and screwed up his eyes against the blinding Arizona sun.

He was sixteen years of age, the youngest rider in the little detachment of soldiers patrolling the vast and lonely desert lands. He was too young, though the Army didn't know it when he joined in 1891, to be serving with the toughest cavalry division in the West.

All at once the humid air was rent with war cries and from the rocks to his left he saw a wildly-riding band of Apaches bearing down on him. Instantly, his carbine was out and he heard the sergeant shout: "Stand and fire!"

Grimly he and his companions blazed at the oncoming Indians who retaliated with gunfire and arrows.

The youngster saw several companions fall, but coolly continued to shoot, firing at the leader of the band, a courageous warrior who was the finest rider he had ever seen. At last the Apaches retreated to the hills.

"Who was that?" asked the young man, admiringly.

"That, sonny boy," said the sergeant, "was Geronimo—the greatest War Chief in the Apache Nation."

Years later, the young man was to write about the Apaches in two books: *The War Chief* and *Apache Devil*, both sympathetically written from the Indians' point of view. But these were not to be his best known books—for the youngster was Edgar Rice Burroughs, famous as the creator of Tarzan, lord of the jungle.

Burroughs was discharged from the cavalry when it was discovered that he was under age.

He drifted down to Idaho where he worked on a ranch, living the rough hard life of the cowboy without complaint. But there was too much routine and not enough thrills to suit him, so he moved on. *The Bandit of Hell's Bend* and other Westerns were the outcome of this experience.

He opened a store in Oregon, found the life monotonous and the profit small, so became a railroad policeman in Salt Lake City. Even this bored him soon, so he headed for the Oregon gold-fields to become a miner. It was all mining and no gold.

By the time he was thirty-five, Burroughs regarded himself as a failure. While looking through some magazines one day, he decided to try writing.

His first book was *Tarzan of the Apes*.

It told how John Clayton, an English nobleman, and his wife were marooned on the coast of Africa by a ship's mutineering crew. They managed to exist for a while in the wild jungle but, soon after the birth of their son, they died.

The child was found by a tribe of apes and reared by them as one of their kind. The story proved a terrific success and readers begged for more. Burroughs wrote over twenty Tarzan novels, a dozen Martian yarns, four tales set on Venus and several set in Pellucidar, the world at the Earth's core.

Apart from these he wrote "serious" novels and adventure novels of all kinds— western, detective, historical and science fiction.

He sold every story and in ten years had become a millionaire. He built his own ranch called Tarzana, in California, and formed himself into Edgar Rice Burroughs Inc., a company which still exists making big profits from "hiring out" the name Tarzan alone.

He was capable of writing a full-length novel in a weekend—he did so once for a bet.

Over forty films were made of his books, half of these being about Tarzan. The novels were translated into nearly every modern tongue, and more than thirty million people still read comic-strips about Tarzan all over the world.

War Correspondent

HIS books have never been out of print—a British publisher has been reprinting them for nearly fifty years!

At the age of sixty, during the last war, Burroughs went to the East as a war correspondent.

Those who worked with him were astonished by Burroughs' courage and stamina.

Only one novel was the result of his experiences in Java—*Tarzan and the Foreign Legion*, thought by many to be the best, most "sophisticated," of his Tarzan books.

When he died in 1950 at the age of seventy-four, newspapers all over the world reported his passing and millions of people who had been relaxed and thrilled by him felt the loss as if they had known him personally.

Unpretentious to the last, Burroughs wanted nothing more than to entertain. He did this and more in his Tarzan books, for his stories of the "noble savage" have enthralled the world—and the world repaid him with a fortune.

JUNGLE BOY IN PERIL

He had been reared by a tribe of savage apes, and now found himself face to face with Sabor, the lioness, one of their most deadly enemies.

TARZAN'S FIGHT TO THE DEATH

THAT night Tarzan slept in the forest not far from the village, and early the next morning set out slowly on his homeward march, hunting as he travelled.

Only a few berries and an occasional grub worm rewarded his search, and he was half-famished when, looking up from a log he had been rooting beneath, he saw Sabor, the lioness, standing in the centre of the trail not twenty paces from him.

The great yellow eyes were fixed upon him with a wicked and baleful gleam, and the red tongue licked the longing lips as Sabor crouched, worming her stealthy way with belly flattened against the earth.

Tarzan did not attempt to escape. He welcomed the opportunity for which, in fact, he had been searching for days past, armed with bow and arrow and even a knife.

Quickly he unslung his bow and fitted a well-daubed arrow, and as Sabor sprang, the tiny missile leaped to meet her in mid-air.

At the same instant Tarzan of the Apes jumped to one side, and as the great cat struck the ground beyond him another death-tipped arrow sank deep into Sabor's loin.

With a mighty roar the beast turned and charged once more, only to be met with a third arrow; but this time she was too close upon the ape-man for Tarzan to sidestep the onrushing body.

Tarzan of the Apes barely had time to draw his knife before he went down beneath the great body of his enemy. Rapidly the gleaming knife struck home.

For a moment they lay there, and then Tarzan realized that the inert mass lying upon him was beyond power ever again to injure man or ape.

With difficulty he wriggled from beneath the great weight and placed a foot upon the body of his powerful enemy. Then, throwing back his fine young head he roared out the awful challenge of the victorious bull-ape.

From his earliest days this was how Tarzan had learnt to cross the jungle, swinging high overhead from branch to branch. ▶

THE French schoolboys who decided, one day in 1940, to go for a walk among the gorse and bracken at Lascaux, near the little town of Montignac in the Dordogne, were careful where they were treading.

The whole area is limestone country, and because limestone is porous the action of rain over thousands of years has made the land a kind of huge sponge, full of hidden caves and grottoes. Some are quite near the surface, and many an unwary hiker has broken an ankle in a bracken-concealed opening.

On this occasion it was a dog belonging to one of the boys who was unlucky, because after a surprised yelp it disappeared down a narrow crack. In order to rescue their pet the boys enlarged the crack, and one by one they slipped through it.

They found themselves in a huge cavern whose walls were covered with perfectly preserved paintings of horses, deer and bison. By accident they had discovered the finest known example of the art of Palaeolothic, or Stone Age, man.

Awed Experts

Although the experts who later inspected the find were awestruck by the boys' discovery, they were not altogether surprised, because for a long time it had been said that to drive down into the Dordogne region on the main road to Paris was like stepping back into the Stone Age.

Ever since a lawyer turned anthropologist named Edouard Lartet had started exploring caves in the area a century before, numerous traces of early man had been found. In fact, the Dordogne was known to have been not just inhabited but fairly densely populated for thousands of years.

It was acknowledged as the most important and rewarding place in the world for prehistoric research, but the technical brilliance and as-new condition of the paintings at Lascaux made them absolutely unique. These were not just prehistoric relics but works of art in their own right. What kind of man was it who could produce work of such high quality, between 15,000 and 20,000 years ago?

They were, in fact, known as the Cro-Magnon people (the word comes from an old local dialect name for the place where their skeletons were first discovered) and they probably took the place in Europe of the earlier Neanderthal man.

Cro-Magnon man was still a hunter, but a hunter with vastly increased skills, which was hardly surprising, considering that his brain capacity was much the same as that of a modern European. And he seems to have arrived with an artistic talent so powerful that its quality is timeless.

The cave paintings found in such places as Rouffignac, Pech-Merle and elsewhere all portray animals of various kinds, but none are as impressive as those that cover the walls of the caves at Lascaux.

Beyond the cave entrance, which seems to have been sealed about the time the paintings were completed, is a broad cavern, 15 metres long, with creamy white walls that throw up the painted animals in an almost startling fashion.

There are further chambers, all with similar friezes, and the back of the main hall is dominated by a line of six huge bulls, some of them five metres in length. Some pictures have been superimposed over others, in one spot the paintings are four layers deep, and one question struck everyone who saw them: what was the purpose of this amazing gallery of prehistoric art?

It seems unlikely that we shall ever be certain of the answer, but research has built up an impressive number of probabilities. We know that the Cro-Magnons never bothered to decorate their homes, so the fact that they confined their pictures to special caves suggests that the work had some practical purpose.

Hunting Ritual

Most experts now agree that the paintings in the Lascaux and other caves were part of a magic hunting ritual, perhaps as an offering to the spirit of some particular animal, so that it would allow itself to be killed, or so that it would not return as a ghost to haunt its killer.

Another possibility is that the paintings were made to ensure a steady supply of animals. The Cro-Magnon men were very skilled hunters. They had spears, knives and slings and they knew how to make traps for small animals and pitfalls

Primitive man fashioned weapons with which to hunt. The creatures that were his prey are depicted on the walls of the Lascaux caves.

for large ones. In Predmost, Czechoslovakia, there were skeletons of no less than 1,000 mammoths, which suggests that their killers were not only exceptionally brave but had brought mammoth-hunting to a fine art.

But even the best hunter could do little if there was nothing to hunt. Earlier people travelled constantly as they followed the game, but the Cro-Magnons of the Dordogne had set up fixed homes and possibly over-hunted the areas in which they lived.

Magic Powers

It seems likely that artist-magicians painted a picture of a scarce animal and then used their powers to make it appear. This last theory seems to be borne out by the over-painting of one animal on top of another, as though one picture only served for one occasion.

When the Lascaux paintings were first discovered everyone marvelled at the freshness and brilliance of their colour. The artist had applied his colour with a kind of crayon made up from clays and mineral oxides mixed with charcoal and animal fat as a binder.

Some colours were apparently blown on in powder form, through a reed or hollow bone. Once they were on the wall they were absorbed by the limestone. Then, due to the constant temperature and humidity, they did not fade —

until they were discovered.

When Lascaux was opened to the public after World War Two, the entrance was an artificial one, leading almost directly into the cavern known as the Hall of Bulls. No longer were the paintings insulated from change, for apart from climatic variations they were exposed to an atmosphere polluted by the breathing of 2,000 visitors a day. By the early 1950s experts began to suspect that some of the paintings were deteriorating, and after a further ten years had passed the danger became all too clear.

Some pictures suffered from *mal vert* or "green sickness", a green algae that crept steadily over the walls, others from *mal blanc*, "white sickness" which was a coating of calcite.

The authorities took steps to stop further damage. In 1963 the cave was closed to the public and equipment installed to regulate the temperature, humidity and chemical composition of the atmosphere, and a steel and concrete replica of the cave was constructed with exact copies of the paintings made for general viewing.

The paintings in the Lascaux caves and similar places are more than just fascinating relics, for they fix a time when primitive man was at last able to do more than just hunt. The time came when communities could spare men to serve as full-time painters, and the work they left marks the beginning of the history of the world's art.

When four boys wandered into a cave in France they discovered works of art which had been created by primitive cavemen 20,000 years before

Caves Of Wonder

The light from the torches revealed paintings that had not been seen for centuries.

The warlike Assyrians lived a life of luxury and ease in their capital city of Nineveh, owing to the unlimited slave labour supplied by prisoners of war. King Sennacherib used slaves to construct a splendid palace at Nineveh on an artificial platform of mudbrick and bitumen, diverting the waters of the river Tigris round it.

CAPITAL OF A CRUEL RACE

Revengeful enemies burned down the Assyrians' temples and palaces, reducing them to heaps of rubble

MORE than three thousand years ago the first great empire of the world was established by the Assyrians, a people who lived in the north of the fertile and ancient valley of Mesopotamia between the Tigris and Euphrates rivers.

These Assyrians were a fierce and warlike race who subdued their neighbours by a bloodthirsty reign of terror, torture and death that lasted several centuries. From their mighty cities along the river banks, the Assyrian kings held sway over the rest of the civilised world, keeping detailed records of all their conquests and cruelties.

When at last in the 7th century B.C. the Assyrian empire began to totter, the fate of its ruling people was as terrible as that which they had inflicted upon other lands.

Revengeful Babylonians, Medes and Scythians poured into Assyria, sacking cities and murdering the inhabitants. For four years the capital city of Nineveh, once the metropolis of the eastern world, held out against the invaders. Then in 612 B.C. it, too, gave way.

So great was the hatred of the invading armies for the oppressors that, in their triumphant fury, they turned upon the very stones of Nineveh, reducing vast palaces and temples to mere heaps of rubble.

A time came when only two mounds marked the site of Nineveh, in what is now northern Iraq. But the city was never quite forgotten. The smaller mound was popularly believed by local Arabs to be the tomb of Jonah, the Prophet who, according to the Bible, warned the Assyrians to repent of their wickedness before it was too late. Quyunjik, the larger mound, was supposed to be haunted by demons, and stories were told of monstrous creatures, half-bull, half-man, that guarded treasures within.

There were other similar mounds scattered along the banks of the Tigris near which Nineveh had stood. Ten miles to the north of Quyunjik lay a place called Khorsabad and thirty miles to south was Nimrud.

Both these places were once believed to be Nineveh. It was a reasonable mistake: the Bible had spoken of the city as being so huge that it took three days to cross it. Quyunjik, Khorsabad, and Nimrud marked the sites of three separate cities, but the kings of Assyria

moved from one to the other and the area between must have resembled, to some extent, the enormous area of town and country that we call Greater London.

In 1842, Paul Botta, a French diplomat, began excavating at Quyunjik. Three years later his work was taken over by Henry Austen Layard (1817-1894), the true discoverer of Nineveh.

The Nineveh which he uncovered was built on the orders of one man—Sennacherib (705-681 B.C.). He was the king whom the Bible remembers as having attempted to destroy Jerusalem, but who was prevented when his army was wiped out by an epidemic—probably influenza! Like Nebuchadnezzar in neighbouring Babylon, Sennacherib did not hesitate to destroy the buildings of his ancestors in order to erect his own beautiful palaces.

Slave Labour

Sennacherib's city was roughly rectangular in shape, about two and a half miles long and a mile wide, protected by great walls. Royal palaces, approached by enormous flights of steps, stood where later only those two mounds rose.

The palaces were very simply planned, consisting of a series of very long, narrow chambers. The walls were immensely thick in comparison to the width of the rooms: one of the halls had walls 15 feet thick. Only the lower parts survived, and it was supposed that their great width was designed to support columns which would form the second storey.

To build their city, the Assyrians used slave labour on a scale equalled only by the Egyptians. Sennacherib himself boasted that: *"I caused the inhabitants of foreign countries and the peoples of the forest to drag the great bulls to my palace."* The bulls were the winged, man-headed statues which aroused the superstitious awe of the Arabs of later centuries, and even affected Layard when he viewed them in the dim half-light of the excavations.

Many of the sculptured slabs (bas-reliefs) which lined the walls of the palaces, show how these colossal statues were moved from the quarries to the city. They were floated on barges down the Tigris and then laboriously transferred to sledges, for no wheeled vehicle

could take their weight. Hundreds of slaves were harnessed to the sledges: an officer directing the operation would stand on the statue itself while subordinates directed the activities of the various gangs. Layard himself employed similar means of transport to move the statues to the coast for shipment to London.

The Assyrians, unlike the Babylonians, had access to quarries of stone in the nearby mountains. They constructed their buildings of bricks, but faced them up to a height of 10 feet with sculptured slabs of stone. There were two miles of these slabs at Quyunjik alone and they tell, in wonderful detail, the story of a vanished people.

Most of the subjects concern the king, showing him at worship, at war, and at hunting, but the artist was free to introduce minute details of everyday life. Typical of the Assyrians is the fact that, while animals and human beings are sculpted to the life, flowers and fruit are carved with careless crudeness.

The dominant theme of these reliefs is killing, by war or hunting. Here heads are being brought in as trophies: there prisoners are being tortured: here a lion coughs out its life: there a foal is being brought down by a hound. The Assyrians saw themselves exactly as their neighbours saw them—as a ferocious, bloodstained people.

And yet it was in this same Nineveh that one of the most precious literary finds was made—the library of Ashurbanipal (668-626 B.C.). He was one of the last kings of Assyria and devoted much time to the collection of the clay tablets which both Assyrians and Babylonians used as books.

More than 12,000 fragments of tablets were found in the ruins of Ashurbanipal's palace at Nineveh. They proved to contain a remarkable range of literary work, including treatises on astrology, medicine, law and chemistry, as well as romances, jokes and dictionaries.

Most important of all this literature was the great poem known as the Epic of Gilgamesh, which told the Babylonian version of the Creation, and of how a man built an ark to save himself when a great flood destroyed the land.

When Greek Fought Greek

The ambitions of the Athenians and the jealousy of the warlike Spartans led to a long and bitter conflict

ACROSS the blue waters of the Aegean sped an Athenian trireme. There was scarcely a pause in the rhythmic swing of its oars, as a double crew of oarsmen rowed and slept by turns. Their voyage was a matter of life or death.

For four years Athens had been at war with Sparta and her allies, and some of the cities in the Delian League which Athens led were beginning to challenge her authority. One of these was Lesbos, off the north-west coast of

As the Athenian ship sped across the Aegean Sea, the oarsmen took their meals while they rowed, so as to lose no time on their life-or-death mission.

Asia Minor. Though treated as free associates rather than as subjects, the Lesbians boldly renounced the alliance.

The Athenians struck swiftly, blockading the island's capital, Mytilene. A Spartan fleet sent to its relief arrived too late to save it from surrender in 427 BC.

In Athens at that time one of the popular leaders was a tanner by trade, named Cleon, whose fiery speeches were enthusiastically received in the Ecclesia. At his urging, it was decreed that every adult male in Mytilene should be put to death.

Next day the people, appalled at what they had done, reversed their decision. But the ship carrying the sentence of death had already sailed. At once another trireme

was commissioned to go after it. Despite the efforts of its crew, it failed to overtake the other ship; but, racing into the harbour at Mytilene as the executions were about to take place, it delivered its message just in time.

Tragedy was averted in this instance. But, during the long conflict with the Spartans, the Athenians' system of popular government often produced disastrous decisions. It was Cleon who had opposed the wise leadership of Pericles towards the end of that statesman's life. And it was Cleon who called for a more aggressive conduct of the war.

Cleon himself won his greatest triumph on the west coast of the Peloponnese. An Athenian force, under the experienced general

Demosthenes, had trapped some hundreds of Spartan hoplites on an island off the town of Pylos. Fearful of losing so many of their

CONTINUED ON NEXT PAGE

A pottery fragment used as a "ballot paper".

small body of citizens, the Spartan government asked for a truce.

Cleon opposed this, and criticised Demosthenes for delay in capturing the blockaded Spartans. He boasted that he could do it himself in 20 days. His challenge was accepted — and, thanks to his energy and Demosthenes' co-operation, he succeeded in making

A vote to ostracise, or exile, an unpopular leader was recorded on an *ostrakon*, or pottery fragment. The one pictured on the left, bears, in Greek characters, the name of Thucydides. This exiled leader wrote a history of the Peloponnesian War.

good his boast.

With the captured hoplites as hostages, Attica was spared the threat of Spartan invasion for the time being, though the war still raged elsewhere. Despite Cleon's success, the policy of pursuing the war on land as well as at sea was proving a costly one. The Athenians' numbers, greatly diminished by an epidemic of plague which had struck them during the last years of Pericles' rule, were further reduced by losses in battle.

Cleon himself was killed in a vain attempt to capture Amphipolis, a town on the north Aegean coast which had sided

against Athens. In 421 BC a peace party won temporary control in Athens, and a treaty was signed with Sparta. But this fragile peace did not last long.

The pro-war party in Athens, led now by Hyperbolus, a lampmaker, and an aristocratic adventurer named Alcibiades, recovered the ascendancy. Alcibiades recklessly led an expedition into the Peloponnese to raise opposition to Sparta. The Spartans, thus challenged in their own homeland, won an overwhelming victory over the Athenians, and the war was on again in earnest.

The gravest threat to Athens' survival came from the interruption of her trade, especially with the Black Sea ports, from which came much of her grain. The Athenians now looked for another

The "police force" at Athens was traditionally recruited from the northern land of Scythia and its members retained the distinctive costume and arms of a Scythian archer.

The shepherd god Pan (right) was the legendary inventor of the flute; but the single and double-piped flutes generally used by the Greeks were very different from the multi-tubed "Pan pipes".

The Greek lyre was a simple form of harp. It consisted of a resonator — a tortoise shell was often used for this — with two horns joined by a crossbar. The strings, stretched between the bar and the resonator, were plucked either with the fingers or with a *plektron* (plectrum).

source of supply; and the choice they made was astonishing — and catastrophic.

They planned to send an expedition to Sicily, in the western Mediterranean. There they hoped to find the vital supplies of food, and timber, which they needed. There were a number of Greek settlements in that distant island. Chief of these was Syracuse, which was on friendly terms with Sparta, and this city the Athenians intended to capture.

Despite their terrible losses of men and material, the Athenians fitted out a fleet of 100 ships, joined by 30 from their allies. Hundreds of citizens lined the quays at the Peiraeus as the expedition left port to the sound of trumpets and religious incantations. Victory in the West, they were sure, would solve their problems, and restore their city's prestige and power.

The expedition, which was commanded by a competent but cautious general named Nicias, was doomed to failure. Help expected from other Sicilian cities did not materialise, and Nicias' force proved too small for its task. To begin with he gained some successes, but the Syracusans, led by a Spartan general, Gylippus, frustrated his efforts.

In answer to Nicias' appeals, the Athenians managed to send a powerful reinforcement. But the Athenian fleet was itself trapped in the Great Harbour at Syracuse, and soon the besiegers were themselves besieged. The enterprise ended in ignominious defeat and surrender.

Appalled though they were by this terrible blow, the Athenians still had the courage to fight on, and actually succeeded in building

another fleet. There was plenty of work for it. Members of the Delian League were now in open revolt against Athens.

The Spartans had established a fortified camp on Attic soil, and from this they constantly harassed the Athenians. They and their allies were also becoming more powerful at sea, thanks to a pact with Greece's old enemy, the Persians, who helped to pay the cost of the Peloponnesian fleet.

Backed by the unquenchable spirit of the people, Athens' democratic leaders maintained the struggle for ten more years, against ever-increasing odds. It was not until 404 BC that the conflict, rather misleadingly known as the Peloponnesian War, came to an end.

After the Athenian fleet had been destroyed in a surprise attack

at Aegospotami, on the Hellespont, the Peiraeus was cut off by sea, and the city besieged on land. The Athenians were finally forced to yield.

One of the terms of the treaty that followed was that the city walls and the Long Walls should be dismantled. Despite the humiliation of defeat, peace came as a relief to most ordinary Athenians, and it was to the music of flutes that they set to work to demolish the fortifications they had defended so long.

Relieved to have peace at last, the defeated Athenians set to work to demolish their defensive walls to the accompaniment of flutes.

The MAUSOLEUM

Everyone has heard of a mausoleum, the word used for a particularly impressive tomb, but did you know that the original Mausoleum was one of the seven wonders of the ancient world? It was the tomb of King Mausolus of Caria and was erected at Halicarnassus in south-west Asia Minor by his widow, Artemisia, in 353 B.C.

It no longer survives, since it was destroyed by the Crusaders during the Middle Ages, but excavations of the site have shown that it was probably made up of five parts. These were the base, made of greenstone and cased with marble, a collection of columns, a pyramid, a pedestal and a statuary group of Mausolus and his wife in a chariot. By repute, there were 36 columns with statues standing between them and these surrounded a square area known as a "cella".

It was probably between 150 and 200 ft. tall and measured 100 ft. by 80 ft. There is a model of the Mausoleum in the British Museum, London.

Mausolus himself was a Persian and became ruler of Halicarnassus during the 4th century B.C. He made Halicarnassus a really great city and increased its population by the inclusion of six towns belonging to the Leleges tribe.

Most of the site of Halicarnassus is now occupied by the town of Budrum, a seaport of Turkey.

The picture shows a reconstruction of the Mausoleum.

Defeated in battle, the British sent an envoy to Caesar to plead for peace, promising to send hostages and to do as he commanded.

Julius Caesar Lands In Britain

DURING a series of campaigns under the generalship of Julius Caesar, the power of Rome was extended across Gaul (France).

When Rome could claim that her empire reached the boundary of Gaul—the Channel—she began to wonder about the misty land called Britain which lay beyond.

Caesar talked with merchants and travellers who had crossed to this mysterious land. He sent one of his men to take a look: to see if this could be an untapped field of glory.

Fresh conquests were essential: Rome was not kind to those who failed. She had no time for stalemates: she wanted to hear of new victories.

If Caesar lacked substantial information about the people of Britain, he did know that they had sent help to the tribes he was trying to keep down in Gaul. That was enough.

Late in the year 55 B.C., Caesar ordered his ships to assemble for a short excursion across the water.

He sailed to the coast of Kent with two legions, but the local tribes had seen him and were ready to contest the beach. They were nearly successful, for they were quick and lightly armed, and the Roman soldiers had to struggle out of their ships into the water, laden with armour and weapons.

If fortune went against the Britons in a straight fight, the bad weather and strong tides of the Channel favoured them. While they were suing for Caesar's peace and offering hostages, the Roman ships were dragging their anchors in a storm that severely damaged the fleet.

Caesar was in a vulnerable position and the British chiefs knew it. First they organised an ambush, startling the Romans as they gathered corn in the fields—but it was not decisive.

Then, during several days of bad weather, the tribes gathered their men and chariots together.

A short battle ensued in which the British were overpowered and again sued for peace. Caesar demanded more hostages, and then departed in his patched-up ships.

In fact he had not really achieved much, but his report of the invasion of a new land thrilled the Romans. They rejoiced with 20 days of festivities and holidays.

Caesar was shrewd enough to know the true worth of his expedition, and before the year was out he was preparing to come again.

He designed and built new ships, which he hoped would cope better with the Channel, and set out with five legions and 2,000 horses.

The second invasion was scarcely more fruitful than the first, although it lasted longer (three months). Caesar disembarked without trouble and, after a skirmish, settled down to organise his camp.

In the meantime, the Channel took its toll, for in the night a great storm blew up, carrying off many of his ships. Forty and more were lost and much work was needed on those surviving.

The British were assembling their forces under one of their chiefs, Cassivellaunus. But the strength of the Romans was too much for them, and they were driven through the woods and fields. Caesar followed Cassivellaunus across the Thames and sacked the headquarters of the chief (near St. Albans).

Some tribes began to offer their submission to Caesar, and Cassivellaunus himself sent envoys of peace. Realising that summer was nearly over, Caesar made peace, exacting tribute and hostages. Then he went back to Gaul, and the Romans did not attempt to conquer Britain again for nearly 100 years.

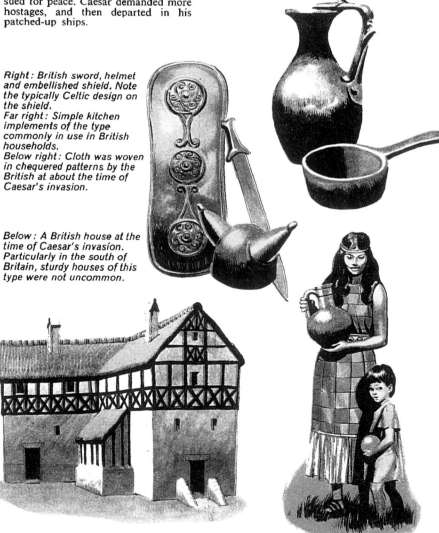

Right: British sword, helmet and embellished shield. Note the typically Celtic design on the shield.
Far right: Simple kitchen implements of the type commonly in use in British households.
Below right: Cloth was woven in chequered patterns by the British at about the time of Caesar's invasion.

Below: A British house at the time of Caesar's invasion. Particularly in the south of Britain, sturdy houses of this type were not uncommon.

I SAW THE SIGN IN THE SKY

I studied the stars—and I knew at once that this one was different. For a Persian like me that star could mean only one thing . . .

I MUST admit that I was on the point of turning back from what all my advisers had regarded as a dangerous journey, until I saw the men who were destined to be my travelling companions for the rest of the way. When I found that they, too, were following the strange new star, I regained my courage, and we decided to go on together.

Two nights previously I had been astonished when, as is my nightly custom, I climbed the stairs of the highest tower in my palace, to study the sky.

Perhaps it is because the nights are so often cloudless and the stars so brilliant that we men of the East study them so carefully. We have our maps and our charts, and can sail our ships or guide our caravans far more accurately by our knowledge of the sky than we can by any of the landmarks which are visible by day.

Birth of a King

WHAT so astonished me that night was the sight of a new star. It shone low down on the Eastern horizon, but with a greater radiance than any other in the sky. According to our ancient lore this could only mean one thing: somewhere a Prince had been born, and one destined to be the greatest of all monarchs.

As I watched the star I noticed that it did not move in the fixed pattern of the other stars but that it was climbing the sky along a path of its own. I knew that within a few days it would have crossed the sky to sink below the Western horizon, so I determined to follow its guidance, in the hope that it would lead me to the birthplace of the King whose birth it heralded.

Far across the desert there was, I remembered, the kingdom of the Jews. Could it be among them that a new King had been born?

MADONNA AND CHILD BY MICHELANGELO

It was an easy matter for me, as ruler of my own kingdom, to assemble a caravan of camels, and to have them loaded with all the necessities for the journey.

I decided to take only a handful of old and reliable servants with me. My court officials were perturbed. I dare say they thought I was mad, but of course they could not say so. All did their best to dissuade me, but I ignored their warnings of the dangers of the desert route or the bitter cold of the season. Within a few hours I was on my way.

Next day, when the sun rose, I felt much less certain of my intention. Weary with the night's travel, I spent the afternoon at a *caravanserai*, or

resting-place for travellers. As the sun set the strange star reappeared, and I felt the same urge to follow it. But when, with the break of day, its light faded, my doubts returned again.

I had almost decided to turn back when we reached a well, and there I was surprised to see a troop of camels with their riders, among whom were two noblemen with their servants.

After the exchange of salutations we declared our business, and I was delighted to find that these noblemen were in fact princes from distant kingdoms, both of whom had seen the star in the East, and had also set out to follow it. They agreed that it signified the birth of some great monarch, to whom they wished to pay appropriate honour.

A Visit to Herod

BOTH of them had set out independently, but their ways had crossed, and they had decided to journey on together. They were delighted to welcome a fellow-seeker to their company.

It would take a long time to describe the rest of our journey, which was a hard one indeed. Yet so sure were we of our purpose that we pressed on gladly. The star still led us westward, and when we had crossed the desert we agreed that our best plan would be to call upon King Herod, for we were now in his dominions. So we therefore presented ourselves at his court in Jerusalem.

I confess that we did not like King Herod, nor did we trust him. He was very attentive to us, and from his own wise men we learned that the nearby town of Bethlehem had long been considered a place from which a Jewish King might one day come.

Gifts and Homage

THERE we determined to go. Herod begged us to come back and tell him if we found the Prince whom we sought, but privately we agreed to avoid another meeting with him, and to return home by a different route.

At Bethlehem we could find no one to help us. The little town was crowded, but no prince was known to be there. We passed right through the town, and were going beyond, when we met a company of shepherds from the hills. It was they who sent us to the village inn, for they had already been led by a vision to visit a child born there that same night.

We were confused and bewildered. This inn was no King's palace! Yet there was a royal dignity about the man and woman who watched over the sleeping child whom we saw in the stable there. And the light of the star we had followed fell softly on his face.

In turn we knelt and did homage, and each of us left the richest gift in our possession. Silently we left the inn, and as we rode away I remember we heard the shepherds in the valley below, singing to the praise of the new-born King.

Who were the Wise Men?

MANY legends have grown up about the mysterious strangers who appeared at Herod's Court in Jerusalem, and then went on to Bethlehem at the time when Jesus was born. St. Matthew neither says that they were three in number, nor calls them Kings. This is assumed only from the three valuable gifts which they brought, and from other Biblical references.

By the eighth century the names had been given to them which have since become traditional. These were Caspar, Melchior and Balthazar. There are also legends of a fourth wise man who turned back.

The travellers were almost certainly Persian astrologers, who followed a new celestial object from East to West. Old Chinese records mention a star which suddenly appeared at about this time, and similar new stars have been observed on other occasions.

It is also known that the "conjunction" of the planets Jupiter and Saturn, normally seen only once in 800 years, occurred three times just before the date of Christ's birth.

Although there is this interesting evidence that the star of Bethlehem was a reality, it was from the personal recollections of Mary, the Mother of Jesus, that the first Christians probably learned the story, and repeated it to the writers of the Gospels towards the end of the first century.

HADRIAN'S WALL

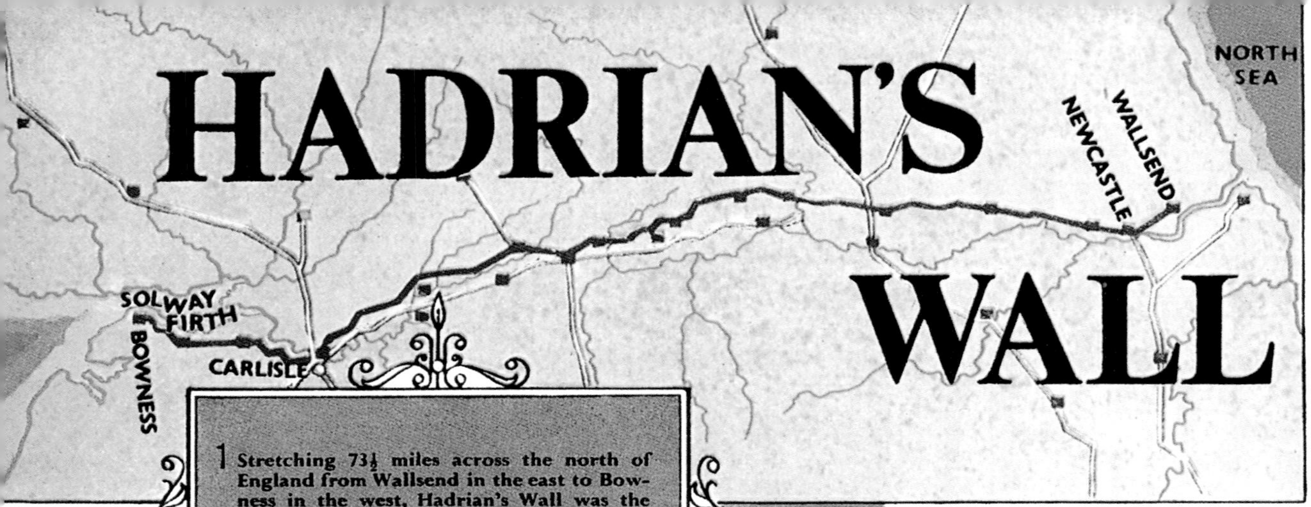

NORTH SEA

WALLSEND
NEWCASTLE

SOLWAY FIRTH
BOWNESS
CARLISLE

1 Stretching 73½ miles across the north of England from Wallsend in the east to Bowness in the west, Hadrian's Wall was the farthest northern outpost of the Roman Empire and the most formidable defensive system ever built in Britain. Occupied by the Romans for over two centuries, it is now an ancient monument, and today only hikers tread its ramparts. Much of the wall is as impregnable as it was in the days of the Romans.

Hadrian's Wall at Housesteads in Northumberland

4 ... If anything, the tribesmen regarded the fortifications as a challenge and carried on raiding as before. More often than not the Roman patrols arrived too late to prevent their attacks.

5 The audacious Scots even attacked garrisoned forts, massacring the defenders and retreating back to their isolated villages long before reinforcements could arrive.

9 Work was started on his wall immediately and Hadrian stayed to supervise the building until it was completed four years later. By that time it stretched for 73½ miles. Along it were seventeen forts housing between 500 and 1,000 men each and many observation and signalling turrets.

10 It proved to be an impregnabl For the first time the Scots wer in their own wild country Romans and Britons living in could go about their busines

ans and Scots fought many a fierce battle.

2 In the first century A.D. the Southern British settled down peacefully under Roman rule; but in the north it was a different story. The savage Scottish tribes resisted all the Roman attempts to subdue them. Despite patrols by legionaries they launched regular attacks across the border, looting and killing wherever they could.

3 At first the Romans thought a show of strength would frighten off the tribesmen so they fortified many towns like York and Chester. They were wrong . . .

any young Britons joined e Roman army and earned e reputations as soldiers t, even with their help, the mans could not afford to ep the bulk of their army gaged in constant guerilla warfare with the Scots.

7 They desperately sought some way of keeping out the Scots not calling for vast numbers of troops. A visiting emperor—Hadrian—provided the answer.

8 Hadrian was forty-six when he arrived in Britain in the year 122. An experienced soldier, he knew the only solution was to seal the border with impregnable fortifications. A bronze head of Hadrian, who was the first Roman emperor to wear a beard, was found in the Thames and is now in the British Museum.

11 Instead of having to keep several large armies along the border the Romans found they could keep the peace by sending out cavalry patrols as the American army did against the Indians in the days of the "Wild West."

12 It was not until the Romans left Britain that the Scots finally succeeded in breaching the wall to terrorize the north again—two hundred years later.

The TRIGAN EMPIRE

Countless light years away from Earth is the galaxy of Yarna, and in that galaxy is the planet Elekton. Of all the empires on Elekton, that of Trigan was the greatest. Today we begin a new story in the fantastic history of the Trigans . . .

Driven far from its own galaxy by a space storm, a strange craft was caught up in the gravity field of the planet Elekton, and drawn towards it . . .

It fell in the rocky countryside of Hericon . . .

Night fell, and in the gloaming three luminous spheres emerged from the craft and hovered above it . . .

Some distance away, a herd of gelfs lay sleeping after a day of browsing on the sparse grass of the hillside. Silently, the three spheres drifted towards them . . .

The luminous globes hovered over the heads of the three gelfs . . . disintegrated . . . *and vanished into the animals' ears!*

Instantly, the three creatures awakened . . . and *communicated* with each other!

What are these creatures whose minds and bodies we have occupied?

A very low order of species.

Perhaps not the highest species on this planet.

At dawn, an old gelfherd came up to the pasture and drove his herd down the hillside.

Move, you lazy creatures . . . *move!*

The old man would have died of shock if he had known the evil intelligence at work in the minds of three of his flock.

He is a higher creature.

When he sleeps, one of us will take him over.

Two days later, two men came riding through the valley; they were Janno and Keren . . . on their way to the Court of King Kassar of Hericon with a message from the Trigan Emperor.

We'll camp here, Keren, and we should reach Hericon City by tomorrow midday.

Nights are chill in the hills of Hericon, so the two friends made a fire. Later, they saw shapes moving in the darkness towards them, and their hands flew to their swords . . .

WHO'S THAT?

LOOK!

Only an old gelfherd, masters . . . seeking the warmth of your fire, and a bite of food if you can spare it.

The young comrades readily agreed, and the trio ate together. Later, Keren and Janno lay down to sleep.

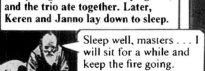

Sleep well, masters . . . I will sit for a while and keep the fire going.

Later, when all was silent save for the steady breathing of the two youths, the old man whispered to the two gelfs . . . who also slept . . .

Take them over!

Two spheres rose from the sleeping gelfs and hovered above Janno and Keren!

Next Episode: Plan For Evil

BUILDING THE GREAT

THE Prince of Ch'in, who in 221 B.C. declared himself First Emperor of a united China and took the title of Shih-huang-ti, was one of the most awesome and ruthless rulers the world has known. He broke the power of the feudal families of China and appointed military and civil officials to administer the great areas of land within his power. The vigour and authority of his rule knew no bounds. The type of government which he set up survived in China until this century.

Within a year of assuming power, Shih-huang-ti turned to the north of his lands to defend them from barbarian enemies—the Hsiung-Nu—ancestors of the warlike Huns who later invaded Europe.

Some sections of defensive walling had already been built to keep out the Hsiung-Nu. Shih-huang-ti resolved to build a wall that would not only keep the barbarians out, but would keep the Chinese in and firmly mark the frontier.

Very little was recorded about this monumental and extraordinary Wall. What now remains of it has been often rebuilt and repaired.

In just 10 years, Shih-huang-ti built about 1,500 miles of Wall. It stretched from the east coast, near the site of Peking, for hundreds of miles westwards, crossing the great Yellow River.

The Emperor who commanded that the Wall be built had little regard for the lives of his subjects. Like ants, they were sent in giant flocks to work on the Wall—perhaps a million men and women died in the years of its construction. Prisons disgorged their inhabitants, and prisoners of war were sent there to toil—and probably die.

The work went on through all changes of climate: the heat of desert summers, the icy winters. The Wall rolled on, through sand and mud and scaled giddy mountainous heights. It was not allowed to cease.

The immensity of the task staggers the imagination—and the savagery of it. Where human labour was available in infinite measure, nothing was impossible, no task too great to be undertaken. If the materials for construction were not at hand, then they had to be brought from no matter how far away, at no matter what expense.

The Wall was really a double wall. Hard brick outer walls were filled with clay and built on foundations of stone. About 30 feet up, along the top of the Wall, was a roadway wide enough for eight men to march abreast and for horses and chariots to travel along. Every 100 yards or more there was a watch-tower, standing out from the Wall. From these strongholds, signals could be sent to warn soldiers along the Wall of imminent enemy attack. Probably about 25,000 of these towers were built along the Wall.

China is a land that preserves her memories in tales and legends. Within them is a germ of the truth. Stories are told of the men who fell ill as they worked and how they were trampled into the Wall along with the clay; of those who died and were thrown in also.

One of the most famous legends tells of a princess whose beloved husband had been sent off to labour on the Wall. He died there and was buried in the Wall.

The princess was beside herself with grief and she journeyed to the Wall determined to find where her dead husband lay. But no one could tell her. Then a spirit came and told her to cut her finger, hold it before her and follow the trickle of blood. She did as she was bidden and the drops of blood led her to her husband's grave. She took his body back with her so that it might be buried in his homeland.

WALL

Illustrated by Angus McBride

Bronze weapons of the period.

Map showing the Great Wall

Shih-huang-ti, the man who was determined that it should be built.

Lightweight carriage of the period. Note the harness of bronze and the flimsy framework of the carriage.

The Wall was edged with a parapet which gave protection to archers when attacked from below.

ACCORDING to legend, the city of Rome was founded by Romulus in 753 B.C. Around this city was built the greatest Empire the world had known.

The grandeur of Rome was reflected in her conquests which, at their greatest extent (under the Emperor Trajan, A.D. 98-116) included Italy, Gaul, Spain, Britain, Western Germany, Greece, Asia Minor, North Africa, Egypt, Mesopotamia, Palestine and the Mediterranean islands. The greatest of her rulers—Julius Caesar, Augustus, Marcus Aurelius, Constantine—rank among the greatest rulers of all time. Her scholars—Cicero, Virgil, Horace, Livy and Ovid —are still widely read.

Everyone has heard of the tremendous courage of the Roman legions and of the brilliant organisation of the Roman law and civil service. The bold and vigorous work of her artists and architects can still be seen in Rome, in the Colosseum, the Pantheon and the many temples and forums.

Of course, Rome went through hard times, and periods of bad government, but, in general, she remained strong while she was organised for expansion, and while the morale of her people was high. But having reached the fullest extent of her power, she outgrew her strength and her eventual decline was then inevitable.

Rome had internal problems. There was no fixed method of choosing the next ruler. The principle of hereditary monarchy was feared. This sometimes meant that a period of uncertainty and chaos attended the choice of a new Emperor. The imperial throne was within the reach of every ambitious soldier and many tried to win it.

Another growing problem for the Empire was the decline in the population of Italy. This basic pool of manpower for the Empire's needs had been depleted by war.

What Rome lacked most of all was money to keep her civil administration and military system running smoothly. These had been the basis of her success.

THE FALL OF THE ROMAN EMPIRE IN THE WEST

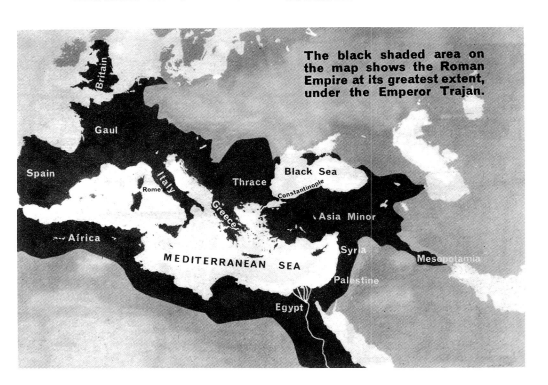

The black shaded area on the map shows the Roman Empire at its greatest extent, under the Emperor Trajan.

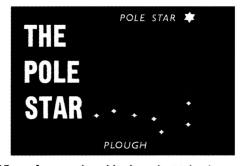

WHAT IS:

THE POLE STAR

POLE STAR ★

PLOUGH

IF you face north and look at the night sky you will see a group of seven stars arranged in the shape of a saucepan with a curved handle. Astronomers call this group the Plough, because it is also shaped like an old-fashioned plough.

The two stars farthest from the handle point to the Pole Star, or North Star.

Although the Plough, which acts as a pointer to the Pole Star, is easily picked out, its position changes according to the time or season of the year.

Thus at nine p.m. in spring, the Plough is directly overhead, but at nine p.m. in the autumn the Plough is low down and near the horizon. In summer, the Plough appears to stand on its handle in the west, but in winter it stands on its handle the other way round towards the east.

Whatever its position, the Plough and the other stars appear to move from east to west in twelve hours. It is not the stars that are moving, however, but the Earth, which turns round once every day.

Because it is so bright and easily found, the Pole Star has been used by navigators since very early times to find their way at sea.

The 3rd century A.D. marked a very low ebb for the Empire. There had been no large-scale loss of territory, but many districts had suffered from the backlash of war and famine, and plague had further decimated the population. Lands lay uncultivated, commerce was disrupted, and taxes collected with difficulty.

Two Emperors who did much to delay Rome's progress along the downward path were Diocletian and Constantine the Great. Diocletian divided the imperial power between himself and three other men. The administrative reforms he put in motion were worthwhile but expensive, as were the four imperial courts, which cost a great deal to maintain.

Diocletian abdicated in 305 and 19 years later, Constantine, having defeated a number of rivals, gained sole power. Constantine's reign is famous for two things: his adoption of Christianity as the religion of the Empire; and the building of a new capital, which he named Constantinople, on the Greek city of Byzantium.

Even from the time of Augustus, it had been the practice to allow barbarian tribes to settle within the frontiers of the Empire. This policy had been continued by succeeding Emperors. Barbarians found a place for themselves at court and made up a large proportion of the armies that were now fighting Rome's battles for her.

The reason why these tribesmen turned so suddenly and so vigorously against the Empire at that particular moment was partly because it was so pitifully weak and partly because they themselves were being threatened from behind by the merciless and terrifying Huns. The barbarian people, called the Visigoths, appealed to Rome to be allowed to cross the Danube to escape from the Huns, but so many thousands of them crossed that it was impossible to settle them peaceably and they took up arms against Rome. The Roman Empire had now been divided into two parts, and the west Roman Emperor, Valens, was killed by the Visigoths on the field of Adrianople. The Visigoths then turned eastwards to Constantinople, then under

the rule of Theodosius. Theodosius provided them with territory and they settled for a time peacefully. But when Theodosius died in A.D. 395, he was succeeded by his two ineffectual sons: Honorius in the west and Arcadius in the east. Honorius was under the thumb of an able barbarian general named Stilicho.

At about the same time, the Visigoths chose Alaric as their King. Alaric invaded Italy in A.D. 400, but was defeated by Stilicho. In 408, after Stilicho's death, Alaric came back again and marched to Rome. The city was saved by the payment of a heavy ransom. Alaric wanted lands for his people, but Honorius would not grant him any. After further negotiations had failed, Alaric marched to Rome, took the city and sacked it. Shortly afterwards, Alaric died and the Visigoths left Italy.

Honorius died in 423, by which time a large part of the western Empire had passed out of his hands. Barbarians had settled in Spain and Gaul, and in 429, Gaiseric, King of the Vandals, crossed to north Africa. He built a fleet which terrorised Rome from the sea.

In 451, Attila the Hun invaded Gaul but, being defeated there, he turned to Italy instead, and his army ravaged the country. The Huns turned back from Rome without fighting and shortly afterwards, Attila died.

In Italy, the last of a line of shadowy Emperors was one named Romulus Augustulus. He was deposed by his German military chief, Odovacer, in the year 476. In that year the Roman Empire in the west is formally considered to have ended.

The sack of Rome in 410 by the barbarian Alaric and his horde of Visigothic warriors was a profound shock to the civilised world. Mighty Rome had ruled the Western world for hundreds of years. Men could not imagine that a time would come when the Roman Empire would no longer exist.

THE WORLD 'GROWS'

The world was turning out to be a much more complicated place than early geographers had thought. In the fifth century B.C. the Greek historian Herodotus explored the Nile and its Temples, Persia and Babylon.

Greek generals were the first men to publish surveys of the regions through which they marched. Under Alexander the Great (356-323 B.C.) they journeyed through Persia to unknown India beyond, in the hope of conquering the world. Their explorations in south-east Asia were invaluable to geographers.

In the fourth century B.C., Pytheas of Masillia sailed beyond the Pillars of Hercules, westwards into the unknown Atlantic. He explored the European coastline, studied tides, and sighted the shores of Iceland.

In the second century B.C. a globe existed in the royal library at Pergamum in Asia Minor which showed all the known lands crowded together, the rest of the globe as sea. One geographer there, Crates, believed that three unknown continents existed to the south and west.

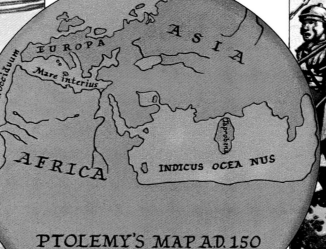

PTOLEMY'S MAP A.D. 150

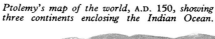

Ptolemy's map of the world, A.D. 150, showing three continents enclosing the Indian Ocean.

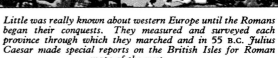

Little was really known about western Europe until the Romans began their conquests. They measured and surveyed each province through which they marched and in 55 B.C. Julius Caesar made special reports on the British Isles for Roman maps of the west.

An attempt to chart the earth was made in A.D. 150 by the Alexandrian geographer Ptolemy. His map showed three continents, with the Indian Ocean as an inland sea. Although he misjudged the world's size, his map was a standard reference for seamen until the Middle Ages. It listed about 8,000 places, compiled from travellers' records.

With the fall of the widespread Roman Empire the Dark Ages descended upon the world, and the lands of the East and West were once more unknown to each other. In the West terrible legends revived of monsters, balls of fire, intense heat and other mysteries to be encountered by travellers in the East. Sailors believed that if they sailed beyond a certain point they would fall off the world.

The next explorers were missionaries, spreading the new Christian faith. Some were women like St. Helena, wife of a Roman emperor, who in the fourth century A.D. made a pilgrimage to Jerusalem, and Etheria of Aquitaine, who travelled in the East. St. Brendan of Ireland, probably reached the Arctic Ocean in 573, for his accounts include descriptions of icebergs.

TINTAGEL CASTLE
IN CORNWALL

The first building at Tintagel was a farmhouse erected in the third century A.D. This had disappeared early in the fifth century when a Celtic missionary called Juliot founded a monastery on the headland. According to the Norman Domesday Survey the monastery was deserted and in ruins in 1086.

Reginald, Earl of Cornwall, started building a castle at Tintagel in 1145. The castle stood on the isthmus or narrow strip of land that then connected the Tintagel headland with the mainland. During the next two centuries the castle was enlarged and strengthened. But as it was seldom occupied it had fallen into neglect when it was granted to the Black Prince in 1337. The Black Prince put it into repair, but after his death it was again neglected.

THE KING ARTHUR LEGEND
There is no historical evidence that King Arthur had any connection with Tintagel. It was an early writer of romances called Geoffrey of Monmouth who started the traditional story in the twelfth century. The real King Arthur was a Celtic hero of the fifth century who stopped for a time the Saxon invasion of England. So little is known of him that the scene of his exploits has been placed as far apart as Cornwall and the North of England.

EDWARD, PRINCE OF WALES
Eldest son of Edward III, he was also Duke of Cornwall and popularly called the Black Prince. He won many battles in the Hundred Years' War with France and died in 1376.

Towards the close of the fourteenth century extensive alterations and repairs were made to Tintagel Castle. It then became a state prison to which traitors and political offenders were sent from all over England. Amongst those who were shut up in the castle dungeons was John of Northampton, a Lord Mayor of London who had earned the Royal displeasure.

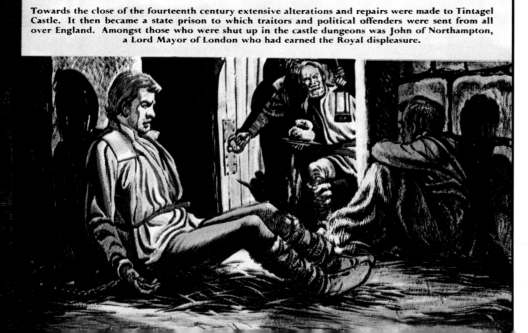

According to the famous legend, King Arthur and his knights sat at a round table. There the king held court and planned with his devoted followers the defence of the weak and the destruction of tyranny and oppression.

Tintagel Castle as it stands today in its wild and mysterious setting of legend and romance. The Castle attracts visitors from all over the world. The ruins are partly on the island and partly on the mainland.

The castle had very little history during the fifteenth century. According to contemporary historians, most of Tintagel Castle was in ruins by the mid-sixteenth century. The stone bridge that once led to it had disappeared and been replaced by a few elm logs.

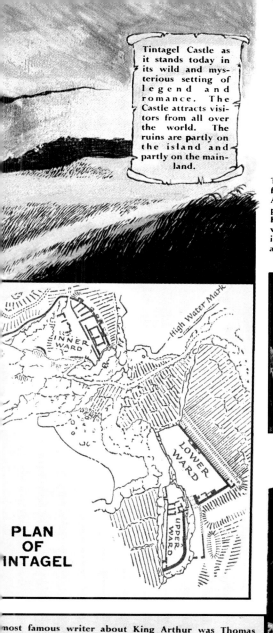

PLAN OF TINTAGEL

The castle stood crumbling and forgotten until 1859, when Alfred Tennyson published his poetic history of the legendary King Arthur and associated him with Tintagel. Public interest in the ruined castle was aroused and repairs were carried out.

The cliffs around Tintagel are the haunt of a rare, crow-like bird called the chough. According to tradition, King Arthur still lives as a chough, and will one day become a man again.

ALFRED LORD TENNYSON
Born in 1809. Tennyson's great narrative poem "Idylls of the King" aroused tremendous interest in the King Arthur legends. In 1850 Tennyson was appointed Poet Laureate.

...most famous writer about King Arthur was Thomas ...ry. He collected a number of English and French hero ...ds and published them in a book called "Morte ...hur"—"Death of Arthur." Published by William ...n in 1485, this was one of the first books printed in ...nd and is one of the finest examples of fifteenth century prose.

The legend tells us that King Arthur had a famous sword called Excalibur. When he was dying he ordered the sword to be thrown into a pool. The sword had originally come from the pool, and as it fell, a ghostly hand caught it and drew it down.

The Post Office at the village of Tintagel, or Trevena as it should be correctly called, is in a stone house dating from the fourteenth century. It has been National Trust property since 1903.

Perched high on the cliffs overlooking Tintagel is the Church of St. Materiana. It is so buffeted by Atlantic gales that even the tombstones have to be buttressed to prevent them from being blown over.

King Arthur's Hall was built in 1933 as headquarters of a society called the Fellowship of the Round Table. Over fifty different kinds of Cornish stone were used in its construction. It contains a valuable collection of ancient manuscripts and a library of books dealing with the King Arthur story. The drawing on the right shows the granite Arthur Throne at one end of the Hall.

REPEL THE DANES!

HALF the island fortress was lost. The eastern bastions were gone. East Anglia had been surrendered without a fight. Northumbria had been conquered by savagery and trickery. Half of Mercia had been betrayed.

At this time, A.D. 871, Alfred, 22 years old, was offered the throne of Wessex, the only Saxon kingdom that survived from the seven that had once been England. Now Wessex was in daily danger of destruction.

The Viking raiders were gloating in their triumph.

Alfred was suddenly a king only because his elder brother had died, probably from wounds, after a series of battles against the invaders. Now a rich realm lay before the greedy invaders. The great army of Danes scoffed at the Saxon countrymen and their young king.

Alfred looked at his inheritance, its position and its plight. It was a kingdom that reached from Kent in the east to Cornwall in the west. The Thames made a winding boundary to the north.

From the sea a few raiders would sweep in from time to time and leap with wild heathen cries from their longships. This they had done intermittently for the past 125 years.

The greatest danger lay to the north-east, where prowled the Viking Danes, their wild, roving eyes ever watchful for rich kingdoms to loot and plunder.

They had come first to the peaceful, almost slumbering isle of Britain merely as passing raiders. They sought easy pickings. They fought savagely when they came, their wolf-skinned warriors howling in battle like the animals whose pelts they wore. Others, the *berserks*, raged without mailcoats in the belief that they were protected by their strange northern gods and needed no armour. They terrorised their foes and because of their wildness and ferocity their name became an English word for madness.

Alfred was soon to realise that if the thieving Danes were resisted they would go to some other place where the loot was easier. He knew how the king of Paris had given in to their demands and paid them a huge price to go away and leave his city in peace. The Viking leader took his prize and went. A year or two later his warlike sons returned, demanding even more gold or else . . . !

So it was that Alfred decided to resist, rather than pay and pray for peace. He had fought the Danes at Ashdown, and beaten them whilst his elder brother prayed. This was only a few weeks previously, and he had shown that a Saxon army could take on and defeat the raiders.

Before that he had been in an attack on their defensive stronghold at Reading. Here the Saxons had suffered heavily to no avail. The Saxons always lost many men whenever they assaulted a Viking fort.

From this Alfred learned two lessons. The first: that it would be impossible to drive the Danes right out of Britain. The second: that if Danes could not be harmed in strongholds, then neither could Saxons.

Therefore the clear-sighted young king decided to hold on to and defend as much of the island as still remained to the Saxons, and to defend it by means of a string of forts.

First line of defence

First of all, he decided to defend his long coastline. Ships were built much like those of the Danes, only larger. Some accounts say that they were twice the size and carried as many as 60 men. The intention was to fight the invaders at sea, and so prevent the need for combatting them on land. When five years a king, a great army of Danes drove treacherously deep into Wessex in spite of a treaty of peace, and made a strong camp at Exeter. They also had a fleet in Poole harbour, but when this attempted to move to Exeter it was caught by a storm off Swanage headland, and Alfred's ships did the rest. It is said that 120 Danish ships were lost with about 5,000 men. As a result the army had to withdraw from Exeter and Wessex. Thus, for the first time in history, ships had become England's first line of defence as they would be again and again in the centuries to come.

In the years that followed there were many battles. Some of Alfred's allies collapsed disastrously for him, and treaties made with the Danes were often heedlessly broken by them.

At long last a boundary was set on Danish rule. It reached from London, followed the River Lea to near Bedford, thence across country to the Roman-built Watling Street (now the A5) which it followed to Chester.

Behind this slender line on the map, Alfred began organising his defences.

First he had to re-build his army, a part-time affair in which the men were called to arms whenever an emergency arose and went home when it no longer existed, or when they felt tired of fighting, or became worried about the wife and children and the farm, or ran out of food.

The Danes never had this problem. They were men without homes, except the rowing bench on their ship or a shelf in the great hall at their camp. They were professionals . . . but they were not to be the last professional soldiers to be defeated by an amateur spare-time British Army.

Alfred organised his manpower on a relief basis, so that there would always be a fighting force standing by, but each man in turn was relieved by another when his term of duty was done.

He issued a royal command that towns and districts should build fortifications of a size which could be defended by the number of men available. The scale was four men to every pole (5½ yds.) of wall. Crumbling Roman walls and ramparts were restored and strengthened. New ditches with earthen, turfed walls occasionally faced with timber were constructed. Defensive towns were set up. These were called *burhs*.

Wessex, in Alfred the Great's time, became the impregnable citadel of our beleaguered island fortress.

Above: The young King Alfred. This noblest of English kings was a mighty warrior, a brilliant ruler and a fine scholar. Right: A typically ferocious battle between the Saxons (in the foreground) and the Danes. The central figure is a "berserk." Berserks were Viking champions. The word either meant going into battle without mail coats, or wearing animal skins.

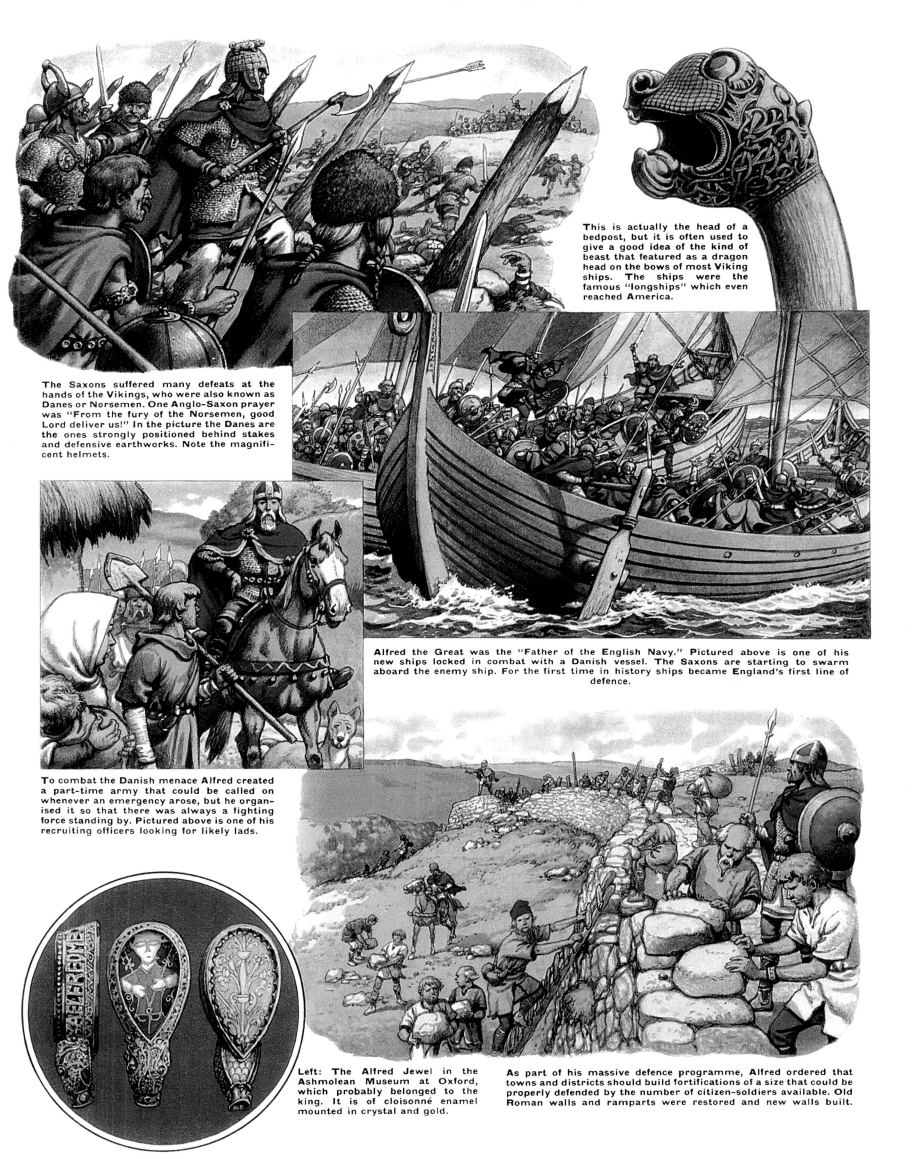

This is actually the head of a bedpost, but it is often used to give a good idea of the kind of beast that featured as a dragon head on the bows of most Viking ships. The ships were the famous "longships" which even reached America.

The Saxons suffered many defeats at the hands of the Vikings, who were also known as Danes or Norsemen. One Anglo-Saxon prayer was "From the fury of the Norsemen, good Lord deliver us!" In the picture the Danes are the ones strongly positioned behind stakes and defensive earthworks. Note the magnificent helmets.

Alfred the Great was the "Father of the English Navy." Pictured above is one of his new ships locked in combat with a Danish vessel. The Saxons are starting to swarm aboard the enemy ship. For the first time in history ships became England's first line of defence.

To combat the Danish menace Alfred created a part-time army that could be called on whenever an emergency arose, but he organised it so that there was always a fighting force standing by. Pictured above is one of his recruiting officers looking for likely lads.

Left: The Alfred Jewel in the Ashmolean Museum at Oxford, which probably belonged to the king. It is of cloisonné enamel mounted in crystal and gold.

As part of his massive defence programme, Alfred ordered that towns and districts should build fortifications of a size that could be properly defended by the number of citizen-soldiers available. Old Roman walls and ramparts were restored and new walls built.

THE VIKINGS STRIKE AT FRANCE

When the fierce men from the North sailed up the Seine in their long ships they came as the forerunners of a dynamic new breed of northern Frenchmen who, within a few generations, were to humble England

JUST as the Vikings from Denmark had plundered, looted, pillaged and burned the coasts of England, now, in the ninth century, under their leader Hasting, they turned their fierce gaze upon the coast of France.

When the Vikings had gained a foothold on the land they went one day to the Bishop of one of the seacoast towns and told him sadly that Hasting was dead.

"His last wish was to be buried as a Christian," they chorused sadly. "Unless this happens, how can he enter Paradise?"

The Bishop was touched. Here was a golden opportunity to introduce Christianity to these warring pagans. Eagerly he called his parishioners to a funeral service for the great Hasting in his church and solemnly the coffin was carried in before a procession of Vikings and Christians.

When everyone was inside and the doors closed, up popped the coffin lid and out came a very much alive Hasting, sword in hand. The Vikings closed in on the Christian "mourners" and killed them all. Then they rifled the Church of its treasures and sailed away.

Over the years not all the Vikings were content to make such hit-and-run bandit raids. Thirty thousand of them under their chief Rollo, sailed, up the Seine in their long ships to Paris and laid siege to the city while the King, Charles the Fat, was away in Germany.

The Parisians, under their leader Count Eudes, drew up their drawbridges and prepared to keep the invaders at bay.

The Weak Kings

A year went by—a year of tightening belts, of starvation and of famine. Still the Parisians held on grimly, watching from the city walls as their tormentors roasted fine lean meat on spits upon the ground below and ate their fill.

Then one night Count Eudes escaped from the city. Undetected, he galloped through the besiegers and rode as fast as he could go to the King in Germany. Having obtained the pledge of Charles the Fat to return with a large army and raise the siege, he rode back to Paris and again under cover of night got back into the city.

But Charles the Fat was also Charles the Coward. When he did come back to Paris, and he was a long time coming, instead of attacking the Vikings he paid them a large bribe to go away.

The agony of Paris was over but its fury with the King had just begun. Charles the Fat was deposed and Count Eudes then became King.

When Eudes died Rollo the Viking was still foraging in northern France. But even roving Vikings eventually liked to settle down somewhere, and now he accepted the offer from King Charles the Simple of a handsome grant of land, a title, baptism as a Christian, and a French princess for his wife—in return for his allegiance to the crown of France.

The title Charles gave to the fearless Viking

Racing his warhorse through the besiegers, Count Eudes got back into the city of Paris.

was Duke of Normandy. In due course Rollo's great-grandson William was to succeed to the title and emblazon his name on a page of English history as William the Conqueror.

While the Vikings were at the peak of their activities France was ruled by a succession of weak kings—made the weaker by the strong line taken by all the dukes and barons who ruled over their territories like kings themselves and who feared no man—least of all a king whom they themselves were so often in a position to order about. Weakness, too, had sprung from the enmity of the family to which Count Eudes belonged (called the Robertians after one of their number, Count Robert the Strong, a great landowner) and the royal Carolingian house.

Some of these Robertians in fact had actually been kings themselves, alternating with the Carolingian kings. In the year 987 the Robertians finally emerged the stronger party when their candidate for the throne, named Hugh Capet, was elected. Hugh took his surname from the fact that he liked to wear a cape or cloak, and his dynasty marked the election of a new dynasty of kings called the Capetians.

King Hugh tried hard to stem the power of the barons, but they never let him forget that they had elected him and therefore expected him to favour them.

"Who made thee a count?" demanded the King of a baron who was not treating him with proper respect. "Who made thee a King?" retorted that nobleman. And that exchange aptly summed up the royal position.

An interesting little story told about Hugh's son Robert serves to show firstly how weak were these early Capetians and secondly, by contrast, how powerful the authority of the Pope was becoming.

Robert, already married to a woman much older than himself, had fallen in love with his cousin Bertha, and as soon as he became King, married her. For this the Pope excommunicated him—that is, cut him off from the Church.

Noble Scholar

King Robert, hurt though he was by this punishment, continued to regard cousin Bertha as his wife, with the result that the Pope put the whole of his kingdom under an interdict, which meant that no services could be held in any of the churches. At length Robert yielded; he sent Bertha away and the interdict was lifted. And although he went personally to Rome to ask if he could take Bertha back, the Pope was adamant in his refusal—and the papal verdict was accepted.

Now we are in the eleventh century—a vibrant 100 years for France. Just as the Romans had once integrated themselves with the Gauls, so the Vikings had now integrated themselves with the French, and from that union had come Normandy, and from Normandy Duke William, who in 1066 took the crown of England and found himself king of a foreign land yet only a duke owing homage to another king in his own country.

Before he sailed for England William asked the King of France, Philip the First, to join him in his expedition. But Philip was an indolent man who lived only for pleasure and was not interested in a foreign war. When William triumphed over King Harold of England, though, Philip was jealous and saw the danger of having one of his vassals as a king and therefore an equal.

There was not much that lazy King Philip could do to hamper resourceful King William but he did take advantage of the Conqueror's divided interests in England and Normandy to stir up rebellion in the northern dukedom. For this William angrily went to war with his King. It was during this war that William burned one of Philip's towns. Riding through the smouldering debris the new King of England's horse slipped on a piece of burning wood and threw its rider. A few weeks later William the Conqueror died from the effects of the fall.

If Philip was a lazy, useless King, the rest of France did not follow his example. With the

◄ **In a war against King Philip the First of France, England's William the Conqueror burned one of Philip's towns. Riding through the smouldering debris the King of England's horse slipped on a piece of burning wood and threw its rider. A few weeks later William died from the effects of the fall.**

continued on next page

THE STORY OF FRANCE

continued from previous page

words of Pope Urban the Second ringing in their ears, Frenchmen from all over the land banded together in a fever of excitement to launch the First Crusade to free the Holy Land from the Saracens.

The causes and effects upon Europe's story of the exciting Crusades to the Holy Land we need only record. This we must do, because France led the Crusades; she was the organizing spirit behind them after the papal call to action and although the Crusades were truly an international movement, France supplied the majority of the knights and soldiers who fought for the Cross.

The reign of Louis the Sixth, called Louis the Fat, saw the extension of the growth of towns and cities which was an important development of France, and indeed, of Germany and Italy, in the Middle Ages. During the time of King Philip and King Louis towns, or boroughs, had been built around market places to protect them; the inhabitants of these boroughs were now called *bourgeois*.

Other towns grew up for a different reason. They had been built originally around a feudal lord's castle and were natural places for municipal development. When Louis the Fat was fighting his barons in an attempt to curb their power, these townspeople helped him and were rewarded for their loyalty to the monarch by being granted certain important privileges, like making their own laws and appointing their own magistrates. These self-administering groups came to be called *communes*.

Third Estate

The idea of semi-independent townships jealously guarding the privileges they had won was not confined to France. In Italy communes like Venice, Milan and Florence, and in Germany an association of cities known as the Hanseatic League, actually became independent republics, raising their own armies and fighting their own battles.

Louis the Fat minded none of this. By giving some power to the bourgeois who could now work for their own improvement, he created a newly-felt loyalty towards the sovereign and at the same time curbed the barons' power.

But there was one striking difference in the growth of power among merchants and traders in France and the parallel occurrence in England. In our country merchants and knights mingled without much difficulty into the Commons, creating a two-tier structure of government in the Lords and the Commons. In France there was no such unity of the lowest orders, and the bourgeois, although gaining great freedom and power, remained the "Third Estate," a name that was a constant reminder that they were socially the lower class.

Much medieval history is the story of the lives of a succession of kings, for, in comparison with later ages, scant accounts have been left to us of the lives of ordinary people. One important medieval Frenchman whose story we do know,

"Who made thee a count?" demanded King Hugh of the disrespectful nobleman. "Who made thee a king?" retorted the Count roughly.

CAROLINGIAN KINGS OF FRANCE
From Louis II

	Years	From	To
Louis II	2	877	879
Louis III and Carloman	3 / 5	879 / 879	882 / 884
Charles II	4	884	888
Count Eudes	10	888	898
Charles III	24	898	922

(In 922 Count Robert was acknowledged by the barons as their monarch, but he was killed in 923.)

	Years	From	To
Rudolf	13	923	936
Louis IV	18	936	954
Lothaire	32	954	986
Louis V	1	986	987

CAPETIAN KINGS
To Louis VI

	Years	From	To
Hugh Capet	9	987	996
Robert	35	996	1031
Henry I	29	1031	1060
Philip I	48	1060	1108
Louis VI	29	1108	1137

however, was a teacher by the name of Abélard.

Of all the medieval universities of Europe, that at Paris had become the most famous and in the twelfth century it was attracting pupils from all over the Continent. This success it owed to the brilliance of its teachers and most of all to Abélard, a man who rejected the comforts of a noble birth to become a scholar.

Abélard studied hard and soon so outshone his teachers that it was he who became the master, commanding great audiences. Nothing, he argued, could be accepted unless it could be *proved* true, and in religion faith should be arrived at by reason. Topics he discussed and argued included questions like, Is God a substance, or not?

To Abélard's lectures came a beautiful and intelligent girl of 17 named Héloise, and Abélard soon fell in love with her. The couple eloped and married, but because marriage would harm Abélard's career in the Church, Héloise kept it secret. Like all secrets, however, it was discovered and Héloise fled to a convent.

With his bride gone, Abélard went into a monastery. To him there, Héloise wrote some of the most beautiful letters in European literature: letters of pure love and nobleness of character that have become famous.

Abélard continued to teach, but he had many enemies and he was condemned by them as a heretic. His health never recovered from this blow and he died a year later.

ENGLAND IN THE SAME PERIOD

871	Alfred the Great	1035	Harold I
901	Edward the Elder	1040	Hardicanute
925	Athelstan	1042	Edward the Confessor
940	Edmund the Elder	1066	Harold II; Battles of Stamford Bridge and Hastings
946	Edred		
955	Edwy		
958	Edgar the Peaceful	1066	William I
975	Edward		(The Conqueror)
978	Ethelred the Unready	1087	William II
1016	Edmund Ironside	1100	Henry I
1016	Canute	1135	Stephen

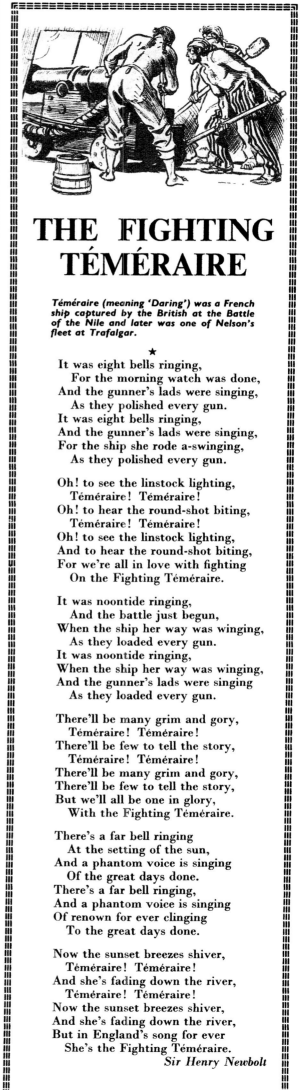

THE FIGHTING TÉMÉRAIRE

Téméraire (meaning 'Daring') was a French ship captured by the British at the Battle of the Nile and later was one of Nelson's fleet at Trafalgar.

★

It was eight bells ringing,
  For the morning watch was done,
And the gunner's lads were singing,
  As they polished every gun.
It was eight bells ringing,
And the gunner's lads were singing,
  For the ship she rode a-swinging,
  As they polished every gun.

Oh! to see the linstock lighting,
  Téméraire! Téméraire!
Oh! to hear the round-shot biting,
  Téméraire! Téméraire!
Oh! to see the linstock lighting,
And to hear the round-shot biting,
For we're all in love with fighting
  On the Fighting Téméraire.

It was noontide ringing,
  And the battle just begun,
When the ship her way was winging,
  As they loaded every gun.
It was noontide ringing,
When the ship her way was winging,
And the gunner's lads were singing
  As they loaded every gun.

There'll be many grim and gory,
  Téméraire! Téméraire!
There'll be few to tell the story,
  Téméraire! Téméraire!
There'll be many grim and gory,
There'll be few to tell the story,
But we'll all be one in glory,
  With the Fighting Téméraire.

There's a far bell ringing
  At the setting of the sun,
And a phantom voice is singing
  Of the great days done.
There's a far bell ringing,
And a phantom voice is singing
Of renown for ever clinging
  To the great days done.

Now the sunset breezes shiver,
  Téméraire! Téméraire!
And she's fading down the river,
  Téméraire! Téméraire!
Now the sunset breezes shiver,
And she's fading down the river,
But in England's song for ever
  She's the Fighting Téméraire.
        Sir Henry Newbolt

The DOVER ROAD

WRITTEN AND DRAWN BY
PETER JACKSON

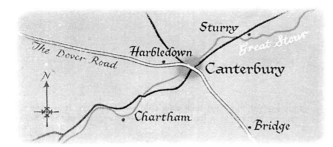

CANTERBURY
Historic city honoured as the birthplace of Christianity in southern England.

In the year 597, Saint Augustine and a company of monks landed on the Isle of Thanet to bring the Christian message to the heathen people of Kent. Ethelbert, King of Kent, had married a Christian princess named Bertha, who was allowed to practise her faith. She persuaded her royal husband to hear the teachings of St. Augustine. Ethelbert became so impressed that he was converted to the Christian faith and was baptized on June 2, 597, in St. Martin's Church. *(See number 1 in the plan below.)*

SAINT MARTIN'S CHURCH

It is the most ancient place of Christian worship in the whole of England. Here, long before St. Augustine and his monks came, was the oratory of Queen Bertha. Although its appearance has greatly changed, some of the original building is still standing, notably the font.

It was from this very font that King Ethelbert received his baptism.

FYDON'S GATE
(Number 2 in plan sketch.)
Fydon's Gate dates from around 1300 and leads to the ruins of the great abbey founded by St. Augustine. In the year 1538 the abbey surrendered to Henry VIII when threatened by attack from his artillery, and became a royal residence. Later, it was used as a brewery until 1843. It is now the entrance to St. Augustine's college for the training of missionaries.

Other monastic remains are the hospital of St. Thomas (number 3) where poor pilgrims spent the night; Black Friars (4) founded in 1236; the poor priests' hospital (5), rebuilt in 1373 and the Grey Friars (6), of which the quaint building shown on the left still spans the river as it has for the past 700 years.

THE WEAVERS' HOUSES
(Number 9 in plan sketch.)
It was here that Huguenot weavers set up their looms when, on the invitation of Elizabeth I, they came to England as refugees from bitter religious persecution in France. The looms are still in use.

Much of Canterbury's city wall still remains, but its gates were demolished in 1781, with the exception of the West Gate. *(Number 7 in plan.)*

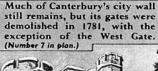

The West Gate, too, was nearly lost. In 1850 Wombwell's circus came to the town, led by a pair of elephants which could not get through the gate. The corporation debated whether to pull it down, but it was saved by one vote.

Adjoining the King's School (8) is this gem of Norman architecture. It dates from about 1160 and is the only staircase of its kind to be seen in England. It is worth a visit.

THE BUILDING OF
ST. DENIS

MANY of the beautiful cathedrals and parish churches in England are built in a style of architecture that is known as 'Gothic'. This style developed in Europe between the 12th and 15th centuries. 'Gothic' buildings were scorned at the time of the Renaissance, when architects harked back to the classical proportions of ancient Greece. They scoffed at the artistry of the medieval world, which they considered barbaric and rudely labelled it 'Gothic', after the barbarian Goths who overran Europe in the 5th century.

Nowadays, these cathedrals and churches all over Europe are widely visited and admired. Certainly, like all styles of architecture, the Gothic style tells us a good deal about the people who built in it.

For one thing, they had a marvellous sense of humour. Look out for the hideous faces of the gargoyles that stick out from the walls, with their eyes rolling and their tongues hanging out! You can be sure that the craftsman delighted in representing his enemies in such guises. Look, too, in unexpected places: the misericord or hinged seats in the choir stalls are often delightfully carved, sometimes with scenes from everyday life (see Henry VII's chapel in Westminster Abbey, and also in the choir-stalls of Exeter cathedral).

Medieval carvings are quite unselfconscious: the ugly things in life are depicted as naturally as the beautiful.

Despite the attitude of Renaissance times, which despised all things medieval, there was a genuine revival of learning in the 12th century. Europe had by this time emerged from that period which is sometimes depressingly called

the 'Dark Ages', and the appearance of the Gothic style went hand in hand with this new intellectual vitality.

Gothic supplanted the style known as 'Romanesque'. In a Romanesque church, the weight of the stone masonry, the immensity of the columns, the thick walls and the small windows, created a stern and forceful atmosphere. This atmosphere was supported by many of the sculptures: Christ in judgement upon the world, and the fate of the Damned being favourite subjects. The building impressed upon the Christian that God was to be feared and obeyed.

Light and airy

What a difference there is when you step into a Gothic cathedral! You are greeted by a vision of light, height and airiness. Slender columns soar upwards to dizzy heights. (This fact, combined with the natural rivalry which existed between one architect and another, sometimes led to disaster!)

What is so different about the Gothic church is the approach to God. All of a sudden, he is shown to be approachable. With arms outstretched, he is the God of love. Horrors are left behind and, as sinful men look around them, what they see is a gentle and sympathetic encouragement to turn over a new leaf.

The elements of the Gothic style—the pointed arch, the ribbed vault and the flying buttress—were not Gothic inventions. They had all been seen before, especially in Armenia, Persia and other eastern regions. The pointed arch can be seen at Durham, but that cathedral is not Gothic.

What was new in the Gothic style was the combined and purposeful use of these things to create a particular effect: to reduce the wall-space and increase the size of the windows to let in light and create a feeling of height. It is an immediate reaction in a Gothic church to look upwards; the horizontal emphasis is minimal.

The Gothic style came into being in the Ile de France, that small region around Paris, ruled by the King of France, from which his power eventually spread all over the country. Compared with the south of France, the region was very backward in intellectual matters, but the fortunes of the French monarchy were on the upgrade, and the guiding hand behind the throne in the reigns of King Louis VI and Louis VII was the talented Abbot Suger of St. Denis. It was he who strove, above all things, to increase the power of the French crown; and it was he who acted as Regent when Louis VII went on crusade.

Suger had several reasons for wanting to build a new abbey church at St. Denis. To start with, the present one was in a bad state of repair; but, mostly, he wanted his King to have a church that was worthy of him. The creation of this church was very dear to Suger's heart, and he was absorbed in the project from beginning to end: he even wrote a little book about it.

It is generally agreed, as far as one can say that Gothic 'began' at any one moment, that it did so in 1140, when the foundation stone was laid for the new choir at St. Denis.

The very rich and grand manner in which Suger proposed to build his abbey brought him into sharp conflict with the greatest spiritual force of his day, St. Bernard, who was a monastic reformer and the friend of popes and kings.

They eventually became friends, but not before there had been a sharp exchange of letters between them, with St. Bernard doing the attacking.

In church architecture, St. Bernard resisted all temptations to decorate in any way whatsoever. He regarded the ornamentation of places of worship as 'fit only to distract the idle from their books'. During his lifetime, the Cistercian Order of monks, of which he was the principal member, built the plainest of churches imaginable. There were no wall-paintings, no stained glass, no sculpture, and the altar was of plain wood. There was nothing, therefore, to distract the mind from spiritual matters.

Suger, who wanted to enshrine both riches and decoration in his abbey, defended himself against Bernard, drawing references from Scripture to assist himself. The sight of such beauty, he argued, would draw men's minds from mundane everyday things and lead them to think of the wonders of heaven.

Both of these points of view marked out the paths which Gothic architecture and art were to follow. The enormous spread of the Cistercian Order brought with it the spread of the Gothic style in an unsophisticated form which is now much admired. But Suger, gathering together the finest artists from far and wide, sparked off the more familiar branch of the style, whose flowering can be seen all over Europe.

Precious stones

Suger supervised every stage in the building at St. Denis with loving care. When his carpenters came to him and expressed their doubts about finding 12 enormous wooden beams for the roof, and carpenters in Paris were not able to help either, Suger took the dimensions and his carpenters and set out to the forest, where, to the amazement of everyone, he found 12 trees of exactly the size needed, and then arranged for ox-carts to transport them to the site.

Kings, princes and noblemen supplied much of the enormous treasure which went to decorate St. Denis. The high altar was covered in gold and encrusted with what Suger himself described as "a great and valuable variety of precious gems; hyacinths, rubies, sapphires, emeralds and topazes, and also a selection of various large pearls". Suger was also very proud of the stained glass windows which, he said "we caused to be painted, by the exquisite hands of many masters from different regions".

Sometimes, in his book, Suger's enthusiasm over the contents of his abbey runs away with him. He is like a cook, licking his lips over the delicious ingredients he is putting into a splendid confection. Then again, it seems, he sometimes remembers St. Bernard's stringent comments and rises in defence of his abbey.

The day of the consecration of St. Denis in 1144 was a great one for Suger. Nineteen archbishops and bishops consecrated the 20 altars, and the abbey was packed with capacity crowds who came to see King Louis VII and 12 of his knights act the parts of Christ and the Twelve Apostles in the ceremony.

Just as Suger must have wished, the abbey at St. Denis was a 'trend-setter'. In the years that followed, the Gothic style blossomed in northern France (and quickly spread to England) and found its full expression in the magnificent cathedral of Chartres.

Abbot Suger chooses trees for the roof beams of his new abbey church.

This medieval-style pictorial representation by LOOK AND LEARN artist Dan Escott of a scene from the First Crusade shows the Crusaders trapped by the Saracens between the two peaks known as the Horns of Hattin by the Sea of Galilee.

When the Crusaders set up their camp between these two peaks they were quickly surrounded by the Saracen army of Saladin, who rained arrows at the Christians from the surrounding rocks. Saladin added further to their discomfort in the intense heat by getting his men to set fire to the parched grass in the pass.

Flying from the red striped tent are the arms of Jerusalem and the standard held by the Crusader knight shows the arms of their leader, King Guy of Lusignan. On the flag over the white tent you can see how King Guy has quartered both these arms on his personal standard as King of Jerusalem.

Foreground left, is a Knight Templar of about 1145. Right is a Knight Hospitaller of the same period.

CRUSADERS WHO NEVER FOUGHT A BATTLE

LOUIS THE SEVENTH

WITH a Christian King on the throne of Jerusalem at the end of the triumphant First Crusade, the Europeans who had settled down in the Holy Land after the terrible three-year struggle to capture it looked forward to the dawning thirteenth century with high hopes and abundant enthusiasm.

Life was certainly good. The constant sunshine warmed their homes, nurtured fresh fruits for their tables and brought a mellowness into their lives that had never been there when they lived in cold, hard Western Europe.

For all these bountiful blessings the Crusaders desired to give thanks. Although they were soldiers at heart their Christian faith was as deep as ever and it was from this combination of soldierliness and saintliness that they formed themselves into two knightly bands known as the Hospitallers and the Templars.

The full title of the Hospitallers was "The Order of the Knights of St. John," the name *Hospitallers* being derived from the hospital or hostel of St. John which had been built as a shelter for pilgrims to the Holy Land. The *Templars* received their name from their headquarters—Jerusalem's Temple of Solomon.

Both these groups were made up of deeply religious, God-fearing men who as civilians led simple, abstemious lives but who were quite capable of donning armour at the least sign of trouble and fighting with all the old ferocity that had made the Crusaders feared among Saracens. Both groups, too, were founded with the object of protecting Christian pilgrims to the Holy City, and both very soon wielded so much power and influence throughout the Holy Land that they, rather than the monarchy and government, were the real rulers of the Near East.

Besides acquiring power, the Templars and Hospitallers acquired riches. They developed the land and built superb castles and, like good settlers, they merged into and became part of their new country, where they came to be known as the Franks.

The Saracens Swoop

The Saracens, of course, disliked the Franks almost as much as when they were Crusaders. They still regarded these Christians as foreigners in their land, although the necessities of trade made them bury their differences. Like all smouldering, aggrieved people, they needed only a leader to put a match to their gunpowder, and when this leader emerged in the person of a man named Zengi the Saracens swooped gleefully on to the important Christian city of Edessa. They captured it by the novel device of lighting fires under the walls so that the flames ruined the mortar between the stones and the walls collapsed. Then they burned the city and put its Christian inhabitants to the sword.

Europe was first numbed, then galvanized by the news of Zengi's victory. Clearly it was the signal for another Crusade.

Just as had happened when Pope Urban preached the First Crusade half a century earlier, the knights and peasants of France this time gathered in a French field to hear the oratory of Bernard of Clairvaux. Again the crowd was

When the huge and brilliant new army reached the Holy Land everyone suddenly decided that instead of fighting they would all go home!

swayed and soon the Second Crusade was under way.

These Frenchmen who set out in the year 1147 for the Holy Land had their own King, Louis the Seventh, to lead them. But Bernard of Clairvaux, realizing that still more Crusaders were necessary, went ahead of them into Germany and persuaded the German King, Conrad the Third, to start out with a second force.

The French and the Germans finally linked up in the Holy Land a year after they had set out. Constant skirmishes with the Saracens had depleted their ranks, but they were fit and well fed by comparison with the soldiers of the First Crusade when it had reached the same point.

They had, too, the additional advantage of the strong alliance of the Franks, descendants of those First Crusaders, now led by Baldwin, King of Jerusalem, who had all the men and supplies he needed, as well as the armies of the Hospitallers and the Templars. When all these forces came together the army of the Second Crusade was huge enough to strike fear into the most ferocious Saracen.

Objective number one, their leaders decided, would be the Saracen-held city of Damascus, to which they now marched with pomp and ceremony. The procession, spangled with red crosses, stretched for miles over the heat-tortured ground. Shields, armour and lances glinted in the strong sunlight; banners, drapes and knightly coats of arms added colour to the splendid scene. It must have seemed unbelievable then to these enthusiastic soldiers of the Holy cause that within a few weeks their Crusade would collapse in a complete débâcle.

For in that short time the fiercest twin enemies of Crusades—hunger and disease—struck with deadly effect. Thousands died daily, and thousands more deserted the cause. At Damascus the Crusaders camped outside the city walls and settled down for a siege. Still their numbers were depleted with alarming rapidity. They had not been there for very long—and had achieved nothing at all—when the leaders of the Franks, and the Hospitallers and the Templars decided that they were all wasting their time.

They had good reason to lose heart. Within a few days' ride were their lands and estates, urgently demanding their peaceful attentions. At Damascus there were now so few Crusaders that victory was an unlikely prospect, and even if they achieved it there would not be sufficient men to carry on. So they called King Louis and King Conrad into the conference tent and calmly

continued on next page

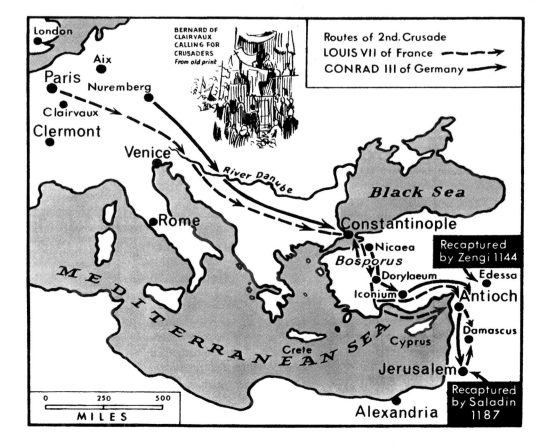

Routes of 2nd. Crusade
LOUIS VII of France - - - ➤
CONRAD III of Germany ——➤

BERNARD OF CLAIRVAUX CALLING FOR CRUSADERS
From old print

London
Aix
Paris
Nuremberg
Clairvaux
Clermont
Venice
Rome
River Danube
Black Sea
Constantinople
Nicaea
Bosporus
Dorylaeum
Iconium
Edessa
Antioch
Damascus
Cyprus
Jerusalem
MEDITERRANEAN SEA
Crete
Alexandria

Recaptured by Zengi 1144
Recaptured by Saladin 1187

0   250   500
MILES

CRUSADERS WHO NEVER FOUGHT A BATTLE

continued from previous page

◀ Left: Conrad the Third, King of Germany, whose army linked up with the French in the Holy Land.

Right: Bernard of ▶ Clairvaux. His fiery oratory swayed the French and began the Second Crusade.

announced that they were all going home.

With that decision the Second Crusade melted away.

Among the Saracens, however, new and vital events were happening. Two years previously Zengi, their leader, had been stabbed to death by one of his slaves after he had caught the man stealing. Eventually their leadership was inherited by a man whose name is etched on the story of the Crusades: a young man named Saladin, who was intelligent, educated, honest and fair—an altogether different brand of enemy to Christendom.

As a boy Saladin's unusual abilities had been spotted by his uncle, a successful Saracen noble who had taken him under his wing. Saladin had served under the Sultan of Syria with success and in time had succeeded his master. In due course he added to his titles the Sultanship of Egypt; and the leadership of these two lands made him the most powerful Muslim in the East and the natural leader of Islam, their religion.

From his youth Saladin had a burning ambition—to deliver Jerusalem from the Christians. The foolhardy antics of one Christian in particular, Raynald de Chatillon, soon gave him the opportunity to fan the flames of hatred between his supporters and the Christians. Raynald was an avaricious nobleman who lived in a great castle near the Dead Sea; he had come to the Holy Land to seek his fortune and he did not care how he found it.

Ignoring the truce then in existence between Saladin and the Christian King Baldwin, Raynald attacked and pillaged a Muslim trading caravan as it was crossing the desert. Then he sank a Muslim passenger ship in the Red Sea and mocked the Muslims as they drowned. Next he raided another caravan—a caravan filled with treasures that were destined, it was said, for Saladin's own sister.

The Trap

Saladin's fury was complete. He mustered a huge Saracen army on the northern border of the Holy Land and prepared to attack. In alarm the Franks, whose King Baldwin was now dead, gathered under the new King of Jerusalem, Guy of Lusignan, and marched to meet their age-old enemy.

When they met the Franks made a terrible and fatal tactical mistake. The ground they chose for their camp was the high pass between two hills, called the Horns of Hattin, close to the Sea of Galilee. When the Saracens came up to them they simply surrounded the pass and held the Christians in a trap—a trap which contained no water and no means of getting any.

As the sun beat down the Franks screamed with thirst. To add to their discomfort Saladin fired the grass around the pass. Frying in the heat now, the Christians had to attack. The Saracens threw them back with ease and followed them up the hillside with volleys of arrows. The Franks had no more strength left for battle and surrendered with pathetic eagerness.

Saladin waited at the foot of the hill, knowing that his men would bring King Guy and the vile Raynald de Chatillon before him. When they were brought in both prisoners pleaded for water. Saladin allowed King Guy to drink, but when the cup was handed to Raynald the angry Saracen leader dashed it out of his hand and felled him to the ground. Then he ordered his men to take Raynald out of the tent and cut off his head.

Saladin noted the worried look on the face of King Guy and hurriedly reassured him. "I would not order the execution of an honourable enemy," he said. And Guy and his other noblemen were eventually allowed to go—for a King's ransom.

But their defeat on the Horns of Hattin had ruined the Franks' resistance to the Saracens. Swiftly Saladin swept through the Holy Land to Jerusalem. In October, 1187, the city surrendered.

For 88 years, since the end of the First Crusade, the city had been in Christian hands. Now once again the Muslim flag flew from its walls. But at the moment of his great triumph Saladin's humanity brilliantly surpassed that of his Christian enemies. Not a Christian in the Holy City was put to the sword; instead, all those who could afford to ransom themselves were allowed to go, while those who could not pay were sold as slaves.

But the mere fact that the Holy City was again in Saracen hands meant that there must be another great Holy War. Eagerly the knights of Western Europe tested the points of their spears and prepared themselves for battle.

BENJAMIN FRANKLIN is commemorated by a square-looking red tablet with gilded lettering at No. 36 Craven Street, near Trafalgar Square, where he lived for a number of years when on official visits to England.

He liked London, in spite of his saying that "The whole town is one great smoaky house. . . ." In all he spent 16 years in England and might have settled here but for the War of Independence.

Franklin spent much time trying to avert this war, but this did not prevent him taking an active part in achieving his country's independence once he realized that the struggle was inevitable.

He returned home to America in 1775, and was immediately appointed to the committee which was drawing up the Declaration of Independence. Afterwards he went to France to secure military aid, and remained there as his country's representative throughout the war.

Have you ever noticed any small plaques on the walls of old houses and other buildings? Those in London look like the one shown in the photograph, and they mark the places where famous men or women have lived. Look for them the next time you are in town.

Franklin rendered almost his last public service when, as president of the Pennsylvania executive council, he played a leading role in drawing up the American Constitution. The final document was not entirely to his liking. Nevertheless, he thought it important that the final decision should be

Franklin disliked the ideas in the book, so he wrote one of his own to disprove them!

unanimous, a result he achieved by skilful diplomacy and goodwill.

The tenth son of a soap and candle maker who had emigrated from Banbury, Oxfordshire, in 1683, Benjamin joined his father's business at ten years of age. This he did not like, so he became apprenticed to one of his elder brothers, who was a printer. At sixteen he ran his brother's paper, the *New England Courant*, for a month while James served a jail sentence for being too outspoken about Massachusetts officials and their lack of speed in suppressing piracy.

Afterwards Benjamin quarrelled with his brother and set off for New York. He found no work there, so he again set off on a journey, this time to Philadelphia, where he arrived virtually penniless. He had a job there for a time in a local print shop, and then came to London, where he found similar work.

It was in London that he first showed his real mettle when he had to set up the type for a book containing theories he felt bound to refute, and proceeded to do so in a book of his own.

Returning to America in 1726, he set up his own business and made sufficient money to retire at an early age, with the intention of writing and studying science. He was responsible for a number of inventions, but he is particularly famous for his experiments with electricity. He was the first to link lightning with electricity, and he invented the lightning conductor. Many terms now commonly used in electrical work originated from him.

Benjamin Franklin's ideas were very advanced for his time. "The rapid progress true science now makes," he once wrote, "occasions my regretting sometimes that I was born too soon."

Royal Beasts

From ancient times it was a common practice for men to take some emblem or device to represent themselves. In medieval times when knights were encased in armour, coats of arms became increasingly popular as a means of identification. These coats of arms were also used on flags and standards in battle, and appeared on seals and badges of livery. The Royal Beasts are heraldic animals: some real, some mythological. They are the monarch's personal emblems. Sometimes the right to display them passes from father to son; sometimes it is inherited through marriage.

THE LION OF ENGLAND

The crowned Lion of England holds a red banner charged with three gold lions 'passant guardant' (which means walking with their heads turned). With his other paw, the golden lion grasps the red cross of St. George on a white shield.

KING RICHARD I of England had a new Great Seal cut in 1195. This showed for the first time the three lions 'passant guardant' which have remained the 'arms' of England ever since. King Richard (seen above storming the walls of Acre during the Third Crusade), carried a shield emblazoned with the lions of England.

The earliest recorded royal shield of arms bearing lions is that which King Henry I gave to his son-in-law, Geoffrey Plantagenet, Count of Anjou, when he married Henry's daughter, Matilda, in 1127. From this marriage began the line of English sovereigns from Henry II to the present Queen.

The English lion was not only to be found on shields. A great war 'helm' of the time of Edward III (left) uses the golden lion of England as its 'crest'. The royal crest used today is still the same, except that the lion stands on, and is wearing, a modern interpretation of a crown.

Kings of England made great use of their heraldic lions. One was placed proudly on the bridge at Rochester by King Henry VIII, amongst other royal beasts. Lions were flown from the King's ships (see right). Here, for instance, they have been painted on the sail of a royal sailing vessel of the early 13th century, for easy identification.

FOUNTAINS ABBEY
IN THE COUNTY OF YORKSHIRE

Built by the monks in the twelfth and thirteenth centuries, Fountains Abbey is unsurpassed in beauty among the ruins of this country. It stands in the West Riding of Yorkshire, north of the Valley of the Nidd, some four miles away from the town of Ripon. The pleasant surrounding countryside makes a wonderful setting for the noble Cistercian abbey, more complete than any other in Yorkshire, a county particularly rich in ruined abbeys. The Cistercians were an order of monks who were vowed to piety and extreme poverty. Their architecture was severe and devoid of all unnecessary ornament. The white robe with a black cowl was simple. The lay brothers were responsible for the building and the rest of their time was spent in study and agriculture. This aerial view shows Fountains Abbey as it stood in the fourteenth century.

Fountains was a wilderness at the end of the twelfth century, when twelve Benedictine monks and their Prior arrived to start a new Order. For two years they lived in hardship with poor food and no roof above them except great yew trees, until Saint Bernard of France requested them, poor as they were, to start building the Abbey.

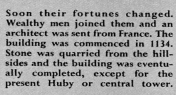

Soon their fortunes changed. Wealthy men joined them and an architect was sent from France. The building was commenced in 1134. Stone was quarried from the hillsides and the building was eventually completed, except for the present Huby or central tower.

After the election of Henry Murdac to the See of York in 1146, partisans of his predecessor set fire to the Abbey in their disappointment, and a large part of it was destroyed. Later the predecessor, William, was again elected, but soon died, after drinking wine from a poisoned chalice.

A—HUBY'S TOWER
B—GUEST TOWER
C—CLOISTERS
D—CHURCH
E—CELLARIUM
F—ABBOT'S HOUSE
G—CELLS
H—REFECTORY
I—KITCHENS
J—CHAPTER HOUSE
K—MONKS' DORMITORY

During the remainder of the twelfth century, work of rebuilding went on ceaselessly. The Cellarium, with its roof vaulting borne on eighteen slender pillars is 300 feet long—20 feet longer than Ripon Cathedral. It is one of the remarkable survivals of the twelfth and thirteenth centuries, and there is no sight in all England like this immense hall, divided into two vast tunnels. It was built in three compartments, one of which may have been used as a refectory, or dining-room, by the lay brothers, the monks who did manual work.

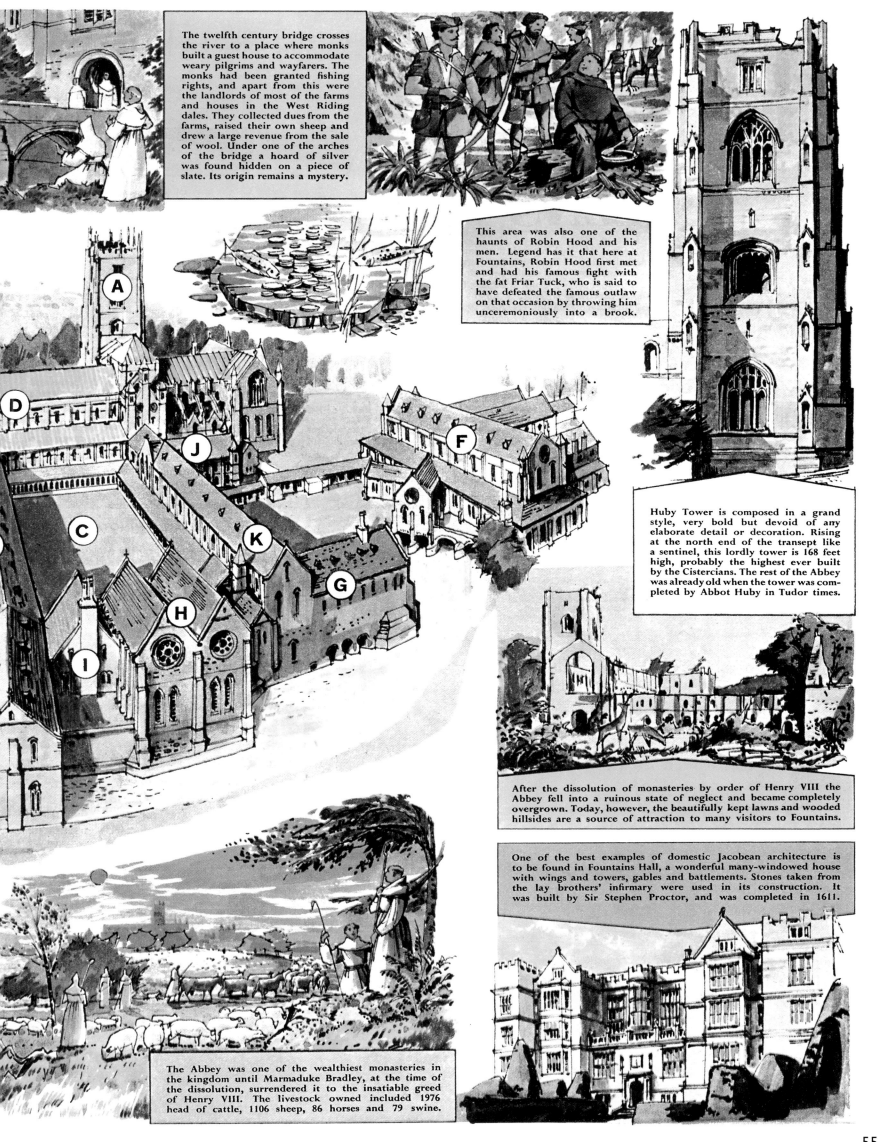

The twelfth century bridge crosses the river to a place where monks built a guest house to accommodate weary pilgrims and wayfarers. The monks had been granted fishing rights, and apart from this were the landlords of most of the farms and houses in the West Riding dales. They collected dues from the farms, raised their own sheep and drew a large revenue from the sale of wool. Under one of the arches of the bridge a hoard of silver was found hidden on a piece of slate. Its origin remains a mystery.

This area was also one of the haunts of Robin Hood and his men. Legend has it that here at Fountains, Robin Hood first met and had his famous fight with the fat Friar Tuck, who is said to have defeated the famous outlaw on that occasion by throwing him unceremoniously into a brook.

Huby Tower is composed in a grand style, very bold but devoid of any elaborate detail or decoration. Rising at the north end of the transept like a sentinel, this lordly tower is 168 feet high, probably the highest ever built by the Cistercians. The rest of the Abbey was already old when the tower was completed by Abbot Huby in Tudor times.

After the dissolution of monasteries by order of Henry VIII the Abbey fell into a ruinous state of neglect and became completely overgrown. Today, however, the beautifully kept lawns and wooded hillsides are a source of attraction to many visitors to Fountains.

One of the best examples of domestic Jacobean architecture is to be found in Fountains Hall, a wonderful many-windowed house with wings and towers, gables and battlements. Stones taken from the lay brothers' infirmary were used in its construction. It was built by Sir Stephen Proctor, and was completed in 1611.

The Abbey was one of the wealthiest monasteries in the kingdom until Marmaduke Bradley, at the time of the dissolution, surrendered it to the insatiable greed of Henry VIII. The livestock owned included 1976 head of cattle, 1106 sheep, 86 horses and 79 swine.

THE GREAT CHARTER

LIKE most English monarchs, King John was often short of money—the more so after he had lost his Continental lands, with all their revenues, to the King of France.

John had other problems too. He succeeded his brother, Richard I, who had spent only six months of his 10 years' reign in England. Richard had bled the country dry to finance his crusading expedition, and England had to pay an enormous ransom to release him after he had been captured on the way home.

After Richard's absence, England had to grow used to John's presence: to the rule of an active and ingenious King who was on the spot to govern.

As feudal lord of England, John enjoyed certain rights over his tenants and could expect certain services from them. John stretched his recognised feudal rights to unrecognisable proportions. In his code of honour there was little that money could not buy.

At first, resistance to John's rule was disorganised. It came from barons like Robert Fitz-Walter and Eustace de Vesci, who were no better, and probably worse, than John himself. Many barons realised that the King had real problems to face in a period of rapidly changing conditions.

As opposition from the barons grew and became organised, John played for time—another of his talents—getting the Pope on his side as he went along.

But the Pope in Rome was far away, and the determined barons were near at hand. On 17th May, 1215, they captured London, which put them in a strong bargaining position. John had to give way temporarily and agree to the limitation of his powers. He did this when he sealed the Great Charter at Runnymede on 15th June.

The Great Charter is a technical, feudal document whose clauses were designed to stop the particular abuses, of a particular time. The Great Charter—so called because of its length, not its contents—was not a revolutionary document. It was partly an attempt to define the King's rights, both as King and as feudal overlord; and partly a commentary on John's imaginative methods of government.

What are we to think, for instance, of the King at whom Clause 39 of the Charter was directed? *"No freeman,"* it says, *"shall be arrested or imprisoned or disseised* (deprived of his possessions) *or outlawed or exiled, or in any way molested, neither will we* (John) *set forth against him, or send* (others) *against him, except by the lawful judgement of his peers and by the law of the land."* In other words, John was forbidden to intimidate those of his subjects who were out of his favour, without first having established their wrong by law.

John found tremendous advantage in the vagueness of his feudal rights. The barons—the most powerful of the tenants who suffered by John's capricious practices—wanted the King's rights and theirs defined and put down on paper.

The King, for instance, was entitled to choose husbands for heiresses who were his tenants. No woman had much say in choosing her husband anyway, and since the husband of an heiress would be the King's new tenant, it was fair that the King should choose someone he could trust.

In return, the King was expected to use his judgment and choose the husband from the same social rank as the heiress. But John had done a terrific 'trade' in heiresses (not to mention widows) accepting the highest offer he could get, and then rushing through the marriage before the poor girl's relatives could find out and complain. Clause 6 of the Charter forbade such practices.

Baron Fitz-Warin, one of the most important barons who pressed for the Charter and who is mentioned in the Charter as a witness.

The King's activities bore down on every rank of society, and some of the Clauses in the Charter relate to the rights of merchants and towns. Take Clause 13, for example. John promised that *"the city of London shall have all its ancient liberties and free customs . . . Furthermore, we will and grant that all other cities, boroughs, towns and ports shall have all their liberties and free customs."* But really, the King was not *granting* anything at all. He was just saying that he would abide by earlier promises.

The most important Clause in the Charter was the one which attempted to enforce its provisions. It was one thing to get John's consent to the Charter, but quite another to see that he observed it. This last Clause set up a Council of 25 barons who were authorised to organise rebellion against the King in the event (which everyone foresaw) of his failure to keep his promises.

The barons were justifiably suspicious, for John wasted no time in setting counter-measures in motion. War was not long delayed and did not end until John's death in October, 1216.

But John's death was not the end of the Great Charter. The Charter formally accepted the principle that the King must accept the law like everyone else, and that if he did not, then he was nothing but a tyrant and his subjects would be justified in rebelling against him.

The Charter has retained its popularity among the people for centuries because it recognised the legality of opposition to the Crown in certain circumstances, and was the first step in the process which led eventually to the formal recognition of Parliament as first the regulator and then the dictator of the King's policy.

King John did not actually sign the Great Charter; he affixed his royal seal to it. The illustration on the right shows the seal, inscribed with the words 'John, by the Grace of God, King of England; Lord of Ireland.'

We do not possess the Charter which John sealed, but four of the copies which were sent round the country have survived. Each was written on a piece of parchment measuring about 15 by 20 inches. Two of the copies are now in the British Museum, one is in Lincoln Cathedral and the other is in Salisbury Cathedral.

THE MODEL PARLIAMENT

The road to London could be difficult and dangerous—and when he got there, the knight had to pay for his own board and lodging. Being elected to Parliament was sometimes a very mixed blessing!

AFTER King John had signed Magna Carta, Parliaments became regular in England, although at first only the most powerful of the King's subjects attended them. Soon however the King's chronic shortage of money once more forced a change.

At that time the Kings of England also ruled over the huge province of Gascony in the south-west of France. War with France was almost continuous. England relied more and more on mercenary troops, and these had to be paid.

Henry III of England feared an attack on Gascony by France's ally, the King of Castille. He needed money to hire more soldiers, but this time the English barons refused to allow further taxation unless the people of the country agreed.

In market places and city squares throughout the land Royal Heralds proclaimed the summoning of a Parliament. But this was to be a Parliament with a difference. Two humble knights from every county were to be called. This was only fair since they, after all, bore the brunt of both war and taxation.

King Henry got his money, of course, and thereafter the knights of the counties were summoned to Parliament.

The election of these knights was a rough-and-ready affair, but it provided a fine excuse for a village fair. The knight who was elected may not have been so happy. The journey to Westminster was difficult and dangerous. Roads were no more than tracks, and could be knee-deep in mud if it rained.

In London, the new Member had to pay for his own food and lodging, and even when he attended Parliament there was little he could do except

agree to further unpopular taxes.

Yet over the years he found that his influence was growing. During the civil war between Henry III and Simon de Montfort, both factions needed the support of the knights. After defeating the King's forces at the battle of Lewes in 1264, Simon de Montfort called a Parliament of his own. Four "discreet knights" from every shire were summoned to discuss the state of the realm.

Next year, Simon summoned another Parliament to Westminster. This time he also called for two representatives from every borough. The knights and barons of the aristocracy were horrified to find themselves associating with mere merchants, but Simon knew what he was doing. He realized where the money now lay—and just who could be taxed! For their part, the merchants were honoured to have their new status

recognised.

In the Middle Ages, most MPs were illiterate. Few people apart from clerics could read or write, and whenever a member wanted to present a petition he had to have it drawn up for him by a clerk.

Only a few years after Simon de Montfort's Parliaments, another important change took place. The Royal Clerks started to keep regular records of these petitions which they called the "Rolls of Parliament." They were in fact in the form of a long roll of parchment, and can still be seen in the Public Records Office in London.

In those days, summoning Parliament was a highly complicated business, so in 1282 Edward I tried out a new scheme. He summoned two Parliaments at once. One, representing the north of England, met at York. Another, representing

the south, met at Northampton.

Then the king realized the danger in this. In the 13th century, England was not as unified as it is today, and the great barons of the north were almost independent. The experiment was not repeated.

Edward I has been called the "Father of Parliament." It was he who summoned the famous "Model Parliament" of 1295, upon which most later Parliaments of the Middle Ages were modelled. The King summoned barons, archbishops, bishops, representatives of the lower clergy, two knights from every shire and two citizens from every borough. It was the first assembly to be really representative of England as a whole, and from that time on Parliament grew rapidly in power and prestige.

With Wallace

SCOTLAND was under the conqueror's heel. The rout of Dunbar was complete, Balliol was deposed and Edward's lieutenants were everywhere. As the English king handed over the seal of government to John de Warenne, he made it clear that Scotland was to be kept in abject servitude.

But resentment of the English yoke remained very much alive. In the hearts of the Scottish people—if not in its nobles'—there was a spirit of defiance. All that was needed was a leader.

In William Wallace the Scots found that leader.

★ ★ ★

The approach of summer seemed only a small release from the winter of Scotland's despair. Admittedly there had been disturbances in the Western Highlands, Aberdeenshire and Galloway, but there was no sign of a co-ordinated uprising against the English. Not until Wallace struck.

With 30 men, Wallace attacked and slew the sheriff in his residence, then set fire to Lanark itself. In those flames was illuminated the hero the Scots had hoped and prayed for, the wholehearted patriot whose methods they could understand and to whom they could all rally.

Much has been written about Wallace, only to prove that not very much is known about him. He seems to have been so active a figure in so troubled a period that his reputation has grown with later hearsay rather than from contemporary recorded sources. Even so, we can piece together enough of Wallace's history to see that he was the sort of man who could stir Scotland's passion and pride.

Probably born at Elderslie, near Paisley, William Wallace was the son of Sir Malcolm Wallace, who owned modest lands which made his sons neither of noble nor of mean birth. As to William's date of birth, we can infer that he was quite young when he killed Hesilrig, possibly between 25 and 30. Reputedly huge, and credited with superhuman strength, he appears to have fitted the image of all epic heroes. And to his heroic physique were added the qualities of intelligence and generalship.

As the people took up arms and trooped to his side, Wallace turned them into a reliable fighting force, kept together by strict discipline. Declaring that he fought in the name of the deposed king, John Balliol, he set out on his mission of liberation. Aided by William de Douglas, the first noble to support his cause, he marched on Scone and attacked the court of the justiciar, William de Ormesby, who only just managed to escape with his life while Wallace took valuable booty.

While Wallace went on to take Lennox and Galloway, resistance was being shown in other parts of the country. Warenne had to send a force under the command of Percy and Clifford to confront the rebels, and it was then that Wallace's few noble supporters deserted him, surrendering at Irvine in July, 1297.

Whether Wallace was at or near Irvine we do not know, but the next we hear of him is in the forest of Selkirk, where Hugh Cressingham, the pompous, hated treasurer, dared not follow. All the time, Wallace's army was growing, and in August he was besieging Dundee.

It must have been at about that time that he was joined by Andrew de Moray, whose men had been carrying all before them in other parts of Scotland.

Together, Wallace and Moray became joint leaders of the Scottish army. And, as they joined forces, Edward I sailed for Flanders, refusing to believe or not caring to listen to Warenne's reports that Scotland was in turmoil.

Wallace's unforgettable hour was nearing.

"Ready to Fight"

Whoever has heard of Wallace has heard of Stirling Bridge. Warenne and Cressingham knew that the threat from the north could no longer be ignored, and advanced with an army said to have numbered some 50,000 foot and 1,000 horse. They reached the Forth and found that Wallace and Moray had occupied a strong position on the north side. Wallace was at the foot of Abbey Craig, the huge rock where his monument can now be seen, and with forces arrayed on the foothills of the Ochils. From this strategic position, he stared down on the plain below, and on the English forces who were positioned between the river and Stirling Castle.

Apparently there were three attempts at mediation, but Wallace's defiant reply was that "we have not come for peace, but ready to fight to liberate our kingdom". It was provocation enough. The English army charged its way across the narrow bridge, two or three abreast. Wallace waited patiently. Only when as many English as he could safely hope to defeat had crossed did he give the order to attack.

Raced upon from both flanks, the English were slaughtered in huge numbers. The bridge was blocked by dead and wounded; the cavalry could not manoeuvre on the swampy ground and was speedily cut down; many who tried to flee were drowned in the river. Cressingham was killed, and his skin cut in strips for trophies; Warenne barely managed to escape to Berwick. It was the first occasion on which a lightly-armed peasant army had overwhelmed a trained feudal army, and the defeat was total.

Inspired by this victory, Wallace and Moray set about restoring Scotland, though Moray died a few months later from wounds sustained at Stirling Bridge. The army grew, both by volunteers and by forcible methods.

After taking Dundee, Edinburgh, Roxburgh, Berwick and Stirling, Wallace raided northern England, burning many of the English towns.

Probably around Christmas, he returned to Scotland, and about the same time was either elected or declared Guardian of the kingdom. A short time after that he may also have been knighted by one of the earls.

But, though Wallace set about his duties as Guardian diligently and diplomatically, time was running out for the Scottish patriot.

Edward had finally realised the threat to his authority and had returned from France. In March, 1298, he moved the seat of government to York and issued writs for men and supplies. By early July, he had crossed the border at Coldstream and by mid-July he was approaching Edinburgh with 80,000 foot and 4,000 horse.

Wallace should surely have harassed the English, rather than risk a pitched battle. But he may have received reports that Edward's army was lacking supplies and that his Welsh troops were on the point of mutiny. Then, too, there seems to have been a possibility of desertion from Wallace's own army, which left him with no alternative but to fight.

And so the English and Scottish armies met, on 22nd July, 1298, at Falkirk.

At the crucial moment before the battle, misfortune overtook Wallace. The few nobles he had with him began quarrelling over the supreme command, and eventually left the field. What followed was little less than bloody slaughter. Wallace's generalship with the forces available to him could hardly be criticised. His spearmen were drawn up in schiltrons—bodies of men kneeling with their spears outstretched before them—and his archers were interspersed between them. But with a force only a third the strength of the better-equipped English, he stood little chance. The English archers shot down the Scots effortlessly, then the knights charged at them and completed the defeat.

So ended Wallace's brief but heroic leadership. Robert Bruce and John Comyn became Guardians of the country, and after that little is known of Wallace's whereabouts. It is certain that he went to Paris to try to win French sympathy, and he may even have gone to Rome in support of the Scottish protest to Pope Boniface against Edward's claim to the overlordship of Scotland. There seems no evidence that he was in Scotland between 1299 and 1303, but he reappears later as an implacable foe, harassing Edward's troops at every opportunity.

By Edward and the English, Wallace was regarded with a contempt and hatred verging on obsession. There was not even a suggestion of admiration for a brave

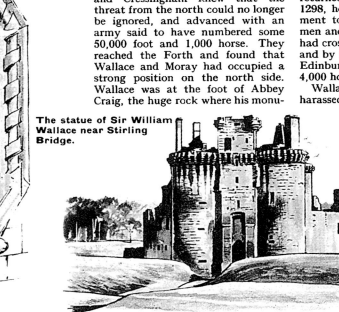

The statue of Sir William Wallace near Stirling Bridge.

Caerlaverock Castle was made famous by its resistance to Edward I in 1300.

for the Cause

While the country's fortunes were at their lowest, one man refused to be daunted by English oppression —— one of the greatest Scottish patriots.

enemy. To them, Wallace was a pillaging brigand—most likely because he was not of noble blood—and he was pursued relentlessly. Records show numerous instances of claims for expenses(!) incurred by people hunting him.

At last, in 1305, he was taken, most certainly through the treachery of his own jealous countrymen. Probably betrayed to Sir John de Menteith by a man he trusted, he was caught somewhere near Glasgow.

Taken swiftly to London, where he was met by a howling mob, Wallace was brought for trial to Westminster Hall on 23rd August. Forced to wear

a laurel crown in mockery of his alleged but unestablished boast that he would wear a crown there one day, he was charged with being a traitor to Edward. Although this was untrue, because he had never sworn allegiance to Edward, he was sentenced to the ghastliest of fates and died in agony the same day.

By extinguishing Wallace's life, the English had far from extinguished the spirit he had aroused. Even while the pursuit of Wallace was in full cry, that same spirit of independence was pursuing the young Robert Bruce, whom destiny had chosen to continue the struggle.

In May, 1297, Wallace led 30 men to Lanark, slew William Hesilrig, the English sheriff, and burnt the town. Stirling Castle (illustrated as it is today) was one of the most strategically vital castles in Scotland. The cannon (foreground) would not have been in use until later.

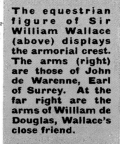

The equestrian figure of Sir William Wallace (above) displays the armorial crest. The arms (right) are those of John de Warenne, Earl of Surrey. At the far right are the arms of William de Douglas, Wallace's close friend.

At the Battle of Stirling Bridge (1297), Wallace waited until "as many of the enemy as he believed he could overcome" had crossed the narrow bridge. Then, while some of his men held the northern bridgehead, the others attacked those who had crossed. This formalised drawing shows the English crossing the bridge two or three abreast; though the bridge would have been made of wood. The present stone bridge was built in the 15th century, upstream from the site of the battle.

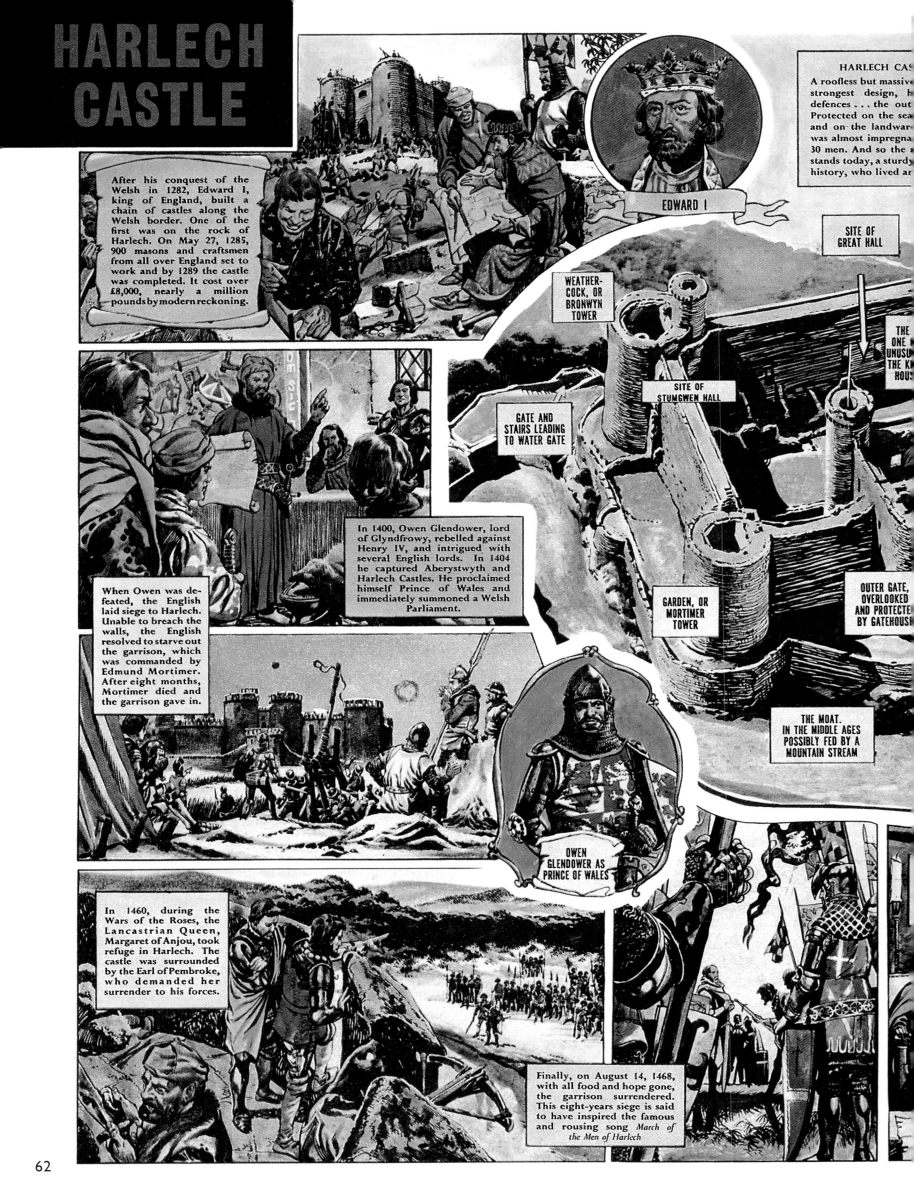

HARLECH CASTLE

After his conquest of the Welsh in 1282, Edward I, king of England, built a chain of castles along the Welsh border. One of the first was on the rock of Harlech. On May 27, 1285, 900 masons and craftsmen from all over England set to work and by 1289 the castle was completed. It cost over £8,000, nearly a million pounds by modern reckoning.

EDWARD I

HARLECH CAS
A roofless but massive
strongest design, h
defences ... the out
Protected on the sea
and on the landward
was almost impregna
30 men. And so the
stands today, a sturdy
history, who lived an

SITE OF GREAT HALL

WEATHER-COCK, OR BRONWYN TOWER

SITE OF STUMGWEN HALL

GATE AND STAIRS LEADING TO WATER GATE

THE ONE UNUSU THE KN HOUS

In 1400, Owen Glendower, lord of Glyndfrowy, rebelled against Henry IV, and intrigued with several English lords. In 1404 he captured Aberystwyth and Harlech Castles. He proclaimed himself Prince of Wales and immediately summoned a Welsh Parliament.

GARDEN, OR MORTIMER TOWER

OUTER GATE, OVERLOOKED AND PROTECTE BY GATEHOUS

When Owen was defeated, the English laid siege to Harlech. Unable to breach the walls, the English resolved to starve out the garrison, which was commanded by Edmund Mortimer. After eight months, Mortimer died and the garrison gave in.

OWEN GLENDOWER AS PRINCE OF WALES

THE MOAT. IN THE MIDDLE AGES POSSIBLY FED BY A MOUNTAIN STREAM

In 1460, during the Wars of the Roses, the Lancastrian Queen, Margaret of Anjou, took refuge in Harlech. The castle was surrounded by the Earl of Pembroke, who demanded her surrender to his forces.

Finally, on August 14, 1468, with all food and hope gone, the garrison surrendered. This eight-years siege is said to have inspired the famous and rousing song *March of the Men of Harlech*

GARDEN TOWER

BRONWYN TOWER

CAUSEWAY AND MOAT

PRISON TOWER **CHAPEL TOWER**

POSTERN GATE TO OUTER WARD

OUTER WARD

STAIRWAY TO WATER GATE

In medieval times the sea came right to the foot of Harlech. The castle is shown, its roofs intact, shortly after completion. The ship is bringing supplies, to be landed on the beach and brought into the castle through the water gate and up the stairway.

WATER GATE

...STANDS TODAY
...the building was of the
...al massive rings of
...and inner wards, etc.
...y an almost sheer cliff
...deep moat, the castle
...led a garrison of only
...ruin of Harlech Castle
...to the makers of Welsh
...in its grey stone walls.

CHAPEL, OR ARMOURER'S TOWER

RUINS OF THE CHAPEL

SITE OF THE BAKEHOUSE

THE WELL

PARLIAMENTARY SOLDIERS

ROYALIST SOLDIER

At the outbreak of the great Civil War most of Wales supported Charles I. Sir Hugh Pennant garrisoned the castle and withstood the siege of a large Puritan force under Colonel John Jones, Oliver Cromwell's brother-in-law. Forced to surrender in 1647, Harlech was the last Royalist stronghold in England and Wales.

MAIN GATE

PRISON, OR DEBTORS' TOWER

CAUSEWAY. ORIGINALLY A BRIDGE WITH ONE OR TWO DRAWBRIDGES

HARLECH CASTLE GROUND PLAN

RAMPART WALL

N W E S

CAUSEWAY

STAIRS TO BEACH

MOAT

The Puritans blew in the gate and removed the roofs of Harlech castle, and for 250 years it stood in peace. One of its chapels became a house, and its ivy-covered walls were the subjects of many nineteenth century paintings. Today the castle is featured in almost all the souvenirs bought by visitors to the historic Welsh town

...e to Harlech during the
...ears and parts of the
...into ruin. The local
...held in the castle and
...tower served as a jail.

Harlech castle is now in the care of H.M. Office of Works and thousands of visitors come each year to admire the magnificent view of Snowdonia from its worn, grey stone battlements.

The TRIGAN EMPIRE

A strange craft has landed on the planet Elekton in the country of Hericon. The three occupants of the craft—visible only as luminous spheres—have taken over the minds and bodies of a gelf-herd and two of his flock . . . and now two of them are about to take over Janno and Keren . . .

Janno and Keren awakened, but alien minds directed their thoughts and their speech.

The mind and body of the creature I occupy belongs to one named Janno.

. . . And mine is called Keren. Like the other creature, an officer in the service of the Trigan Empire.

The three set off at dawn.

This mind of Janno tells me that we are on our way to the Court of King Kassar of Hericon.

Excellent . . . you have both much improved your position in the species of this planet.

He is a great ruler.

The cunning intelligence that controlled the mind of the old gelf-herd seized upon the opportunity.

As we are stranded on this planet, we must occupy the minds and bodies of the highest and most powerful creatures possible, so that we can dominate the planet . . . I shall take over this King Kassar!

Shortly before midday they came in sight of Hericon city, and were soon at the gates of the royal palace.

Janno and Keren . . . officers of the Trigan Empire, with their servant! We bring a letter for your king!

Pass, Trigans!

Stern-faced Kassar of Hericon received the letter which 'Janno' handed to him.

From my master, His Imperial Majesty the Emperor Trigo!

On reading the letter, King Kassar's harsh features relaxed in a smile of pure pleasure.

Ha! My friend the Emperor tells me here that he is on his way to visit us for the celebration of the Great Games. That is excellent news!

© 1967 IPC, a Division of Time Inc. All Rights Reserved. Used with permission of DC Comics

Kassar ordered a feast to be instantly served in honour of the messengers ... and the three newcomers exchanged a muttered conversation.

Tonight, when he sleeps, I will take over the king!

Yes!

The Emperor Trigo is a great one also ... the greatest ruler on the planet. When he comes here I will take him over!

The feast began, and went on far into the night.

During a pause in the huge meal, matched pairs of Hericon warriors entertained the guests with fights to the death, after the barbaric manner of that country.

He has him!

Well thrown ... now strike with your sword, man!

Not till the dawn of Elekton's twin suns was there silence in the vast hall, and King Kassar slept where he sat.

Now!

From the ear of the sleeping gelf-herd rose the luminous sphere ...

Aaaah!

It hovered for a few moments over the head of the sleeping king ... and then ...

Next Episode: The Courage of Trigan's Emperor!

65

The Long Road To Cathay

Marco Polo

The lure of silks and treasure drew Marco Polo on a journey of a thousand days to reach China — where he was to remain for over twenty years

RUSTICIAN, a prisoner from Pisa incarcerated in Genoa Jail, gasped in astonishment when he heard the name of the new prisoner who had been sent to share his miserable cell. "So you're the famous Marco Polo!" he exclaimed. "We've all heard a great deal about you!"

As the two prisoners got to know each other, Rustician implored Marco Polo to tell his story. "I'll write it down for you," he said. "Then you'll be as famous after you're dead as you are now!"

The story that Marco Polo began to relate drove Rustician's pen across the thick paper with a heavy scratching sound that seemed to sweep all the dreariness out of that prison cell, as the prisoner-scribe recorded adventure and travel on a scale undreamed of in that autumn of 1296 . . .

Marco's father, Niccolo Polo, and his uncle Matteo, were Venetian brothers with a zest to reach the fabled land of Cathay — China as we call it — where legend claimed that enormous riches awaited the first bold traders.

It took 15 years for the Polo brothers to travel to the Court of the great Kublai Khan of China and back again. When they returned after incredible adventures, Niccolo's wife had died and his son Marco, whom he had left behind, was 15 years old.

For hours Marco listened with other Venetians to his father's tales of that amazing journey that included snowstorms, warring Tartars, mighty floods, the scorching Gobi Desert and the strange splendour of the oriental Court.

"We have given a pledge to return to the Court of Kublai Khan," Niccolo Polo said. "The Khan has asked our Pope to send him a hundred missionaries to teach Christianity to the Chinese people. He also asked for a jar of oil from the Holy Sepulchre at Jerusalem."

Marco Polo was 17 when his father and uncle set out on their second journey — and

there was no question but that he would go with them. It proved a good deal harder, though, to find a hundred missionaries ready to brave the unknown perils of an Asian journey. Eventually, two friars agreed to join the expedition — and both of them decided to give up when they heard that Armenia, a country they had to cross, had been invaded by a despotic Sultan.

The three Polos pressed on. Marco fell ill and his sickness delayed the journey for a whole year. When he recovered the march continued, taking the family on a month-long crossing of the Gobi Desert. Four days from the Khan's Court, messengers sent out to meet them embraced them with a heart-felt welcome and listened awestruck to their tales of a journey that had lasted a thousand days.

CONTINUED ON NEXT PAGE ▶

Without maps to guide them, Marco Polo and his companions had to cross burning deserts and high mountain ranges. Much of the land along their route remains uncharted to this day.

"Who is this man?" asked Kublai Khan when his eyes fell upon young Marco.

"My lord," replied Niccolo, "he is your servant, and my son."

"He pleases me," said the Khan, "and he is most welcome."

Marco did indeed please the Chinese Emperor. The Khan liked him so much that he sent him on a mission that lasted six months.

Time after time after that Marco was sent on secret missions or trading trips all over the East. He tells us about the then unknown islands of Cipango — the land we call Japan. "The people have great stores of precious metals. They are fair and civilised in their manners . . ."

He tells us, too, about Tibet, Bengal and India, all places where he was sent to do administrative work in the provinces ruled by the Khan.

"The Chinese Empire is composed of 34 provinces," Marco recorded. "At regular intervals on the roads that span it are posts for travelling messengers. At each post is a room with a bed covered with silk and everything useful for a traveller . . ."

As the years went by all the Polos became the special favourites of the Khan and they grew rich as a result. But they had good reason to become anxious as Kublai Khan grew old and feeble, for the Court was a web of jealous intriguers and the Venetians feared for their lives if the Khan died. But the Khan liked the Venetians far too much to allow them to go. Then fate played them a good hand.

The King of Persia, the grandson of Kublai Khan's own brother, had asked the Mongol ruler to send him a wife chosen from his own royal family. Princess Kogatin, who was 17, was selected, and the envoys sent to fetch her were so taken with the Polos that they begged the Khan to let them travel with the bridal party.

In the circumstances, not even Kublai Khan could refuse. Reluctantly, he agreed to let them go as Kogatin's escort. The journey began with 14 ships manned by nearly 2,000 men.

Stormy Voyage

After three months at sea they reached Java, then Sumatra, where storms delayed them for five months. It took another 18 months to reach the Persian port of Ormuz.

Several of Princess Kogatin's servants had by then succumbed to the rigours of the journey and died. The Princess herself survived only to discover in Persia that the King, her intended husband, had also meantime died. In true medieval style, Kogatin was then presented to his son.

The Polos had to make their way from Persia onwards to Europe by the most difficult routes, because so much war and devastation lay across the easiest way. The journey home from Peking took three years altogether and the Polos counted themselves lucky to have left the Khan's court when they did, for they learned that Kublai had died after their departure.

At last the magnificent water city of Venice was in sight. But the Polos had not bargained for the surprise they found there. After 24 years' absence, burned by the desert sun and wearing Tartar clothes, they were unrecognisable.

No one was convinced that the strangely-attired travellers were the three Polos until the trio held a banquet and there, before the assembled guests, tore open the linings of their clothes to let flow the cascade of gold and jewels they had brought from Peking.

A few months later the Venetians and the Genoese were at war, and Marco Polo sailed in a galley against the Genoese fleet.

The ships from Genoa swooped down on those from Venice and in the skirmish that followed Marco's ship was dismasted. The Genoese swarmed aboard her and Marco and his sailors were taken as prisoners to Genoa Jail. There, of course, he met Rustician the scribe, to whose efforts we owe the story of Marco Polo.

After three years Marco was ransomed and returned to Venice, where he lived for another 25 years on his fame and fortune.

Marco Polo's capture by the Genoan fleet was a happy accident for posterity, for while he was in captivity a fellow prisoner wrote down the tale of his travels in the East.

WESTWARD HO!

The chief geographers of the Dark Ages were the Vikings, who extended their horizons west and north in search of fresh lands to loot and conquer. They explored Britain and cruised northwards, locating Greenland and Iceland, which they colonized.

The Swedes surveyed the European coastline thoroughly. Later they navigated the rivers of Europe, sailing inland as far as Russia. There they captured Kiev and journeyed southwards to the Black Sea. But they did not explore the Far East.

In the Far East the Arabs reigned supreme, spreading across Asia and the Mediterranean lands. In 900 the Arab geographer Jakoubi explored Russia, central Africa and sailed into the North Atlantic ocean, sighting a land to the west.

Most geographers did not believe that more land existed in the west. But in 1000 Vikings sailed farther westwards and reached a country which was probably America. They colonized it, but later returned home for unknown reasons, leaving the pastures once more to Indians. It became a forgotten land.

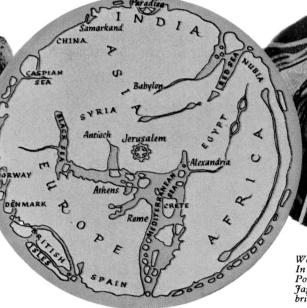

Medieval mapmakers believed the world was flat and that unwary seamen might sail off the edge. This Hereford map (1280) is typical of their religious beliefs, showing a flat world ringed by water and centred on the Holy Land.

Western explorers now ventured out to rediscover the East. In the thirteenth century the Venetian traveller Marco Polo went overland to China, explored Asia and put Japan on the map. He gave detailed accounts of his routes, bringing back fantastic tales of the wealth to be found in eastern lands.

As the East opened up again, new sea routes for trade were needed. Prince Henry of Portugal, a great geographer, fitted out a fleet in the 1400s to chart the oceans and sail off the known map. His crews discovered several Atlantic islands.

Portuguese seamen explored the African coast and opened it up for trade as far as Sierra Leone. In 1498 Da Gama charted a new sea-route to India by rounding the dreaded Cape of Good Hope. There was a growing conviction that the world was round.

The Genoese sailor Columbus tried to prove the world was round by sailing west to reach the East in 1492-8. His passage was blocked by a land-mass he thought was China. In fact it was the rumoured land in the west—America.

The story of Africa... 'Towards the Setting

D URING the 3rd century A.D., the great Negro kingdom of Kush, in the eastern Sudan, fell before invaders from Axum in Ethiopia, who had grown rich and strong from their gold trade with the Arabs. The people of Kush had to flee for their lives and many, according to an

Early in the 4th century, the camel was brought to North Africa from Asia. The advent of the camel encouraged Mediterranean traders to send more frequent caravans across the Sahara desert to trade with Ancient Ghana, which grew prosperous and powerful.

Arab historian, "marched towards the setting sun", spreading into the central and western Sudan. Here they founded kingdoms with organizations similar to Kush: and Kush, in its time, had derived its organization from Ancient Egypt.

The earliest of these ancient African kingdoms are probably at Darfur, which lies about half way between the valley of the Nile and the Niger. One of the most important kingdoms was Ancient Ghana, founded early in the 4th century. It was many miles to the north-west of modern Ghana, between the head-waters of the Senegal and Niger rivers.

It was about this time that the camel was introduced to North Africa from Asia. Mediterranean traders were able to send more frequent caravans across the Sahara, and Ghana, having gained control of the rich gold deposits of the region, became rich and powerful.

Egypt and North Africa were by now part of the Roman empire, and Christianity was coming to north-east Africa. In the 4th century, the Emperor of Ethiopia and his people were converted, and very soon afterwards, during the reign of the Roman Emperor Constantine, Christianity became the religion of the Roman empire. The pagan temples of Egypt gradually fell into disuse and some were destroyed.

In the 5th century, however, Rome fell before the attacks of the Goths and the great days of the western part of the Roman empire were over. During these troubled years, nomadic Berbers living in the Sahara began to raid northwards, on their newly-acquired camels, pillaging the lands of the settled agricultural Berbers of the North African plains. These nomads were the strange, veiled Tuaregs, who had a rigid caste system, with an hereditary

aristocracy who were warriors, and they kept Negro slaves.

In the year A.D. 570, the prophet Mohammed was born in Arabia and on his death his followers began a warlike campaign to convert people to the Mohammedan faith. They overran Arabia and Syria and then Mesopotamia and Persia. Early in the 7th century, they invaded Egypt and Nubia and then turned north-westwards, eventually occupying the whole of North Africa and crossing to Spain.

After a few years, there were only a few Christians, known as Copts, left in Egypt, for the bulk of the people had been converted to Mohammedanism, and when the Arabs invaded Spain, there were many Berber converts to this faith in their armies. Ethiopia, however, cut off and aloof in her highlands, was not invaded and remained Christian.

Also unaffected for many years were the ancient African kingdoms deep in the heart of Africa. Some time during the 8th century, or even earlier, the first Mande kingdom arose, in the valley of the Upper Niger. To the north-east of Lake Chad was Kanem, which a 9th century Arab described as "a great kingdom among the kings of the Sudan . . . They spend their time cultivating and looking after their cattle; and their religion is the worship of their kings . . ."

This worship of the king, who was believed to be divine, had existed in Ancient Egypt. In all these ancient African Kingdoms, the king was regarded as a god, and at his death both animal and human sacrifices were offered.

By the 11th century, an Arab historian recorded that "the king of Ghana can put 200,000 warriors in the field, more than 40,000 of them being armed with bow and arrow." The capital city was "a very large city with

Sun'
by Mary Cathcart Borer

Illustrated by: Angus McBride

several markets, many date palms and henna trees as big as olives . . . filled with fine houses and solid buildings.''

In 1062 — four years before William the Conqueror landed in England — the Tuaregs, who had become fanatical followers of a Mohammedan leader called Ibn Yasin, launched a movement to convert the kingdoms of the Sudan, first attacking Ghana. Fighting was long and bitter and in the end Ghana disintegrated, but by the beginning of the 13th century the kingdom of Mande, by now converted to the Mohammedan faith, emerged to take its place, with a new capital, Mali. One of its greatest emperors was Mansa Musa, who came to power in 1307. He captured the cities of Gao and Timbuktu, on the Upper Niger, and at Timbuktu ordered many new mosques and houses to be built.

Mali, Gao and Timbuktu became centres of Arab culture and learning as well as for the camel caravans which carried their valuable loads of gold and ivory northwards to the Mediterranean. Amongst the merchandise they brought back from the Barbary coast were books in manuscript for the learned judges, doctors and clerics of Timbuktu, who were maintained by the emperor and visited by students and scholars from as far away as Cairo and Baghdad.

One of the greatest emperors of the kingdom of Mande was Mansa Musa. He came to power in 1307. The cities that he built became centres of Arab culture. Here, in his capital city of Mali, Mansa Musa is borne on a litter by subject chiefs, and attended by the court poet (wearing the bird-head and feathers). ▶

The bloodshed must have seemed endless to our ancestors who endured this

"I MEAN TO SETTLE A ACCOUNTS WITH THEM IF I CAN"

Above: This is our artist's impression of a 15th century manuscript painting, and it shows King Edward III with some of his subjects. The shield has the French fleur-de-lis on it as well as the royal lions. It was painted about a century after the event. **Below:** In 1338, just after the Hundred Years War had started, Southampton was ruthlessly pillaged by the French. It was the beginning of a long series of battles, sieges, sackings, victories and defeats on both sides.

PERCHED on a column of old wine-barrels filled with sand, the look-out was cold and cramped. He heard the bells of the churches in the port some miles away summoning the faithful to Mass, and grinned. Not long before he was relieved now! He peered seawards again—and nearly fell off his perch in astonishment. A fleet of ships had appeared from nowhere and was moving steadily towards the harbour. The look-out scrambled down, fired the beacon of pitch to spread the alarm, and scampered back to his village.

Soon the clangour of battle rose from the narrow streets of the port. It pursued the look-out as he ran. Then came an ominous silence. From the outskirts of the town the look-out looked back. Plumes of smoke were drifting from every house and long lines of townsfolk, laden with their belongings, were

This shows the type of armour used during the war. On the right is a "coat of plates" opened out and from the inside. Once the head was put through the central hole, the small plates protected the shoulders and the body armour wrapped around—and was secured over—the back flap. The iron plates were riveted to the strong material. A rich knight might have a splendid suit covered with velvet. This type of armour had been used for 150 years and soon the complete breastplate was worn.

The map shows France at the beginning of the Hundred Years War. Aquitaine is on the South-West coast, shown in red, the other English possession, also in red, being Ponthieu

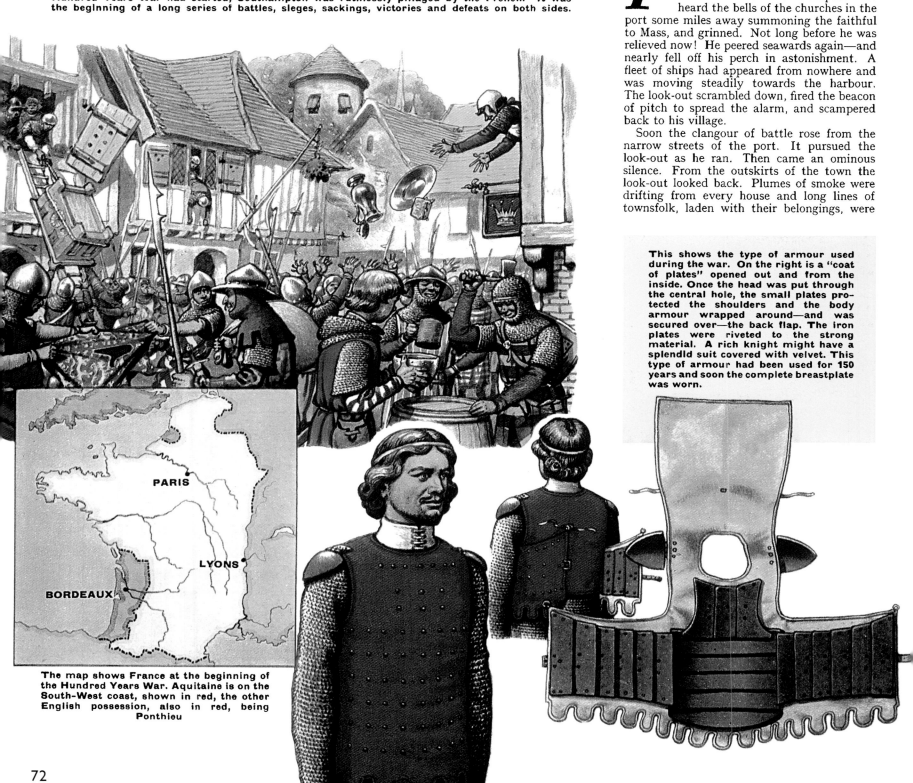

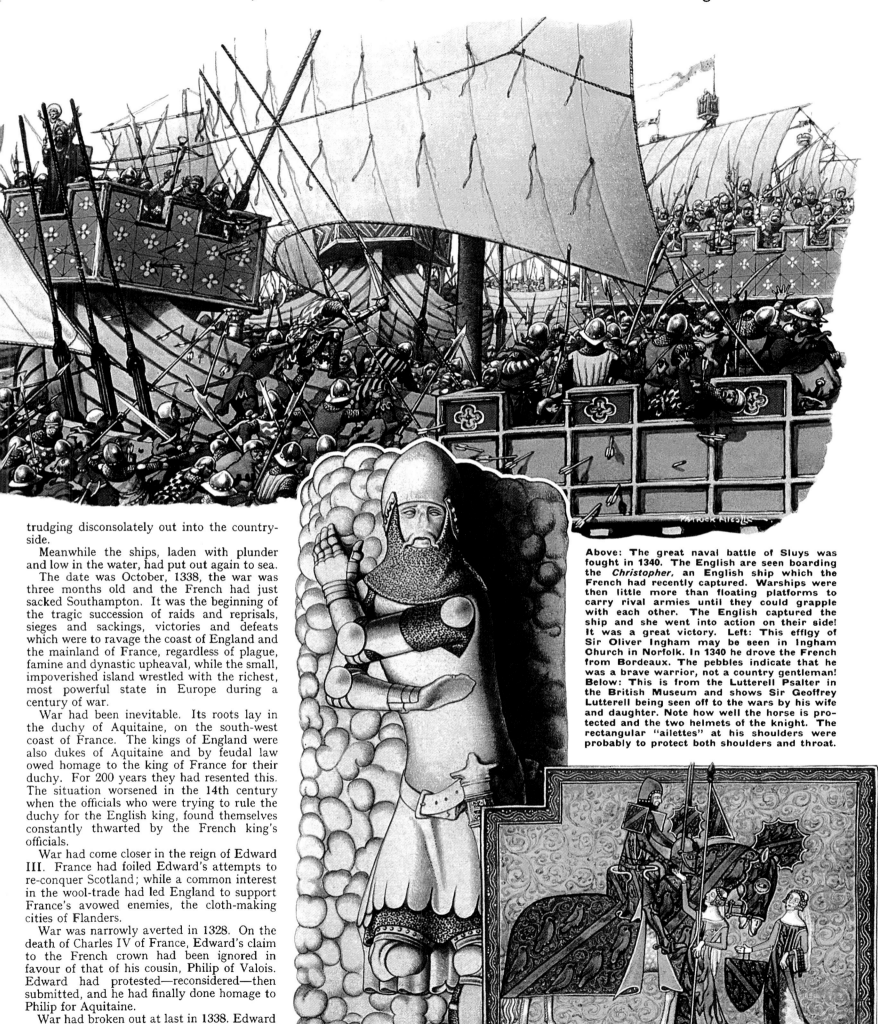

trudging disconsolately out into the country-side.

Meanwhile the ships, laden with plunder and low in the water, had put out again to sea.

The date was October, 1338, the war was three months old and the French had just sacked Southampton. It was the beginning of the tragic succession of raids and reprisals, sieges and sackings, victories and defeats which were to ravage the coast of England and the mainland of France, regardless of plague, famine and dynastic upheaval, while the small, impoverished island wrestled with the richest, most powerful state in Europe during a century of war.

War had been inevitable. Its roots lay in the duchy of Aquitaine, on the south-west coast of France. The kings of England were also dukes of Aquitaine and by feudal law owed homage to the king of France for their duchy. For 200 years they had resented this. The situation worsened in the 14th century when the officials who were trying to rule the duchy for the English king, found themselves constantly thwarted by the French king's officials.

War had come closer in the reign of Edward III. France had foiled Edward's attempts to re-conquer Scotland; while a common interest in the wool-trade had led England to support France's avowed enemies, the cloth-making cities of Flanders.

War was narrowly averted in 1328. On the death of Charles IV of France, Edward's claim to the French crown had been ignored in favour of that of his cousin, Philip of Valois. Edward had protested—reconsidered—then submitted, and he had finally done homage to Philip for Aquitaine.

War had broken out at last in 1338. Edward

Above: The great naval battle of Sluys was fought in 1340. The English are seen boarding the *Christopher*, an English ship which the French had recently captured. Warships were then little more than floating platforms to carry rival armies until they could grapple with each other. The English captured the ship and she went into action on their side! It was a great victory. Left: This effigy of Sir Oliver Ingham may be seen in Ingham Church in Norfolk. In 1340 he drove the French from Bordeaux. The pebbles indicate that he was a brave warrior, not a country gentleman! Below: This is from the Lutterell Psalter in the British Museum and shows Sir Geoffrey Lutterell being seen off to the wars by his wife and daughter. Note how well the horse is protected and the two helmets of the knight. The rectangular "ailettes" at his shoulders were probably to protect both shoulders and throat.

"I MEAN TO SETTLE WITH THEM IF I CAN"

had become convinced that France intended to fight on behalf of the Scots and that an invasion fleet was being assembled in Normandy. At once he had sought and found allies in the Low Countries and Germany. Philip, in response to these defiant moves by his vassal, had confiscated Edward's land in France, which was virtually a declaration of war. Thereupon, Edward revived his claim to the French crown and sent a challenge to King Philip. "We give you notice," he wrote, "that we shall claim and conquer our heritage of France by armed force and from this day forth we challenge you." Then, taking advantage of a revolt among the cities of Flanders against the French, Edward sailed for the Low Countries from Orwell in Suffolk in July, 1338. In every church in England, priests led their congregations in prayer for the success of his expedition.

Their prayers were not immediately effective—on land, at any rate. England's allies proved unreliable, the French refused to risk a major battle, and the campaigns of 1338-40 were inconclusive. Although Edward was proclaimed king of France in the market-place of Ghent in January, 1340, and although his new Great Seal displayed the lilies of France quartered with the leopards of England, his title was still a hollow one.

At sea, however, it was different. In spring 1340, while Edward was back in England raising more men, Philip assembled at Sluys on the coast of Flanders a fleet of almost 200 ships, ready to invade England or to intercept Edward when he set out again. When Edward's advisers learned of the French fleet, they urged the king to defer his departure. Edward rounded on them: "I will cross in spite of you," he snapped, "and you who are afraid, where no fear is, may stay at home."

The battle begins!

Edward and his new contingents sailed in June. On the 23rd they came in sight of Sluys; a forest of masts showed them that the enemy was still there. Remembering Southampton, the king was pleased. "I have long wanted to fight them," he smiled. "They have inflicted so much damage on me that I mean to settle accounts with them if I can."

Slowly the two fleets took up battle formations. The ships themselves took no part in the struggle; they existed merely to provide a floating platform on which men at arms would fight as they did on land. The English formed up in threes, one vessel containing men at arms between two containing archers. The French were arranged in four lines, each vessel clamped and chained to its neighbour.

In front was the *Christopher*, the flagship in which Edward had sailed from Orwell two years previously. The French had captured her a year later; now, crammed with Genoese cross-bowmen, mercenaries in the service of France, her presence in their line of battle was a calculated insult to the English.

The shipmasters delicately coaxed the two blocks of ships towards each other. Soldiers, lining the decks, nervously fingered their weapons; archers tested their strings; and trumpeters moistened their lips, ready to give the signal to board. Suddenly with a juddering impact the ships came together; sailors flung grappling hooks on chains over the ships opposite them and made them fast. Battle was joined.

Avenged!

The fighting was fiercest around the *Christopher*. Heedless of the bolts from the crossbows which tore through their ranks, the English swarmed over the great ship giving the Genoese no time to re-load. Swiftly they cleared her decks, forcing the enemy over the side. Soon the *Christopher* went into action again, this time in her rightful place in the English van.

Heartened by their early success, the English pressed home their attack. Their archers sent flights of arrows thudding into the massed French soldiery; then their men at arms closed in, trampling over writhing, moaning figures which clutched vainly at the shafts which transfixed them, and drove the French into the sea.

Eventually all but 24 of the French ships had been captured. The English were triumphant; the French humiliated. King Philip's jester joked bitterly about it at court. "Why, Sire," he asked his master, "are the English cowards? Because, unlike the French, they dare not jump into the sea."

The battle of Sluys avenged the sack of Southampton; it removed for the time being the threat of a French invasion; and it gave Edward control of the Channel. Now he could land his armies in France wherever and whenever he wanted.

STORIES WITHOUT WORDS

L ONG ago, before man lived on the Earth, the Goddess of the Sun had a quarrel with her young brother. The Sun Goddess was so angry that she hid in a cave and pulled a stone slab over the entrance so that no one would bother her while she sulked. The result was that the world was plunged into darkness.

The rest of the gods held a meeting to try to find a way of coaxing the Sun Goddess out of the cave, and at last it was decided that Ame-no-Iwato, the Goddess of the Dance, should perform in front of the cave to the sound of beautiful music.

After Ame-no-Iwato had been dancing for a while, the Sun Goddess grew curious and opened the door of her cave. Immediately the God of Strength ran forward and, putting his fingers in the crack, managed to force the slab open. The gods then begged the Sun Goddess to leave the cave and bring sunshine to the world again. At last she agreed and things were as they were before.

So runs an old Japanese legend, and the steps of Ame-no-Iwato's dance form the foundation for Japan's traditional dances.

Today in Japan, there are two main forms of dance, the classical Noh dancing, which is difficult to appreciate unless one has studied it, and the more popular Kabuki. Both are forms of dance drama, telling stories, and incorporating pantomime.

Temple Dancers

The Noh dance is said to be the perfection of all the ancient aristocratic Japanese dances. It goes back five centuries, to the days when troupes of dancers were attached to Shinto and Buddhist temples. It was then taken up by the Japanese court, and still has a small but enthusiastic following.

In Noh dancing, the performers wear masks for the characters they play, and their costumes are gorgeous and full of colour, but the stage on which they perform has little decoration.

The dancers usually move slowly, rather like characters in a slow-motion film. Women characters in particular are expected to demonstrate smoothness of movement. When girls are being trained, they have to do their dance exercises with pitchers of water balanced on their heads. They must not spill any of the water and, so that they take small steps, they have to practice with a piece of cardboard held between their knees.

Because Noh dancing is traditional, no innovations are permitted. Each character in the dance must always be portrayed in exactly the same way, and dancers usually specialise in a few parts each. These parts are handed on from generation to generation of families which have devoted themselves to certain Noh characters.

Noh parents begin training their children as soon as they can walk. The toddlers must learn to copy the older dancers exactly, and not find styles of their own.

First entertainment

The most popular form of dancing in Japan is that performed in Kabuki theatres. This began in the 16th century and was the first entertainment of this sort the common people of Japan had. The first performances were given in dried up watercourses, and often took the form of mimicking temple ceremonies, to the amusement of peasant audiences. Then, as they grew more popular, the Kabuki dances told stories borrowed from puppet plays.

Today there are Kabuki theatres all over Japan. The dancing is characterised by gaudy costumes, brightly lit stages and the flowing movements of the women dancers. Male dancers perform in exaggerated postures, in contrast to the grace of the girls. As in Noh dancing, gesture is very important. The movement of a fan can suggest a butterfly in flight, while another movement can suggest a spear being hurled and so on. Great use is made of the wide sleeves of the costumes to indicate the personality of the character.

THE MAN AND THE MOMENT

TAMERLANE'S LAST BATTLE

A RAW-EDGED wind moaned through the tent stays. Sleet and flecks of snow reinforced its sting. Groups of shaggy ponies stood side by side, nose to tail, seeking to shelter themselves from its bite. Soldiers drew their heads between their shoulders to escape the agony of cold that ached in their joints and cracked their cheeks.

Inside the largest tent of all, in the central cluster of the encampment that sprawled for miles across the dull plain, an old man lay dying.

The scene was Central Asia, some three hundred miles from Samarkand.

The aged warrior beneath the furs was Tamerlane, now 70 years old, born the son of a minor chieftain in the fertile land of Cash. From this humble origin, not much better than that of a peasant, his ambition, energy and ruthlessness had driven him ceaselessly to conquer kingdom after kingdom. In his long life he soldiered on 35 campaigns and among the fruits of victory had some 27 regal crowns placed upon his prematurely white head.

As a young man he became a rebel in a land that was then in disorder. The khans of Transoxiana had died out and his leaderless homeland had been invaded by Uzbecks. He organised a rising against the foreign tyranny and waited with 60 warriors in the hills above Samarkand for the war chiefs of Transoxiana to rally to his aid.

They did not come, and after waiting seven days he and his loyal band took to the desert, where they were forced to battle with a thousand pursuers. They beat them off with a ferocious slaughter. After the battle Tamerlane was left with but seven companions and four horses . . . and a reputation as a courageous and terrible fighting man.

Timur the Lame

It was said that during his desert wanderings he received a wound in the foot that left him lame for the remainder of his days. (*Timûrlenk* means Timur the Lame, which has been corrupted into Tamerlane.) Other authorities say that he was born with a crippled foot and arm.

Tamerlane spent several years wandering and fighting in the desert. Gradually his band of followers grew until they were strong enough to drive the Uzbecks right out of the kingdom. Thus at the age of 36, Tamerlane had won his first crown, the fertile kingdom of Transoxiana. Fabulous Samarkand was his capital.

One kingdom was not enough for Tamerlane, a man of voracious ambition. He claimed descent or kinship from the mighty Genghis Khan, the conqueror of all Asia from China to the gates of Europe.

For over 40 years the vast lands of Persia had been without a ruler. Tamerlane set out with his army to end that state of disorder.

One by one he defeated the petty chieftains that opposed him, cities opened their gates to him or were starved and battered into submission. His troops advanced to the mouth of the Persian Gulf and captured the fabulously wealthy city of Ormuz. He then set out on a merciless Holy War against the Christians who lived in the mountains around Tiflis between the Black and Caspian Seas.

In 1390, when over 50 years old, he marched his warrior armies across the Russian plains and through the endless forests of Siberia. This mighty host of invaders lived off the land, stripping it of crops and game animals, for none could escape. Villages vanished beneath pillars of smoke, the occupants were slaughtered and their farm animals devoured.

Triumphant armies

After months of wandering in the Russian domains of the Golden Horde of Tartary, the massive armies met in headlong conflict at the battle of Urtupia and again four years later on the banks of the Terek. Laden with vast quantities of spoil, his triumphant thousands abandoned the desolate landscape without actually reaching Moscow.

Now the old man who had conquered kingdoms and empires from the Persian Gulf to Muscovy lay restless with fever and delirium. His servants chilled his perspiring body with icy water. He shuddered and fell back to his dreams of glory. He had many.

For Tamerlane had marched his great armies across the mountains and deserts into India. He arrived before the gates of Delhi in 1308 and lured the Sultan Mahmoud and his 50,000 warriors from the fortress to do battle on the plain.

One hundred and twenty elephants advanced with the Sultan's army, but turned in panic when faced with ditches filled with fire, and ramparts of iron spikes and bucklers. The monstrous beasts caused more havoc in their own army than among the invading foe.

Delhi was captured and admired enough by Tamerlane for him to copy its style in Samarkand, before he levelled it to the ground!

CONTINUED ON NEXT PAGE

THE MAN AND THE
MOMENT
continued

Hunger for power and conquest burned fiercely throughout the long life of Tamerlane. Already his armies had ranged far to the north, the south and the east.

In the west was the powerful Moslem empire of Sultan Bajazet, and beyond that the great powers of Europe.

Tamerlane marched into Turkey, besieging and destroying cities that barred his way. Four thousand Armenian defenders were buried alive for daring to oppose the armed might of Tamerlane.

He swung south into Syria, and with elephants and Greek fire he routed the crack regiments of Mamelukes who rushed to the defence of Allepo. The city was entered, almost the entire population was slaughtered and their skulls piled high in grotesque pyramids in honour of the Mogul victory. The ancient city of Damascus was later reduced to smouldering ashes.

Nothing could withstand the terror and the destructive power of Tamerlane. Baghdad he laid in ruins in the summer heat of July, 1401, and 90,000 heads were stacked in a gruesome triumphal pyramid on the débris.

He fought the decisive battle of Angora (Ankara) against the Sultan Bajazet, the scourge of the Christians, who even then had forces besieging Constantinople (Istanbul).

By this time Tamerlane had the experience of 30 years of almost continual warfare behind him. His massed foot soldiers advanced in disciplined order. His squadrons of cavalry swirled around the enemy like flames destroying blades of dry grass.

Bajazet, so it was said, was captured and placed in an iron cage until he died. The ravening hordes of Tamerlane were let loose to plunder and burn the wealthy cities of the Sultanate.

Great feasts

Tamerlane returned to Samarkand in triumph. There were celebrations, carnivals, feastings and the marriage of six grandsons. Massive quantities of meat and flasks of wine were gathered for the occasion, whole forests were cut down to provide cooking fuel, tents and pavilions crammed with the spoil looted from many nations and empires covered acres of ground. Thousands attended the banquets which lasted for two joyous months!

Although now 70 years old, Tamerlane's ambition would not let him rest content. He must move on, many kingdoms and empires were his, but not the whole world. His spies had informed him of disunity and weakness in the great Empire of China.

A campaign was organised. Depots were set up along the intended line of march.

In the winter of 1405 he set out, with 200,000 veteran warriors following his standard. Five hundred wagons carried baggage and supplies. China would soon be listed among the conquests of Tamerlane. . . .

. . . But 300 miles from Samarkand, age and fever struck him down. He died in his tent, and with him died the empire that had been built at the cost of unknown millions of lives, the destruction of cities by the score, villages and settlements by the thousand.

One of Henry V's standards that flew at Agincourt.

AGINCOURT:

The Impossible Victory

HENRY V

Between two woods in the north of France ten thousand exhausted Englishmen faced a French army four times bigger. The French had all the armour and all the food—the English, only a dynamic, determined king to lead them. . . .

D'ALBRET, constable of France, tore open the note that a messenger had brought to his tent and roared with laughter.

"A message from Paris," he chuckled at his senior officers gathered around him. "The commander of the Citizen Militia offers us six thousand crossbowmen to help us beat the English on the morrow."

As one, the French officers took up the laughter of their commander. "Six thousand crossbowmen! Sir, at that rate our army should slaughter them before nine-tenths of us even had a chance to see them!" And again the officers roared with mirth.

The French, encamped fourteen miles from St. Pol, near the coast of Calais, that night of October 24, 1415, could afford to laugh, could afford to see the joke in the message from Paris. For in front of them was a tired, miserable, depleted and utterly exhausted English army.

Tired and Footsore

THE French were between the English and the coast their enemy needed to reach in order to struggle back to England. And the French army was fit, ready to fight, and at least *four times* larger than the English army.

No wonder d'Albret laughed. No wonder he scorned the offer of another six thousand crossbowmen.

Outside the tents rain fell unceasingly, soaking the sentries and churning the ground to mud. It fell on the ploughed-up gap between the woods of Tramecourt and Agincourt, the gap which the French guarded and through which the English must pass to reach the coast.

It fell on the other side of the gap, where the English, tired and footsore, were camped.

King Henry V of England surveyed the dismal scene and refused to acknowledge the gloom of his officers.

He stepped from his tent and all that night walked among his men, cheering them up for the next day's battle.

Henry's Claim

AND as they lay down in the wet, covering the strings of their longbows to keep them dry, many of them must have relived the past weeks in their minds—the weeks since they set out, fresh and eager, with King Henry for France. . . .

When Henry V succeeded his father, Henry IV, one of his first proclamations was to claim the throne of France.

The English loved the gay Henry V. He was generous, too, and paid his soldiers well. So, although he had little right to be king of France, they readily joined his army preparing to cross the channel.

In France Henry's army had besieged the town of Harfleur and eventually captured it. But the fight weakened his men, and when disease broke out among them they were in trouble.

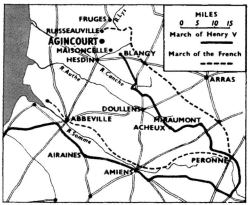

The English and French routes. At Péronne Henry turned back towards the coast again, the French army marching parallel. At Agincourt the French called a halt, blocking the route to the coast—and battle commenced.

Henry realized that he would have to return to England, but decided to show his strength to France by taking the long route across the north of the country to Calais.

The march had been a slow one, in the worst of weather. And by the time the English army—about 10,000 of them—came up to that gap between the woods of Tramecourt and Agincourt, the French were waiting for them with at least *forty thousand* first-class soldiers. . . .

Cavalry Charge

WHEN the new day dawned over that muddy scene it was St. Crispin's Day, October 25. The English, up early after their uncomfortable night, cut long stakes from the woods on each side of them and sharpened the points. The French forsook their horses because of the mud and ranged themselves in three lines along the gap through which the English must pass.

Henry ordered his men to fix their pointed stakes into the ground and stand behind them. But the French refused to move.

So the English longbowmen uprooted their stakes, moved forward, replanted the stakes and sent a whistling shower of arrows into the enemy. The French response was a cavalry charge, but in all that mud their horses floundered and the English longbowmen, reloading their bows, picked off many of them.

But there were still many more French than English, and the French, now on foot, pressed into the invaders' ranks. Henry's men surged back and the king's brother, Humphrey of Gloucester, was beaten to the ground. At once Henry jumped to his aid. A French knight, seeing the English king, aimed a great blow at his head. Henry reeled, recovered, and ran his sword through the man.

For a time the hand-to-hand fighting was desperate. But soon the French were hampered by the overwhelming press of their own numbers.

Handicapped

THEN the battle turned dramatically. The English longbowmen, seeing how handicapped the French were by their heavy armour in the mud, charged on to the French flanks with their swords and cut down the enemy. Into the disorder poured the second French line: again the English charged upon them, wielding sharp steel.

When the third French line came through they gazed with horror upon the scene and those who were not bogged down in the mud by the weight of their armour fled ungallantly.

Henry gathered his soldiers and met the final French onslaught.

When the sun went down on Agincourt in the evening of St. Crispin's Day the gap between the two woods was filled with eight thousand French dead. The English losses were a few hundred, including, tragically, the Duke of York, who had been stifled in his armour by the weight of the dead.

Henry and his battle-stained army sailed with their prisoners from Calais. Then the victors of Agincourt marched through London, cheered by huge, happy crowds. How England loved this gay, dynamic king!

Philip "The Good"

NEWS of the assassination of John the Fearless, at Montereau, came as a great shock to his son and heir, Philip, who was staying at the time in Ghent, with his young wife, Michelle of France.

Philip was totally unlike his father in appearance. He was tall, handsome and distinguished, with a thick mane of dark hair, a broad brow and keenly proud eyes. He moved in such a dignified way that it was said of him: "His appearance alone proclaimed him emperor, and his natural graces made him worthy of a crown."

Philip loved pomp and display, and he also employed the chronicler Chaestillain for the sole purpose of recording the events of his life, for he had a feeling that he was to play an important part in the destiny of Europe.

As a result of the death of his father at French hands, Philip the Good drew closer to the King of England, Henry V. France, divided under the leadership of the Armagnacs, was heading for disaster, and failing miserably in making headway against the English invaders.

The mad King of France, Charles VI, and his wife, Queen Isabella, were staying at Troyes, and from there the King issued letters patent, forbidding the citizens of Paris to obey any orders of his son, the Dauphin. By the Treaty of Troyes (May, 1420) King Henry V of England was made Regent and heir to the throne of France, and he married Catherine, the French King's daughter.

All was well as long as Henry V was alive. Philip the Good fought hard and well for Henry, heedless of the final outcome of the alliance. Philip had to face the forces of the Dauphin, who threatened the Burgundian domain.

With the help of contingents from the Duke of Bedford (Henry V's brother), and from Savoy and Lorraine, the Dauphin's army was driven westwards. At this point, the Duke of Bedford took his leave and headed for Paris. News had reached him that his brother, the King of England, was critically ill.

Henry V died at the castle of Vincennes, to the east of Paris, on 31st August, 1422. He was only 34 years old.

A regency had to be formed at once to govern for the two Kings: Charles VI and Henry's infant son, Henry VI. Philip declined to be Regent, so the Duke of Bedford shouldered the task. In October of the same year, Charles VI died, and young Henry was proclaimed King of France and England.

At Charles's funeral, Philip's absence was conspicuous. Philip was annoyed that Bedford thought that he could take precedence over him. Feelings ran sufficiently high for a premature attempt at reconciliation between Philip and the Dauphin, to be made, to no avail.

On 30th October, 1422, the Dauphin proclaimed himself King Charles VII of France. At this time, Philip was torn between his obligations to his English allies and his patriotic feelings as a Prince of the Royal House of France.

However, with the Dauphin's renewed onslaught against Burgundian territories, Philip had no time to delay, and a joint Anglo-Burgundian force took to the field and routed the Dauphin's army. From that time onwards, Philip used the defence of his own territories as an excuse for disassociating himself from the affairs of his acknowledged lord, Henry VI.

Philip turned his attention towards extending his own frontiers. Between 1426-28 he secured ownership of the county of Namur, and lands in Holland, Zealand, Friesland and Hainault. In 1426, he also obtained Brabant, adding to his already impressive list of titles those of "Duke of Lothair, of Brabant, and of Limburg, and Marquis of the Holy Empire."

During this time, the English armies under the Duke of Bedford were in conflict with the forces of the Dauphin, Charles. Then, when Joan of Arc came to Charles's aid the tables began to turn against the English.

When Joan was captured at Compiègne, she was handed over to John of Luxembourg, commanding the Burgundian troops outside the besieged town. Luxembourg immediately notified Philip the Good, who hastened to the spot to see Joan. Having no illusions as to the divine mission of "The Maid", Philip handed her over to the English in return for an enormous sum of money.

Joan's imprisonment, trial and death at the stake caused a flood tide of patriotic fervour to sweep France. Philip felt the backlash of this as his armies met with setbacks against the forces of Charles VII.

Change of Heart

Bedford tried to bolster the alliance with Philip by manoeuvring him into a favourable third marriage, but for the English armies in France it was the beginning of the end. Bedford sustained one set-back after another, with a weakening army and severe financial difficulties. The national feeling which Joan had created carried all before it.

Philip, meanwhile, was undergoing a change of heart. He had always regretted not having fought against the English at Agincourt. Now, he felt, was the time to become first and foremost a Prince of France.

At a meeting at Nevers in 1435, the Burgundian and French courts began talks of reconciliation. They were all tired of war, and longed for peace and a united France once again. Later, at the Treaty of Arras, amidst splendid tournaments and banquets, peace was at last sealed.

Turning again to the expansion of his own territories, in 1441 Philip took possession of Luxembourg, persuading his extravagant aunt to lease him the rights of the country. Later he bought Luxembourg for 120,000 Hungarian florins.

About this time, the Emperor Frederick III of Hapsburg offered to make Philip King of Brabant. Philip in turn requested that he should have enough land to merit the title of King and suggested that he should occupy lands from Holland to the Rhine and to the Jura Mountains. The Emperor did not like the idea of so powerful a state neighbouring his lands, and the idea was dropped. In any case, Philip was virtually a king in all but name.

Charles saw to it that the Duke had little to say or do in the domestic affairs of France, so Philip was never to see his cousin Charles VII alive again.

When Charles died, in 1461, Philip attended the coronation of Louis XI at Rheims cathedral, and as usual outshone the new King with his magnificence. Philip journeyed back to Paris with the King and put on lavish entertainments.

Philip died five years later, in 1467. His body was eventually buried in the family mausoleum at Champmol, Dijon.

Philip the Good left behind him an impressive record of territorial aggrandisement, out of which grew a powerful new state. Like his father, he surrounded himself with able councillors and soldiers. To his fabulous court, he attracted musicians and men of learning.

(Left) England's King Henry V (1413-22) was the great fighting ally of Philip the Good against the forces of the Dauphin and the Armagnacs. Henry renewed Edward III's claim to the throne of France, and in two campaigns brought France to her knees. By the Treaty of Troyes (1420) Henry arranged to marry Catherine, daughter of the half-mad French King, Charles VI. Henry was also to be Regent of France until Charles died, after which Henry and his heirs were to succeed to the French throne. It was at the signing of this Treaty that Henry V and Philip the Good (right), realised that in their hands lay the destiny of France: but neither realised for how short a time.

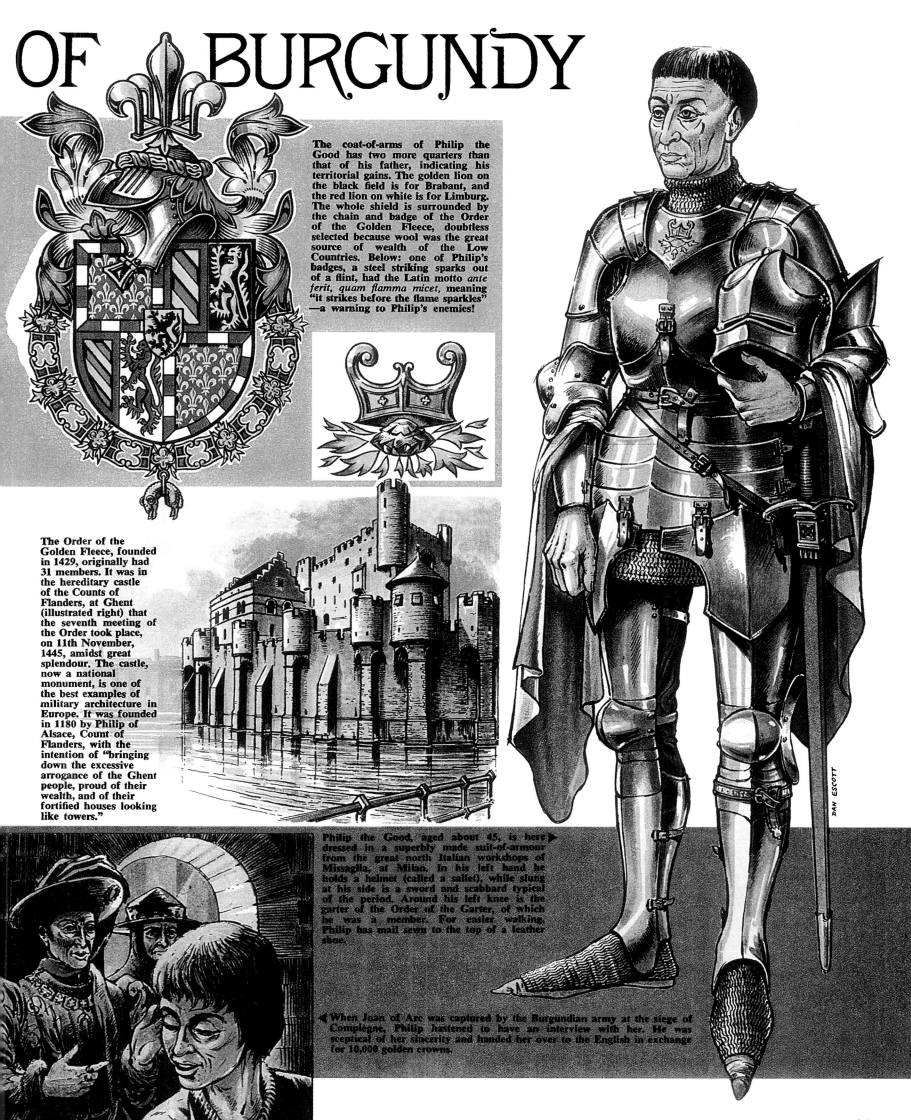

OF BURGUNDY

The coat-of-arms of Philip the Good has two more quarters than that of his father, indicating his territorial gains. The golden lion on the black field is for Brabant, and the red lion on white is for Limburg. The whole shield is surrounded by the chain and badge of the Order of the Golden Fleece, doubtless selected because wool was the great source of wealth of the Low Countries. Below: one of Philip's badges, a steel striking sparks out of a flint, had the Latin motto *ante ferit, quam flamma micet*, meaning "it strikes before the flame sparkles" —a warning to Philip's enemies!

The Order of the Golden Fleece, founded in 1429, originally had 31 members. It was in the hereditary castle of the Counts of Flanders, at Ghent (illustrated right) that the seventh meeting of the Order took place, on 11th November, 1445, amidst great splendour. The castle, now a national monument, is one of the best examples of military architecture in Europe. It was founded in 1180 by Philip of Alsace, Count of Flanders, with the intention of "bringing down the excessive arrogance of the Ghent people, proud of their wealth, and of their fortified houses looking like towers."

Philip the Good, aged about 45, is here dressed in a superbly made suit-of-armour from the great north Italian workshops of Missaglia, at Milan. In his left hand he holds a helmet (called a sallet), while slung at his side is a sword and scabbard typical of the period. Around his left knee is the garter of the Order of the Garter, of which he was a member. For easier walking, Philip has mail sewn to the top of a leather shoe.

When Joan of Arc was captured by the Burgundian army at the siege of Compiègne, Philip hastened to have an interview with her. He was sceptical of her sincerity and handed her over to the English in exchange for 10,000 golden crowns.

DAN ESCOTT

THE FALL OF CONSTANTINOPLE

a) Turkish gunner with slow-match wound around a pole. He used it to ignite his cannon.

b) A Janissary—a member of the elite corps of the Turkish army.

WHEN the Emperor Constantine in A.D. 328-330 built a new capital upon the old Greek city of Byzantium, he gave the Roman Empire two capital cities. Rome in the West and the new Constantinople in the East. This division was made more complete under his successors who ruled as separate Emperors from these two capitals.

The two halves of this divided Empire had entirely different futures and for this the barbarian invasions of the 4th and 5th centuries were responsible. When the Huns began their sweep across central Europe, only a few areas of the Eastern (Byzantine) Empire felt the ripples of the disturbance. The Goths merely brushed up against Constantinople, laying waste the Balkan regions; they did not settle there permanently, but moved on to attack Rome's western regions. Gaul, Spain, Britain, North Africa and finally the Italian peninsula itself fell under barbarian rule.

The Roman Empire in the east lasted independently for 1,000 years, during which time it suffered great changes of fortune ranging from times of brilliant vitality to periods of pitiable weakness. For these ten centuries, Constantinople was a Christian bulwark for the West against the threatening Goths, Slavs, Persians and Saracens. While the Empire was forced to surrender lands, it upheld every one of its claims to pre-eminence. Among its genuine achievements was the maintenance of a high standard of culture—which was the more impressive because of the general lack of it elsewhere—and the transmission of the Christian religion to Russia and the Balkan states.

Mohammed II—the conqueror of Constantinople.

Though the Empire ceased to exist in the west in the 5th century, it reached one of its greatest periods in the east under the 6th century Emperor, Justinian. Besides regaining for a time some of the provinces that had been lost in the West, Justinian undertook the mighty work of systematizing Roman Law, a work which had a profound effect on the intellectual life of Western Europe in later centuries, and which still arouses admiration and respect.

During the 7th century, the Empire lost much territory to the Arabs who, spurred on by their new-found religion, Islam, were steadily building themselves an empire. For the next century, the eastern Empire was to look in vain for a man who could restore some of its bygone glory. With corruption rife at Court, and with Emperors falling like ninepins at the hands of assassins, it was little wonder that the Moslems overran Palestine, Syria, Egypt and Mesopotamia, and continually menaced Asia Minor.

The downward slide was arrested by the work of Leo the Isaurian (717-41). His reforms were felt in every sphere of government, and in particular in the army. Leo's work prepared the way for a new period of conquest and a revival of learning which reached its zenith in the reign of Basil II (976-1025).

Unfortunately, this upsurge did not last. During the 11th century, the eastern Empire was again on the verge of collapse. It was the Emperor Alexius Comnenus who appealed to the Pope in Rome to send troops to help him against the Seljuk Turks who had conquered Palestine. But the First Crusade which arrived at the gates of Constantinople was not at all what Alexius had expected, or what he wanted. He wanted a mercenary army which would do his bidding, not a force of self-seeking volunteers

The Crusaders eventually turned to attacking the Empire itself. The Fourth Crusade (1204) was diverted to Constantinople to reinstate the deposed Emperor, Isaac Angelus and his son, Alexius. But when this had been done, Alexius was not in a position to hand over the huge sum of money that he had promised in payment, and the waiting Crusaders, growing restive, stormed and took the city and committed appalling barbarities.

A western Emperor sat on the Byzantine imperial throne for 50 years after the taking of Constantinople. Then it was recaptured by Michael Palaelogus in the name of the Byzantine aristocracy. But the Empire never fully recovered from the shock of the western attack and, although it survived for nearly 200 years, it was never more than a shadow of its former self.

At the end of the 13th century, the Empire had to face the hostility of two formidable enemies: the Ottoman Turks in Asia, and the Serbs in the Balkan peninsula. It must have been with intense relief that the Empire witnessed the defeat of the Serbs by the Ottomans in 1389, and the annihilation of the great Ottoman army by the Mongols under Tamerlane in 1402.

Characteristically, the Empire made no constructive effort to restore its fortunes in the few years' respite that events had given it. The Ottoman Turks did recover from their disastrous defeat and, on this occasion, it was to the Hungarians under their great soldier King, John Hunyadi, that the eastern Empire had cause to give thanks.

Hungary, menaced by the raiding sorties of the Turks, gathered an army and drove the Turks out of Serbia with such vigour that they sued for peace. Unfortunately, the Hungarian King did not pursue his advantage, but agreed to peace, and a year later, in 1444, the tables were turned and his army was defeated at Varna.

Nine years later, the stage was set at Constantinople for the final scene. In April, 1453, the Turkish ruler, Mohammed II, laid siege to the city with a land and sea force of 150,000 men. The Emperor, Constantine XI had only 8,000 men, but he was assisted by a brilliant Genoese soldier, John Justiniani.

Constantinople had never fallen before an enemy horde and some believed that it never would. But little was done to back this up.

The defence of the city was mainly in the hands of Italians, Germans and Spaniards.

The end came on the night of 29th May, 1453, when the Turkish cannon breached the wall. As dawn broke, the last of the Roman Emperors died the death of a hero in battle, and the Turks took the imperial city.

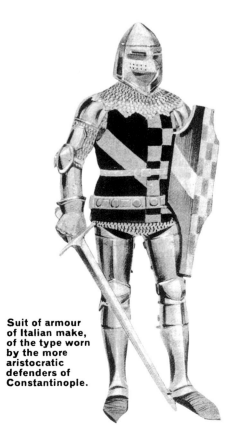

Suit of armour of Italian make, of the type worn by the more aristocratic defenders of Constantinople.

THE word 'Renaissance' (meaning 'rebirth') is applied to various phases of artistic and intellectual activity from medieval times to the present day. For instance, we speak of a renaissance having taken place at the time when Charlemagne was Emperor in the 9th century; and of the '12-century Renaissance' of medieval Europe. But when we talk of *the* Renaissance, we refer specifically to a period of artistic and intellectual vitality which, generated in Italy in the 15th and 16th centuries, spread all over Europe.

The Italian Renaissance was more than just a rebirth of ancient Greek and Roman styles in art and literature; it was the birth of something entirely new. Certainly the glories of Greece and Rome were discovered afresh but, what was more important, the Renaissance accepted beauty for its own sake, and in this way, turned its back on the ideals of the medieval world.

Just as the Gothic style satisfied specifically religious needs in an age when religion dominated men's lives, so the work of the Renaissance artists was a response to the demands of the rich Italian merchant class.

There were many rich patrons in 15th century Italy, but none provided an atmosphere more stimulating to artistic production than the Florentine merchant-banking family of Medici, between the years 1434 and 1492.

Florence, an independent, republic city-state, both wealthy and prosperous, inevitably turned away from the austerities of religion to embrace worldly and material values. The Florentine people found nothing in pagan classical writings that clashed with their Christianity. Plato's works were translated, and the ancient philosophers were honoured. The Medici set the pattern for not only employing artists, but also for seeking their company and appreciating them as individuals, which was a complete break with the anonymous role of medieval artists.

Cosimo de' Medici, the first of the Medici to rule the turbulent Florentine republic, was an enlightened patron of arts, besides being the founder of the political power of the Medici family.

The shrewdest of businessmen, Cosimo also had an intense appreciation of beauty, and he liked the company of scholars and artists. He was surrounded by an atmosphere of experi-

The Italian Renaissance

FLORENCE AND THE MEDICI

The house of the Medici (today the Palazzo Riccardi) in the Via Cavour, Florence, was typical of large Florentine houses of the time. It has heavy walls and barred ground-floor windows in case of riots. Here the Medici entertained many of the great men of the period.

ment. Brunelleschi, the architect, was discovering and writing about the laws of perspective; Masaccio was creating new visual effects in painting, and Donatello was giving new realism to the human form in sculpture.

This was Cosimo's environment, and his purse was never closed to the needs of artistic endeavour. He spent an enormous amount of money on the enlargement of the church and monastery of San Marco, and endowed the monastery with a valuable collection of books for their library. The abbey and library at Fiesole, and the building of the church of St. Lorenzo in Florence, are only a few instances of his generosity.

In 1430 began the building of Cosimo's fine palace in Florence to a design by the architect Michelozzi. In it were housed his priceless collection of antiques and manuscripts.

Two painters, both friars, were closely associated with Cosimo. One was the gentle, pious Fra Angelico. In spite of his attachment to the cloisters, Fra Angelico was well aware of the new ideas being circulated outside the walls of his monastery. Gradually, he came to look closely at nature and copy what he saw, giving his works roundness of form and greater animation.

Fra Angelico's finest achievement was the frescos he executed at San Marco. Amongst these is one showing the Adoration of the Magi, which he painted at Cosimo's request.

Cosimo's sympathetic treatment of the wayward friar, Fra Filippo Lippi, was quite consistent with Renaissance practice. Applauding his genius, Cosimo was patient when the artist's behaviour was whimsical and erratic. Fra Lippi's temperament was quite unsuited to the cloister; indeed, it often interfered with his work.

On one occasion, Cosimo, after remonstrating with the friar, locked him in a room and told him that he would not be allowed out until the work was done. Undeterred, Fra Lippi knotted his bedding together to make a rope, escaped out of the window, and disappeared for a considerable time. Cosimo did not censure him on his return, but opened his purse to the improvident artist.

Not surprisingly, Fra Lippi was the architect of his own ecclesiastical downfall when one more indiscretion proved just too much for the Church.

In his old age, Cosimo became more and more interested in philosophy. He had founded the Platonic academy under the scholar Marsilio Ficino, and its meetings were often held at Cosimo's family house just outside Florence.

Cosimo died in 1464. In the following year, his young grandson—soon to be dubbed Lorenzo the Magnificent—began to come into prominence.

Lorenzo's many-sided abilities make him a perfect specimen of the ideal 'Renaissance Man'. He surrounded himself with artists, architects and philosophers. He was no mean poet himself, and his interest in architecture was detailed and technical. He was an excellent judge of talent. For example, he had only to see one piece of Michelangelo's work, before bringing the young artist into his household, giving him board, lodging and an allowance until he was 18 years of age.

Sandro Botticelli, the renowned artist whose fluid interpretation of female beauty was entirely original, was Lorenzo's court painter. For the Medici, his chief work of interest was The Adoration of the Magi, which shows three generations of Medici—Cosimo, his son, Piero, and his grandsons, Lorenzo and Guiliano—kneeling before the Christ child.

While Lorenzo ruled Florence, peace in Italy favoured the arts; and Florence was at this time a star-studded city. What other state could claim the distinction of nurturing two of the greatest creative geniuses—Leonardo da Vinci and Michelangelo—at about the same time?

These two will always be remembered as the most brilliant of those enquiring minds which dwelt successfully on many subjects. They were the greatest of the many men who were curious about all that they could see in the world and much that they could not; who continually experimented and questioned, and who delighted in witnessing and creating things of beauty.

Delight and pride is obvious in the words of Marsilio Ficino, Cosimo's protégé, who wrote: "This century, like a golden age, has restored to light the liberal arts, which were almost extinct: grammar, poetry, rhetoric, painting, sculpture, architecture, music . . . and all this in Florence."

After Cosimo's death, young Lorenzo was sent ▶ on a tour of Italy by his father, Piero. He visited Bologna, Ferrara, Venice and Milan. Wherever he went he was magnificently entertained.

On 26th April, 1478, Lorenzo de' Medici and his brother, Giuliano, were attacked by members of the Pazzi family, powerful rivals in Florence, during High Mass in Florence cathedral. Giuliano was stabbed and killed, but Lorenzo escaped and subsequently took a terrible revenge on the Pazzi family.

ENGLAND'S CROWN

THE barons of fifteenth-century England were plotting. A dozen of them, their horses steaming after a hard ride, galloped over a drawbridge and into a grim turreted castle.

Their planning behind those walls had only one object: the unseating—or if you like, the murder—of Richard Plantagenet, King of England.

Shakespeare has painted Richard III as a deformed tyrant whose hands were stained with the blood of relatives who had stood in the way to the throne.

In fact, he was a handsome, courageous king who believed above all in his country. But his enemies—and he had plenty of them—were always busy spreading malicious stories about the young king.

They whispered that he had murdered his nephews in the tower, and poisoned his beautiful wife.

And now the barons found that their powers had been curbed by Richard, whose new laws helped to protect the common people. So they lined up behind Henry Tudor, a dour Welshman who had spent most of his life in hiding.

Hour of Decision

Now, sensing that the hour of decision was near, Henry had returned from Europe early in 1485, landed in Wales, gathered up an army, and marched across the country to the Midlands.

So it was that on August 22 in the fields near the little Leicestershire town of Market Bosworth, the stage was set for a drama that was to change the course of English history.

King Richard was an excellent military commander, with a number of successes to his credit. And yet, even with the larger army, he was not happy about the approaching struggle.

Henry's fifth column had already been nibbling and nagging at Richard's supporters. His staunch friend John, Duke of Norfolk, had been receiving anonymous letters advising him to desert his master.

Others were tempted by offers of lucrative posts.

Left: Described as a wicked hunchback Richard III (1452–85) was supposed to have murdered his two young nephews in the Tower of London to gain the throne for himself. In fact he was a handsome man and a good leader. But he lost the support of his people after the murder, whether he was guilty or not. Above: Richard's rival for the throne was Henry Tudor. As a child he was taken to Brittany where many loyal Englishmen rallied round him. He was crowned Henry VII in 1485 after the Battle of Bosworth.

★★

As the sun rose over Bosworth Field the trumpets sounded the call to arms. The clank of armour, the cough of horses, the words of command broke the stillness of the dawn.

The knights in their heavy armour were lifted clumsily into their saddles.

Infantrymen picked out their sharpest swords and spears, tested the braces of their shields, and moved forward to the flags marking out the regimental positions.

Richard posted his forces on the top of a small incline, his cavalry wings on either side of the main line. Henry grouped his army on level ground some hundreds of yards away.

On a small hillock to the right of the field stood the treacherous Sir William Stanley. He professed to being one of the king's allies, but he was actually waiting to see which side was likely to win before committing his small force.

The order to charge was sounded on Richard's ground—and forward rolled the mass of soldiery, swords drawn, teeth clenched, shields braced.

The hideous din burst open the countryside as the first wave of men clashed with Henry's front ranks. Yells, cries and groans were mingled with the clanging of

steel and the swishing of arrows and spears.

For an hour or more they fought, neither side giving way to the other. Then, seeing his men hard-pressed, Richard urgently signalled Stanley to bring reinforcements.

At first Stanley flatly refused to stir. When he finally did, he brought his men charging towards the flank of the king's army.

When Richard saw this act of treachery his heart filled with despair. But from that despair grew courage seldom seen on the field of battle.

Gathering his staunchest supporters Richard charged towards the centre of the battle, wielding his sword with all his might, slaying right and left, and even reaching within striking distance of Henry Tudor himself.

Richard Unseated

His charger reared as Richard plunged on. Two of Henry's men jumped at him. With a sweep of his sword he cut them down.

Two more, and suddenly he was unseated. Hacking desperately about him Richard continued the fight on foot. Now he struggled like a man who knows the end is near.

A dozen Lancastrians cornered him near a tree. He fought them single-handed and slew them one by one.

But he himself, mortally pierced with many wounds, was overcome by exhaustion. Richard, King of England, fell to the ground breathing out his last.

As he fell on that blood-stained field the crown of England tumbled off his helmet and rolled along the ground into a hawthorn bush.

There it lay, glinting brightly in the sunlight, for a moment of history, until a Lancastrian soldier picked it up and carried it to Sir William Stanley.

To the roars of the victorious army he put it on the head of Henry Tudor, the new King Henry VII.

Arms of Richard III of England, who assumed power after Edward IV's death.

Arms of Henry VII, first Tudor king of England, once Earl of Richmond.

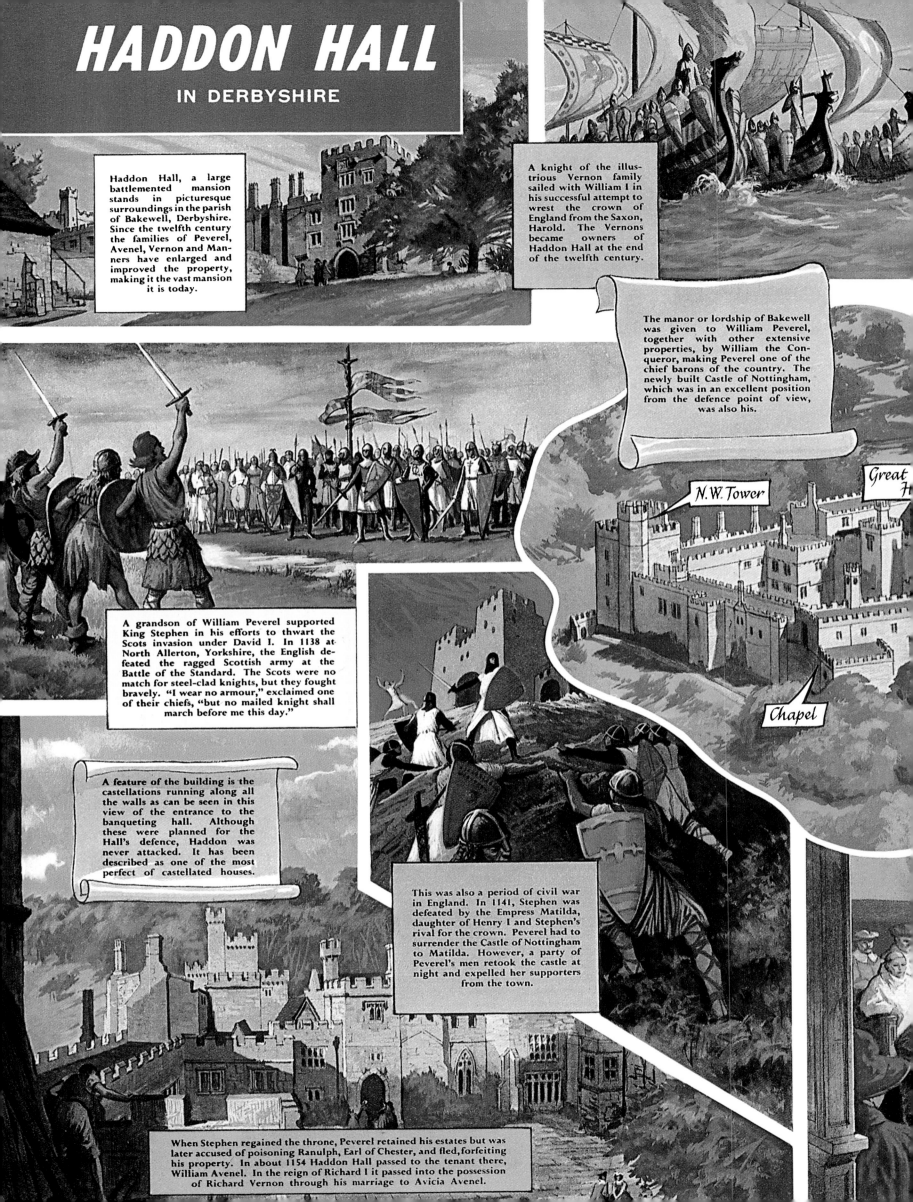

HADDON HALL
IN DERBYSHIRE

Haddon Hall, a large battlemented mansion stands in picturesque surroundings in the parish of Bakewell, Derbyshire. Since the twelfth century the families of Peverel, Avenel, Vernon and Manners have enlarged and improved the property, making it the vast mansion it is today.

A knight of the illustrious Vernon family sailed with William I in his successful attempt to wrest the crown of England from the Saxon, Harold. The Vernons became owners of Haddon Hall at the end of the twelfth century.

The manor or lordship of Bakewell was given to William Peverel, together with other extensive properties, by William the Conqueror, making Peverel one of the chief barons of the country. The newly built Castle of Nottingham, which was in an excellent position from the defence point of view, was also his.

N.W. Tower

Great H

Chapel

A grandson of William Peverel supported King Stephen in his efforts to thwart the Scots invasion under David I. In 1138 at North Allerton, Yorkshire, the English defeated the ragged Scottish army at the Battle of the Standard. The Scots were no match for steel-clad knights, but they fought bravely. "I wear no armour," exclaimed one of their chiefs, "but no mailed knight shall march before me this day."

A feature of the building is the castellations running along all the walls as can be seen in this view of the entrance to the banqueting hall. Although these were planned for the Hall's defence, Haddon was never attacked. It has been described as one of the most perfect of castellated houses.

This was also a period of civil war in England. In 1141, Stephen was defeated by the Empress Matilda, daughter of Henry I and Stephen's rival for the crown. Peverel had to surrender the Castle of Nottingham to Matilda. However, a party of Peverel's men retook the castle at night and expelled her supporters from the town.

When Stephen regained the throne, Peverel retained his estates but was later accused of poisoning Ranulph, Earl of Chester, and fled, forfeiting his property. In about 1154 Haddon Hall passed to the tenant there, William Avenel. In the reign of Richard I it passed into the possession of Richard Vernon through his marriage to Avicia Avenel.

The property eventually passed to John Manners, son of the Earl of Rutland, on his marriage to Dorothy Vernon. Local tradition says that they eloped during a masked ball at Haddon, John having waited in the woods disguised as an outlaw. There is a doorway in the Hall called Dorothy Vernon's doorway and a bridge is also named after her.

The VERNON CREST A Boar's Head

Eagle Tower

Long Gallery

In early times, when inns were seldom to be found except in towns or cities, the Lord of Haddon in addition to presiding over banquets in the beautiful fourteenth century Banqueting Hall ensured that provision was always ready for the hungry traveller. Sir George Vernon, Dorothy's father, was famous for the magnificence of his style of living and his vigorous personality.

John Manners supported James I's claim to succeed Elizabeth I to the throne of England. There were several claimants but in 1603 James was proclaimed king on Elizabeth's death. One of his first acts was to knight John Manners.

te Apartments

er Garden

In 1641 a descendant of John Manners became Earl of Rutland and the Hall has remained in this family until now. By 1703 Haddon was no longer occupied, so it escaped the rebuilding which so many great houses underwent in the Georgian period. Early in the present century the ninth Duke of Rutland restored the Hall to its former condition in order to make it his home.

Nothing can convey a more complete idea of the old way of life than Haddon. Many great dwellings have disappeared completely; others are merely a heap of ruins, but this has been preserved complete.

Vernons, known as the "Kings of the Peak," ed Haddon for nearly four hundred years during ch time they prospered, and succeeding genera- s added to the buildings. In 1426 Sir Richard on was appointed Speaker of the Commons in the Parliament held at Leicester.

The Man Who 'Discovered' Russia

Richard Chancellor.

Richard Chancellor had originally been part of an expedition to find a north-east passage to China. Instead, he landed in Russia and sealed an important trade agreement with its Tsar, Ivan the Terrible

HOW do you get to China? A question simple enough to answer today. But over 400 years ago it was one of the most talked about problems among thinking Englishmen.

You could, of course, go south, then east or west, following routes already tracked by the Spanish and Portuguese. The English, however, believed that there were other ways — not along the bottom of the world, but over the top of it. They thought a way to China lay to the north.

The problem: was it north-west (the way that John Cabot had partly taken) or north-east?

It was the temperamental, aged Italian explorer, Sebastian Cabot, son of John, who finally persuaded Englishmen to look for a north-east passage. They liked Cabot. At 74 he was as alert and as crafty as ever, but he had mellowed. He had settled in England and he had a bank of nautical experience to draw upon that was second to none.

Cabot, now too old to explore, had to content himself with fitting out the expedition.

The command of the three ships was given to Sir Hugh Willoughby. His second-in-command was Richard Chancellor, who was to play the principal role in the events that followed.

The little fleet was watched by a big crowd as it sailed down the Thames from Greenwich in May, 1553. These were times of great change in Tudor England. Once again the boy King Edward VI was seriously ill and soon to die. His most likely successor, Mary Tudor, was committed to returning England to Catholicism. A Catholic England or a Protestant one — this was an even bigger problem than the north-east passage to China.

At Harwich there was a week's delay because the wind did not blow in the right direction. Then Willoughby led the way to the Norwegian coast.

At a group of small Norwegian islands, the commander called his captains together and gave them precise instructions about what to do if they should be separated by a sudden storm. Only hours later that was exactly what happened. The seas, Wil-

loughby wrote, "became so outrageous that the ships could not keep to their intended course."

One of them was never seen again. Another, the *Bona Esperanza*, commanded by Willoughby himself, was tossed about in the icy-cold Arctic Sea for six weeks. Finally she made a landfall on the Murmansk coast of Russia.

Willoughby sent out scouts this way and that, but there was no one to be seen. There was nothing for it but to settle down and pass the winter there. An Englishman could not turn back — although, had Willoughby known something of the severity of an Arctic winter, he might have done so.

The end for Willoughby and his crew must have been like that of Captain Scott on

CONTINUED ON NEXT PAGE ▶

Hammered by the storm, Richard Chancellor's ship found a safe anchorage at Vardo, the expedition's agreed rendezvous in an emergency. But none of the other ships arrived to join him.

his South Pole expedition. One by one they died. Five months after leaving England, some were still alive — a month later all were dead. Only Willoughby's diary, lying on the desk at which his body was found still in a sitting position, survived to tell the heroic tale.

The third ship hammered by the storm was the *Edward Bonaventure*, commanded by Chancellor. He had made a safe anchorage at Vardö, the agreed rendezvous for such an emergency, but as the days went by he realised that Willoughby and the third ship must be lost.

What to do? Chancellor had no doubts about that. He resolved "either to bring that to pass which was intended, or else to die the death."

So Chancellor sailed on into the eerie frozen north and the land of the white bear and the sea-horse to "a place where he found no night at all, but a continual light and brightness of the sun shining upon a huge and mighty sea." Presently, he entered the White Sea, which is like a great bay almost completely surrounded by land, in northern Russia.

At sight of the *Edward Bonaventure*, the local fishermen, near where modern Archangel stands, dropped their nets and raised their sails in terror. Never had they seen anything as colossal on the sea. It took Chancellor a long time of patient reasoning to indicate that he meant them no harm, that he wanted only to trade.

Thus reassured, the simple White Sea folk crowded around the *Edward Bonaventure*. They gave the Englishmen food, but as for trade, they said, they would first have to ask their Tsar. It was soon clear to Chancellor that, more than anything else, these fur-clad fisherfolk had the most profound respect for their Tsar.

He was Ivan the Terrible, who fortunately at this time was enjoying the halcyon

So severe was the Arctic winter, that, after reaching the Russian coast, the crew of one of the ships were overcome by the cold and perished to a man.

period between his cruel youth and savage middle-age. Chancellor, determined to meet him, was undeterred by the 1,500 miles of ice and snow that lay overland between Archangel and Moscow. He cajoled the fisherfolk into giving him sledges and set out for the capital.

He had not gone very far before he met an emissary of the Tsar, who gave him post-horses and provisions, for, he said, the Tsar had learned of the coming of the English and was anxious to be in touch with Western Europe.

It was a strange procession that finally rode into snow-covered Moscow. Chancellor had set out as second-in-command of a fleet to seek the north-east passage to China and instead was now arriving as the commander of an overland party that was "discovering" Russia.

Ivan the Terrible was delighted at the twist of fate that had brought the English to his court. He listened enthusiastically to Chancellor, then gave him a letter to send to King Edward VI in London. "If you will send one of your Council to treat with us, your country's merchants shall have a free market through my whole dominions, to come and go at their pleasure," Ivan wrote.

Queen's Interest

By the time Chancellor had taken this letter back to London, King Edward was dead and his half-sister; Mary Tudor, was on the throne. Mary was determined to restore the old religion of Catholicism. To this end, heretics were being burnt at the stake and rebels hanged, drawn and quartered, but Mary's advisers had time to regard the Tsar's letter with interest.

They remembered that the Pope had assigned all the Unknown, swimming like new planets before men's eyes, either to Spain if it were west of the Azores or to Portugal if it were east of them. They annulled that decree at once and gave a charter to a "Muscovy Company" to create trade between England and Russia.

Within weeks of the company being formed, Chancellor was preparing to sail again for the White Sea. Following his earlier route, he was back in Moscow in October, 1555, and stayed there for eight months to establish trade connections. When he set out again the Tsar sent with him a Russian ambassador.

Chancellor was almost home again when disaster struck. While anchored in a Scottish bay one November night, the *Edward Bonaventure* was caught in a sudden storm and thrown upon some rocks.

Chancellor got the ambassador and his attendants into a small boat and made for the shore. It was dark and the sea heaved in the storm; soon the little boat was turned over by the onslaught. Chancellor and the ambassador's attendants were all drowned; only the ambassador survived the ordeal.

But the good work for which Chancellor had given his life was now well started. The Russian trade prospered and the quest for the north-east passage to China went on vigorously. It was finally found, over a century ago, by a Swedish explorer hardly recalled today.

He was Baron Nordenskjold from Stockholm and was the first man ever to bring a ship around the north coast of Asia.

With their boat overturned by the storm, Chancellor and the ambassador were thrown into the tempestuous sea.

The TRIGAN EMPIRE

A strange craft has landed on the planet Elekton, and the three occupants of the craft—visible only as luminous spheres—have taken over the minds and bodies of an old herdsman and two young Trigan officers, Janno and Keren. Then—while King Kassar of Hericon is asleep—a luminous sphere moves from the old herdsman to the king . . .

Kassar of Hericon awoke . . . but now an alien intelligence controlled his mind and body. He glanced at his two companions.

Good! . . . With every move we improve our position amongst the species of this planet. Soon we will be the masters here!

The three turned to regard the old herdsman, who lay asleep.

He will awaken himself. He will know . . . and tell . . . everything!

Then we will eliminate him at once!

Two of them carried the herdsman from the hall, quelling his frantic struggles and shutting off his cries so that the sleeping feasters were not awakened.

Outside was a sheer drop over the ramparts to the gorge below.

The creature will not be a danger to us now.

Later, the twin suns of the planet Elekton rose in the lurid dawn sky, and the three looked out with grim satisfaction over the towers and domes of Hericon.

As King Kassar, I rule all this . . . but it is not enough!

The evil intelligence that controlled Janno answered . . .

The Emperor Trigo is on his way here . . . I will take him over and then we shall be masters of the Trigan Empire also . . . and after that . . . who knows?

Three days later, a formation of Trigan atmosphere craft swooped low over the city.

The Trigan Emperor stepped out of his craft and was greeted by 'King Kassar'.

Welcome, Trigo. You do Hericon a great honour by coming here for the Games.

I much look forward to seeing the contests, Kassar.

All Hericon packed the vast arena for the Great Games which were held annually.

Long live the King! Long live the Emperor!

Trigo frowned, but kept his thoughts to himself. He had long ago forbidden the barbaric so-called 'games' in his Empire . . . but it was politically necessary to remain on good terms with the warlike Kassar . . .

You will enjoy the first item, Trigo . . . a contest between a wild Zargot and a giant slave armed only with a short spear!

The watching multitude waited in tense silence for the unequal contest to begin . . .

Twice the big man skilfully evaded the beast's furious attacks, but the third time he was sent spinning to the dusty earth!

Trigo had been watching the contest with growing fury and impatience. In a trice he leapt into the arena!

By the stars, I'll not see him perish!

He snatched the unconscious man from under the descending talons of the Zargot . . . and was himself struck down!

Aaaaaagh!

Next Episode: Trigo loses his 'mind'

IN THE DAYS OF OUR FOREFATHERS
THE ELIZABETHANS AT PLAY

WE hear a lot today about international money, borrowed or lent to governments across the world. In Tudor times the monarch was the government, and when the monarch wanted cash he or she raised it, as happens today, through taxes.

But sometimes the taxes were not due when the money was wanted, or perhaps more money was wanted than was due. In that event the monarch raised a loan from the merchants of Antwerp, then the "money capital" of the Continent.

Unfortunately for the Kings of England, the Antwerp merchants demanded 14 per cent interest on their loans—a considerable rate by any standards. In addition, the merchants paid some of the loan in cash and some in jewels, and the jewels afforded them a further large profit.

In order to raise the money, the monarch kept a "Royal Agent" in Antwerp to manage the "King's Loans." In the middle of the 16th century the Royal Agent was Sir Thomas Gresham, son of a wealthy Norfolk family, Cambridge educated, and a member of the Mercers' Company.

As agent, Gresham went regularly to the Bourse, the Antwerp money market. He did a good job for England. Not only did he succeed in lowering the interest rate to 12 per cent, but he managed to obtain the Royal Loans completely in cash.

But Gresham did more than that. He realised that what was being done in Antwerp could just as well be done in London, where there were plenty of merchants, but without any unifying power.

So Gresham came back to London and there built the Royal Exchange, the "Bourse" for the merchants of London. At a time when England's explorers and merchant adventurers were discovering new markets

and opening up great areas for foreign trade, the activities of the merchants in the Royal Exchange galvanised European trade.

Coincidentally, the Low Countries were ravaged by Spain in terrible years of religious wars. As a result, the world's trading centre moved from Antwerp to London, which, thanks to Gresham, was ready to receive it. The delighted English merchants, rising to the occasion, built ships and warehouses and formed companies to handle the huge volume of goods coming to and passing through their Port of London. So, when we think of Britain ruling the waves, we should spare a thought for the enterprise of Thomas Gresham, who made London the greatest port in the world.

Elizabethan Englishmen did not spend all their time getting rich by trade. They had their amusements and enjoyed them immensely. Although the bow as a weapon of war was giving way to guns, archery was still popular as a sport. So, too, were football and hockey, and bull and bear baiting.

On May Day everyone danced around a maypole

on the village green to the tune of a Morris dancer's fiddle. The Morris dancers—you still see them in some parts of Britain—dressed up as Robin Hood characters and formed a procession. In the procession was a man tied to the figure of a horse, in such a way that he appeared to be riding it. As he galloped about he blew peas from a bladder at the spectators, who didn't seem to mind at all.

Pageants and tournaments were held on special occasions and were great crowd-pullers. When a pageant was held by night, hundreds of people marched with burning torches to illuminate the armour of parading knights, and to show up the fancy dresses. People watching from their windows hung out candles of all colours, and had a fine view of all that was happening.

Such a Tudor pageant was described by Sir Walter Scott in *Kenilworth*: "A broad glare of light was seen to appear from the gate of the park, and, broadening and brightening as it came nearer, advanced along the open and fair avenue that led to the Gallery Tower. . . . Onward came the cavalcade, illuminated by two hundred thick waxen torches, in the hands of as many horsemen, which cast a light like that of broad day all around the procession. . . ."

Just as everyone was not getting rich by trade, not all the time was spent at play. The Elizabethan age saw a great upsurge in industrial activity. The

forests of the Kent and Sussex Weald were chopped down and burned in iron-making furnaces; all kinds of metal were mined in the North and West, salt was mined in Worcestershire, ironworks flourished in, and destroyed, the Forest of Arden, coal, or sea-coal as it was called, because it was inevitably transported by sea, was coming into its own on household hearth and in factory furnace.

In Elizabethan days church-going on Sunday was enforced by law. But the parson, who in previous years had been all-powerful, then was despised for abusing his power, was regarded by Elizabethan times as a rather pitiful fellow. The Queen had allowed parsons to marry again, but it took a little time for people to accustom themselves to parsons with families, and sometimes they were objects of ridicule. Churchgoers heckled the sermon on Sundays if they didn't like it—and even the Queen joined in the abuse, shouting at the parson in his pulpit if she objected to his message.

Enforced by law, too, was the eating of fish on Fridays and during Lent. The purpose appeared to be religious, but it is a reflection on the buccaneering spirit in Elizabethan times that that wasn't the purpose at all—it was to protect the fishing industry, because the fishing industry was the finest training ground for the Royal Navy.

This business of paying lip service to the Church angered those who were daily joining the growing numbers of severe Puritans, a new and powerful religious force. One of them wrote indignantly: "Never hath all kind of sinne and wickedness more universally raigned in any nation at any time, yet all are received into the Church, all made members of Christ."

Were all the Elizabethans outside the Puritans as wicked as that? Perhaps not, for while they prayed by compulsion in the Church, many of them prayed of their own volition in their own homes, and family prayer, which was certainly a popular way of communicating with God, helped to provide a healthy balance to Merry England.

In the long years of the Tudor peace, men no longer had to think of their homes as fortresses and instead of building castles, those who could afford to built brick or stone manor houses with lofty gables, oriel windows and lots of magnificently carved wood ornamentation.

A paradise—for some!

As visitors went to the door of the great hall, they rode down long straight drives with gardens of lawns and flower beds on either side. The rooms inside the house were spacious but still furnished in spartan style. Above the family's rooms, in the attic, were the cramped quarters of the servants. England, said a contemporary writer, was "the purgatory of servants and the hell of horses," because servants were wretchedly treated and horses were made to toil all their lives.

The ladies of such Elizabethan houses were described for us by a Dutchman: "They are well dressed, fond of taking it easy, and commonly leave the care of household matters to their servants. They sit before their doors, decked out in fine clothes, in order to see and be seen by the passer-by. They employ their time in walking and riding, in playing at cards, visiting their friends, making merry with them at childbirths, christenings, churchings and funerals. That is why England is called the paradise of married women. The girls who are not yet married are kept much more rigorously and strictly than in the Low Countries."

The young unmarried women, says another writer, loved "to show coyness in gestures, mincedness in words, gingerliness in tripping on toes like young goats, demure nicety and babyishness," when they went out in their silk scarves "cast about their faces fluttering in the wind, or riding in their velvet visors, with two holes cut for the eyes."

Town life was of necessity a little more realistic. Craftsmen lived in small houses in narrow lanes, while merchants lived in narrow houses four or five stories high. No matter how wealthy they were, there was always the shop on the ground floor and the gathering of apprentices living in it; the Elizabethan merchant would not live apart from his work. All the floors were strewn with rushes, and flowers abounded to sweeten the air from the stench that was everywhere in the streets.

In town and in country the expansion of wealth led to much greater demands for luxury and extravagance. The Tudor table still groaned with great joints of meat, but people wanted to broaden the scope of their meals and to try new ideas in eating. Thus vegetables and roots—pumpkins, salads, radishes, carrots—were reintroduced to the family fare; "they be looked upon as dainty dishes at the tables of delicate merchants, gentlemen and the nobility, who make their provision yearly for new seeds out of strange countries." And these "dainty dishes" were an excellent thing, for they provided the balanced protein diet which the bread and meat eating, beer-drinking English had lacked for so long.

But Merry England, the long peace, the paradise for married women and the land of good living was not to last. An austere age was coming, and with it the worst ever civil war in our island's story.

Edinburgh's Royal Mile
Written and Illustrated by Peter Jackson

It is the "high street" of old Edinburgh, the ancient centre of the city, the mile which links the Castle with the Palace of Holyrood house. To walk along it is to live in Scottish history, for every yard recalls the glorious past.

A. HOSPITAL
ST. MARGARET'S CHAPEL & MONS MEG
C. GOVERNOR'S HOUSE
D. PORTCULLIS GATE
E. NATIONAL WAR MEMORIAL
H. OLD PALACE
B. NEW BARRACKS
F. MUSEUM
G. GREAT HALL

The Castle

Perched on a rock 443 feet above sea level, it is an impressive sight from below. There has been much re-building, but parts of the ancient castle still remain. In its time it has been a fortress, a treasury, a refuge for Sovereigns and a prison for their enemies. During Festival time a Floodlight Tattoo is held on the Parade ground. *(The plan below shows the situation of the Castle and its buildings.)*

THE ESPLANADE was declared to be part of Nova Scotia by Charles I ~ and legally it still is

OUTLOOK TOWER ~ from which you get a wonderful view.

LADY STAIR'S HOUSE. A museum of local material and relics of Robert Burns.

CASTLEHILL   LAWNMARKET

To Lady Stair's House

MERCAT CROSS ~ Royal Proclamations are made here

St. Giles' Church

St. Giles', which stands on the site of a Norman church destroyed by Richard II of England in 1385, was built between 1387 and 1462. The square central tower is surmounted by the famous Crown of St. Giles. Here in 1638 Jenny Geddes, threw a stool at the preacher in protest against the Scottish Church adopting Anglican ceremonies.

The Encyclopædia Britann— was first published her— in Anchor Close in 177—

HIGH   STR—

This house was accidentally hit by a cannon ball in 1745 and it is still in the wall.

Here lived William Brodie ~ Church Deacon by day and burglar by night who was hanged in 1788.

GEORGE IV BRIDGE

Greyfriars Churchyard

CANDLEMAKER ROW

PARLIAMENT HOUSE not used as such since 1707. Though re-fronted it still has its original interior finished in 1640.

Site of BOYD'S INN where D— 1773 and threw his lemonade out — the waiter put a lump of sugar in —

St. Margaret's Chapel

This is the oldest place of worship in Edinburgh, and one of the smallest in Britain. It was once used as a gunner's storehouse. In front of the chapel is a famous cannon ...

Mons Meg

The cannon barrel consists of iron bars joined by hoops and it was made at a place in Scotland called Mollance, later corrupted to Mons. It could fire a stone ball to a distance of two miles and was first used in 1455.

"Greyfriars Bobb—

Bobby was a Skye terrier belonging to — named Gray who came to market every — day. Gray died in 1858 and was buried — friars Churchyard. This fountain was — American admirers in memory of —

Greyfriars Churchyard

In 1638 Charles I imposed the ceremonies and rules of the Church of England upon the Scots. Many objected and drew up a declaration swearing to defend their own faith. It was first signed in Greyfriars Church, and 5,000 people added their names in the churchyard. Here were imprisoned for five months the 1,200 prisoners captured at the Battle of Bothwell Bridge in 1679. Amongst the famous men buried in the churchyard was the Regent Moray, who died in 1581.

The Abbey of Holyrood

It was founded in 1128 by David I, King of Scots. The legend is that when he was out hunting he was unhorsed by a stag. Before it could attack again a cross miraculously appeared between its antlers and it ran away. In gratitude the King founded the Abbey and named it after the Holy Rood (or Holy Cross) which had saved his life. Several of the Scottish kings were crowned and married in the Abbey of Holy Rood.

Today only the Nave remains, and this is in ruins due to the collapse of the heavy stone roof in 1768.

Canongate Tolbooth

Tolls were collected here for many years. It was also a council chamber, a court house and prison. The Tolbooth was built in 1591. The Treaty of Union between England and Scotland was signed near here in 1707.

Huntly House

This is the city's largest museum of local antiquities. Built in 1591, it is the only timber-fronted house left in the city.

Whitehorse Close

This inn was built in 1623, and until the early nineteenth century the London stage coaches arrived at and departed from it each day.

y Knox's House

bout 1490, its tion with the eformer is un-; he may have here in 1572. it contains a n of Knox relics.

CANONGATE CHURCH. 1688. THE CHURCHYARD CONTAINS MANY INTERESTING GRAVES.

QUEEN MARY'S BATHHOUSE WHERE, LEGEND TELLS US, MARY QUEEN OF SCOTS BATHED IN WINE & MILK.

CALTON ROAD · ABBEYHILL

JEFFREY ST. · NEW ST. · CANONGATE

ST. MARY'S STREET · PLAYHOUSE CLOSE

COWGATE

lodged in w because fingers.

Here was Edinburgh's first theatre opened in 1747

The Royal Palace of Holyroodhouse

Begun by James IV of Scotland, it was enlarged to its present size by Charles II.

In the original part of the palace you can see the rooms where Mary Queen of Scots lived.

remembered because for 14 his master died he sat on the refused to leave it. He died l was buried close to the grave d faithfully watched over for so long.

Here on March 9, 1566, Mary was dining with her secretary, David Rizzio, when conspirators, suspicious of his influence over the Queen, murdered him. Leader of the conspiracy was Lord Darnley, husband of the Queen.

On the first floor is what has been called "the world's worst picture gallery." There are 111 portraits of Scottish Kings and Queens, real and mythical, painted by a Dutchman Jacob de Wet in 1684-86. This was real mass-production—he had to paint one a week at a fee of two guineas each! In his spare time he painted fireplaces! The gallery was originally a banqueting hall where, in 1565, Queen Mary was married to Darnley. In 1745 The Young Pretender gave a ball there. In the hall, Scottish representative peers are elected to Parliament.

VIEW FROM A TREE-TOP THAT LED TO FAME

Shimmering in the distance was the Pacific Ocean. Francis Drake saw it and determined to become the first Englishman to sail upon it . . . an act that was to make his name immortal

Sir Francis Drake

FRANCIS DRAKE was alone and wandering in the hills of what is now Panama when, on an impulse, he climbed the tree that was to point the way to his destiny and fame.

It was, we are told, "a goodlie and great high tree", and from its upper branches the young ship's captain could see on one side the mighty Atlantic, which he already knew so well, and on the other, the Pacific, shimmering in the distance.

Drake came down from the tree, fell on his knees, and prayed that he might one day become the first of his countrymen to sail on the Pacific. It was a bold prayer, for the Spaniards regarded the Pacific Ocean as all their own and it was unthinkable to them that any foreigner would dare to enter it.

Drake, born in Devon, took to a seafaring life while he was still a boy. Like all English seamen of Elizabethan days, he quickly learned to hate the Spaniards — England's arch enemies.

He was still a young man when he won modest fame for himself by seizing a quantity of Spanish gold at the Isthmus of Panama. It was then that he went for a walk in the mountains and climbed that tree to see the Pacific for the first time.

Five years later, in 1577, his dream was fulfilled. Queen Elizabeth, protesting her friendship for King Philip of Spain but privately hating him, gave Drake most of the money he needed to sail secretly into the Spanish seas. With it Drake fitted out the *Golden Hind* and three other ships. Pretending that the Mediterranean was his destination, he sailed to the Cape Verde Islands, and then westwards across the Atlantic.

Drake thought that the only way through to the Pacific was via the Strait which the Portuguese explorer Magellan had named and discovered and through which no English ship had ever passed. He had no

CONTINUED ON NEXT PAGE▶

After sailing through the Strait of Magellan, Drake and some of his crew rowed towards the island of Mocha off the coast of Chile. They were given a hostile reception by the islanders, so one story goes, and Drake was wounded by an arrow.

maps or charts and the fierce cold of that rough southern sea added to the hazards of the journey.

It took 16 days to get through the Strait of Magellan and Drake turned his ships hurriedly up the west coast of South America, hoping for warmer weather. Instead, terrible storms followed one after the other. The ships were scattered and one was blown away and never heard of again. Another, after being separated from the *Golden Hind,* sailed back through the strait to England and announced that Drake had been lost. A third was wrecked, and only one of its crew escaped.

Alone now, the *Golden Hind* sailed on.

Along the coast, native fishermen had told Drake of the Spanish harbour of Valparaiso, where a galleon with a valuable cargo was anchored. As the *Golden Hind* sailed defiantly into the harbour, the Spaniards, who had never seen an enemy ship there, imagined she was a Spanish ship and hoisted their flags in welcome.

Calmly, the *Golden Hind* sailed alongside the galleon and moments later Drake's men swarmed over the side on to her decks. The Spaniards, too surprised to resist, were overcome, and all the gold, wine and jewels in their holds was taken on board the English ship.

Drake hoped to get his richest booty at Lima, capital of the Spanish colony of Peru. Nearby he captured a small Portuguese ship and offered to let it go free if the captain would pilot him into Lima harbour. Thus, in the dead of night, the *Golden Hind* sailed into Lima, where 17 Spanish trading ships rode at anchor.

An attack? It was the last thing the Spaniards expected. Drake didn't even have to fire a shot. He plundered the ships of their cargoes of silk and linen, but it was gold he was really after.

But then a Spaniard blurted out the news that Drake wanted to hear: a large Spanish treasure ship had just sailed off to Panama. Drake unfurled his sails; the wind was in his favour and as the hunt began the captain offered a gold chain as a reward to the man who first saw the Spanish ship.

Huge Haul

Ten days later a shout rang out — the enemy ship lay dead ahead. Thinking the *Golden Hind* was a friendly ship, the Spanish captain waited calmly for her to come up with him. It was to prove a costly error, for an arrow from the *Golden Hind* wounded him and the English gunners shot his mast overboard.

The Spaniards surrendered without a fight and this time Drake found all the plunder he wanted. There was gold, silver, and jewels worth £90,000 — as much as the *Golden Hind* could carry.

There could be no turning back — the Spaniards would now certainly be on the look-out for the Devon buccaneer. Drake decided to keep going northwards. He held to the popular belief of his times that there must be a sea-passage round the north of North America.

Leaving the Spanish settlements behind him, he sailed farther north up the coast of North America than any man before him, but he could find no way back into the Atlantic. His men did not like the colder weather, either, so he turned southwards again.

On the coast of California, in what is now the harbour of San Francisco, the *Golden Hind* dropped anchor for some much needed repairs. Here the natives came crowding round to stare at the "white gods".

The only safe way home now was across the Pacific and round the Cape of Good Hope. It needed all the brilliant seamanship of which Drake was so capable to bring his men safely home.

Few could believe their eyes in Plymouth when, three years after she had set sail, the *Golden Hind* sailed back into harbour. Drake and his gallant company had been given up for lost 18 months before — now here they were, laden with jewels, like some fairy tale come true.

When the captain had told his story several times, he sailed off to Deptford in the Thames to report to the queen. How, with the complaints of the Spanish ambassador still ringing in her ears, would she receive the bold buccaneer? For a long time Elizabeth hesitated. Then the queen bade Drake kneel before her and taking a sword, knighted him.

Drake and his crew sailed into Plymouth Sound in September, 1580. He and his gallant company had been given up for lost 18 months earlier. Now here they were, laden with jewels, like some fairy tale come true.

WHEELS ACROSS THE WORLD

PRIMITIVE
The early cart, like this Persian one of 4000 B.C., was simply a seat on wheels. The wheels were tree-trunk segments, revolving round spindles.

Later the cart evolved into a more elaborate chariot, like the one in this painting of King Tutankhamen who ruled Egypt in 1400 B.C. Made of wood, leather and rope, it has a floor of woven fabric to prevent jolting. Reins attached to the driver's hips leave his hands free to use weapons such as a bow or spear in battle.

Once the principle of the wheel became widespread, chariots were used for travel as well as war. This Etruscan chariot of 500 B.C. was found at Fabriano in Italy.

ROMAN
The Romans developed the chariot still further. The two-horse triumphal chariot was made of wood, had metal-rimmed wheels and was ornamented with gold.

When the Imperial army was on the march, loads were carried in a cart called a carrus. Its front wheels were pivoted.

For long journeys the Romans had a covered wagon (carruca dormitaria) in which they could sleep at night.

For sports events, a light-weight racing chariot was used, drawn by two horses. The driver perched perilously between the wheels.

MEDIEVAL
After the fall of the Roman Empire, European roads became neglected and vehicles on wheels were rare. Transport was by litter, carried by men or animals. About A.D. 1200 wheeled carriages reappeared, but only for rich people, like this decorative but bumpy tent-on-wheels.

In King John's time small carriages were curtained, not only for privacy, but to keep out dust and flies. Springs had not yet been invented.

Wheel axles were bolted direct to the carriage body, so that even this ornate French carriage of 1300 was a real "bone-shaker."

ELIZABETHAN-JACOBEAN
The fairy-tale carriage above is similar to the State Coach of Queen Elizabeth I. Massive and heavy, it moved rather slowly and was probably very uncomfortable to ride in.

By 1600 springs had been invented. The coach body rested on great straps which were fixed to the wheel axles, relieving the bumping caused by appalling roads of the time.

At last, after a thousand years, wheel-pivoting was rediscovered. Coaches no longer made a wide arc round corners, but took them smoothly and more comfortably.

The Countess Olivia gave an amazed gasp when her steward Malvolio swaggered up wearing his bright new yellow stockings with cross-garters. Had the stern and humourless servant gone mad?

CALL IT WHAT YOU LIKE

▼▼▼▼▼▼▼▼▼▼▼▼▼▼▼▼▼▼▼▼▼

. . . that, in effect, was what Shakespeare said when
he finished this play. The title he gave it had nothing
to do with the tangled plot, and the play was presented
as TWELFTH NIGHT—OR WHAT YOU WILL

▲▲▲▲▲▲▲▲▲▲▲▲▲▲▲▲▲▲▲▲▲▲▲

OF all William Shakespeare's plays, *Twelfth Night*, written about 1599 or 1600, has one of the most complicated plots. It is a comedy in which mistaken identity plays a dominant part, and is the story of the "eternal triangle" of love. Many of the terms used in the dialogue are topical, which an audience of the sixteenth century would have appreciated, but which are wasted on the modern audiences of today without explanation. The play was probably written as an entertainment to be presented at Christmas time, on the last day of the traditional feast—hence the title *Twelfth Night*.

Viola, disguised as a nobleman, goes to the court of the Duke Orsino, ruler of Illyria, and wins his trust and affection as a faithful messenger to the Countess Olivia, with whom Orsino is in love. When it becomes obvious that Olivia refuses all contact with him, the Duke is thrown into despair. But then Viola reveals that she is really a woman, and has been in love with him for some time. So Orsino, thwarted in one love affair, is successful in another, and marries Viola.

Source of Money

SEBASTIAN is Viola's twin brother. She had believed that he was drowned in the shipwreck which stranded them in Illyria, but at the end of the play she discovers that he is alive. He marries Olivia.

Sir Toby Belch is the Countess Olivia's uncle who, with his two friends Maria and Sir Andrew Ague-cheek, enrages the steward Malvolio with his noisy drinking-bouts. He is made responsible for Malvolio's safety when the Countess believes her steward to be mad. When the steward is eventually released, Sir Toby marries the servant girl Maria.

Sir Andrew, a great friend of Sir Toby Belch, is the idiot of the play. Sir Toby has led him to believe that he has some prospect of marriage to Olivia, and he stays for months at the Countess's house, waiting for a chance to woo her, but finds none. Sir Toby, meanwhile, drinks away Sir Andrew's money, being sure that he has found a lifelong source of income.

Well Rewarded

MARIA the servant girl warns Sir Toby and Sir Andrew when they try Olivia's patience too far. In the end she is well rewarded for her labours, for she marries Sir Toby.

Malvolio, Olivia's self-righteous steward, is an important man in the household, who threatens to turn Sir Toby Belch out of the house for his rowdy behaviour, so earning the knight's hatred.

Malvolio falls victim to a trick devised by Maria to bring him into disrepute with the Countess. He finds a letter in the garden where he takes his afternoon walk, which he takes to be from Olivia. In it the Countess declares her love for him, and instructs him to wear yellow stockings with cross-garters to please her—a fashion that Olivia in fact really hates.

Malvolio does not know that Maria, the servant maid, has devised this way of bringing him into disgrace with his employer. Obediently following the instructions Malvolio appears before Olivia wearing yellow stockings. The Countess believes him to be mad, and orders Sir Toby to take care of him. Eventually Malvolio is released, but he has paid the price for being so overbearing.

Feste the Clown might well be termed the great onlooker in *Twelfth Night*. He knows most of the characters in the plot, plays on the weaknesses of some, while offering friendship to others. Olivia's father had taken a great delight in Feste's wit, but Olivia herself, mourning for her dead brother, sharply reproves the Clown when his gentle taunting becomes too much for her.

The baiting of Malvolio he enjoys, although he is at heart a kind person who will only torment people to a point. Eventually it is he who supplies the steward with pen, ink and paper in order that he may write to the Countess and tell her that he is not mad, but was deceived by the letter which he believed had come from her.

**Viola, as Orsino's messenger, visits Olivia,
who is in mourning for her brother.**

There is no land like England

There is no land like England
  Where'er the light of day be;
There are no hearts like English hearts,
  Such hearts of oak as they be.

There is no land like England
  Where'er the light of day be;
There are no men like Englishmen,
  So tall and bold as they be.

And these will strike for England,
  And man and maid be free
To foil and spoil the tyrant
  Beneath the greenwood tree.

There is no land like England
  Where'er the light of day be;
There are no wives like English wives,
  So fair and chaste as they be.

There is no land like England
  Where'er the light of day be;
There are no maids like English maids,
  So beautiful as they be.

And these shall wed with freemen,
  And all their sons be free,
To sing the songs of England
  Beneath the greenwood tree.

*Song from "The Foresters," by
Alfred, Lord Tennyson*

TO CELIA

Drink to me only with thine eyes,
   And I will pledge with mine;
Or leave a kiss but in the cup
   And I'll not look for wine.
The thirst that from the soul doth rise
   Doth ask a drink divine;
But might I of Jove's nectar sup,
   I would not change for thine.

I sent thee late a rosy wreath,
   Not so much honouring thee
As giving it a hope that there
   It could not withered be;
But thou thereon didst only breathe,
   And sent'st it back to me
Since when it grows, and smells, I swear,
   Not of itself but thee !

Ben Jonson, Poet and Playwright, and his great friend, Shakespeare

BEN THE BRAWLER

IN the year 1598, at Hog's End Fields, Shoreditch, two men faced each other with rapiers ready. One was Gabriel Spencer, a bad-tempered actor. The other, older, with a pock-marked face, was Ben Jonson, poet.

Nobody knows the cause of their quarrel. Spencer had the longer sword and wounded Jonson in the arm. The poet then drove his blade under the actor's guard and Spencer fell dead.

Ben Jonson was tried at the Old Bailey and found guilty of murder but reprieved.

In the sixty-four years of his brawling, but learned, life, Benjamin Jonson was imprisoned many times, angered everyone that mattered, including King James I, and even in death did not lie at rest, for his coffin was set upright in Westminster Abbey. His plays, his poems, his dauntless spirit, are honoured to this day.

He was born in 1573, lived in Charing Cross and daily walked through the grounds of the Royal Palace of Whitehall to Westminster School, where his tutor, the scholar William Camden, revealed the classic world of Greece and Rome. His parents were poor, and when he failed to get a scholarship he was apprenticed to a bricklayer.

Ben's heart was set on the theatre, but he wanted to mirror life in classical style without the airy fancies he criticized in the plays of his actor friend Will Shakespeare.

His first classic play, *Every Man In His Humour*, was a success. Other plays were not, but he was undismayed, and in his epilogue to *Cynthia's Revels* cheekily wrote his own verdict: "By God, 'tis good."

His masterpieces, *Volpone* and *The Alchemist*, both attacked greed—"the evil glitter of gold." He drew inspiration from the classics, and his famous poem *To Celia*—"Drink to me only with thine eyes"—was written not in ardour for a lady fair but fashioned out of five prose passages by the Greek writer Philostratus.

Truly Ben Jonson was a contradiction—a scholar but a red-blooded one. He drank mightily, roistered with his cronies in the Mermaid Tavern, had a large collection of riddles and enjoyed hearty jokes.

He died in 1637 an honoured man of letters, and the apt inscription on his tomb in the Abbey says simply: "*O rare Ben Jonson.*"

MYSTERY OF THE SONNETS

Who was the Dark Lady of Shakespeare's haunting verses?

IN considering the theatrical difficulties with which Shakespeare was faced in writing his plays we have so far in this series dealt with his casting problems, like the way in which he wrote for certain accomplished actors of his time, and his handling of women's characters, which were, of course, always played by boys.

Another thing we must remember is the style of the Elizabethan theatre. The audience sat or stood on three sides of the forty foot by thirty foot stage, and some of those in the upper gallery were actually *behind* the stage. This gave an immediacy of contact with the audience not often possible in the theatre today.

Shakespeare's plays were acted at a very fast pace, with lavish costumes, but no sets and no intervals. Rapid changes of action and emotion that sometimes make Shakespeare puzzling to us when we think of his plays, or see them on a "picture frame" stage, become understandable in the context of the big but very intimate theatre he wrote for.

At the Globe, the 3,900 lines of *Hamlet* took three hours. Today, were it not for the cuts usually made by directors, it would take at least four hours.

No places for scenes were ever specifically given by Shakespeare outside the dialogue. If your edition says before a scene "A street in Venice" or "A woodland glade," these are insertions by editors.

Shakespeare never meant you to know until the moment he was ready and gave the clue in the text, exactly where the action was taking place. No edition of his play published before the eighteenth century gave any indication of place. Nor were the plays fully divided into acts and scenes.

Antony and Cleopatra and *Romeo and Juliet* were given no divisions whatever. In fact, the modern divisions we have in these plays and in many others are ruinous to Shakespeare's intentions. There are often forty or more scenes in *Antony and Cleopatra* as produced today, and this spoils the flow of the action.

If we really believe that Shakespeare was the greatest dramatist that ever lived, should we not also believe that he knew what he wanted and did not want? Should we not go back to producing the plays as *he* meant them to be produced?

Now for a moment, let us turn to the sonnets. These are the 154 poems published in 1609. In

this edition they are full of glaring errors, and Shakespeare obviously had nothing to do with the printing. He could not have even read the proofs.

The first seventeen are addressed to a young man urging him to marry; the next 109 are mainly addressed to some adult man; and the remaining twenty-eight are about a woman.

We know nothing of the reason Shakespeare wrote the sonnets in this way, and scholars have pondered for a century on the problem—especially the one posed by the last twenty-eight . . . who was the woman, the Dark Lady of the Sonnets, as she is called?

Few Illusions

MANY volumes have been written about her, but it is enough here to say that the evidence of the sonnets points to her being a real woman whom Shakespeare loved almost to madness.

She was no dainty maiden. She loved him and tormented him, drove him to the heights of passion and the depths of misery. He writes tender passages about her, and he insults her with all the deadly verbal venom at his command.

Perhaps she was Anne Whateley, the Stratford girl he deserted—after applying for a marriage licence—to marry Anne Hathaway instead. Perhaps she was Mary Fitton, one of the Queen's maids of honour. Perhaps she was a girl he met in the theatre. We just do not know until some further evidence comes to light.

Ben Jonson, who was considered in his lifetime as Shakespeare's peer as a writer, had few illusions about him. In the First Folio he wrote a poem "to the memory of my beloved, the author Mr. William Shakespeare, and what he hath left us." In the poem these lines occur:

"*. . . I confess thy writings to be such*
As neither Man, nor Muse, can praise too
*   much . . .*
I therefore will begin. Soule of the Age!
The applause! Delight! The wonder of our
*   Stage!*"

More than three hundred years later, Ivor Brown wrote of Shakespeare:

"*He was not for throne of pomp or the dais of the intellectual; he preferred to be the Gentleman in the Parlour, the vagrant lodger, the man in the wings, the reporter in the royal gallery. In these positions of spectatorship he mingled three elements: a common-sense philosophy of moderation, deep feeling for all folk suffering and all things gay or beautiful, and unfailing*

Did Shakespeare first see his "Dark Lady" as she watched the plays performed at the Globe?

power to find the word perfect to each place and subject."

There we have the measure of Shakespeare in two quotations centuries apart. But in centuries to come, will the praise still be for Shakespeare, or will some new discovery prove what some scholars suspect . . . that Shakespeare did not write the plays at all?

This is the exciting question we shall examine in next week's article.

HATFIELD HOUSE
IN HERTFORDSHIRE

For more than three hundred years, Hatfield House, in Hertfordshire, has been the home of the distinguished Cecil family. It is a house containing treasures which bring the past vividly to life. It is built of red brick and Caen stone and is one of the best examples of a Jacobean mansion in England. The house stands in an extensive park. Hatfield House has been in turn a bishop's palace, a royal palace, a private mansion, and during the two World Wars, a convalescent home and hospital.

THE OLD PALACE

Hatfield House stands in the parish of Bishop's Hatfield. In a nearby church is the tomb of Robert Cecil who built Hatfield. He was the son of Elizabeth's great minister, William Cecil, Lord Burghley.

In the early seventeenth James I visited Robert house, Theobalds, and li so much that he insisted o it for Hatfield. Cecil pu but one wing of the ol used the bricks to buil mansion. It was built li honour of Elizabeth an years hard work. But lived in it. He died be move into the magnifice

ROBERT CECIL

In Saxon days the land belonged to the monks. In the late fifteenth century Bishop Morton built a fine palace of timber and brick here which became the palace of the Bishops of Ely. Part of the old palace still stands by the side of the present Jacobean mansion.

BISHOP MORTON

The bishops' palace became a royal residence after the dissolution of the monasteries. Henry VIII kept it as a nursery palace. Here Mary, Elizabeth and Edward spent much of their childhood, and when he became king, the young Edward granted the palace to his sister Elizabeth. She was living here when Edward died.

During Seymour's trial Elizabeth was kept at Hatfield. The testimony of her servants helped to convict Seymour. When Elizabeth's half-sister Mary became Queen in 1553, Elizabeth was sent back to Hatfield Palace. This time she was kept in "honourable detention" during Mary's reign.

In 1558 Mary died. A brilliant cavalcade of gentlemen rode post-haste to Hatfield to proclaim Elizabeth queen. They found her sitting under an oak tree in the park reading her Bible, and here she received the first news of her accession. An oak tree is still preserved in the park which is known as Elizabeth's Oak.

Thomas Seymour, Lord High Admiral, wanted the hand of the young Elizabeth. An ambitious man, he made many enemies. Persistent rumours of their love-affair led to an investigation. Seymour was tried, convicted of treason, and executed in 1549.

MARY TUDOR

Robert Cecil's son, the second Earl of Salisbury, spent the family fortune in lavish furnishing and entertaining. The third, fourth and fifth Earls, impoverished by this extravagance, were forced to sell many of the treasures which the house contained. The sixth Earl spent little time at Hatfield and the house became practically derelict.

Lady Emily, masterful wife of the seventh Earl (who was created a marquess in 1789), restored Hatfield to its former grandeur. She would gamble until the floor was thick with playing-cards, and she was said to be fond of throwing golden guineas to the poor. A beautiful portrait of her, painted by Sir Joshua Reynolds, still hangs at Hatfield.

Lady Emily was always a keen horsewoman. Even when elderly and almost blind she still rode to the hounds, strapped to the saddle, and with a groom alongside. Returning from the hunt one day at the age of eighty-five, she retired to her room to write letters, and overturned a candle. In the fierce fire, which spread from her apartments to the rest of the house, Lady Emily died.

Hatfield was one of the first private houses to have electric light. The power plant was in the park and the electric fittings often exploded, showering the guests with sparks. Loose cushions were kept around the house to be thrown at faulty fittings.

The Second Marquess, receiving word of Queen Victoria's intention to visit the house in 1846, made great preparations, and had extensive redecorating done. As the Queen's cortège entered the drive the men were just putting the final touches to their work.

The house contains, among the treasures preserved in it, a large number of historical portraits. Also to be seen are the cradle of the infant Charles I, and a garden hat which belonged to Elizabeth I.

A valuable collection of manuscripts and state papers is preserved at Hatfield and a genealogical tree, drawn up for Elizabeth I can be seen. It traces her descent back to Adam and it is 42 ft. long. An early tank of the First World War stands in the grounds. It commemorates the trials held there in 1915 of the prototype Mark I tank. The tank was finally put into service and used extensively in the war.

The Pilgrim Fathers

MASSACRE—AND VENGEANCE

At the head of every Company of Militia was a Captain, directly responsible to the Colony's Government. Under him was a lieutenant, an ensign, a clerk and several sergeants. The rank and file were either pikemen or musketeers. The drill was patterned on European methods, but, as the militiamen adapted themselves to the conditions of Indian warfare, a pattern of their own gradually emerged, and the long, unwieldy pike and European battle formations were abandoned.

THE threat of an Indian war was hanging over New England like a storm cloud in the early 1670s. By now the settlers had spread out far beyond Plymouth, the original colony of the Pilgrim Fathers, and were living in isolated townships and farms scattered over a vast wilderness and connected only by a network of forest trails.

The towns were organised into counties, each with its own county court room. The counties made up the colony.

The elected leaders of the counties were solid businessmen, most of them staunch Puritans, and they watched over the economy and administered justice. Trade was increasing. Vessels sailed out of the growing ports of New Haven, Newport and Boston, carrying produce from the farmlands and furs from the interior, and sailed in bringing imported goods from England.

In 1643, three of the colonies banded together under an alliance called the New England Confederation. These were Massachusetts, Connecticut and Plymouth, who drew up an agreement for mutual defence.

The fourth New England colony, Rhode Island, differed from its neighbours in that it was a refuge for those settlers who, quite simply, were not Puritans and did not want to be!

Within the Confederation every male of military age was a member of the militia. His gun and powder horn hung at the ready in his cabin, and he was expected to take part in regular training sessions.

Back in 1622, the colony of Virginia to the south had suffered the horrors of an Indian uprising, and among the many reasons given for the near ruin of the colony was a lack of military discipline. The New Englanders were determined not to suffer a similar disaster, and knew that their security depended upon their ability to put an efficient force into the field at a moment's notice.

In 1674 the situation around Plymouth Colony was tense. The Indian leader, King Philip, was growing steadily more angry and hostile.

The Indians, infuriated by the spread of settlers over their lands, and conscious that they were losing their old way of life, were at last uniting under Philip to try and drive the white men into the sea. The Plymouth Government was aware that something was afoot as reports of bands of Indians in the vicinity of Mount Hope started coming in. The most isolated frontier village was Swansea, near King Philip's fortress on Mount Hope. It was at these few dozen scattered houses that painted war parties first struck.

Some of the houses were already empty as their frightened occupants had already fled. The Indians began by ransacking the cabins, then set fire to them. Settlers, huddled for protection in the block houses, heard their terrifying yells and hastily despatched riders to sound the alarm through the settlements. Soon New England was up in arms. At Swansea nine men were killed and two fatally wounded, and, as the months went by, town after town went up in smoke and flames.

To combat the alliance of King Philip's Wampanoags, the Narragansetts and the Nipmucs, the United Colonies put an army of 1,000 men in the field with orders to attack the Great Narragansett Swamp Fortress in Rhode Island. In December, 1675, it was destroyed and 3,000 Indians were killed or forced to flee, many later dying of hunger and exposure. However, attacks on the settlements continued in all their savage fury. The following July Philip's wife and son were captured, but the King escaped into the forest.

A party of soldiers under Benjamin Church kept up the pursuit, and finally Philip was killed at Mount Hope. His head was mounted on a pole and displayed at Plymouth. The war was now over and the giant task of reconstruction began. Thousands of people had lost their homes and the economy was shattered. But it was only a setback. For the Indians, however, the war had been a disaster. Their lands were gone and they became mere tenants and hired servants. They were the refugees now. Their power in New England was broken for ever.

THE cruel death of the great King Henry the Fourth of France by the dagger of the assassin Ravaillac as the King was riding in his carriage through the streets of Paris left Henry's nine-year-old son on the throne.

This awkward, sullen-looking boy, Louis the Thirteenth, was of course too young to rule. Until he came of age, therefore, his mother, Marie de Medici, assumed the title of Regent.

Marie could have chosen her dead husband's adviser, the Duke of Sully, to be her minister. Instead she rejected that wise man and in his place she put a vain Italian upstart named Concini.

When the noblemen of France rebelled against the policies with which Concini fed Marie he simply paid them huge bribes to pacify them. And all the time the Italian increased his own wealth at the expense of the country.

Concini knew that his days of power were numbered unless he could contain the growing boy King. Through Marie, therefore, he supervised the boy's upbringing along lines that he hoped would make Louis a completely ineffectual ruler.

A famous French writer has told us how Concini's plan for Louis worked:

"The King was left in complete idleness, and provided with no instruction whatever. He often complained of this and later in life frequently referred to the fact that he had not even been taught to read. A scrupulous watch was kept that no courtiers should gather around him. The young King saw no one but his attendants, who were at once dismissed as soon as the slightest sign of friendship with Louis became apparent."

The attentions of one courtier, however, were missed by the artful Concini until it was too late. Left with nothing to do for most of the week but hunt, Louis found a friend in his falconer, Albert de Luynes.

Everyone, in fact, misjudged Albert de Luynes, who was much older than the King. No one saw in this amiable, pleasant fellow the craving for power that the simple falconer was later to exhibit.

Meanwhile another commoner at court was

RICHELIEU
The Great Cardinal

An all-powerful King with an all-powerful minister—this was the aim of Cardinal Richelieu, the man who rose from a humble country priest to hold the highest position in France after his sovereign

beginning to show signs of the personal genius which he was soon to emblazon on the story of France. Armand du Plessis of Richelieu had, unlike the King, received an education which his brilliant mind had seized upon. He had studied theology and very soon was confounding learned and experienced men with the breadth of his knowledge and his ability to discuss the scriptures.

At twenty-one, Richelieu, who was destined to be truly great, was made a bishop. In due time he was introduced into the court of Marie de Medici where he soon gained a complete influence over the Regent. Despite his youth, it was a shrewdly calculating influence, and one that Richelieu used for the time being to defend Concini against the anger of the nobles and the people.

Luynes, the falconer, too, was using his influence in a calculating fashion as he nursed his master's hate for Concini the adventurer. One day at the palace of the Louvre in Paris the young King called the captain of his guard and told him that he wanted to be rid of the Italian minister, who was still his mother's favourite.

The captain and his men approached Concini as he entered the inner courtyard surrounded by his admirers. A word passed between them; then the guards drew their pistols from under their cloaks and fired point-blank into Concini's face.

Marie was distraught when she was told that her favourite was dead. Weeping she moaned: "For seven years I have been a ruler; now all I can hope for is a crown in heaven!"

Louis, of course, was delighted. He announced that he would now rule the kingdom alone, and sent Richelieu from his mother's court off into the country. Luynes was created a Duke and became Louis's chief adviser.

Family Quarrel

By promoting his old falconer to such high office Louis was courting rebellion among his noblemen. It was not long in coming. The disaffected nobles drove a wedge between Louis and his mother, both of whom were holding courts in different parts of the country. As the quarrel between mother and son was fanned Louis was obliged to raise an army to march against the supporters of his own mother.

Who could prevent the catastrophe of a battle between the royal family—the kind of civil war that no one believed belonged to seventeenth-century France? The exiled Richelieu was the man, it was decided. The young bishop was recalled and hastening to the Queen Mother's court ahead of Louis's soldiers, he arranged a brilliant reconciliation. So successful was he that Louis and Marie embraced each other when they met.

Marie now fell completely under the spell of the clever young Richelieu, whom Luynes, the King's man, was beginning to see as a serious rival. While Richelieu nursed his ambition to become a Cardinal, Luynes saw his ambition fulfilled when the King promoted him to the

office of Constable, the highest in the land.

Louis, like Luynes, was not anxious to see Richelieu get his Cardinal's hat. "I know this man," he told his mother after Richelieu had successfully persuaded Marie to give up her own court and return to her son in Paris. "He is a man of unlimited ambition."

It was at this point that the bishops of the Catholic Church in France demanded that their religion should be practised in the province of Béarn where, since the days of Henry the Fourth, the Huguenots (French Protestants) had been allowed to worship freely. They asked the King to back them and Louis agreed; accordingly he marched into Béarn and proclaimed the Catholic faith there.

What would the Huguenots in the rest of France do now?

Their strongest settlements were the city of Montauban in the south and La Rochelle on the Atlantic Ocean, and at once they began to arm. The royal reply to this was to send an army against the city of Montauban under the command of Constable Luynes, but before anything was achieved the Constable caught a fever and within three days he was dead.

Determination

Louis had to have a new adviser, and since the religious wars were beginning again he had to choose quickly. Richelieu was his choice; within a year of the Constable's death the man of unlimited ambition was created a Cardinal.

Richelieu was even more determined than the other Catholic leaders to destroy the Huguenots and straightaway he began a siege of their stronghold of La Rochelle. From that city the Huguenots appealed to England to help them, and King Charles the First sent over a fleet under the command of his worthless favourite the Duke of Buckingham.

Ruthless determination, a desire to achieve his objective at any cost—these were the forces that drove the tall, frail Cardinal, and the foppish Duke of Buckingham was scarcely the man to stop him. The French fleet sailed to the attack and swept the English away, forcing Buckingham to return to England to face the anger of every Englishman in the land.

The Huguenots of La Rochelle continued to hang on grimly. The Cardinal walked with steadfastness among his besieging soldiers, his

Deprived of the company of courtiers, the boy king found a friend in his falconer, Albert de Luynes.

After quarrelling with her son, King Louis the ▶ Thirteenth, Marie de Medici, the Queen Mother of France, left the royal château at Blois and formed a party strong enough to defy the King. Then Richelieu (background) was recalled to court to effect a reconciliation between mother and son. How successfully he did so you can see from this picture of their meeting. Instead of attacking his mother's soldiers, Louis embraced her. "How your Majesty has grown!" said Marie when they met. "Grown for your service, madame," was the young King's gallant reply.

eagle eyes ready to fix on any fault, any laxity in the Catholic camp. For a time, too, Louis came to watch the siege; he noted the Cardinal's meticulous preparations and he was impressed.

Slowly the Huguenots starved. For two long years they held out until famine forced them to ask for terms. Then the walls of their city were broken down and although they were allowed to continue practising their faith, all their other privileges were taken away.

For Richelieu the surrender of La Rochelle was a magnificent triumph. Now the Cardinal was all powerful.

It was in the field of foreign policy that Richelieu really made his political name, so let us now have a look at the situation that existed in Europe in the early part of this seventeenth century.

You will remember that in the first half of the sixteenth century the struggle for power was between the Kings of France and the Holy Roman Emperor Charles the Fifth, who was also King of Spain. When Charles abdicated his son Philip the Second received his Spanish kingdom and his brother Ferdinand received his possessions in Austria together with the title of Emperor of the Holy Roman Empire.

Charles, Philip and Ferdinand were members of the Hapsburg family which had been powerful in Europe since the thirteenth century. By the time Louis the Thirteenth was on the French throne Ferdinand's Hapsburg descendants had made the family and its empire to the east of France all powerful in Europe. Their principal possessions were Austria, Hungary and Bohemia, and from these countries they were the complete controllers of international diplomacy. This was the power which Richelieu, in the name of France, was determined to reduce.

Day of Dupes

After the siege of La Rochelle Richelieu and the King set out on a series of campaigns. With the sword they were successful, but after they returned Louis became ill and during a fever he was persuaded by his artful mother to send the Cardinal away from the court. The King was soon to regret this hasty action, for he found that there was not a man in France with half of Richelieu's ability.

But Marie, the King's mother, was overjoyed at the Cardinal's banishment. Lately she had been growing jealous of Richelieu's power and when he was gone she made the mistake of promising his job to each of her favourites in turn. The Cardinal, however, was not so easily crushed: returning to Paris in due course he presented himself before Louis who, despite the ravings and protestations of his mother, took the Cardinal back as his minister.

"I honour my mother, but my obligations to the State are greater than towards her," said Louis grimly. Thereafter the time in which Marie wrongly imagined that she had got rid of the minister for good and was happily giving his job to all her callers was called "The Day of the Dupes."

Richelieu could see then that his most implacable enemy at court was the Queen Mother. Now it was his turn to whisper to Louis that she was the troublemaker, with the result that the King banned Marie from his court. For a long time she wandered aimlessly through Europe until, friendless and nearly penniless, she died in the house of a German shoemaker.

Meanwhile the Cardinal was made a Duke and from this lofty position he set about realizing another of his dreams—to make France great by concentrating power in the hands of an absolute monarch and his minister. To do this he could not have fractious noblemen forever causing

upsets, so gradually the nobles' power and privileges were whittled down by the minister's policies.

The nobles seethed with anger; at last they decided to rise in rebellion against Richelieu. But the Cardinal, as ever, knew everything that was going on in the kingdom; his spies were everywhere and he heard about the nobles' plans even before they were completed. Their leader Montmorency, son of the famous old Constable of France, was speedily captured and executed as a traitor. Nothing and no one was allowed to stand in the way of the great Cardinal.

In the German Empire the Thirty Years War had been raging since 1618. Primarily it was a religious war caused by the Protestant princes in Germany quarrelling with their Catholic emperor. Richelieu saw a way of turning this purely German war to French advantage—it meant that he would have to support the Protestants whom he despised but if he were successful the borders of France could be extended. And, as ever, he was successful.

Successful, too, was his crusade of intrigue against the Hapsburgs. Richelieu was prepared to give money to any opponent of that mighty house, even sending funds to the Protestant King of Sweden to pursue his enmity against the empire.

At home a new rival to the Cardinal was feeling his way to power. Cinq-Mars, although already himself a favourite of the fickle Louis, was prepared even to betray his country to Spain in order to bring about the Cardinal's downfall.

But Richelieu's ability to discover everything that was going on around him again saved him. As soon as the Cardinal had received an assurance from Louis that the King would stand by his minister in all things, Richelieu presented Louis with a copy of the secret treaty that Cinq-Mars had made with the Spanish.

Cinq-Mars, together with his friend De Thou, was arrested by the King's command and both men were executed.

"Too many Kings of France have failed because they did not support good ministers," declared Louis as he conferred a new title—Lieutenant-General of the Realm—on the Cardinal. But the new Lieutenant-General was a sick man; he had never been strong or physically fit and in December, 1642, one of his many illnesses caused his death. Louis, the King whom he had made all-powerful, survived him by only a few months.

Richelieu has been attacked and praised both in history and fiction and he remains even today a controversial figure. What is beyond doubt is his significance, for his ambition to make the King a supreme ruler and his country a great one to the exclusion of all else, paved the way for two important events in the story of France.

The first was the most glorious reign of all in France—the reign of the supreme King Louis the Fourteenth. And the second was that by making the monarchy so absolute Richelieu stifled the political development of his country, a fact which at last bred the French Revolution.

The Slave's Dream

Beside the ungathered rice he lay,
His sickle in his hand;
His breast was bare, his matted hair
Was buried in the sand.
Again, in the mist and shadow of sleep,
He saw his Native Land.

Wide through the landscape of his dreams
The lordly Niger flowed;
Beneath the palm-trees on the plain
Once more a king he strode;
And heard the tinkling caravans
Descend the mountain-road.

He saw once more his dark-eyed queen
Among her children stand;
They clasped his neck, they kissed his cheeks,
They held him by the hand!—
A tear burst from the sleeper's lids
And fell into the sand.

And then at furious speed he rode
Along the Niger's bank;
His bridle-reins were golden chains,
And, with a martial clank,
At each leap he could feel his scabbard of steel
Smiting his stallion's flank.

Before him, like a blood-red flag,
The bright flamingoes flew;
From morn till night he followed their flight,
O'er plains where the tamarind grew,
Till he saw the roofs of Caffre huts,
And the ocean rose to view.

At night he heard the lion roar,
And the hyena scream,
And the river-horse, as he crushed the reeds
Beside some hidden stream;
And it passed, like a glorious roll of drums,
Through the triumph of his dream.

The forests, with their myriad tongues,
Shouted of liberty;
And the Blast of the Desert cried aloud,
With a voice so wild and free,
That he started in his sleep and smiled,
At their tempestuous glee.

He did not feel the driver's whip,
Nor the burning heat of day;
For Death had illumined the land of sleep,
And his lifeless body lay
A worn-out fetter, that the soul
Had broken and thrown away.

By HENRY WADSWORTH LONGFELLOW

PROUD AS A PEACOCK

The ancient Greeks called him Juno's bird—and his feathers were once a badge of honour

WITH his gorgeous plumage of bronze, blue, green and gold glittering like polished metal, it is not surprising that the peacock has for long been the symbol of pride and splendour.

In the days of knightly chivalry, solemn oaths were taken "on the peacock." For anyone to be described as "proud as a peacock" meant that that person was the last word in dignity.

The Ancient Greeks called the peacock Juno's bird. This was because the eye-like markings on his display feathers were thought to represent the hundred eyes of Argus, ordered by Juno to guard Io, daughter of the king of Argos.

The famous peacock throne of the Mogul emperors at Delhi was of glittering magnificence, for it had as background the figure of a peacock with spreading feathers made of gold and precious stones. In China, the Emperor could bestow no greater honour upon a mandarin than to give him a fan of peacock feathers.

India and Ceylon

ALTHOUGH peacocks have been common in Europe and kept as decorations in the gardens of the wealthy since the earliest times, the peafowl is native to India and Ceylon.

In their wild state peafowl live in flocks of one cock and four hens. The hens are rather drab and colourless birds compared with the magnificent male.

Peafowl build an untidy nest on the ground or in the low branches of trees. The hen lays six eggs. Both the male and female have identical plumage until they are two years old, when the cock develops his magnificent display of feathers.

Strictly speaking, the peacock's fan-like tail is not his tail at all. The colourful feathers actually grow above his tail, which consist of quite short feathers.

Moreover, the colours of the peacock's so-called tail are not so brilliant as they seem. The "tail" only appears brilliant and glittering because the surface of the feathers reflects light brilliantly.

One species of peacock now native to Japan has wings of a particularly brilliant blue. This is the true "peacock blue" we hear about. The hen of the Japanese species is a dirty white.

The BATH ROAD

WRITTEN AND DRAWN BY
R. S. EMBLETON

Cherhill · Avebury · Marlborough
← Bath   R. Kennet

The origins of the settlement on which Marlborough stands go back far into pre-history. It is certainly as old as Stonehenge and it is said that Merlin the Wizard was buried under the mound on which Marlborough Castle, built by the Norman kings, once stood. The town's motto is "Ubi nunc sapientes ossa Merlini?"—"Where are sage Merlin's bones?"

The Bath Road runs *through* Marlborough College, for it is bridged by an arch which joins the school buildings. The famous Castle Inn, an old coaching inn, is now part of the school. The great Lord Chatham created a sensation when he locked himself in a room there for three weeks in 1767 because an attack of gout had been aggravated by his uncomfortable journey.

Leaving Marlborough we move on to the village of Avebury which is enclosed within a huge circular bank nearly fifty feet high. Here the remains of temples built by prehistoric man can be seen. Huge stone pillars trace the outline of the temples.

In 1653 the town was practically destroyed by fire. It started in a tanner's yard and spread rapidly across the thatched roofs of the houses. Since then no thatched roofs have been allowed in Marlborough.

It was at Cherhill that Dr. Christopher Alsop made his famous white horse in 1780. He outlined the horse with flags and directed operations from a nearby hill with a trumpet.

Silbury Hill is a prehistoric mystery. Built before the Romans came, it covers an area of five acres and is 130 feet high—the largest artificial mound in England.

The quiet village of Cherhill was the home of the Cherhill Gang. They terrorized the surrounding countryside for much of the eighteenth century.

CARISBROOKE CASTLE
ON THE ISLE OF WIGHT

The Romans had a fort at Carisbrooke to command the approaches to their port of Clausentium (Southampton). It was rebuilt in 530 by the Anglo-Saxons and named Wihtgarasburgh. After the Norman Conquest William Fitz Osbern was Lord of the Isle of Wight and began the present castle.

In 1071 Roger Fitz Osbern led an unsuccessful revolt against William I and Carisbrooke was forfeited to the Crown until 1100, when it was granted to Richard de Redvers, who enlarged the castle.

CARISBR
The castle is
Ministry of W
historical sho
and is oper

March to April
May to September
October
November to Feb

The c
castle

The castle well is 161 feet deep and has supplied the castle with water for 750 years. The water is raised by a wheel built in 1587 and 15 feet 6 inches in diameter. It is worked by a donkey which treads inside the wheel, turning it.

Earl Baldwin, son of Richard de Redvers, supported Matilda against King Stephen. Baldwin retreated to Carisbrooke, and was besieged. Exiled, he returned in 1153 and built the keep.

Countess Isabel, last of the de Redvers, greatly enlarged the castle, which in 1358 passed to the Earl of Salisbury. In 1377, Carisbrooke was besieged by the French, but they were defeated in a battle beneath the castle walls.

In the troubl
15th cent
three Lord
Carisbro
were c
victed of
treason :
Duke
Glouceste
1446; Duk
Somers
1461; Lo
Scales, 14

The castle passed to the Crown in 1483. In 1587 it was heavily fortified to resist the Spanish invasion. Some ships of the Armada were actually destroyed off the island.

A gun called the Carisbrooke falcon is a rare example of 16th century artillery.

Army officer in the reign of Elizabeth I

This part of Carisbrooke Castle was constructed by the Normans.

Made 500 years ago, these oak doors at the inner end of the gatehouse passage are still in good condition. They originally led to the inner gate, which is now destroyed.

After the Royalist cause was lost, Charles I was imprisoned in Carisbrooke Castle from November 1647 until September 1648, when he was removed to the nearby town of Newport.

CHARLES 1

King Charles I attempted to escape from his prison room in Carisbrooke Castle. The story goes that he was jammed in the window and discovered by the guards. This plot was the excuse for Charles' execution.

The great hall of the castle is now a museum and contains many relics of Charles I, including the key of the room in which he was imprisoned. He was beheaded four months after he left Carisbrooke.

Carisbrooke Castle in the reign of Edward III

1. MAIN GATE AND GATEHOUSE.
2. WELL.
3. KEEP.
4. DOMESTIC BUILDINGS.
5. MOAT.
6. GARDENS.

Key to Charles I's prison room.

Colours of the Isle of Wight Militia in the Napoleonic Wars.

TLE TODAY
the care of the one of the great the Isle of Wight lic as follows:

kdays   Sundays
p.m.   p.m.
5.30   2 to 5.30
7   2 to 5.30
5.30   2 to 5.30
4   2 to 4

An Old Blind Man Sits Thinking

The helpless poet dictates "Paradise Lost" to one of his daughters.

THE old man dressed in black sits still and quiet in the room hung with heavy green curtains.

The furniture in the room is old and dismal. And the old man, seated in his armchair and with his long hair falling on his shoulders, seems a natural part of his surroundings and his time— England in the years after the Civil War.

There is a desk before the old man, but he pays no heed to the papers upon it. For if we look hard we can see that the man, whose name is John Milton, is blind.

What is he thinking of, this sightless man, as he sits there?

Perhaps of his boyhood in Bread Street, London, where, despite his weak eyes, he wrote poems in Latin and pamphlets in English denouncing King Charles I and the clergy.

Or perhaps the old blind man is thinking of more settled days when, after his first and disastrous marriage, the great Protector Cromwell himself appointed him "Secretary for Foreign Tongues," on account of his fluency in European languages.

And here the poet's forehead furrows. For it was at this stage in his life that his doctor had warned that unless he eased up on his work he would lose the sight of his eyes.

How could he have eased up? Had he not been appointed to serve his country in the hour of its freedom by Oliver Cromwell himself?

Here the old man fingers his blind eyes. Perhaps he is thinking now that, after all, his blindness is in vain. Thinking, perhaps, of the bitterest pill of his life, the death of Cromwell and the Restoration of the Stuart kings to the throne.

And his own unceremonious removal to prison, where they took him sightless and uncomplaining, for being an enemy of the monarchy.

The old man smiles. He is out of prison now. Mercifully the king has had him released.

The blind poet leans forward and pulls at a bell rope. A girl comes into the room. She is one of his daughters. At his dictation she writes.

He talks about Satan and about God and about the Serpent and the archangels, and about the Eden that Adam and Eve lost. The blank verse of his majestic words thrill, and is catchingly beautiful.

John Milton is composing another of the twelve books of *Paradise Lost*. He does not yet know that this amazingly imaginative work, written to "justify the ways of God to man," is to become the greatest epic poem of our language.

Besides the genius of *Paradise Lost* even Milton's other brilliant works pall. This one great story developing the Bible's account of the Fall of Man places him at the head of the English poets. Yet ironically this, the greatest poem in the English language, earned for John Milton a miserable ten pounds! And when he died he was lonely, scorned and forgotten.

How Milton Saw Satan

PARADISE LOST, written in blank verse, is a sheer effort of the imagination. The materials in the Bible for the Fall of Man are scanty enough, yet from this slender outline Milton built up in twelve books or chapters, a poem of 10,565 lines.

Most of the narrative is directly given by the poet, but in the middle part of the epic there is much recital of things past, and some foretelling of things to come, by angel visitants who supply Adam with knowledge and advice.

In his opening chapter Milton pictures the overthrow of the rebel angels in Heaven; their rally in the nether world under Satan, and their determination to continue their rebellion. Then he describes "their dread commander," Satan. The passage stands out as a triumph of description:

He, above the rest
In shape and gesture proudly eminent,
Stood like a tower. His form had not yet lost
All its original brightness, nor appeared
Less than an archangel ruined, and the excess

Of glory obscured; as when the sun new risen
Looks through the horizontal misty air
Shorn of his beams, or, from behind the moon,
In dim eclipse, disastrous twilight steals
On half the nations, and with fear of change
Perplexes monarchs. Darkened so, yet shone
Above them all the archangel. But his face
Deep scars of thunder had intrenched, and care
Sat on his faded cheek, but under brows
Of dauntless courage and considerate pride,
Waiting revenge.

The effect of Satan's oratory in rousing again his dispirited followers is mirrored in these magnificent lines:

He spake; and to confirm his words outflew
Millions of flaming swords, drawn from the thighs
Of mighty Cherubim. The sudden blaze
Far round illumined Hell. Highly they raged
Against the Highest, and fierce with grasped arms
Clashed on their sounding shields the din of war,
Hurling defiance towards the vault of Heaven.

◄ Adam and Eve in the Garden of Eden. "About them frisking playd All Beasts of th' Earth . . . Sporting the Lion rampd, and in his paw Dandl'd the Kid . . ."

Puzzle in the Corner

ONE of the first laws of geometry, or theorems as they are called, to be established arose out of an old Egyptian problem.

When an Egyptian builder wanted to build one wall at right angles to another, he would first measure out a triangle on the ground with a piece of rope. He would make the first side of the triangle three cubits long (a cubit was about two feet long), the next side four, and the last three, each cubit being measured by a knot in the rope (Figure 1).

The builder quickly learned that if he used these measurements his triangle would contain a perfect L, a right angle of 90 degrees. He could then build his walls along the lines marked out by the rope.

But he could not explain *why* his triangle gave him a right angle.

The explanation was provided by a Greek mathematician called Pythagoras, and his explanation is called "Pythagoras' Theorem," after him.

The answer has nothing to do with the fact that the numbers 3, 4 and 5 follow each other, because a triangle with sides of length 6, 8 and 10 yards would also contain a right angle.

What Pythagoras found in the Egyptian's triangle was that when

FIG. 1

3

5

4

90°

he squared the short sides (multiplied them by themselves), and then added them together, they equalled the long side (called the "hypotenuse") when it was squared. Put simply, he found that $(3 \times 3) + (4 \times 4) = (5 \times 5)$. If you work this out, you can see for yourself.

He also found that this relation was true for *any* right-angled triangle. If we give the letters a, b and c to the sides of a triangle, then in any right-angled triangle, $a^2 + b^2 = c^2$, where c is the hypotenuse.

If you find this relation between the sides is true in a triangle, then you know it must be a right-angled triangle. The mathematicians express this by saying that in a right-angled triangle the square on the hypotenuse is equal to the sum of the squares on the other two sides.

The Egyptian builder had simply chosen the right lengths for the sides of his triangle for constructing a right-angled triangle.

Figure 2 shows a nice proof of Pythagoras' Theorem. The side a of the triangle is also the side of a square, whose area is a^2 (the area of a square is found by

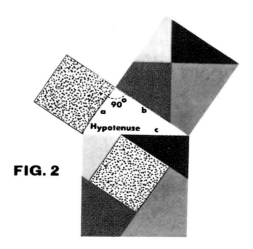

FIG. 2

90°
a b
Hypotenuse c

squaring its side). The sides b and c of the triangle are also sides of squares, whose areas are b^2 and c^2.

As we know by Pythagoras' Theorem that $a^2 + b^2 = c^2$, we should find that there is enough material in the two smaller squares to fill the large square. And we can see that there is!

The Dictator Who Stopped A Country Dancing

The execution of King Charles I in 1649 plunged England into ten dismal years of Puritan rule when sports, dancing and most forms of pleasure were forbidden

SNOW was falling on the morning of 30th January, 1649, as King Charles I set out on foot from St James's Palace to the Banqueting House in Whitehall. He walked briskly between his guard of Cromwellian soldiers, telling them to step out, as the morning was cold. On his arrival, Oliver Cromwell was waiting for him, with the royal death warrant in his hand, a warrant for which he had found the necessary number of signatures only with the greatest difficulty.

At one o'clock in the afternoon, Charles was led out through a window in the Banqueting House on to the scaffold that awaited him, where the executioner severed his head with a single blow. A great moan of horror drifted up from the thousands of spectators. It was not the sight of the execution that worried them, for they were well hardened to horrors of that kind. It was simply that Cromwell had done the unthinkable, the ultimate act against the Crown. He had killed the king.

Oliver Cromwell, the future Lord Protector of England, had no such qualms about his behaviour. So far as he was concerned, this was the inevitable outcome of a conflict between a monarch and his people. Charles had believed wholeheartedly in the Divine Right of Kings, had flouted the cherished privileges of Parliament and eventually split the country into two factions during the Civil War. Once Charles had been forced to admit defeat, his execution had become inevitable and almost symbolic. For Cromwell, this was to be the dawn of a new age, one in which England would be ruled fairly and decently by men elected by the people.

Cromwell has never been an easy character to understand — certainly his appearance did not work in his favour. He was a big man, with features so heavy and highly-coloured as to be positively ugly, while his voice, which one might have expected to be deep, was high and struck a jarring note. He never wore anything but the plainest clothes, made for him by a country tailor, and those who knew him reported that his shirts were seldom clean.

However, it is possible that Cromwell deliberately tried to look unattractive in order to provide a contrast with his foppish predecessors. Certainly he kept very quiet about his passion for horses, his love of music and the good humour he showed when he was with his family, all of which would have seemed far too human to have pleased his extreme Puritan followers. But there is no doubt that he was a tough, determined man, and one who was a great deal better educated than he pretended to be, with a technical grasp of warfare that was highly professional.

Ruthless Action

For a man who had always fought for the rights of Parliament against the king, it must have been a strange experience for Cromwell to discover that the Parliament which he inherited had passed a Bill behind his back enabling it to last for ever without being disbanded. But the Members had misjudged the character of the man they were dealing with, because Cromwell marched into the House of Commons with troops at his back and cleared everybody out.

By 1653, Cromwell was Lord Protector of the Commonwealth of England, Scotland and Ireland, with only a small council to assist him. Britain had become a republic, with Oliver Cromwell as virtual Dictator.

It is doubtful whether Cromwell relished the position. Within a few years there was a proposal to make him king, which he unhesitatingly refused. He genuinely wanted peace and prosperity for his country, and yet there was a ruthless streak in his nature. Today, even his greatest admirers find it hard to justify the manner in which he waged war in Ireland, and his sacking of the city of Drogheda, where he cold-bloodedly slaughtered most of the town's population.

But what was life like under Cromwell? The Lord Protector could claim quite fairly that many injustices had been swept away, but like many dictators he was at the mercy of the men who had put him in power. The Puritans, with their hatred of elaborate Church rituals, had managed to convince themselves that almost anything enjoyable was sinful, and to be stopped at all costs. Alehouses were shut down, sports were forbidden, and a man who used bad language was fined on the spot.

All over the country, maypoles were cut down in case they should

Charles I steadfastly refused to recognise the validity of a court to try the head of the realm. He was found guilty of treason and executed outside the palace of Whitehall on the morning of 30th January, 1649.

encourage dancing, and it was illegal for women to wear ornaments or jewellery of any kind. To walk anywhere on a Sunday, except to Church, involved a heavy fine, and Christmas Day was especially frowned upon, as it was considered to be no more than a pagan festival. Special detachments of soldiers travelled round London at Christmas time, with the power to enter any house and confiscate any festive food.

Not surprisingly, the ordinary people of England bitterly resented this interference with their traditional customs, and they began to feel a real hatred for the army of petty officials who enforced the nonsensical rules. Nor did it make them any happier to learn that the higher officials were living in the luxury that they were so ready to condemn.

It was not long before the Government, which had set out to be fair to all men, became the most unpopular body of lawmakers the country had ever known. In the past there had been bad kings and unjust barons, but at least they had been real people whom the common folk could blame. Under the Commonwealth, however, the land seemed to be ruled by thousands of nameless officials.

Unaware of all this, Cromwell himself ruled with dignity and common sense. But ill health and the strain of office began to take its toll. He became obsessed with the idea that enemies were plotting his death, and he took to wearing a shirt of mail beneath his coat and sleeping in a different room every night. When he died in 1658, he named his son as his successor, but Richard Cromwell was a quiet country gentleman who had little taste for politics. Within a couple of years, Prince Charles had been invited back from exile.

The Commonwealth was a strange interlude in British history, and one that has never been repeated. But on paper at least, there seems no reason why it should not have worked. Indeed, had it worked, we should probably still be a republic to this day. So what went wrong? Almost certainly the chief cause was Cromwell's almost total disregard for the feelings of the ordinary man and woman in the street. Personally brilliant, he delegated his authority to an army of fanatics, who set about destroying the most cherished freedoms and customs of the British people. Eventually, the long-suffering public refused to take any more, and Charles II was welcomed back with almost hysterical joy.

Oliver Cromwell

Having overthrown the monarchy, Cromwell was determined that the new Parliament should rule efficiently. When, in 1653, self-interested MPs attempted to pass a law enabling them to rule indefinitely, Cromwell simply marched in with a body of troops and cleared the building.

KENILWORTH CASTLE

Written and illustrated by C. L. DOUGHTY

We usually think of castles as being built of stone, but in earlier days they were mounds surmounted by wooden palisades. Kenilworth is an example. In the early years of the twelfth century the manor of Kenilworth was granted by Henry I to his Chamberlain, Geoffrey de Clinton, and the castle he built may well have looked like this. The Norman Keep, the first stone building, was erected between 1150 and 1175. King John strengthened the defences and it became a royal stronghold. Later it was one of the four castles which he offered to the barons as a guarantee of his good intentions over the Magna Carta.

John's son, Henry III, made the fatal mistake of giving Kenilworth to the man who was to become his greatest enemy, Simon de Montfort, Earl of Leicester, who led the insurgent barons against the king. Henry was defeated and taken prisoner at the Battle of Lewes in the year 1264.

THE NORMAN KEEP

JOHN OF GAUNT'S HALL, 14th century

Here are the ruins of the castle as they appear today on a site between Warwick and Coventry in the county of Warwickshire. It was once protected by a great artificial lake covering more than 100 acres.

Henry III's son, Prince Edward, was imprisoned in the castle, but escaped. He then prepared to do battle with de Montfort. Taking his rival's men by surprise, Edward utterly routed them. De Montfort escaped by swimming across the lake in his nightshirt, and with the remnants of his forces was besieged in the castle for six months. Despite the use of battering rams and a great wooden tower holding 200 bowmen, with attacks by barge across the lake, all assaults failed. It was hunger and sickness that finally made the rebels surrender. Henry III then granted Kenilworth to his son Edmund.

JOHN OF GAUNT

John of Gaunt, Edward III's fourth son, spent money lavishly on restoring and extending the castle, and it was he who transformed the medieval fortress into a palace. The Great Hall, measuring 90 feet by 25, is generally considered to be one of the finest examples of medieval architecture to be found anywhere in England.

THE GREAT HALL

The era of Kenilworth's greatest magnificence and extravagance will always be linked with the name of Robert Dudley, Earl of Leicester, the favourite courtier of Queen Elizabeth I, who made several visits to the castle. One visit lasted nineteen days, and Leicester is said to have spent the fantastic sum of £100,000 on entertaining his sovereign during her stay.

The vast lake around the castle in those days provided wonderful scope for water sports and floating tableaux. On Elizabeth's arrival she was welcomed by "The Lady of the Lake" with attendants on a floating island ablaze with torches. It is interesting to think that on such an occasion an eleven-year-old boy from Stratford-upon-Avon, named Will Shakespeare, might have been an onlooker.

LEICESTER'S GATEHOUSE, 16th century

'S BUILDINGS, century

LONG BARN, 16th century

In 1588, while England was rejoicing over the defeat of the Spanish Armada, Leicester died on his way to Kenilworth. He wrote to Elizabeth just before his death, and on the paper she inscribed "his last letter." With the passing of Leicester the great days of Kenilworth Castle came to an end. After the Restoration of Charles II in 1660, it passed on to the Earls of Clarendon and remained theirs until presented to the nation in 1937.

From James I, who purchased it for the low sum of £14,000, the castle eventually passed to Charles I. After changing hands twice during the Civil War, it was finally secured by the Parliamentarians in 1642. Cromwell, fearing that it might become a Royalist stronghold, blew up parts of the keep and walls.

In the 1820's Kenilworth was a desolate ruin, its many glories forgotten. But Sir Walter Scott in his novel of that name graphically re-created those days. Once more the castle caught the popular imagination, and from Victorian times onward it has been very popular with tourists and holiday-makers.

The TRIGAN EMPIRE

A strange craft has landed on the planet Elekton, and the three occupants—visible only as luminous spheres—have taken over the minds and bodies of King Kassar of Hericon and young Janno and Keren. During the Great Games of Hericon, the Emperor Trigo tries to save an unarmed man from a savage beast, and is himself struck down . . .

Hericon guards rushed into the arena and beat off the snarling Zargot, while others dragged clear the Trigan Emperor and the man he had saved.

Thank the stars the Emperor is still alive . . . whatever possessed him to do such a foolish thing?

There's no accounting for these soft-hearted Trigans!

The alien intelligence that controlled the mind of the Hericon King saw its opportunity, and gave an order.

Take the Emperor to the Palace and make him comfortable. He will soon recover.

Then, turning to his companions . . .

Naturally!

He will be unconscious for some hours . . . you know what you have to do!

And you know what you must do!

Yes!

Presently, the thing that controlled Janno's mind and body directed him to lie down on the balcony outside the room where Trigo lay unconscious.

In a short space of time I shall be the emperor of the Trigans!

Soon he was asleep, and then . . . . . . the luminous sphere arose from out of his ear . . .

. . . drifted into the room, and took over the mind and body of the unconscious Trigo!

A short while later, Janno awoke with a start. He was himself again . . . *and he remembered everything!*

The thing . . . the *thing* has left me . . . and gone to . . . *Trigo!*

A shadow fell across him as he leapt to his feet. He saw the face of his friend Keren . . . and the pistol aimed at his chest!

Keren! . . . Aaah!

You know too much . . . *and you must be eliminated!*

Janno knew that it was not his friend's mind that directed the finger that pressed the trigger . . . and he smashed his fist against the other's jaw.

He gazed down at the crumpled figure, *all unaware of the peril behind him!*

Keren . . . Keren . . . how can I set you free of the thing that has taken you over?

A smashing blow brought him crashing to the flagstones!

Aaaaah!

He recovered consciousness a few minutes later, to find himself held by a pair of brawny Hericon guards . . .

This traitor tried to assassinate me! . . . Take him down to the courtyard and execute him!

What has happened, Imperial Majesty?

. . . and the harsh voice of Trigo dinned in his ears!

Next Episode: A vain search for a friend!

The Soldier Who Conquered The Seas

Colonel Blake was a complete stranger to naval matters when he was pitched into the battle to win maritime supremacy for England

Robert Blake

WHEN the bloody head of King Charles I was held aloft for the crowd to see on a cold January morning, men might have been forgiven for thinking that at least the terrible English Civil War was over. Brothers could now bury differences with brother, and friend with friend. A new life could begin in peace.

Such was the wishful thinking, but it was far from the case. The war went on. The Royalists fanned out across the land and — to the consternation of England's new republicans — across the sea, too.

What was worse, most of the captains in England's relatively new navy decided to support the Royalist cause. They united under the King's cousin, Prince Rupert, who was the most famous of all the Royalist generals, and raided England's shipping until they became a serious menace.

With the shrewd eye of the brilliant strategist that he was, Oliver Cromwell considered that if the Royalist navy could be led by a land general with no experience of seagoing matters, then so too could the Parliamentary navy.

A few hours later, Colonel Robert Blake, of Bridgwater in Somerset, read his new orders in astonishment. He was 50 — old for those times — yet he was to be England's new "general of the seas", and his job was to seek out and hunt down Prince Rupert's Royalist fleet.

Thus the next great naval battle of our islands' story was fought between generals who had hardly ever been to sea.

The idea seemed as unlikely to some of the people of that time as it does to us today. A writer of the Cromwellian era declared: "A boisterous sea and stormy weather will make a man not bred to it so sick that it bereaves him of his legs, stomach and courage. In such weather, when he hears the cry 'starboard' or 'port', or to 'bide aloof' or 'haul home a clue line' he thinks he hears barbarous speech which he conceives not the meaning of."

Robert Blake was not in the least bit worried about that. A staunch Parliamentarian, he had achieved fame during the Civil War chiefly through the seizure and year-long defence of Taunton, which enabled the Parliamentary party to maintain itself in the

CONTINUED ON NEXT PAGE ▶

In one of the darkest days in Britain's naval history, the Dutch fell upon Blake's little fleet off the Goodwin Sands. For several months, the Dutch admiral Tromp sailed with a broom at his masthead, boasting that he would sweep any English ships from the Channel. But Blake was to have his revenge.

Blake's last battle was fought against the Spanish in the Canary Islands. His little fleet escaped almost unscathed, while the wrecks of the Spanish galleons littered the harbour at Santa Cruz. Sorely wounded in the conflict, Blake was to die before reaching home.

West of England for a considerable time. Blake, short, squat and not very handsome was sure that his sea legs would serve him as well as his land legs had done.

Prince Rupert was operating his Royalist fleet from the Irish coast, to where Blake now led the Parliamentary ships, sailing himself in the *James*. For six months Blake blockaded the Royalists in Kinsale harbour and then, under cover of bad weather, they escaped to Lisbon.

Blake at once gave chase and, when he got too close, Rupert moved on to Cartagena in Spain. Blake stayed on his tail and it was clear that there would have to be a fight. Off Malaga Rupert turned and faced his pursuers and the results for him were disastrous. At the end of the battle only two of the Royalist ships were still seaworthy.

With the Royalist threat at last obliterated, Oliver Cromwell determined to make more use of his new "general of the seas". The English Channel was currently commanded by the Dutch and, using Blake, the English resolved to wrest that mastery from them.

The trick that Blake used to provoke the Dutch was a very cunning one. When their Admiral Tromp took shelter in Dover harbour with 50 sailing ships, Blake fired a warning to remind him that he had not saluted the Castle — a traditional point of honour that had fallen into disuse. For answer, Tromp, who considered that he had been insulted, let off a broadside, which was supposed to remind Blake that the Dutch were his superiors. At that, Blake's 15 ships fell upon him.

Mast after mast fell on the Dutch side as the English gunners tore away at them. By nightfall, Tromp was obliged to sail his battered fleet away, like a broken man limping

away from a fist fight. He had never been beaten before — and he must have wished that he had saluted the Castle.

The Dutch brought in another admiral, De Ruyter, to deal with Blake. The two fleets met on a September afternoon in the North Sea and continued fighting until long after nightfall. Several of De Ruyter's ships were sunk and none of Blake's, although both sides claimed the victory.

Only weeks later the Dutch sent back Tromp with a huge fleet of 95 ships to seek out Blake. With a far smaller fleet — caused by the fact that Oliver Cromwell had taken steps to reduce the size of the navy — Blake sailed out to meet his old adversary off the Goodwin Sands.

English Battered

But this was to be no heroic-style action. Outnumbered and out-gunned, the English fleet was given a fearful battering and the delighted Tromp thereafter sailed the English Channel with a broom at his masthead — a symbol of his determination to sweep the English from the Narrow Seas.

Cromwell and his governing Council hastily conferred. They decided to repair and reinforce the wrecked fleet and to keep faith with Blake. So, early in the following year, 1653, Blake went to sea again in search of Tromp. The English now had 73 fighting ships and, when they found the Dutchman leading a convoy up the Channel, they saw that the enemy had just about as many.

The battle started off Portland on February 18 and for three days the Hampshire and Dorset coastline reverberated to the sounds of shot and shell as the two biggest navies in the world fought to see which was

the master. Blake was repeatedly in the most extreme danger and on the third day he was wounded. But his valour inspired his men and the Battle of Portland was among England's finest naval victories.

Blake's wounds kept him out of the final showdown that caused the Dutch to withdraw from the contest with England, but he was back again for another great exploit after Cromwell had declared war on Spain.

Blake, in the *George*, had 23 ships, and his target was a Spanish fleet holed up in the strongly fortified harbour of Santa Cruz in the Canary Islands. The English fleet swept through the narrow harbour entrance so quickly that the guns of the fort could only fire twice before Blake's ships were out of their range.

Seven big Spanish galleons lay waiting for them — so badly positioned that they hid the guns of many smaller ships waiting behind them.

Fire and gunsmoke filled the harbour as the two sides fought it out. One of the galleons blew up, leaving a gaping wound in their ranks. Soon the others were on fire and sails and masts hurtled skywards.

With the shore batteries raking the English ships, which needed to get away through the harbour mouth on the tide, Blake had to abandon the idea of taking a galleon or two with him as a prize. Instead, he ordered all the enemy ships to be set on fire. Then, still hammering away at the shore guns, he ordered his ships — only one of which was lost — away in triumph.

The English people impatiently waited for the return of their new national hero, when they heard the news. But he was a sick man, and his health failed so rapidly that he died only two hours before the *George* entered Plymouth Sound.

THEIR DIARY OF THE WEEK . . .

From the triumphant diaries of PEPYS and EVELYN

**Pepys
25th May, 1660.**

By the morning we were come close to the land, and everybody made ready to get on shore. . . . I went . . . and one of the King's footmen, and a dog that the King loved (which dirtied the boat, which made us laugh, and we think that a king and all that belong to him are but just as others are), in a boat by ourselves, and so got on shore when the King did. . . . Infinite the crowd of people. . . . The shouting and joy expressed by all is past imagination. . . .

**Evelyn
29th May, 1660.**

This day, his Majesty Charles the Second came to London, after a sad and long exile. . . . This was also his birth-day, and with a triumph of above 20,000 horse and foot, brandishing their swords, and shouting with inexpressible joy. . . . I stood in the Strand and beheld it, and blessed God. . . .

Illustrations by R. Embleton.

Samuel Pepys and John Evelyn were close friends in life. Fortunately for us, they were in different places at the Restoration of Charles II, which Sir Winston Churchill has called "England's supreme day of joy." Evelyn watched the King enter London on Restoration Day itself, while Pepys had had the thrill of landing with the King at Dover, a few days before.

Pepys had been lucky. His cousin, Edward Montagu, later Earl of Sandwich, who commanded the English fleet and had helped engineer the King's return, had asked the diarist to go with him as secretary in the ship that brought Charles back from his exile on the Continent. From that moment Pepys never looked back, and he later helped to found the modern British Navy.

Sir Winston Churchill's remark about the Restoration could not be called an exaggeration. Oliver Cromwell's rule, for all its achievements at home and abroad, had not suited the British, who by nature were opposed to being ruled by a dictator and his all-powerful army, and by intolerant Puritans with their kill-joy attitude to pleasure.

When Cromwell died, his son, a harmless country gentleman, "succeeded" him, but soon vanished into obscurity, and a power struggle developed between the Army and a new Parliament. By 1660, the vast majority of Britons longed for a monarchy again.

UNIQUE IN HISTORY

The welcome to Charles proved this. Never before or since, has there been such an outburst of joy in Britain. Charles must have been amazed to find that even the famous Ironside Army was drawn up to greet him. (It later disbanded, the soldiers becoming model citizens, as they had once been the New Model Army !)

Pepys was overwhelmed by the King's reception at Dover. As for the scenes in London, Evelyn describes how the streets were strewn with flowers and hung with tapestries; the bells rang and the fountains flowed with wine ! He noted that the Restoration was "done without one drop of blood shed," a circumstance unique in history, and thanked God for it.

Charles, the Merry Monarch, had his faults, and his reign had many crises. But two things stand to his eternal credit. He accepted General Monk's advice and refused to allow his supporters to take revenge on their opponents—few lost their lives or suffered because they had supported Cromwell; and he was shrewd enough to see that the power of Parliament had come to stay. He did not want to go on his travels again ! So the bright promise of his Restoration was fulfilled.

The Village That Sacrificed Itself

T**HE** village of Eyam, pronounced *"Eem"*, is remote, even today. Visitors to the Derbyshire Dale country who drive between the typical local drystone walls from Little Hucklow to Great Hucklow, and then on to Grindlow and Foolow, will eventually come to Eyam. There they will find a small village green, which still boasts a pair of rather time-worn stocks, a relic of the days when anyone who misbehaved himself could expect to be imprisoned in them until he had seen the error of his ways.

Further on there is one of the few sheep-roasting spits left in England, a good deal smaller than the traditional apparatus for ox-roasting, but in these days of expensive meat, a good deal more practical. The local building is of stone, typical of the countryside, and the village is well worth a tourist's snapshot for its appearance alone.

However, this is not just another village in the Peak District, this is the "Plague Village", remembered for the steadfast bravery of its people. No special monument commemorates the fact, because the village of Eyam is its own memorial.

London Smitten

In 1665, London was in the grip of bubonic plague, the Great Plague that was to claim more than 65,000 victims in the city before it was done. Plague was not new to London, for there had been odd outbreaks for hundreds of years, as indeed there had been in most parts of Europe. People accepted it as something that came from the East, spread mysteriously, and just as mysteriously went away again.

How it was passed from one person to another they had no idea; certainly nobody knew of a cure. When there was an occasional outbreak one simply hoped for the best, and if the disease looked as though it might be taking hold, anyone who could afford to, fled.

There were a few cases of plague in Westminster during the autumn of 1664, but no more than usual. But in the spring the following year, it crept down Holborn and within six months had travelled from one side of the city to the other. Forty-three people died of plague in May, 1665; 590 in June; 6,137 in July and 17,036 in August.

The summer was an unusually hot one, and the disease bred rapidly in the filthy, tight-packed streets. Even today we have no means of knowing what

When a box of infected clothing brought the Plague to the Derbyshire village of Eyam, the inhabitants voluntarily isolated themselves from the surrounding districts — but at a terrible cost to themselves

caused this particular outbreak, but it seems likely that it was introduced by some Dutch prisoners of war, and then spread by the fleas of the black rat. But once plague broke out in a city, all it needed to spread like a forest fire was heat and dirt, and in 1665 London had an abundance of both.

Two thirds of London's 400,000 inhabitants left the doomed city as quickly as possible. The King and his court went to Oxford, the less well-connected to anywhere that could provide them with a temporary home. In many cases the refugees took the dreaded illness with them, while London literally took on the appearance of a city of the dead. Those who stayed behind were mainly the poor, who had nowhere else to go, and a small number of officials who considered it their duty to stay.

Among the latter was the diarist, Samuel Pepys, who could easily have found an excuse to move with the court, but as a civilian naval official, he felt that to stay at his post was the equivalent of showing cour-

age in battle. He was also driven by an overpowering curiosity that was stronger than fear, and to which we owe his wonderful on-the-spot descriptions of a London where grass grew in the streets and there were not enough fit people left to bury the dead.

Eyam, in far away Derbyshire, was sufficiently remote not to be troubled with refugees, but even so, it was still within reach of the plague. In the late summer of 1665, a London tailor despatched a parcel of clothing to a client who lived in the village. Some of the clothing was second hand, and, like even the costliest of clothing at that time, it carried fleas. By October, no less than 25 of the people of Eyam had died of plague.

The man who took charge of the situation was the rector of Eyam, the Reverend Peter Mompesson. A man of great personal courage, sufficiently educated to realise what the outbreak could mean to the still healthy areas around him, Mompesson summoned the villagers and outlined his plan.

Eyam was in the grip of plague, but there was no reason why they should involve others in their misfortune. Mompesson suggested not only that no inhabitant of Eyam should move beyond the village boundaries, but that no outsider should be allowed in.

It was a harsh rule, but it made sense, and because they respected their Rector the people of Eyam agreed. So stones were erected in a rough circle around Eyam in order to mark the limits of the Derbyshire village. Essential provisions, such as flour and salt, were brought from neighbouring hamlets and left on certain specially-designated stones. These were paid for in money left alongside in troughs kept filled with vinegar in the belief that this would free the coins from infection.

Mompesson also gave orders that the people of Eyam, men, women, and children, should smoke as much tobacco as possible, because this was widely believed to be a safeguard against plague.

Deadly Toll

It does not seem to have been a very efficient solution. Ten months after Eyam commenced its voluntary isolation, seventy of its inhabitants had died. Sunday by Sunday, the Rector gathered a steadily-dwindling congregation on a small, horseshoe-shaped curve of turf and small trees just inside the village circle known as Cucklet Dell, and there in the clean, fresh air he did what he could to strengthen their faith and courage.

Courage they certainly needed, for by the end of the year 259 villagers had fallen victim to the plague, and in such a tiny community this meant that barely a household escaped. Fortunately, in London the pestilence was on the wane, for as often happened the plague burned itself out. The Court returned from Oxford and week by week the city filled up and became alive again.

London would take a long time to recover, but not so long as Eyam, which had sacrificed itself, and suffered so terribly, in order that its neighbouring villages should remain healthy. Probably these simply Derbyshire men and women never considered that they were doing anything out of the ordinary, but their neighbours remembered them with gratitude, and over three hundred years later Eyam remains as a memorial to the heroism of ordinary folk.

Whilst the victims of the Plague had to be buried, the survivors had to be fed. Food was left at special stones around the village, and the money to pay for it was placed in troughs of vinegar in the belief that this would free it from contamination.

MONUMENTS TO YESTERDAY

Eyam today is a popular tourist attraction, both for its natural beauty and its unique history. The plaque on the wall of the cottage (left) commemorates the first victim of the Plague.

More than two thirds of the villagers died as a result of their selfless heroism.

THE GREAT FIRE OF LONDON

IN September 1666 a fire broke out in London's City. Fanned by a strong wind, it spread rapidly. Samuel Pepys wrote an account of it in his famous Diary:

2nd (Lord's day). Jane called us up about three in the morning, to tell us of a great fire they saw in the City; but, being unused to such fires as followed, I thought it far enough off; and so went to bed again, and to sleep.

About seven rose again . . . and walked to the Tower; and there I did see the houses at that end of the bridge all on fire, and an infinite great fire on this and the other side of the bridge.

The Lieutenant of the Tower . . . tells me that it begun this morning in the King's baker's house in Pudding Lane, and that it hath burned down St. Magnus' Church and most part of Fish Street already.

Everybody endeavouring to remove their goods, and flinging (them) into the river, or bringing them into lighters that lay off; poor people staying in their houses as long as till the very fire touched them, and then running into boats, or clambering from one pair of stairs by the waterside to another.

I to White Hall, and there up to the King's closet . . . I was called for, and did tell the King . . . what I saw; and that, unless his Majesty did command houses to be pulled down, nothing could stop the fire. The King commanded me to go to the Lord Mayor from him.

4th . . . the sky looks all on a fire in the night . . . Now begins the practice of blowing up of houses in Tower Street . . . St. Paul's is burned, and all Cheapside . . .

6th Strange it is to see Clothworkers' Hall on fire these three days and nights in one body of flame, it being the cellar full of oyle.

7th Up by five o'clock; and find all well. Saw all the towne burned, and a miserable sight of Paul's church burned, and Fleet Street.

8th People speaking their thoughts about the rebuilding of the City. I was kept awake in my bed by some noise I heard . . . some people stealing some neighbour's wine that lay in the streets. So to sleep; and all well all night.

The baker at whose shop the fire started escaped hastily over the roof with his wife. Their maid, however, was afraid to follow them, and so became the first victim of the Great Fire of London.

Samuel Pepys, woken at three o'clock in the morning by the maid, could see the glow of the fire across the City. He decided that it was too far away to worry about, and went back to bed again.

When the roof of Inner Temple Hall caught fire, a seaman daringly clambered up and beat out the flames. He was given a reward of ten pounds for his courage in saving this ancient building.

King Charles II, fearing that the fire would spread rapidly, ordered the Lord Mayor to blow up houses in the path of the flames, thus making a wide gap across which the fire could not spread.

The Monument (202 ft. high), in Fish Street Hill, London, was built to commemorate the Great Fire.

RIDDLE of the LAND

"**L**AND HO!" The look-out's cry from the crow's nest of the Dutch sailing ship sent the crew scurrying across to the starboard rail. Admiral Roggeveen looked, too. Then he excitedly consulted his charts. No land was marked at this point in the Pacific Ocean.

As the ship approached and circled the island, the Admiral noted that it was thirty to forty miles in circumference and roughly triangular, with a mountain at each corner.

Admiral Roggeveen inked on his map the triangular blob of land, and wrote beside it "Easter Island." For it was Easter Day, 1722.

Little did he know as he brought his ship in to the coast that he had named the world's most mysterious island.

Roggeveen's own report sets the scene: "This island contains about six thousand souls. And all over the island stand huge idols of stone, the figure of a man with big ears and the head covered with a red crown."

Unusual Carving

ONE can imagine how that report intrigued other adventurers. Many made landings. They tramped the island and counted the statues. There were 230 standing all over the place. And apart from size—varying from fifteen to thirty-five feet high—the statues were all identical.

Legless, they rose from the earth at hip level. The faces were expressionless, with receding foreheads, tight lips, prominent chins and a curious tilt at the end of the nose.

But more curious still were the ears. Long and thin, they hung down to the jaw. On each statue was a hat-like crown of red stone.

About a hundred of the statues stood on and around the slopes of a dead volcano. The rest adorned either side of a five-mile long avenue—the sacred road to the island's burial ground.

They had been carved in an unusual manner. Instead of first hacking out a block of stone and then shaping it, as any of our sculptors would have done, the Easter Island sculptor had chiselled his statues into the living rock. Only when it was complete was it separated from the rock behind and below.

Stone Tablets

THEN it was dragged to its chosen position and slipped into a hole already prepared for it. This in itself was a Herculean task, for each statue weighed between 20 and 40 tons.

Whom do they represent? Why are they there? Why are there so many? Who made them? Questions like these were expected to be answered when explorers discovered that the natives of Easter Island had 67 stone tablets covered with writing. The only trouble was that none of the natives could read them. Nor could the language experts of the civilized world.

So for answers to those baffling questions, scientists studied the islanders' legends, which had been handed down by word of mouth for centuries. This is how their story goes:

"Many years ago there was a fair country called the Kingdom of Maraerenga. The king had two sons named Ko and Hotu Matua. When the old king died, Ko became king of Maraerenga and Hotu Matua was forced to flee and find a kingdom of his own.

"He set out with a fleet of canoes carrying his wife, his followers, servants, seeds and tools. At last he came to this fertile island which he named Rapa Nui. The people prospered and multiplied and Hotu Matua wore the crimson cloak and crown of kingship.

"His followers, all aristocratic long-eared people, and his servants and workers who were short-eared like us, were happy. But when Hotu Matua died the long-eared rulers used the people cruelly and made them slaves.

"So the people rose up and killed the long-eared ones. All of them. But they remembered Hotu Matua with love, and a sculptor named Rapu was inspired to make a statue of him. When they saw it the people were so overjoyed they asked for more statues of their beloved former king, to keep their island safe in case other long-eared people should take revenge."

But if this legend is true, Rapu must have lived about three hundred years! For quite apart from the 230 standing statues, there are 157 more in the quarries in stages of construction.

They are even bigger than the standing statues, but of course, identical in appearance. All the 157 were being worked on at the same time when, for some unknown reason, the project was so suddenly abandoned that tools were left lying all over the quarries.

No one man could have done the job. There must have been a small army of sculptors and a large army of labourers, the experts now believe.

Again, in the burial ground are the bones of many more people than the island could have supported, even allowing for the tombs having been used for many centuries.

Both these facts point to the conclusion that Easter Island must at one time have been near to a much larger island, or series of islands. Some scientists believe that Easter Island was the holy land and cemetery for its bigger neighbour.

In 1576 a navigator named Fernandez reported the existence of a large land area not far from where Easter Island was later discovered. A ship's captain named Davis also saw this extensive land mass a hundred years later. He did not delay his voyage to land, but named the place Davis Land.

Where is Davis Land today?

There is no doubt that it has vanished. Some natural calamity—an undersea volcanic eruption, a tidal wave, an earthquake—destroyed it.

Some scientists believe that the Easter Islanders came originally from Peru in about the year 500 A.D., where the ruling aristocracy were called Long Ears.

The many expeditions that followed the great Routledge Expedition of 1919 have found an increasing number of the statues overthrown and mutilated by the natives.

Why they do it they will not say. They just repeat the legend of Hotu Matua. Why, believing such a legend, do they hate the statues?

If only those 67 stone tablets could talk!

But even that would not be much use now, for the natives have hidden them all. And so well that years of digging has failed to find them.

All that scientists can work on are the copies that were made of a few of the tablets before they vanished. So far their message has been a complete blank. As blank as the stares on the identical faces of those hundreds of Long Ears that watch over Easter Island.

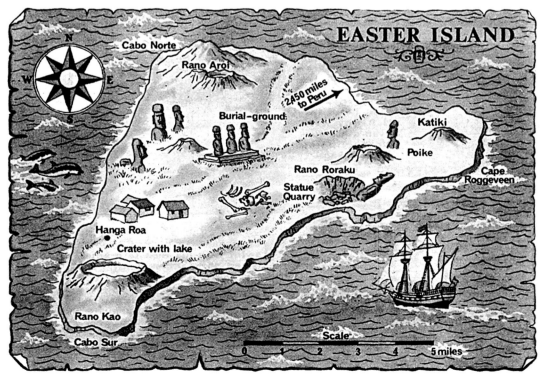

IN THE DAYS OF OUR FOREFATHERS
DAYS OF DANIEL DEFOE

EARLY in the eighteenth century a lone rider journeyed on horseback through the English countryside. He spoke little but observed a good deal—indeed, it was the result of his brilliant observation, among other things, that earned the horseman a place in history.

Daniel Defoe, for he was the rider, is familiar to all of us as the author of *Robinson Crusoe, Moll Flanders*, and many other novels. Among his many jobs in life he was once a newspaper reporter. He had such a quick eye for a "story" that once he wrote a speech for a condemned man and gave him a guinea to read it on the scaffold the following day. When the poor fellow was reciting his speech, Defoe was passing copies of his paper round the watching crowd. Its principal story was the victim's speech—already printed!

Besides his novels, Defoe wrote books about his travels called *A Tour through England and Wales* and *A Plan of the English Commerce*, and they give us an excellent account of life in the eighteenth century.

Defoe found that English farmworkers were reasonably paid and fed, but in Scotland they lived on "a cake of oat bread and a draught of water" and worked to the strains of a bagpipe.

"It was evident," said Defoe, "the poor men had need enough of music to encourage them at their labour; nor would the music do neither, without the Overseer or Steward being in the field too, to see that they stood to their work."

Riding into Halifax, Defoe saw hills and valleys dotted with houses and, as far as the eye could see, there were white patches next to each of the houses—patches of cloth being dried and stretched in the sun. Many of the houses had their own little coal-pit and water-stream, and their owners' families worked inside at their looms or drying vats.

Each week these cottage industrialists took their cloth on horseback to sell in the market, and bought more wool. In the autumn they bought two or three large bullocks which they killed and salted and smoked in the fire of their chimneys, so that they had meat throughout the winter.

Defoe found a few factories—one of them at Derby was 400 ft. long and manufactured silk thread. He reserved some pithy comments, too, for the state of English roads, made impassable for the bulk of trade because more and more livestock was being driven along the muddy ways, making them muddier still, to market towns and cities.

The growth of trade and industry excited much of Defoe's interest. In Norfolk he reported "a face of diligence spread over the whole country; the vast manufactures carried on (in chief) by the Norwich weavers employ all the country round in spinning for them." At Manchester there was trade that "we all know . . . and all that are concerned in it know that it is, as all our other manufactures are, very much increased within these thirty or forty years."

This industrial "explosion", the prelude to the Industrial Revolution period, and its effect on the people, was noticed by another famous traveller, the preacher John Wesley, who observed in his *Journal* about some Bristol brickyard workers:

"As many of them increase in worldly goods, the great danger I apprehend now is their relapsing into the spirit of the world; and then their religion is but a dream."

While small industries were rapidly growing, most people still worked on the land, at the mercy of the harvest for an indifferent life (if it were good), or a destitute one if it were washed away. Daniel Defoe divided the population into seven classes according to their means, and fifth on the list he placed "the country people, farmers and etc., who fare indifferently." Another writer regarded "these small occupiers as a set of very miserable men, working hard,

like a horse, without being able to soften their present lot."

And yet, it was not so many years ago that the land-workers were the salt of the English earth, as well fed as anyone in England. What had happened, therefore, to make them "miserable men"?

The answer is that ranged against any improvement in their present lot was the practise of enclosing land by the great estates, and the rapidly improving farming techniques developed by men like Thomas Coke, of Holkham, Norfolk, and Lord Thomas "Turnip" Townsend.

Townsend, a former ambassador to Holland, introduced to England an idea, called the Norfolk rotation, which represented a revolution on the land. For centuries farmers had allowed their land to lie fallow every third year, or sometimes even every second year. Townsend's Norfolk rotation comprised a four-year crop sequence—clover, wheat, turnips and barley. The system could be immediately re-started in the fifth year, because the clover and turnips broke up the soil, allowing it to recover its nitrogen.

Townsend's idea spread among the other big landowners and made turnips an important English crop. The turnips were fed to sheep and cattle in winter, so that the great autumn slaughter of beasts for which, hitherto, there had been no winter food, was discontinued. This produced a much better quality animal—it is reckoned that the average sheep at market weighed twice as much at the end of the century as its forebear did at the beginning of the century.

Another important innovator on the land was Jethro Tull, who eschewed the old method of scattering seed across the top of the soil and invented a drill, drawn by a horse, which sowed seed at the depth and intervals for which it was best suited. The results were spectacular—Tull's crops doubled, and at the same time his soil was ventilated and much freer of weeds.

Social menace

In the towns the urban population of Georgian England was showing its taste for two pastimes that have always been a feature of English life—drinking and gambling. By the 1740s gin drinking had become a national problem; eight million gallons of spirits were being consumed every year. London had thousands of "gin shops" advertising their wares with the sign, "Drunk for 1d., dead drunk for 2d., clean straw for nothing." It took some time for Parliament to pass an effective Act regulating this social menace.

The gamblers leapt at rumours that the South Sea Company would make fortunes out of the huge trade to be had in South America and the Pacific islands. In three months the company's stock, taken up by speculators, increased its value seven times, and on this great wave of gambling fever many other spurious companies were started to soak up the speculators' money. When the crash came thousands of people were ruined, and the government, which had been implicated in the South Sea Company rumours, was in disgrace.

It is noteworthy, though, that a few men made fortunes in that dramatic period of speculation, by selling their stock for a high price before the crash. One of them was Thomas Guy, who used his profits to found the famous London teaching hospital which bears his name today.

Wealth—the new wealth of enterprise and industry—was the ambition of many men in the eighteenth century. And the wealthy did not set themselves up as a class apart. Like Coke and Townsend, they did not sit back on their laurels, but were willing to try anything new. Some leased their land for mining; others, like the Duke of Bridgwater, built canals to carry their coals directly to their customers. Men with great estates who added to their wealth in the eighteenth century did so on their own initiative, and those without initiative failed to keep their estates.

All the great landowners liked to display their wealth in different ways. Lord Chandos had his own private orchestra of 27 musicians. Lord Palmerston's collection of paintings was worth a large fortune. Sir Robert Walpole had a passion for accumulating wigs, and the Duke of Marlborough, of Blenheim fame, for tapestries. Georgian building, the love of all landowners in the eighteenth century, and Georgian decoration, had an elegance which many people believe has never been attained since.

CULLODEN
THE LAST GREAT BATTLE
ON BRITISH SOIL

1. The struggle that led to Culloden was a glorious but desperate one from which the Scots did not flinch. It began when the last of the Royal Stuarts, the legendary Bonnie Prince Charlie, decided to recapture the English throne for his family line.

2. Prince Charles had ... summer of 1745 he l... He had only seven s... the news spread and ... Highlanders had pledg... Their hopes were hig...

5. News of the Scots victory shocked the English. They realized that they had totally underestimated the danger, so the Duke of Cumberland was ordered to march north with his men to quell the uprising and capture the Prince.

6. Fate stepped in to help the Duke. First the Highlanders started to argue among themselves and the Prince's vital supporters in England failed to rise in his support.

7. The lack of support in England wa... blow to the Prince. Although he ... press on to London he reluctantly ... the pleas of his followers to turn bac... way the Scots attacked Falkirk and ... although the English were now in ho...

9. Because their victory at Prestonpans had been won on a surprise attack the Scots launched an assault on the English that night, but in their weakened state they were beaten off. It was the beginning of the end.

10. And so, on the morning of April 16, the armies faced each other on the bleak moor, eight thousand wet and weary Highlanders against an equal number of well-trained and rested Redcoats. Both opened the battle with cannon fire, but the English achieved the best results.

4. But the Scots moved too fast for Sir John. After capturing Edinburgh they made a surprise attack on the army at Prestonpans. The English were routed. The road to London was open to the Scots.

3. At first the English, under Sir John Cope, were not worried. Their army was well trained and they were confident they would beat the Scots.

...d in France, but in the ...riskay in the Hebrides. ...ut the numbers grew as ...ort time seven thousand ...es to support the Prince. ...used to think of failure.

8. By April 15, 1746, the Scots, although back in their own country, were exhausted, underfed and disorganized. They made camp on windswept Culloden Moor, Inverness, in pouring rain. The English were comfortably quartered at nearby Nairn.

...1. In spite of the accuracy of the English ...ire the Scots were the first to attack. This ...vas what Cumberland wanted, for his men ...ad been trained to meet such tactics. ...lthough the Scots broke through the ...irst line, they were mown down by the ...econd. Over a thousand were killed.

12. Cumberland ordered his men to let no one escape and over a thousand more were hunted down and killed. From then on the Duke was known as "The Butcher." Today (right) all is peace on the moor which was once the scene of deadly massacre.

THE BRITISH ABROAD

Today we are fortunate if we can holiday for two or three weeks abroad. Not so the rich young men of days gone by whose "Grand Tour" would keep them away for months.

BY the time Charles II came to the throne of Britain, foreign travel had ceased to be a daring adventure. Slow, dirty, and uncomfortable it might be, but it was no longer something to be attempted only by soldiers, merchants, or ambassadors. It had now become an important part of a gentleman's education, and unless he could air his views on the fashions of Paris, the picture galleries of Florence, or the ruins at Rome, the young son of a wealthy and titled family was likely to be thought of as very ignorant!

During the time of the Commonwealth (1649-1660) the Stuart royal family had been refugees in France, to which many English and Scottish courtiers followed them, and where, incidentally, they began the fashion for Scottish tartans which have been popular there ever since. While living in exile these people travelled widely in Italy and Spain also, thus with their recollections and advice paving the way for the next generation of travellers, and creating the legend that every British traveller was a "Milord" with plenty of money to spend! On their return to Britain with Charles II there were always those who could recommend the best routes for coaches, give warning of rascally landlords, and advise about the weather, just as the touring motorist does today.

The young men who were sent by their rich but anxious fathers on "The Grand Tour" were not therefore venturing into the unknown, but were, if anything, overloaded with advice, warnings, and—perhaps most important of all—introductions to ambassadors, noble families, and university professors, in the countries they were to visit. But these young men did not travel alone. They were always accompanied by a tutor, who was usually a clergyman attached to their father's household, and who had some knowledge of languages, and knew enough history to help the young men improve their knowledge of art and architecture.

Dodging the tutor

These tutors were also expected to keep a strict watch on the behaviour of their young charges, and to prevent them from getting into trouble. Many tutors seem to have had a very hard time on the Grand Tour. Their young men were far more interested in horse-racing than they were in art-galleries, and preferred taverns to temples. They would give their tutors the slip in order to join in wild drinking parties, and to gamble away far more than they could afford on cock-fighting or some other sport. Sometimes the tutor would be the victim of a practical joke or a bit of horse-play—a fake robbery or a bogus visitor—and as a result some came home in disgust, after handing over their charges to the care of some other British acquaintance abroad. For these unfortunate men the tour

◀ **Britons travelling abroad would be sure of an enthusiastic welcome—they were all supposed to have plenty of money to spend!**

was anything but grand!

Despite all this, the custom grew in popularity, and lasted well into the 19th century. Certain places became a "must" for aristocratic young men, not merely for a quick look round, such as a modern tourist gives, but as a place in which they would settle for two or three months, learn the language, study the monuments, and make friends at court who might be valuable to them later in life. Paris, Florence, Venice and Rome, and to a lesser extent the courts of the small German States, Vienna and Madrid, were all places to be considered when such a tour was planned.

The more enterprising might go as far as Athens, Constantinople, or even the Holy Land, although these were all at the time under the rule of the Grand Turk, as the Sultan of the Ottoman Empire was called, and no Christian felt really safe in his territories.

Difficult journeys

It is worth remembering that as yet, foreign travel had only two purposes. One was to make money, and that was the business of explorers and merchants. The other was to get to know people and the places where they lived, and to admire through their eyes the achievements of the past. This meant seeing their historic palaces and churches, viewing their sculptures and paintings, peering at the ruins of ancient civilisations (mostly those of Greece and Rome)

But it also meant making acquaintance with the leaders of polite society of their own day, meeting polished ladies and gentlemen in elegant drawing-rooms where there was music and dancing, polite conversation, and perhaps a discreet game of cards. When tutors could be evaded there were, of course, other excitements to be savoured and more boisterous company to be enjoyed, but in either case the Grand Tour was from first to last an experience of city life and man-made pleasures.

The journeys between the man-made cities were best forgotten, consisting as they did of dreary coach rides over the roughest of roads, in every kind of weather; nights in draughty and uncomfortable inns; encounters with surly landlords and ignorant peasants (if not with actual brigands) and meals of the poorest kind imaginable. The days when the British man abroad actually enjoyed the *scenery* which unfolded before him were still a long way in the future! For those on the Grand Tour, a mountain was not something to climb, but what one called "a prodigious wild prospect", and the sea could only be described as "tempestuous and unfaithful". In fact, they viewed everything which did not satisfy their idea of home comfort and British manners with an air of disdain which has not entirely disappeared, even among the tourists of today. Only an Englishman of those times could have written an account of his travels and called it:

The Glory of England, or a true description of many remarkable blessings, whereby she triumpheth over all the nations of the world.

That, perhaps, sums up the outlook of so many who made the Grand Tour of Europe, a century or two ago!

THE SIGHTS

Above: When the exiles returned they had plenty of advice to give to would-be travellers about the coaching routes across Europe and the best places to stay. Below: Young men on the Grand Tour often escaped from their tutors, preferring taverns to temples!

With his persuasive pen, Jonathan Swift was able to sway a whole nation's thinking. Even "Gulliver's Travels" was more than just a story. But his arguments failed to get him the power for which he craved.

WRITER WHO TOPPLED A GOVERNMENT

IN the narrow, overhanging streets, sedan chairs conveyed haughty women to regions of gossip. In busy coffee houses, men discussed the topics of the day.

This was London of the early eighteenth century. The reign of Queen Anne was blossoming with romance and intrigue.

One day a writer stepped into the centre of the current political squabbles. His name was Jonathan Swift. Seldom has a writer wielded so much power as Swift did in London from 1710 to 1713.

He launched violent criticism towards the policies of Prime Ministers, Secretaries of State and the Duke of Marlborough. Marlborough was Britain's hero after his victory at Blenheim, but had since grown greedy for power.

The country was fascinated by Swift's outbursts. The Whigs lost their power, the Tories took over, the Duke and Duchess of Marlborough lost their influence at Queen Anne's court. The pen of Swift had been the vital weapon.

What was the story behind this brilliant man who was able to swing the country's mind as powerfully as all the Fleet Street newspapers of today put together?

Swift was born in Dublin on St. Andrew's Day, 1667. His parents were English but he was to spend most of his life in Ireland.

Although a famous writer, he was also a devout churchman and early in life he became the Vicar of Laracor with a congregation of about fifteen "most of them gentle and all simple."

He soon produced his first satires—*The Battle of the Books* and *A Tale of the Tub*, which dealt chiefly with divisions of Christianity.

No Bishopric

WHEN *A Tale of the Tub* reached England the Archbishop of York inferred to Queen Anne that the book was blasphemous. So Swift's hopes for a bishopric were shattered.

But more was soon heard of the Vicar of Laracor. While in London in 1710 he met the great letter writers of the day—Addison and Steele—in coffee houses seething with discussion.

Soon his pen was scratching destructive melodies at Marlborough and the Whigs.

The country responded to his articles in the *Examiner* and Marlborough and his officers fell from office. The Tories rejoiced. Swift was the hero of the hour.

But Swift's campaign did not win him the bishopric he still craved for. He became the Dean of St. Patrick's Cathedral.

The publication of *Gulliver's Travels* in 1726 was greeted with frenzied interest in England and Europe.

The story about the giant and the midgets became a great favourite with children, who enjoyed its fantasy. But this is not what Swift intended. The book was satire, in which Gulliver looked down on the follies of the human race. But the people were not shocked—they were just amused and intrigued by the incongruous situation of the man who suddenly found himself to be a giant.

The last ten years of Swift's life were made miserable by illness. He died in 1745 at his Deanery, and millions mourned.

Sir Walter Scott wrote of Swift: "He lived a blessing, he died a benefactor, and his name will ever live, an honour to Ireland."

At home in England he was a normal sized man. But a storm cast him up in a world of people no bigger than his hand!

SUDDENLY, GULLIVER WAS A GIANT

LEMUEL GULLIVER, a ship's surgeon, was sailing to the East Indies on board the Antelope, when a violent storm drove the ship on to the rocks and wrecked it.

He took to the long boat but it capsized, and Gulliver, carried by the current, found himself on the shore of a country called Lilliput.

Exhausted from his ordeal and believing the land to be uninhabited, Gulliver fell asleep. When he woke up he found that he had been fastened to the ground by hundreds of small soldiers, not six inches in height.

At first they fired arrows at him, but they soon got used to his enormous size and began giving him food and drink. This, unknown to Gulliver, was drugged.

While he slept, the little people constructed a huge platform on wheels, which they used to carry him to their city.

Awakening again, Gulliver found himself imprisoned in chains, and surrounding him were the citizens of Lilliput, headed by their Emperor, who had come to see Gulliver's towering figure.

The Emperor told Gulliver that Lilliput was threatened with invasion from the neighbouring country of Blefuscu, and Gulliver offered to assist him by capturing the Blefuscudian warships.

When the tiny people of Blefuscu saw the giant Gulliver approaching their port, they attacked him with showers of arrows.

Hurriedly Gulliver tied their ships together, shielding himself from their onslaught as he worked.

Then he waded back to Lilliput, towing the Blefuscudian fleet behind him.

On his return Gulliver received a cheering welcome and was highly decorated for services to Lilliput.

But after this great victory Gulliver heard that some of the important officials of Lilliput were accusing him of treason and that they intended to blind him as a punishment.

At once Gulliver fled to Blefuscu, where the Blefuscudians helped him equip a boat with a sail and stores.

At last Gulliver set sail for home again. After two days he was picked up by a merchant ship returning to England.

This is only one of the exciting adventures in Gulliver's Travels. Gulliver made six more visits to strange countries—but they are six other stories!

Gulliver captures a Navy! All he had to do was to tie the enemy ships together and wade back to Lilliput towing the vessels behind him.

DICK TURPIN—

**For over 200 years this highwayman's life has been glamorized and sensationalized.
In fact, he was a cruel and vicious
man who never thought twice about robbery and murder**

THE eyes of John Boyes, landlord of the Green Man inn at Epping, north of London, glistened with excitement as one of his customers leaned over the bar counter and spoke into his ear.

"I've heard about that racehorse," whispered the customer. "He's in the stables at the Red Lion at Whitechapel."

John Boyes spoke to his wife. "I've just heard the whereabouts of that racehorse," said he. "I'm off right away to see if I can find him." A few minutes later he left the inn by a back door and rode hard to Whitechapel.

At the Red Lion Boyes went into the stables. There before him stood a handsome grey racehorse with white fetlocks. Boyes could not fail to recognize the animal from the description the police had circulated all round London: it was the same horse that had been stolen from its owner at gun point a week before in Epping by the rascally highwayman Dick Turpin.

It was the reward, not the merits of good horseflesh, that busied the mind of the innkeeper Boyes now as he feasted his eyes on the horse. There was £100 reward offered for its return to its owner, plus £40 for the capture of Turpin. In those days, more than 200 years ago, £140 was a considerable sum of money—more than enough

Dick Turpin is often credited with an extraordinary number of feats of daring and adventure. Here he skilfully disarms yet another of his countless opponents.

to interest most people. Quickly Boyes fetched a policeman and together they hid in the stable loft above the stolen horse.

Several hours later a man came in and untethered the stolen horse. Boyes and the policeman jumped from the loft in triumph, and beat the man to the ground. Then, in the half light, they saw that their victim was not Dick Turpin but the brother of the highwayman's partner, Tom King.

Fictitious Ride

"WHERE is Turpin, and the other highwayman who rides with him?" shouted the enraged Boyes.

"They are in Red Lion Street, round the corner," replied Tom King's trembling brother.

Boyes rushed into the street and there, coming towards him down the road, were Turpin and Tom King. His mind ever on the reward, Boyes sprang at them. There was a scuffle, Turpin fired, and unfortunately for him hit his own partner in the chest. King sank to the ground mortally wounded, while Turpin fled from the scene. Once again the notorious highwayman had murdered and cheated the law.

Without a doubt Dick Turpin was the most brutal highwayman ever to ride the roads of England. His career has been glamorized and sensationalized many times, notably by the Victorian author Harrison Ainsworth in his famous book *Rookwood*, and everyone has heard of his famous but thoroughly fictitious ride to York. Turpin, in fact, was an evil-tempered brute who thought nothing of murder or of robbery with great violence against anyone who crossed his path, however old, however young. Yet his entire career as a highwayman lasted just two years.

Turpin was born at Hempstead in Essex in 1706, when Queen Anne reigned in England. His father was an innkeeper, and apprenticed young Dick to a butcher. But when Turpin finished his apprenticeship and set up shop on his own he became a little over-zealous, and had to give up his calling after the local farmers found that many of their cattle were disappearing from their land at night-time—and finding their way into the butcher's shop run by Turpin.

Into Partnership

THEFT, smuggling and burglary were the easy steps that Turpin took to becoming a highwayman at the age of twenty-nine. At first he was one of a gang, then one of two partners. Then, until he met Tom King and became a partner again, he plundered alone.

For two years Turpin, a heavily-built, pale-faced man, terrified travellers almost everywhere on the London perimeter. One night he held up a lone rider who laughingly revealed his identity. It was Tom King, already a notorious highwayman himself, and it was King who thereupon suggested the partnership that ended in his own death.

Turpin's favourite haunt, however, was Epping Forest. There he lived in a cave, and when one day a forester followed him to the hide-out and

challenged him the highwayman, ever hasty-tempered, drew his pistol and shot the forester dead in cold blood.

Within two years that temper made the name Turpin feared throughout the land. The extraordinary sum of £200 was offered for his capture—extraordinary because £40 was then the top price paid for the arrest of a highwayman. And then, suddenly realizing that the game could not be played for ever, Turpin retired from the road.

The next we hear of the highwayman was that he was living a respectable life under a new name in Yorkshire. The novelist Harrison Ainsworth romanticizes about how he arrived there, on the famous ride to York, mounted on a horse called Black Bess.

In fact the ride (and Black Bess) is mythical. Ainsworth probably based it on the feat of a certain "Nick" Nevison, who in 1676 robbed a sailor near Rochester in Kent at 4 a.m. and established an alibi by being in York at 7.45 p.m. on the same day. Swift Nick, incidentally, need not have taken so much trouble, for he was still hanged.

Heated Argument

THE story of Turpin's end is nothing if not dramatic. One day in the autumn of 1738 a party of rich people was out shooting game on the Yorkshire moors when one of them began an argument. To everyone in the party the antagonist's name was Mr. Palmer, a newcomer to the district but a man of obvious wealth who was quite acceptable to them.

None of them knew then that Mr. Palmer was in reality Dick Turpin, retired highwayman.

The argument became heated and Mr. Palmer, whose temper had not changed with his identity, threatened to shoot one of the party. Because the matter could not be settled amicably Mr. Palmer was summoned before the local magistrate for causing a breach of the peace.

Then, and only then, did those Yorkshire people fall to wondering about exactly how the mysterious Mr. Palmer came among them.

Inquiries were made and while they were being carried out Turpin wrote to his brother, who was still living in the Essex village where the Turpin children were born. The letter was seen by a local schoolteacher, who remembered Turpin at school in the village and remembered, too, the reward that was out for his notorious ex-pupil.

That evening several of the villagers of Hempstead in Essex rode northwards to Yorkshire and there, in the local jail, they identified Mr. Palmer as Dick Turpin. For Turpin the game was up. He was tried for horse-stealing and convicted.

To the end, though, he remained a braggart. The method of hanging a criminal was to stand him in an open cart with the rope round his neck and then to drive the cart away. When the noose was put round Turpin he did not wait for the cart to move. Instead, he jumped off the side and died.

THE HIGHWAY TYRANT

The popular image of Dick Turpin portrays him as a handsome, idealistic hero. In fact Turpin was an evil-tempered man who committed at least two murders in his two-year career as a highwayman.

ROGERS' RANGERS CODE NAME—SAUGOTHEL

Warfare was taking place in North America between the British and the French and their Indian allies. In 1759, Major Robert Rogers was ordered by the British General Amherst to lead his Rangers on a secret mission with the code name Saugothel. This meant the Abenaki Indian town of St. Francis and Rogers' task was to destroy it.

The Rangers travelled by night and eventually reached Missisquoi Bay at the northern end of Lake Champlain.

On 25th September, Rogers left two of his Stockbridge Indians to watch over the whaleboats and supplies for the return journey and led his men into the Missisquoi swamps. For nine days they struggled in the icy bog and then disaster overtook them. Two of the Stockbridge Indians reported that the French had found their boats and there were 400 French and Indians on their trail. He decided to carry on as planned and try to get back by way of the Connecticut River.

The seven Rangers covered the 120 miles of tangled and unmapped wilderness to Crown Point in nine days. This was a remarkable achievement since their leader, Lieutenant McMullen, was lame. But McMullen knew that the Rangers' lives depended on having the supplies at the meeting place on time.

Meanwhile, Major Rogers continued his march and on the twenty-second day after leaving Crown Point, the Rangers reached the St. Francis River, fifteen miles below the Indian town. The icy water foamed and boiled over the rocks along the banks. The current was swift. The river had to be crossed. Rogers waded in to test its depth (see left). The Rangers still had to attack the town and get back to the meeting place already agreed upon. (Rogers' proposed route is shown in the map on the right.)

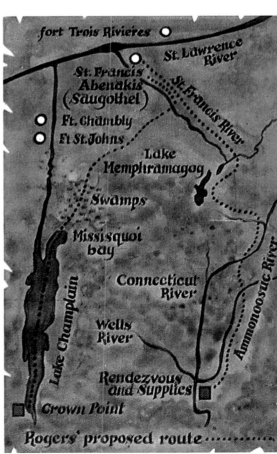

fort Trois Rivières ○
St. Lawrence River
St. Francis Abenakis (Saugothel)
St. Francis River
Ft. Chambly ○
Ft St.Johns ○
Lake Memphramagog
Swamps
Missisquoi bay
Connecticut River
Lake Champlain
Wells River
Ammonoosuc River
Rendezvous and Supplies
Crown Point

Rogers' proposed route ....

ALL THE FUN OF THE FAIR

Originally a fair was a gathering of people who met to trade, seek amusement and take part in religious ceremonies. This is a section of a drawing of an old Mexican fair, showing market stalls and traders with their pottery and basketware.

The Romans held carnivals, or fair days, which included the procession of captured wild animals from all parts of the empire. Later these animals were loosed in an arena to fight to death. Gladiators also fought to amuse the crowds.

This is an Anglo-Saxon fair, where traders sold fabrics, jewellery and pottery from their tables. Livestock was also sold, and there were jugglers, acrobats, like this pole-balancing act, and musicians. The fair would be held in a village.

After the Norman conquest of England, trade with foreign merchants grew. In medieval times the right to hold a fair became a special privilege, given in the form of a Charter. These fairs were held on saints' days, like the St. Valentine Fair at King's Lynn, Norfolk, chartered in 1204. This is a typical medieval fair, with dancing bears, cock-fighting, stalls, jugglers, players and livestock.

Sport was an important part of fairs in the robust Tudor age. Wrestling and archery were popular, and small boys let loose wild rabbits which they chased among crowds. There was a maypole, music, dancing, eating and drinking on the village green. "Pleasure" fairs, at which no trading was done, soon became popular, like the Bartholomew Fair held in London.

The great "frost-fairs" of the seventeenth century were held on the frozen River Thames, which provided an unusually large fairground. Traders sold hot drinks and food to the crowds, for the ice was so thick that fires could be lit upon it.

This small-town fair of the eighteenth century has new amusements. There is a peep-show (right) and an early version of the "big wheel," rope-sliding from the church tower and animal fights. Deformed creatures were also on show.

THE city of Prague was Mozart-mad! The young Austrian composer's opera, "The Marriage of Figaro," had triumphed when it opened there in 1786, and the theatre was sold out for every performance!

When Mozart himself arrived in the city and gave his first concert, there were so many encores that it looked as if he would be there all night. He went to a ball and, to his

piano) at four years old, and at five he started composing. From 1762, he toured Europe with his father and sister, creating a sensation everywhere and being befriended by kings and queens at a time when musicians were usually treated as mere servants.

OPERA'S

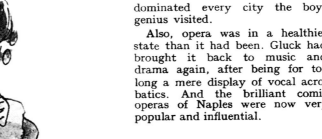

dominated every city the boy-genius visited.

Also, opera was in a healthier state than it had been. Gluck had brought it back to music and drama again, after being for too long a mere display of vocal acrobatics. And the brilliant comic operas of Naples were now very popular and influential.

fashioned style — but a far better piece of work than any of them. More famous is "The Abduction from the Seraglio," about a beautiful Spanish girl imprisoned by a Turkish Pasha in his harem. This one is a comic opera, and contains the first great operatic "character," the fat, greedy, evil, Osmin, who is finally made to look a fool, to everyone's joy.

THE MAGIC FLUTE

But it was "The Marriage of Figaro" which ensured Mozart immortality. His librettist, (the author of the words) was Lorenzo da Ponte, a witty poet, and Mozart and da Ponte chose a dangerous subject. The play they based their opera on, by the French dramatist, Beaumarchais, attacked the aristocracy. (These were the ominous days just before the French Revolution). The opera, for all its beautiful tunes and funny situations, attacked the nobility, too.

Michael Kelly, an Irish singer in the first cast, later wrote of Mozart's face at rehearsals, "lighted up with the glowing rays of genius — it is as impossible to describe as it would be to paint moonbeams."

For Prague, Mozart wrote "Don Giovanni," about the famous lover, Don Juan — he sat up all night before the first performance, writing the overture. Again an aristocrat is mocked — and sent down to Hell! This masterpiece, and "Cosi fan Tutte" (*Thus Do All Women!*) which followed, were great successes.

But Mozart was getting deeper into debt.

It was not simply that the Mozarts could not manage their affairs — in those days composers got too little reward for their work, even when it was successful.

Mozart plunged into work on his last great opera, "The Magic Flute." Unlike its three predecessors, whose librettos were written in Italian, the libretto for "The Magic Flute" was in German. It is a mixture of fantasy, comedy and religion and was to be the ancestor of all German opera.

"The Magic Flute" was a success, but Mozart's health had never been sound, and on December 5th, 1791, he died. His wife could only afford a small funeral. Women did not then attend funeral processions, and because of a storm, no mourners followed the coffin, which was laid in a nameless "pauper's" grave.

The famous composer was only thirty-five. But, of course, that was not the end. Mozart's popularity still grows with the years. Many people would echo his contemporary, Haydn, who said to Mozart's father: "I, as an honest man, tell you before God that your son is the greatest composer I know, in person or by name."

In this scene from "Don Giovanni", musicians appear on the stage, as well as in the orchestra pit.

Mozart was a cheerful, good-natured man—except when he was badly treated, as he was, even when he was very famous, by his "master," the new Archbishop of Salzburg. This spiteful priest continually humiliated him and finally, when Mozart rebelled, had him literally kicked out of his palace!

Mozart married a delightful wife, but she was as hopeless at looking after his affairs as he was, and he was always in debt. And the noblemen, whose favours he so resented having to beg, became less interested in the difficult young man.

But this lay in the future . . .

Mozart's first great opera, "Idomeneo", about a legendary King of Crete, was in the old-

joy, found everyone dancing to waltzes and quadrilles made from his "Figaro" music. "Nothing but 'Figaro' is played, sung or whistled," he wrote to a friend.

Yet, less than five years later, the "perfect musician," as he has been called, died in poverty and was buried in an unknown grave.

It is no exaggeration to say that, as a child, Mozart was the wonder of Europe. He was born in 1756, in the Austrian city of Salzburg, where his father was a musician in the service of the Archbishop. He was playing the clavier (a type of

Mozart wrote his first symphony at the age of eight, on a triumphant trip to London — musicians suspected he must be older than reported, but were astounded to find he was not. At twelve, he wrote his first opera. Though he became master of every sort of music, opera was his chief love from the time he sang in one — aged five!

Mozart was born, operatically speaking, at the right time. Vienna, capital of Austria, had been a centre of Italian opera (there was little German opera then) for over a century, and Italian opera

GREATEST GENIUS by ROBIN MAY

Apparently, Mozart became so engrossed in composing the music for "Don Giovanni" that he wandered into a private garden and was accused of stealing an orange.

The foundation of
THE BRITISH
EMPIRE IN INDIA

THE urge to explore is often motivated by the desire to trade. When Vasco da Gama rounded the Cape of Good Hope in 1498 and landed at Calicut on the west coast of India, he was welcomed by the local rajah, who earnestly desired to trade spices and precious stones with Portugal.

For a century the Portuguese monopolised the trade with India. Their place was taken in the 17th century by the Dutch who carried on extensive commerce with the east, evicting the Portuguese from most of their trading posts.

The first British expedition followed shortly upon the formation of the British East India Trading Company, in 1600. During the first half of the century, the Company acquired a number of coastal trading centres. These included ones at Surat, on the west coast; Madras; and Bombay, which the Company obtained through King Charles II from the Portuguese. At the end of the century, they founded Calcutta.

During this time, the French were building trading stations at Pondicherry and Chandernagore.

The situation in India was very tempting to those whose eyes turned from trade to the prospects of territorial acquisition. In the years that followed the death of Aurangzeb, the last great Mogul Emperor of India, in 1707, the viceroys who ruled great areas of India in the name of the Emperor began to extend their personal power and pay little more than lipservice to the imperial court at Delhi.

The most important of these viceroys were the nawab of the Deccan, the nawab of Bengal and the nawab of Oudh.

There was great scope in this situation for any foreign nation which chose to interfere. It was a question of who would do so first.

While the war of Austrian Succession was under way in Europe, the French governor of Pondicherry, Joseph Dupleix, used it as an excuse to attack and take the British Company's trading post at Madras. The British only regained Madras in the settlement made in Europe by the Treaty of Aix-la-Chappelle (1748).

The French, attracted by the ease of their previous success, were eager to extend their activities and build an empire for themselves in India. The opportunity arose when the choice of a nawab in the Carnatic (a region of the Deccan) was disputed. The French succeeded in establishing their candidate there—for which he paid them a huge sum of money.

Black Hole of Calcutta

The candidate favoured by the British Company had little prospect of gaining power until the arrival of Robert Clive, the brilliant soldier-statesman who rose from the post of clerk in the East India Company to be the founder of the British Empire in India. Clive, seeing that the French pretender had left his capital—Arcot—to try and capture a nearby British station, suggested that he attack Arcot to bring the pretender in haste back to his capital. With only a handful of men and three pieces of artillery, Clive approached Arcot and the frightened enemy garrison evacuated it.

A great army under the pretender's son, supported by the French, came to besiege Clive in the fort of Arcot. After 50 days, a full-scale attack was launched on the fort. In spite of the fact that the walls of the fort were falling down, nothing could suppress the courage of Clive and his men, even though the Indian army was 10,000 strong. After little more than an hour, the enemy were routed and in flight from the scene of battle.

Robert Clive, at 26 years of age, had made his reputation. And the British Company gained control of the Carnatic. From this moment, the

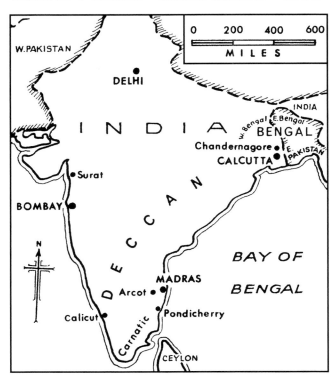

At Arcot, in 1751, Robert Clive and 300 ▶ men faced an Indian army of 10,000. The Indians had many pieces of artillery and their attack was led by armoured elephants. But the encounter lasted only an hour, at the end of which time the Indian army was in flight.

French hopes of an empire in India were doomed.

If the British were established in the Carnatic, their position in Bengal was in danger. The nawab of Bengal, frightened by the British success in the Carnatic, decided to oust them from Bengal before they had a chance to assail his position. This nawab, named Surajah Dowlah, seized Calcutta, took prisoner members of the British Company, and pushed them into the Black Hole of Calcutta, an airless and tiny prison, where, in the course of one night, the majority died from suffocation.

Clive was the obvious choice of leader to avenge this action. He had just returned to India after two years in England.

With a small army, Clive sailed up the Ganges delta into the Bay of Bengal. Fort William, the East India Company's settlement near Calcutta, was taken and then Calcutta itself. Then, after some weeks' delay, in which negotiations of dubious honesty were pressed on either side, Clive made for Plassey, where the army of Surajah Dowlah was assembled. And what a vast army it was. There were 18,000 cavalry and 50,000 infantry supported by more than 50 pieces of artillery. Clive had just over 3,000 men of whom 2,000 were Indian. He had nine pieces of artillery.

Clive took a tremendous risk at Plassey—and won—but it was the sort of risk that was backed up by a sound knowledge of battle tactics. By waiting until the enemy army was nearly upon his own before opening fire, he threw his opponents into disorder, which he followed up by a rapid and devastating advance of his own force.

With Bengal in the hands of the Company, a puppet nawab, Mir Jafar, was installed, from whom vast financial rewards were accepted, and

in addition, the Company gained rights over extensive lands around Calcutta. Clive's soldiers and Company officials were also handsomely rewarded at the expense of the new nawab.

Clive returned to India for the last time in 1765, as Governor of Bengal. The power and effectiveness of the East India Company was now being undermined by the money and gifts which came into the hands of its servants: Bengal was rich and densely populated.

By undertaking extensive reforms in the army and the civil service—raising salaries and forbidding gifts of any sort—Clive made Bengal the base for further British expansion in India.

During the trouble that followed the death of nawab Mir Jafar, Clive secured from the Emperor, at Delhi, a document giving the East India Company sovereign authority in Bengal and the surrounding regions. This meant that the Company administered justice in that area, collected the taxes, and—need it be added—made a substantial profit into the bargain.

The Company was now in the strange position of having imperial power. As a trading company, it had ceased to exist.

The rule of the East India Company was not terminated until the Indian Mutiny (1857), forced the British government to assume full responsibility for the government of India.

India became an independent dominion of the British Commonwealth in 1947, and a sovereign republic in 1950.

EXPERIMENTS YOU CAN DO AT HOME

Why your Bathwater is hot

1

Fill a milk bottle with warm water to which some black ink has been added to colour it. Now fill another milk bottle with cold water. Both bottles must be filled to the brim.

2

Now place a piece of thin but strong card on top of the bottle of cold water. Holding the card firmly against the neck of the bottle, turn the bottle upside down, being very careful that none of the water falls out. Then place the neck of the upturned bottle of cold water on the neck of the bottle of warm water. Make absolutely certain that the necks are exactly in line with each other.

3

Hold the bottle necks together very firmly and carefully pull away the piece of card separating them. In a few seconds you will see the coloured warm water rising up into the bottle of cold water, while the cold water sinks from its bottle into the lower bottle to replace the rising hot water.

*   *   *

The reason why the warm water rose from the bottom bottle into the top bottle is that hot water always rises. Hot water is slightly lighter in weight than cold water, and it rises in the same way that hot air always rises.

This property of hot water to rise is used in houses to provide hot baths, so that you get hot water in the bathroom, although the fire heating the water may be on the floor below.

Don't forget to wash the bottles thoroughly before they are put out for the milkman!

Extracts from
ELEGY IN A COUNTRY CHURCH-YARD

THE curfew tolls the knell of parting day,
The lowing herd wind slowly o'er the lea,
The ploughman homeward plods his weary way,
And leaves the world to darkness and to me....

Beneath those rugged elms, that yew tree's shade,
Where heaves the turf in many a mouldering heap,
Each in his narrow cell for ever laid,
The rude forefathers of the hamlet sleep.

The boast of heraldry, the pomp of power,
And all that beauty, all that wealth e'er gave,
Await alike th' inevitable hour:
The paths of glory lead but to the grave.

Perhaps in this neglected spot is laid
Some heart once pregnant with celestial fire;
Hands that the rod of empire might have swayed,
Or waked to ecstasy the living lyre.

Far from the madding crowd's ignoble strife
Their sober wishes never learned to stray;
Along the cool, sequestered vale of life
They kept the noiseless tenour of their way.

Thomas Gray's Path of Glory

He looked at some old gravestones by a village church—and found inspiration for a poem that has been freely quoted for two hundred years

PROBABLY no poem in our language has been so much quoted as Thomas Gray's Elegy Written in a Country Churchyard.

"The paths of glory lead but to the grave," "far from the madding crowd," "through slaughter to a throne," are expressions from the Elegy that have passed into everyday use in our language.

And the churchyard of Stoke Poges village in Buckinghamshire, the scene of Gray's inspiration, has been given enduring fame as a result of it.

Yet Thomas Gray, a professor of history, wrote comparatively little poetry, and much preferred a quiet life of learning to achieving great fame.

All his life Gray was a shy, sad man with few friends.

He went to school at Eton, and later began writing his odes, a form of poetry which he always preferred, and which made him famous.

An ode is a poem written in a manner resembling a song and composed for some special occasion, or in honour of some event or person.

Gray wrote very little poetry, but once on a holiday visit to his mother's home at Stoke Poges he took up his pen and wrote the beautiful Elegy which has brought him immortality.

The poem concerns Gray's reflections on the people who lie buried in the churchyard. Alive, some of them were wealthy and powerful, others were poor and unknown. In the end, says Gray, their paths all led to the grave.

Gray was offered the Poet Laureateship, an honour which he shyly declined. In 1771 he died at Cambridge, the place where he had worked most of his life, and was buried in Stoke Poges churchyard, the place he had made famous.

Gray's part in our literature is considered an important one because his few poems form a bridge between two kinds of poetry —the "classical" works of men like Dryden and Pope who came before him, and the "romantic" works of Coleridge, Wordsworth and the Lake poets of the nineteenth century, who came after him.

A shy, sensitive man, Gray's path, like everyone's, led to the grave, but not everyone leaves behind them an immortal and very beautiful poem.

The ploughman homeward plods his weary way,
And leaves the world to darkness and to me.

COOK LANDS IN NEW ZEALAND

IT was commonly supposed in the 18th century that a vast continent must exist somewhere in the South Pacific Ocean to 'balance' the known land mass in the northern hemisphere. This theory was based on very slender evidence, but it had the support of influential members of the Royal Society. They wanted to prove to the sceptical that such a continent did indeed exist.

The Society pressured the Admiralty into providing a ship for an expedition of discovery which was also to include the observation of the transit of the planet Venus at Tahiti on 3rd June, 1769.

The man chosen to command the expedition was James Cook, a self-made man, son of a Yorkshire farm labourer, whose extraordinary ability and soundness of judgment were known only to the few who had seen him in action.

Cook chose for this journey a sturdy little collier ship renamed The Endeavour.

The ship was crammed with people when she set off from Plymouth on 26th August, 1768. Apart from officers and crew, a group of scientists headed by Mr. Joseph Banks, the botanist, and Dr. Solander, came as observers.

At Tahiti, the transit of Venus was observed and the ship thoroughly overhauled. A Polynesian guide called Tupia was taken on board and he proved invaluable later in making contact with hostile natives.

Leaving the South Pacific islands behind, The Endeavour struck a westward course. The weather grew colder but there was no sign of the southern continent, Terra Australis, which was supposed to lie in that region. The land which was sighted on 6th October, 1769, was New Zealand, which the Dutch navigator, Abel Tasman had discovered in 1642. Tasman had followed part of the west coast, but no more.

Cook's party were surprised by the vast horizon in front of them. Was this, they wondered, a huge finger of land attached to the unknown continent? Cook was determined to find out.

The Maori inhabitants of the land were not friendly. When they saw *The Endeavour*, they came out in their canoes with their clubs and pikes ready. Cook tried to deter them by firing shots over their heads but several of them were killed before they retreated to the shore.

The following day, three boats were manned and some of Cook's party went ashore. A band of about fifty Maoris awaited them. Fortunately, Maoris, being of Polynesian origin, could understand what Tupia, the guide, said to them. A little trade was done, but the natives were still hostile and Cook named the inhospitable place Poverty Bay.

Cook began to sail south, but the unpleasantness of the wintry weather made him turn north instead. He spent nearly six months sailing round New Zealand. By making the full circuit, he discovered the vital information that New Zealand consisted of two islands separated by a narrow strait, and that it was not attached to any continent. Cook's experience as a coastal surveyor contributed greatly to the value of the charts that he made.

Cook came into contact with many Maoris. Some persisted in hostilities, but most would trade with him and many were friendly and co-operative and took him to their towns and dwellings. He noticed particularly the perfect health of young and old. Even their wounds healed quickly.

Cook was not the only one who found interesting evidence to take back with him. Joseph Banks and Dr. Solander gathered specimens and noted the existence of numerous plant and animal species.

With his mission accomplished, Cook headed for home, spending some time charting the east coast of Australia, which he called New South Wales, on the way. He arrived in England at the end of this, his first voyage of discovery, on 12th June, 1771.

Captain Cook (1728-1779), and above, a Maori fortified town

The RIME of the Ancient Mariner

by Samuel Taylor Coleridge

An old seaman is telling how his ship was dogged by ill-luck after he shot an albatross. His shipmates hang the bird round his neck as a symbol of his wickedness but the ship is becalmed, and Death takes all members of the crew except the narrator. He then sees the beauty of God's creatures all around him and blesses them with all his heart. As he does so, the spell is broken and the albatross falls from his neck into the sea. The poem continues . . .

Oh sleep ! It is a gentle thing,
Beloved from pole to pole !
To Mary Queen the praise be given !
She sent the gentle sleep from Heaven,
That slid into my soul.

The silly buckets on the deck,
That had so long remained,
I dreamt that they were filled with dew;
And when I awoke, it rained.

My lips were wet, my throat was cold,
My garments all were dank;
Sure I had drunken in my dreams,
And still my body drank.

I moved, and could not feel my limbs:
I was so light—almost
I thought that I had died in sleep,
And was a blessed ghost.

And soon I heard a roaring wind:
It did not come anear;
But with its sound it shook the sails,
That were so thin and sere.

The upper air burst into life !
And a hundred fire-flags sheen,
To and fro they were hurried about !
And to and fro, and in and out,
The wan stars danced between.

And the coming wind did roar more loud,
And the sails did sigh like sedge;
And the rain poured down from one black cloud;
The Moon was at its edge.

The thick black cloud was cleft, and still
The Moon was at its side:
Like waters shot from some high crag,
The lightning fell with never a jag,
A river steep and wide.

The loud wind never reached the ship,
Yet now the ship moved on !
Beneath the lightning and the Moon
The dead men gave a groan.

They groaned, they stirred, they all uprose,
Nor spake, nor moved their eyes;
It had been strange, even in a dream,
To have seen those dead men rise.

The helmsman steered, the ship moved on;
Yet never a breeze upblew;
The mariners all 'gan work the ropes,
Where they were wont to do;
They raised their limbs like lifeless tools—
We were a ghastly crew.

The body of my brother's son
Stood by me, knee to knee:
The body and I pulled at one rope,
But he said nought to me.

'I fear thee, ancient Mariner !'
Be calm, thou Wedding-Guest !
'Twas not those souls that fled in pain,
Which to their corses came again,
But a troop of spirits blest:

For when it dawned—they dropt their arms,
And clustered round the mast;
Sweet sounds rose slowly through their mouths,
And from their bodies passed.

Around, around, flew each sweet sound,
Then darted to the Sun;
Slowly the sounds came back again,
Now mixed, now one by one.

Sometimes a-dropping from the sky
I heard the skylark sing;
Sometimes all little birds that are,
How they seemed to fill the sea and air
With their sweet jargoning !

And now 'twas like all instruments,
Now like a lonely flute;
And now it is an angel's song,
That makes the heavens be mute.

It ceased; yet still the sails made on
A pleasant noise till noon,
A noise like of a hidden brook
In the leafy month of June,
That to the sleeping woods all night
Singeth a quiet tune.

THE AMAZING PITTS

TWO hundred years ago a series of bloody and fearful wars changed the map of the world.

First Britain and France fought for the control of India and North America. Then, after Britain's victory, the English-speaking colonists of America rebelled, won their independence and founded the United States.

Finally in Europe the French Revolution sparked off a powder trail of turmoil, violence and war.

Through this half-century Britain's politics were dominated by two towering figures: William Pitt, who became the first Earl of Chatham, and his son, also named William Pitt.

Pitt the Elder became an M.P. after a brief spell as a junior cavalry officer. His first speeches were savage attacks on the Government of Sir Robert Walpole, who remarked angrily: "We must muzzle this terrible young Cornet of Horse."

But Pitt was not a man to be muzzled. His protests against payments of British money for George II's German soldiers in Hanover made him a highly popular national figure. The widow of the great Duke of Marlborough left him £10,000 as a reward for his efforts "to prevent the ruin of his country."

Wonderful Year

Unfortunately Pitt's admirers did not include the King and the all-powerful Duke of Newcastle.

His chance came only after a series of military disasters in 1756.

He declared boldly: "I am sure I can save this country and nobody else can." His enemies decided there was little to lose and took him at his word.

He promoted vigorous, hard-hitting young officers in the army and navy and gave them vital commands. The result was the "wonderful year" of 1759 when the diarist Horace Walpole wrote: "We are forced to ask every morning what victory there has been, for fear of missing one."

In Germany a French army was routed at Minden. In America the French stronghold, Fort Duquesne, was captured and renamed Pittsburg. French fleets were crushed off Lagos and in Quiberon Bay. Wolfe's victory on the Heights of Abraham—where he was killed—wrested Canada from France for ever.

And, as if that were not enough for one year, the last French force in India was destroyed at Wandewash in January, 1760.

Few statesmen have ever been able to boast such a catalogue of triumph. But once the danger was past, Pitt was discarded. He lost much of his popularity by accepting an earldom and a £3,000-a-year pension. The new King, George III, preferred weaker Ministers.

Pitt's mind began to fail. He became crippled with gout. But whenever he was well enough

BRITAIN'S PRIME MINISTERS TO DATE				
Sir Robert Walpole	..	..	..	1721
Earl of Wilmington	..	..	..	1742
Henry Pelham	..	..	..	1743
Duke of Newcastle..	..	..	..	1754
Duke of Devonshire	..	..	..	1756
Duke of Newcastle..	..	..	..	1757
Earl of Bute ..	..	..	..	1762
George Grenville	..	..	..	1763
Marquess of Rockingham		..	..	1765
Earl of Chatham (Pitt the Elder)		..	1766
Duke of Grafton	..	..	..	1767
Lord North ..	..	..	..	1770
Marquess of Rockingham (March)			1782
Earl of Shelburne (July)		..	..	1782
Duke of Portland ..	..	..	..	1783
William Pitt (The Younger)		..	..	1783

he stormed at the pig-headed policies in America, which were losing the empire his victories had won.

"You cannot conquer the Americans," he declared in the House of Lords, where he now sat as the Earl of Chatham. "I might as well talk of driving them before me with this crutch."

In 1778, during one of these speeches, he collapsed, and died a month later. One of the onlookers who carried him out of the House of Lords was his eighteen-year-old son William.

Three years later this young man, known as Pitt the Younger, was himself in Parliament. He was Chancellor of the Exchequer at the age of twenty-three and Prime Minister at twenty-four. When he announced that he had accepted George III's invitation to form a Government, the Commons greeted him with derisive laughter.

Yet he succeeded, repaired the British economy, which had been ruined by the War of American Independence, and stayed in power, with one brief interlude, until he died in 1805.

The prosperity that grew up under his government put Britain in a strong position to resist first Revolutionary France, and later Napoleon, when war broke out in 1793.

But all the Younger Pitt's plans to fight the

WILLIAM PITT THE YOUNGER
a Prime Minister at 24

war ended in disaster. Four times he built up a great European alliance. Four times his allies were forced one after another to make peace with France.

On the fourth occasion Pitt was a dying man, and a disillusioned one. When he was brought the news of Napoleon's victory over Austria at Austerlitz, less than two months after Nelson's defeat of the French fleet at Trafalgar, he noticed a map of Europe hanging in his home and said in despair, "Roll up that map. It will not be needed these ten years."

A few days later he became delirious. "My country," he is said to have muttered as he died, "how I leave my country!"

There is another, more homely, story that his last words were: "I could eat one of Bellamy's meat pies."

Here is William Pitt the Elder (top) who became the Earl of Chatham in 1766, making his last great speech in Parliament in April, 1778. He was speaking against granting independence to Britain's American colonies. Shortly before the end of his oration he collapsed and was carried out of the chamber. He died one month later. In the lower picture we see Lord Nelson on the deck of the Victory at the battle of Trafalgar, 1805. William Pitt the Younger, son of the Earl of Chatham, was then Prime Minister.

LOOKING AND LEARNING IN CHURCH

by The Reverend James Roe

THE CHURCH ROOF

DURING the summer holidays you may perhaps visit the ruins of one of the old abbeys which are to be found all over England. You will probably notice that, although the walls of the abbey church are still standing, the roof has disappeared.

This is because in the Middle Ages such roofs were often covered with lead and when the monasteries came to an end after 1536, this valuable metal was stripped off and sold.

Lead is still used in small quantities to make church roofs watertight, but because the metal is so expensive, most churches are covered with roofs made from local materials such as stone slabs, tiles, or slate. A few are partly thatched with reeds.

Many roofs are supported by great oak beams, which, although they appear so strong, have to be regularly examined for woodworm and other parasites, which can reduce them to a state of decay.

The ends and joints of the roof beams are often carved in the form of flowers, shields or angels, and these carvings are sometimes painted or gilded to bring out their beauty. I have heard it said

that the parts of these carvings which cannot be seen from below are done with no less care than those which can because the wood-carvers were working to the glory of God, and believed that He would see the whole of their work even if men and women did not.

Above the beams the roof may rise to a ridge, or it may be curved with a smooth plaster surface. A fully semi-circular roof is known as a "barrel vault" or, because of its wheel-like structure, a "wagon roof." In some churches a line of very high windows known as the clerestory (that is, a "clear" section) lets in enough light for the beams and ceiling to be seen in detail.

In a few ancient churches, as in many cathedrals, the roof is supported on stone columns which spread out in a marvellous pattern as they approach the roof to form what is called "fan-vaulting."

Look also for a carving of the Royal Arms, which is to be found in many churches just below the roof at the west end; it is there to remind us that the Church of England is the official National or "State" Church.

The TRIGAN EMPIRE

Driven far from its own galaxy by a space storm, a strange craft has landed on the planet Elekton, and the three occupants of the craft—visible only as luminous spheres—have taken over the minds and bodies of King Kassar of Hericon, Keren the friend of Janno . . . and the Emperor Trigo, who has just sentenced Janno to execution!

The Hericon guards seized Janno and dragged him away.

There will be no trial . . . dispatch him immediately!

Still half-dazed from the blow he had received, Janno tried to protest . . .

Listen to me . . . you *must* listen to me . . . the man you see back there isn't *really* the Emperor Trigo at all!

Haw, haw! . . . Do you hear that?

Some curs will tell any kind of story to try to save themselves, but this is the best I've *ever* heard! . . . Not the Emperor Trigo . . . *Ha!*

They took him down to the courtyard. More guards arrived on the scene, one bearing a great executioner's sword.

Well . . . will you kneel and meet your end like a man, or do you have to be forced to your knees?

Then Janno acted!

Hey!

Uuuuuugh!

The way to the high wall was barred by angry, shouting guards. Janno dodged a spear-thrust, and seized the shaft of the weapon, twisting it from the man's hand.

Strike him down!

He's getting away! . . . Raise the alarm!

Twenty swift paces to the wall . . . then, planting the sharp spear-point against the flagstones, he soared into the air . . .

The news was brought to the royal apartments in the palace.

Imperial Majesty, I regret to inform you that the condemned Janno has escaped, and is at large in the city!

Find him! . . . Cut him down on sight!

Alone again, the three alien intelligences who controlled the minds and bodies of Trigo, Kassar and Keren pondered on this new problem.

Janno knows . . . everything!

And he will talk!

So? . . . Who will believe him? . . . By telling the truth, everyone will simply believe that he is mad!

Forget Janno! Back to our plan, which is this . . . the conquest of the planet Elekton!

The Trigan Empire and the Kingdom of Hericon will march against the other inhabitants of this planet . . . there will be no declaration of war . . .

We will strike without warning . . . bomb all airfields . . .

Destroy their sea-fleets in harbour . . .

Meanwhile, having shaken off pursuit, Janno was creeping cautiously through the great gardens surrounding the palace.

If I could only find someone I could trust . . . someone who knows me well, like one of Trigo's staff who accompanied him here to Hericon . . .

Then, peering in through an open doorway, a wave of joy and relief swept over him. There was old Peric, the wisest man in the Trigan Empire. Peric looked up from his scientific work to see the young man.

Janno! . . . Why, my dear young friend, you're torn and bruised. What's happened to you?

Peric . . . there's something I must tell you . . . something you *must* believe, fantastic though it may sound . . .

He told Peric . . . *everything!*

You . . . you don't believe me, do you?

Don't believe that alien intelligences from another galaxy could come and take over our minds and bodies? . . . Why, yes, I think it perfectly possible scientifically . . . we'll talk more of it . . . meanwhile, drink this . . . it will steady your nerves after your terrible experiences.

Janno drank the potion . . . and instantly crashed to the floor!

Poor young fellow, his mind is completely deranged. I will leave him here to sleep for a while while I inform Trigo . . .

Next Episode: Plan for Catastrophe!

H.M.S. VICTORY

by C. L. DOUGHTY

Most of the Victory was probably designed by Sir Thomas Slade, senior Navy Surveyor from 1755 to 1771.

H.M.S. Victory, Nelson's famous ship, now lies in Portsmouth dockyard. A three-decker with 104 guns, she was classed as a first-rate ship-of-the-line. The 2,162-ton ship carried 738 officers and men. She is 226 ft. long from tip of bowsprit to taffrail, with an extreme width of 52 ft. 6 in. The height of her mainmast is 119 ft.

It is impossible to think of the Victory without remembering her most famous admiral, Horatio Nelson, hero of St. Vincent, the Nile, Copenhagen and Trafalgar. Born at Burnham Thorpe, Norfolk, in 1758, he went to sea at the age of twelve. He helped to improve the terrible conditions of seamen. After twenty months at sea in 1805 the surgeon found that only one man was ill.

The Battle of Trafalgar was Nelson's last and greatest achievement. Napoleon had gathered an invading army on the shores of France to conquer England. But this epic sea-battle marked the turning-point in the Napoleonic War and also established the English as masters of the sea. The combined French and Spanish fleets were brought to battle off Cape Trafalgar in southern Spain on October 21, 1805. Nelson's brilliant methods not only threw the enemy into utter confusion but also led to a revolution in naval strategy. The opening shots were fired about noon. An hour later Nelson was hit by a bullet from an enemy sniper. Two and a half hours later, after learning of the triumphant outcome of the battle for the English, the great admiral, idol of the navy and the nation, died in the arms of his friend Captain Hardy.

The Victory, her mizzen and fore topmast shot away, was towed to the shelter of Gibraltar harbour after Trafalgar. Twenty of the enemy's thirty-three ships were taken or sunk that day. Not one of the British fleet of twenty-seven ships was lost.

On January 9, 1806, Nelson's remains were taken to St. Paul's Cathedral, London. The bier on which the coffin rested was covered with trophies. Behind the coffin followed thirty flag officers and a hundred captains. Sorrowing crowds lined the route.

The keel of the Victory was laid down at Chatham Dockyard on July 23, 1759. It was 151 ft. long and 20 in. square. The timber used in her construction probably came from the forests of Kent and Sussex, was transported on ox-drawn wagons to Maidstone and transferred to barges to complete the journey by water to Chatham on the River Medway.

There were frequent halts to work on the ship. Not until Friday, May 8, 1778, did the Victory first put to sea, to become the flagship of Admiral Keppel, Commander-in-Chief of the Grand Fleet.

The Victory first encountered gunfire in June, 1778, when Keppel's fleet fought an action with a French fleet under the Comte d'Orvilliers. Though, officially, England and France were at peace, Keppel's orders were to prevent a merger of the French fleets. At one point during the action d'Orvilliers' flagship, the Bretagne (a hundred and ten guns), and the Victory fought a sharp duel.

The Battle of St. Vincent in 1797 was another major naval action in which the Victory distinguished herself. As flagship of Admiral Sir John Jervis, she played a decisive part in defeating a superior Spanish force. At this battle Nelson first achieved fame. His ship, the Captain, captured two enemy ships. Nelson was congratulated on the quarter-deck of the Victory.

A seaman of Nelson's day. The present blue uniform was not adopted until 1840. Many seamen were "press-ganged," or rounded up, and taken unwillingly to sea in those days.

The Victory's sea-going life did not end with Nelson's death. It was not until 1812 her captain made the final entry in her log-book. In 1922 the Victory was moved from her berth off Gosport into Number Two dock at Portsmouth. She last floated freely in 1925 when, because of the condition of her hull, she was brought permanently to rest on a concrete base.

H.M.S. Victory has been in commission longer than any other ship. She still wears the flag of the Commander-in-Chief of Portsmouth, and she is the sole surviving example of a first-rate line-of-battle ship of her era. In the course of a year she is visited by about a million sightseers. Nearby is the Victory Museum, which contains relics connected with Nelson's flagship and a fine panorama of the Battle of Trafalgar.

MEN FOR SALE!

A CRACKLING, blistering inferno of fire turned the African village into a flaming furnace. From the hungry blaze scampered the terrified natives.

They were fleeing from death into what was to become a life of slavery. The white men who had destroyed their homes were waiting with whips and chains to capture the unfortunate Africans and to ship them to America.

Chained hand and foot, the negroes were taken on board waiting ships, where they were packed so tightly that they could neither sit properly nor stand upright.

This was the slave trade, which developed on a large scale after the discovery of America at the end of the 15th century. The conquering Spaniards, finding themselves short of labour, decided to kidnap and transport into slavery Negroes from Africa.

In the next 50 years, the trade became so profitable that the Elizabethan sailor, Sir John Hawkins, took part in it with the Queen's approval.

But it was the cruellest and most inhumane act that one man could do to another. Why was it allowed? The negroes were powerless to protect themselves. Was there nobody who would save them?

MAN WITH A MISSION

One man made up his mind to try. His name was William Wilberforce, and he was a Yorkshire schoolboy when he first realised the full horror of the slave trade. By this time, nine million Africans had been sold into slavery in America, and at least another quarter of a million had died at sea.

Wilberforce wrote from his school to a newspaper, "Will no one do anything to stop this odious traffic in human flesh?"

No one would. Wilberforce became an M.P. and decided to do all that he could to bring about the abolition of the slave trade.

The tremendous energy with which this slight, frail Yorkshireman threw himself into his crusade against slavery is a story of magnificent dedication.

First, helped by Thomas Clarkson, another zealous abolitionist, he collected evidence about the savage treatment and conditions of slaves.

Wilberforce and his Slave Committee had the support in Parliament of William Pitt, the Prime Minister, and the famous politician Edmund Burke, who became Prime Minister. But as sympathy for their campaign increased, so did the opposition to it.

Merchants in the West Indies vigorously attacked Wilberforce for interfering with the "sacredness of their private property".

In April, 1791, Wilberforce presented Parliament with a motion to end the slave trade. It was heavily defeated. Now came another blow.

Slaves in the West Indies revolted and people in Britain became alarmed. The opposition to Wilberforce and his followers hardened.

Despite this, Wilberforce launched an annual campaign in the Commons which must have seemed like banging his head against a wall.

Every year from 1792 to 1798, despite failing health, Wilberforce presented a motion for the abolition of the slave trade—and every year he was defeated, often with abuse.

Threat of war and reorganisation in Parliament slowed the campaign, but in 1806 he scored a breakthrough when Parliament made it illegal for British subjects to import slaves to any foreign colony.

The following year came the great triumph. In March, 1807, 19 years after Wilberforce pledged himself to see the slave trade abolished, Parliament passed the General Abolition Bill by 283 votes to 16.

The slave *trade* had now been made illegal. But great vigilance was needed to catch the pirate ships that at once turned to smuggling slaves across the Atlantic.

Wilberforce did not cease his campaigning, and three days before he died Parliament passed the second reading of the Bill for the *complete* abolition of slavery. The Bill later became law.

From freedom in Africa to slavery in America was the plight of negroes who were chained and shipped on a nightmare voyage across the Atlantic.

MANCHESTER ROAD

by PETER JACKSON

Since the Middle Ages Manchester has been associated with the textile trade. Its importance as a cloth town began when Flemish weavers settled there in 1363, although a hundred years earlier mills were at work in the district.

England's first library to which the public were admitted was opened in Manchester in 1653. It was founded by Humphrey Chetham. Although at first the books in the library were chained to prevent them being stolen, the chains were removed about 1740. The library still exists, housed in a building dating from 1422.

Manchester's libraries are today among the greatest in the world.

In the eighteenth century machines like Crompton's "mule" and Hargreave's "spinning Jenny" revolutionised the industry. It was in Manchester that Britain's first steam-driven cotton-mill was brought into use.

The mechanisation of cotton-spinning and cloth-weaving led to riots by manual workers, who thought that machines would take over their jobs. In 1817 a group of "Blanketeers" (so-called because each man carried a blanket) prepared to march on London, but it came to nothing.

The industrial unrest came to a head on August 16, 1819, when some sixty thousand people assembled in St. Peter's Field for a demonstration in favour of Parliamentary reform. The local militia were ordered to step in and arrest the speakers, but panicked, and started to wield their sabres among the crowd. The Riot Act was read, but few people heard it. A company of Hussars was ordered to disperse the crowd, with the result that dozens were killed or injured. This event is known as the Peterloo Massacre.

Atomic research was pioneered in Manchester. John Dalton, the true founder of the chemical atomic theory, was a Manchester schoolmaster, and lectured here on the subject.

○ Hydrogen
◻ Oxygen
◉ Water
Sulphur
Zinc

Lord Rutherford occupied the Chair of Physics at Manchester University, where he first split the atom in 1919.

When the distance from Manchester to the sea caused her trade to decline in favour of Liverpool, she had to become a port to survive. This was done by cutting a 35½ mile-long canal to the sea.

The canal was built after years of struggle, and was opened by Queen Victoria on May 21, 1894. It gives ocean-going vessels direct access to the heart of Manchester, making it one of the larger ports in Britain.

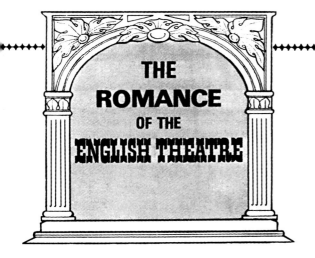
EDMUND KEAN
-Tragic Genius

THERE has been a Theatre Royal in Drury Lane since 1663, and though the present one, built in 1812, has now become the home of American Musicals it ranks as the senior English theatre.

Just beyond its foyer is the Rotunda, the Theatre's Hall of Fame. Here are statues of Shakespeare, of Garrick, the supreme English actor, and of Balfe, whose opera, *The Bohemian Girl* was all the rage in Queen Victoria's reign; there is a plaque to Sir Henry Irving, the first knight of the theatre, and there is a statue of that most exciting of English actors, Edmund Kean.

Before embarking on Kean's tempestuous life-story, we must consider what the state of the Theatre was when he made his sensational début in 1814, as Shylock in *The Merchant Of Venice*.

The great actress, Mrs. Siddons, only performed occasionally now; her brother, John Kemble, looked magnificent, but had little of his sister's genius; there was a scarcity of good new plays, and the new Drury Lane Theatre, built to replace the old one which had been burnt down, was not attracting large audiences.

The other "Patent" theatres—Covent Garden and the Haymarket, the only ones legally allowed to present plays in London—were struggling too. The most popular recent attraction had been a thirteen-year-old actor called Master Betty in various great Shakespearian roles—the House of Commons once adjourned to see his Hamlet!

But Master Betty was only a passing sensation. Clearly a genius was needed—and the Theatre found one in Edmund Kean.

Edmund Kean was born in 1789, and everything was against him. His father went mad and killed himself, his mother abandoned him, and he was looked after by his aunt, an actress called Charlotte Tidswell.

But he soon showed signs of acting ability, and played boys' parts at Drury Lane. When he was eleven, he caught the eye of a Mrs. Clarke, who looked after him and sent him to school. He was already proud and over-sensitive, and when a friend of Mrs. Clarke's indicated that he thought the young man was ill-bred, Edmund was so enraged that he tried to run away to sea.

Great Ambition

He was brought back, but by then Mrs. Clarke had had enough of him, and he returned to the stage. Soon he could dance, sing and play the clown. But that wasn't enough for him. He had an overmastering ambition to become a great tragedian.

At first, success came easily and by the time he was sixteen Edmund was playing leading parts in the Provinces. But he was only 5 ft. 3 in., which was considered too short for a tragedian; and his looks were unremarkable, except for his piercingly brilliant eyes.

So he could make no impression on the important theatres. And then, when he was nineteen, he married an actress called Mary Chambers. The marriage was not a success. Mary was not

suited to the hard life she had to endure as the wife of a touring actor, and she could not understand her ambitious husband—who, in fact, must have been very difficult to live with.

In 1812, with two children now to support, Kean asked for a small-part job at Drury Lane, but was turned down. Then he was engaged by a

Edmund Kean's son, Charles, was a much more respectable figure than his father, but had none of his genius. He is seen here as Macbeth.

non-Patent theatre, which should have meant the end of his chances of real success, because players at these theatres were blacklisted by the major ones, who recruited actors from the Provinces instead.

But by now reports had reached the Drury Lane Committee that the man they had turned down was brilliant! And as things were not going well for their theatre just then, they pocketed their pride and engaged him.

Fate, however, had not finished with Edmund Kean. His elder son died, and then the manager who had signed him up for the blacklisted theatre threatened to hold him to his contract. He was

in despair, but things were finally sorted out, and he made his début on January 26, 1814.

The audience was small, but they could recognize genius. Kean triumphed. He rushed home and called out: "Mary, you shall ride in your carriage, and Charley (his surviving son) shall go to Eton." They did!

Kean triumphed again as Richard III. Lord Byron wrote: "By Jove, he is a soul!" The poet Coleridge said that to see Kean act was like reading Shakespeare by flashes of lightning.

Kean was not in fact a perfect actor, like Garrick, who excelled equally in tragedy and comedy, but in his greatest tragic parts there were moments, "flashes of lightning," which have never been equalled. As the villainous Sir Giles Overreach in *A New Way To Pay Old Debts*, he fell to the ground foaming at the mouth, appearing to go mad. The audience was thunderstruck, Lord Byron was sent into a convulsion, and the other actors were so shaken that one of them had hysterics.

Household Name

Kean was by now a household name, but his nature got the better of him. His other great ambition was to be accepted as a gentleman, but this never happened. He took to drink, and had to make do with wild companions who flattered him. Audiences worshipped him as an actor, but not as a man. He triumphed in America, but then lost all his popularity when he refused to perform one night because the audience was too small.

Finally brandy was the death of him, but before then he had acted Othello with his son, Charles, as Iago. He was not at his best at first, but was proud of his son's success. In the third act, he roused himself and spoke the famous "farewell" speech with all the old glory, but on the words "Othello's occupation's gone," he broke down and fell into his son's arms, moaning: "I am dying . . . speak to them for me." The curtain was lowered on him for the last time.

On May 15, 1833, he died, but he is not forgotten, and if one asks an actor or a playgoer which famous name from the past they would most like to have seen act, the chances are that they will say one magic word: "Kean!"

It is the most important night of Edmund ▶
Kean's life. After years of struggle and disappointment, he is to play Shylock in "The Merchant of Venice" at Drury Lane. The other actors have laughed at the shabby little man during rehearsals, and there will only be a few people in the theatre that night—but they will recognize genius when they see it and realize that theatrical history is being made. But now he tries to keep out the icy blast and makes his way to the stage-door.

The Fish That Became Famous

Schubert's sympathy for the sad fate of a trout at the end of an angler's line spilled over into a beautiful piece of chamber music

IN the summer of 1819, the 22-year-old composer, Franz Schubert, went on a walking holiday with his middle-aged friend and adviser, the singer Michael Vogl. Their destination was Vogl's home town of Steyr, in upper Austria, which was noted for the weapons and armour forged in its famous iron works.

"It is strange to think that the means of so much death and destruction has come from Steyr, one of the most beautiful towns in Austria, if not Europe," wrote Schubert. "I only pray that my stay there will see the production of something more peaceful and humane than guns and swords."

The two hikers were welcomed by Vogl's family and friends, and Schubert became the guest of a barrister, Albert Schellman, who lived in the town's imposing main square. The barrister's house suited him very well, as it was also the home of one of his former school friends, Albert Stadler.

The visitors and their hosts — including a well-to-do mining manager named Sylvester Paumgartner, with whom Vogl was staying — met in the evenings to discuss and play music. Schubert found the countryside delightful, the people warm and friendly, and his only regret was that the weather was so bad.

"Yesterday," he wrote on 13th July to his brother Ferdinand, in Vienna, "we had a really violent thunderstorm. The lightning killed a girl and paralysed two men in their arms."

Then, turning to happier subjects, he added: "In the house where I am lodging there are eight girls, nearly all of them good-looking. This naturally keeps me rather busy. There is one very pretty girl who plays the piano well and is learning to sing several of my songs."

Inevitably, Schubert (who had been known to compose up to eight new songs a day) was asked to write some music for his new circle of admirers. He obliged by composing a piano sonata for the musical girl who had taken his fancy, and by setting a poem specially written by Albert Stadler to mark Vogl's 51st birthday the following month.

These works were much enjoyed and highly praised. But another and more profound work was demanded of him. So Schubert — born in Vienna of a musical family — commandeered Herr Schellman's piano and moved it into his quarters.

New Quintet

"I felt rather guilty about doing this," he confessed afterwards, "as it meant that the young ladies of the house had to give up their dancing parties, which they enjoyed so much — not least of all for the attention paid to them by all the eligible young men of the district."

However, Herr Paumgartner had commissioned a new quintet for piano and strings (violin, viola, cello and bass). He was particularly interested in the cello part, as he played the instrument in a capable if amateurish way.

So Schubert strove to complete the piece before he and Vogl moved on to their next stopping-place, the city of Linz, on the Danube. Seeking inspiration, he turned to the song *The Trout*, which he had written two years previously in a beer garden in Vienna.

Indeed, he had composed many songs while sitting beneath the trees and sipping a tankard of ale — including the famous *Gretchen at the Spinning Wheel*, which he wrote at the age of seventeen, and the macabre and dramatic *The Erl King*, a year later.

Although stout, short-sighted and inclined to untidiness, Schubert was a keen fisherman, at second-hand. He loved to watch men, fitter and better organized than himself, angling for trout in the rivers outside Vienna.

He enjoyed the combat between man and fish, with the trout sometimes wriggling and leaping their way out of trouble. Eventually, when the fishermen renewed their efforts, and plopped the bait in the clear, fast-running waters, the foolish trout would bite on it.

They would then be wound ashore, their scaly bodies writhing with fear and their poor souls, as Schubert put it, gasping and pleading to be thrown back into the stream.

"I was filled with admiration for the sleek beauty and quicksilver movements of the fish," he stated, "and then melancholy overcame me as I watched them being landed. I tried to instil these emotions into my song, which is a celebration and a lament for the shining lives and frantic deaths."

He had written the song quickly and made four copies of it. These he had sent to various musical friends, and he was so tired at the end of his efforts that he scattered the contents of his ink-bottle over the original of the song, mistaking the bottle for his sandbox (this was before the invention of blotting-paper).

When he came to write the "Trout" Quintet he incorporated treatments of his song in the fourth of the five movements (Theme and Variations), and happily accepted the small payment that Herr Paumgartner gave him for the finished work.

The first performance of the quintet was given in Steyr, with the mine manager playing the supporting cello part. Schubert felt he had written a piece that would long outlive him and sang the words of the song to himself.

"I stood beside a river
That sparkled on its way,
And saw beneath the ripples
A tiny trout at play;
As swiftly as an arrow
It darted to and fro,
The swiftest of the fishes
Among the reeds below."

The holiday over, and the quintet a favourite with everyone who heard it, Schubert and Vogl proceeded on their way. The composer recorded that he had greatly enjoyed his stay in the town, and was pleased that such good work had come of it.

He planned to return to Steyr again and again. And he did so; but not as often as he would have liked. For Schubert died of typhoid at the early age of 31, and the inscription on his memorial reads: "Here Music has entombed a rich treasure . . ."

Franz Schubert accidentally poured ink over his score of the song, *The Trout*. But all was not lost: he had made four copies and sent them to his friends. Two years later, the young composer incorporated the song into his famous "Trout" Quintet.

For thousands of years the quickest way to move goods on land was in horse-drawn wagons, which was slow and costly. The Industrial Revolution's first solution to the problem of moving vast quantities of raw materials and manufactures quickly and cheaply was the canal. The first was built in 1761 and soon there were hundreds of miles of these artificial waterways.

The invention of the steam engine did much to bring about the Industrial Revolution. Long before steam locomotives were used to haul trains of wagons on railways, steam engines were at work driving the pumps that kept mines clear of water. This picture shows you one of the first steam engines. It was invented about 1705 by Thomas Newcomen and gave fifty years of service.

The great expansion in the textile industry came about through the inventions of a handful of far-seeing men—James Hargreaves, who invented a machine which spun 120 threads at a time, John Kay, who improved the hand loom, and Samuel Crompton, seen here watching his new spinning machine.

Although it was not the first steam-driven railway lo... George Stephenson's famous "Rocket" finally mad... the development of the railways which the Industri... tion so badly needed for the cheap and rapid tra... goods. Stephenson's engine hauled the first steam... the world's first railway (Liverpool to Manchester... tember 15, 1830, and soon steam trains were a fami...

The Industrial Revolution and its machinery threatened the livelihood of thousands of workers who had made goods by hand. For a time there were serious riots throughout the country when displaced workers stormed and burned down mills and factories in which the new machines had been installed. But in time the machines brought more work for people.

When the Industrial Revolution really got under way, the chief feature of most mills and factories was the steam engine driving the machinery. Power from the engine was taken by leather belting to the various machines. By changing the sizes of the wheels carrying the belting on the machines, the machine's speed could be adjusted.

Goods and raw materials had to be deliv... quickly and by the shortest route throug... the country. So great bridges were thr... across rivers and valleys. The bridges we... first of brick and stone, but as the trains... their loads became heavier, steel and iron bri... spanned the rivers.

The Industrial Revolution brought about an enormous growth of Britain's overseas trade. This needed bigger and faster ships and encouraged the development of the steamer. One of the earliest of these vessels was the Savannah, which was launched in 1819. The first steamship to cross the Atlantic, she made the voyage from America to Britain in 26 days.

Although coal had been used in Britain since Roman times, it was not until the Industrial Revolution, with its steady demand for the fuel to produce steam-power, that the vast wealth of Britain's coalfields began to be exploited. In fact, it was Britain's coalfields and the realization of their value that eventually made Britain the world's workshop.

One of the heavy prices paid for winning the wealth from Britain's coal-mines was the deplorable conditions under which miners worked. Wages were low, hours were long, and the mines were wet and unhealthy. Even boys and girls not yet ten years old were pressed into service to push the heavy tubs of coal along dimly-lit mine galleries.

early iron-workers had to forge and shape metal with hammers wielded by hand. in 1839 James Nasmyth invented his power-team-operated hammer. This was one of the mechanical tools and with it foundries I forge and shape pieces of red-hot iron weighing many tons.

In order to extract iron from its ore, intense heat is needed. This was a slow process until the Industrial Revolution's huge appetite for iron led to the invention of the blast furnace. The great heat needed is obtained by blasts of air blown through the bottom of the furnace on to the glowing ore.

With the rise of the factories and the fall of cottage crafts, many farm-workers migrated to the towns in search of other employment. To replace their lost labour, farmers relied on inventors to produce machines to harvest their crops. One of the first of these reaping machines is shown here. It was invented in 1827 and could do in a day thirty labourers' work, with the aid of two men and two horses.

CAMBRIDGE

Written and Illustrated by C. L. DOUGHTY

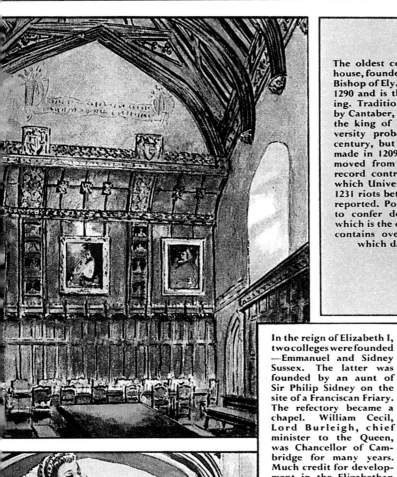

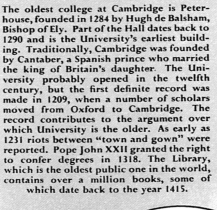

The oldest college at Cambridge is Peterhouse, founded in 1284 by Hugh de Balsham, Bishop of Ely. Part of the Hall dates back to 1290 and is the University's earliest building. Traditionally, Cambridge was founded by Cantaber, a Spanish prince who married the king of Britain's daughter. The University probably opened in the twelfth century, but the first definite record was made in 1209, when a number of scholars moved from Oxford to Cambridge. The record contributes to the argument over which University is the older. As early as 1231 riots between "town and gown" were reported. Pope John XXII granted the right to confer degrees in 1318. The Library, which is the oldest public one in the world, contains over a million books, some of which date back to the year 1415.

In the reign of Elizabeth I, two colleges were founded—Emmanuel and Sidney Sussex. The latter was founded by an aunt of Sir Philip Sidney on the site of a Franciscan Friary. The refectory became a chapel. William Cecil, Lord Burleigh, chief minister to the Queen, was Chancellor of Cambridge for many years. Much credit for development in the Elizabethan era must go to him.

Erasmus, the great Renaissance teacher, was at Queens' College from 1511 to 1515 as Professor of Divinity. He also taught Greek. While there he worked upon his famous translation of the New Testament. Born in Holland, he was looked upon as a leader of English thought. Queens' owes its name to the patronage of two women. Margaret of Anjou, wife of Henry VI, approved the college a few years after her husband founded King's. Elizabeth Woodville, wife of Edward IV, restored the building.

The heart of Cambridge. This aerial view shows the normal plan of colleges, in which buildings are grouped round a hollow square, called a court at Cambridge. Principal features are the gateway, hall, library, masters' lodge, lodgings for Fellows and undergraduates, chapel, and "combination" room or Fellows' common room. On the left is part of King's. Behind King's chapel are Clare and Caius, and part of Trinity beyond. To the right are the classical Senate House and the church of St. Mary the Great.

During the Civil War, Oliver Cromwell held Cambridge as a garrison town for Parliament against King Charles I. The Royalist heads of St. John's, Jesus and Queens' colleges were sent to prison. The gatehouse of St. John's endured a short siege, the doors being renewed after the Restoration.

Sir Isaac Newton, discoverer of the Law of Gravity, was a student and later professor of mathematics at Trinity. At the age of twenty-seven he was hailed as a genius. One of the world's greatest scientists, he discovered, among other things, natural laws upon which today's jet propulsion is based. Experimenting in the cloisters between 1673-1702, he also timed the velocity of echoes.

...hapel, claimed ...e loveliest in ...ixty-nine years ...e laying of the ...e in 1446 by ...then only the ...seen here from ...ngs overlook- ...was complete. ...ft. high roof is ...r Gothic style.

Three symbolic gates were designed by Dr. John Caius, 1510-73, to typify the life of students. They were admitted through the Gate of Humility, now in the Master's garden at Caius, and took up residence through the Gate of Virtue (built 1567). The Gate of Honour led to the Senate House, where the students gained their degrees.

The poet Thomas Gray was a scholar of Peterhouse in 1756. Gray was terrified of fire and begged a friend to give him a rope ladder in case rowdy neighbours fired the buildings. Soon after, the cry "Fire!" was raised in the early hours. Gray descended the ladder in a panic and plunged into a tub of water placed below by hoaxers. Cambridge has produced many poets, including Milton, Wordsworth and Byron.

Magdalene College (pronounced Maudlin) houses the famous Pepys library, bequeathed by the diarist Samuel Pepys who studied there, on his death in 1703. The collection is displayed in his own bookcases. The Diary, in six volumes, forms part of the collection.

The Senate House, built by James Gibbs in the early eighteenth century, is the centre of University Government. Its chief public function is the conferring of degrees upon students.

Cambridge stands on the River Cam about fifty miles from London. There are more than twenty colleges, clergy training houses and other buildings, many of which are open to the public. The students hold bumping races on the river.

The Oxford and Cambridge boat race is the most famous rowing event of the year. Begun in 1829, it became an annual event in 1856. Since then it has been rowed over the 4¼-mile course from Putney to Mortlake, generally in March or April.

dates were:
.. 1768
.. 1505
.. 1960
all) 1326
.. 1352
.. 1800
.. 1584
.. 1887
.. 1348
.. 1496
.. 1444
.. 1542
.. 1347
.. 1284
.. 1448
.. 1879
.. 1473
.. 1511
.. 1882
.. 1594
.. 1896
.. 1350
.. 1350
.. 1925
.. 1881
.. 1897
.. 1869
.. 1949
.. 1954
.. 1873
ome of the
ng clergy.

Among the many Royal visits, that of Queen Victoria and Prince Albert in 1843 was one of the most dramatic. Students threw down their gowns for the Queen to walk on.

The Fitzwilliam Museum, one of the oldest in Britain, was founded in 1816, the year after the Battle of Waterloo, by Richard, seventh Viscount Fitzwilliam.

Lines from

CHILDE HAROLD'S PILGRIMAGE

by LORD BYRON

And there was mounting in hot haste: the steed,
The mustering squadron, and the clattering car,
Went pouring forward with impetuous speed,
And swiftly forming in the ranks of war;
And the deep thunder peal on peal afar;
And near, the beat of the alarming drum
Roused up the soldier ere the morning star;
While throng'd the citizens with terror dumb,
Or whispering, with white lips—"The foe! They come! they come!"

And wild and high the "Cameron's gathering" rose!
The war-note of Lochiel, which Albyn's hills
Have heard, and heard, too, have her Saxon foes:—
How in the noon of night that pibroch thrills,
Savage, and shrill! But with the breath which fills
Their mountain-pipe, so fill the mountaineers
With the fierce native daring which instils
The stirring memory of a thousand years,
And Evan's, Donald's fame rings in each clansman's ears!

Did the great Adventurer lose his way?

Proud, boastful, cynical, conceited—this was the poet Lord Byron. For him life was a great drama, and only between acts did he stop to write his brilliant verses.

LORD BYRON was the supreme egotist. Probably no man was ever more in love with himself. Or pretended he was more in love with himself. For, in a classic contemporary phrase, Byron was all mixed up.

Almost as much as he worshipped himself, women worshipped him. Continentals adored him, society Englishmen loathed him and British working folk slightly admired him.

As a child he was sometimes spoiled yet often bullied by a pepperpot of a mother. He had a magnificent physique and became one of the best swimmers in the land—yet he was born with a club foot. He hated to see or to cause suffering, yet rather than be thought soft he posed as an incorrigible villain, whereas, although he was a villain, he wasn't as bad as all that!

George Gordon Noel, the sixth Baron Byron, was born in 1788. When he was nineteen and at Cambridge University, he wrote a book of poems called "Hours of Idleness."

The poems were not very good, and a writer in *The Edinburgh Review* said as much.

This infuriated proud Lord Byron. Scathingly he attacked the reviewer in a brilliant satire called "English Bards and Scotch Reviewers." Then, disgusted because at the age of nineteen no one had yet recognized that he was a genius, he left England to wander in Spain and Turkey.

Back again in England Byron published in verse his experiences of these travels in two cantos of "Childe Harold's Pilgrimage."

Disastrous Marriage

"CHILDE HAROLD" was a wicked young man who travelled in strange lands. The hero was, of course, supposed to be Byron himself. The poem was rightly a great success, and Byron became the talk of society—which pleased him immensely.

The poet peer followed up this success with *The Corsair* and several more inspired poems, and then made himself a disastrous marriage.

Not only was it disastrous, but Byron insisted upon scandalizing society by talking freely about it until, scorned eventually even by his own admirers, and bitter at heart, he stormed out of England never to return. A huge crowd gathered at Dover to watch his departure.

Byron was the centre of attraction and he loved it.

In the English Channel a fierce storm blew up and threatened to engulf the ship. As the passengers prepared to die Byron strutted the deck proclaiming, "I brought on this storm. This always happens when one of *my* family goes to sea."

Early Death

DESPITE Byron, the ship managed to weather the storm, and the poet went on to Geneva, where he met his friend the poet Shelley, and fell in love with Shelley's sister. France, Switzerland, Italy—Byron wandered on, living gaily, even recklessly, loving foolishly and writing frequently about his great idol—the bad Lord Byron.

And so to Greece. Stripped of his bravado, his panache and his overpowering ego, Byron was in fact a sensitive, freedom-loving man.

When he arrived in Greece that country was throwing off the yoke of its Turkish conquerors in the Greek War of Independence.

Byron the great adventurer threw in his lot with the Greeks. The year was 1824. Three months later, on the eve of the Battle of Lepanto, Byron caught fever and died. He was only thirty-six.

As you can see from the portrait above Byron was an extremely handsome man and must be excused his vanity to some extent. Charles Matthew said that "he was the only man to whom he could apply the word beautiful."

Despite the extraordinary pose he adopted throughout his life, Byron was certainly one of our greatest poets. "Childe Harold" made him famous, and from then until his great final work, "Don Juan," his poems were always exciting. If he had lived a more normal life, and not lost his way along the road, could he have been a much better poet? This is indeed a question to ask about Lord Byron.

For in some of his works, notably "Manfred," and "Vision of Judgement," there are brilliant, memorable passages that lead the reader to think that had the poet spent less time in playing the bitter cynic and more time on the depth of thought of which he was clearly capable, he might have been the greatest of all our poets.

ON THIS SPOT...

Have you ever noticed any small plaques on the walls of old houses and other buildings? Those in London look like the one shown in the photograph, and they mark the places where famous men or women have lived. Look for them the next time you are in town.

TIME and the weather have not improved the old brown plaque which tells observant passers-by that John Flaxman once lived at No. 7 Greenwell Street, near Portland Place.

The son of a man who made plaster casts and models for some of the leading sculptors of the day, John Flaxman was in close contact with artists from the start. He lived, and later worked, at his father's shop 'at the sign of the golden head' in New Street, Covent Garden.

At first there seemed little future for him, for he was puny, crippled and could move only on crutches. His parents allowed him to sit at the back of the shop, where he amused himself drawing, modelling and trying to read Latin. It was his only schooling.

John's activities soon drew the attention and encouragement of the customers, and he received his first commission for a series of drawings at a very early age. His health improved as he grew older, and his talent for drawing brought unusually speedy recognition. At 12, he gained a first prize awarded by the Society of Arts, and repeated the performance three years later. And at the same age, he contributed to the exhibitions of the Free Society of Artists and the Royal Academy. By 1770, he was a Royal Academy student and his work gained him a silver medal.

Through his father's business, Flaxman made contact with Josiah Wedgwood, who employed him to prepare wax models for the classical friezes and the portrait medallions for which Wedgwood chinaware is now famous.

Increasingly, Flaxman felt the urge to see Rome and meet the artists who worked there. He left England for this purpose in 1787, with a commission from Wedgwood to supervise the sculptors and designers he employed in Italy.

He was so excited by Rome that he stayed there seven years instead of the two he had intended. When he returned, he brought with him illustrations he had prepared for works of the classical poets, and these were engraved for him by his friend William Blake.

While in Italy, he had experimented with sculpture in marble. His work was noticed, and by the time he returned he was virtually a free-lance monumental sculptor. His work is to be found in Westminster Abbey, in the cathedrals of Winchester, Chichester, Gloucester and in many smaller English churches.

'The Most Dangerous Man In The Land!'

. . . was he a thief, a murderer, a terrorist perhaps? No, at the beginning of the 19th century this unsavoury description was applied to . . . a poet

EVEN at the age of 25, Percy Bysshe Shelley looked like a scrawny boy whose clothes were too small for him. He had the fair skin and delicate features of a girl; from a childlike face, surrounded by light brown curls, stared two enormous blue eyes.

However, behind this innocent facade there lurked a man who was widely believed to be one of the most dangerous and depraved men ever to have come out of England. In 1818, four years before his tragic death at the age of 29, Shelley took his leave of England, where, he said, "I am regarded as a rare prodigy of crime and pollution, whose look might even infect."

What had this man done to deserve such a reputation?

Shelley was born on the 4th August, 1792, at Field Place in Sussex. His father was a highly respectable Sussex squire and MP, but his grandfather, Sir Bysshe Shelley, was an eccentric baronet, who owned a castle, but preferred to live in a tiny cottage.

Sir Bysshe Shelley had entailed a large part of his estate on Percy. This meant that Percy's father could not threaten him with disinheritance—Sir Bysshe's money was going to Percy and there was nothing Timothy Shelley could do about it.

Shelley's earliest years were spent happily enough at Field Place, surrounded by three sisters who adored him. It was perhaps this idyllic childhood that was the source of his ideas about women which later outraged polite society.

For Shelley was an early supporter of women's rights. He believed that women were equal to and often superior to men in most areas of life. This led naturally to his view of marriage as being a bad idea for most women, since they became tied to their homes and dependent on their husbands.

At the same time that he was formulating these ideas on marriage, other, more dangerous, thoughts were going through his head. He rejected the teachings of the Christian Church and claimed not to believe in God at all. He even began experimenting with magic and going on ghost-hunts.

It was these ideas more than any others that worried Shelley's parents. The authorities at the University of Oxford, where Shelley had gone in 1810, were equally disapproving. At Oxford, Shelley was supposed to be studying chemistry, but his activities were wide-ranging and during his first year at the university he helped write an article which denied the existence of God.

The pamphlet was called *The Necessity Of Atheism*, and Shelley and a friend sent a copy to every bishop in the country. It also went on sale in an Oxford bookshop, where it was soon spotted by one of Shelley's professors, who immediately suspected it as Shelley's work.

Called before the university authorities, Shelley refused to answer their questions and was sent down (expelled) on 25th March, 1811.

The young poet was now in disgrace. His father immediately tried to disinherit him (for it was scandalous that an MP's son should be expelled from Oxford) — only to find that he was prevented from doing so by the terms of Sir Bysshe Shelley's will.

Rightly or wrongly, Shelley now began to feel that he was being persecuted for having ideas that were too advanced for his time. He now did a very foolish thing. A few months after leaving Oxford, he ran away to Scotland and married a girl called Harriet Westbrook. Both were under age—he was 19, she was 16 — and both gave false names. Shelley had now burnt his boats as far as ever being accepted as a respectable member of society was concerned.

Three years after marrying Harriet, the young poet and philosopher fell in love with a girl called Mary Godwin, the daughter of two leading political reformers. He told Harriet that he loved her as well, but, not surprisingly, she left him.

Shelley then eloped to Switzerland with Mary, accompanied by her step-sister, Claire Clairmont. Once on the Continent, Shelley's poetic talent really revealed itself. Previously, he had written some horror stories and one successful poem *Queen Mab* — with Harriet; but now the atmosphere and scenery of Europe, as well as the feeling of being an exile, stimulated his mind to write beautiful poetry.

Over the last seven years of his life, in which he was to return to England only once, he wrote the poems which made him famous. *To a Skylark, Ode to the West Wind, The Mask of Anarchy* — and other verse poured from his pen.

While in Switzerland, the Shelleys and Claire Clairmont met another poet exiled from England for his behaviour — the dashing Lord Byron. Though completely different in temperament, the two men got on straight away. In the evenings in their villa overlooking Lake Geneva, the English expatriates would sit round the fire frightening themselves out of their wits with invented horror stories.

The result of one of these evenings was the creation of one of the world's most famous and horrific characters — Frankenstein's monster, which was the subject of a book written by Mary Shelley.

The Shelleys' restless travelling was not without its sad episodes: several of their children died, either at birth or at a young age. But perhaps the most tragic event concerned Shelley himself, just as he was beginning to consolidate his poetic gifts.

Shelley had always had a strange fascination for water. Once, when sailing with a friend, his boat had become swamped and it looked as if they were going to die. Shelley, his friend remarked, looked perfectly ready to meet a watery death.

But on 8th July, 1822, just before his thirtieth birthday, he did not escape. Once again he had gone sailing with a friend off the coast of Italy, against the advice of the locals, who expected a storm.

Ten days later, his badly decomposed body was washed ashore. In the presence of three friends, among whom was Byron, he was cremated on the shore of Italy.

The "Peterloo" Massacre; in 1819, 60,000 people, demonstrating in St Peter's Fields, Manchester, for parliamentary reform, were attacked by hussars. Eleven were killed and about 500 injured. The incident outraged Shelley, inspiring one of his most forceful poems.

This extract from *The Mask Of Anarchy* shows Shelley's reaction to Peterloo

As I lay asleep in Italy
There came a voice from over the Sea,
And with great power it forth led me
To walk in the visions of Poesy.

I met Murder on the way—
He had a face like Castlereagh—
Very smooth he looked, yet grim;
Seven blood-hounds followed him:

All were fat; and well they might
Be in admirable plight,
For one by one, and two by two,
He tossed them human hearts to chew,
Which from his wide cloak he drew.

Next came Fraud, and he had on,
Like Eldon, an ermined gown;
His big tears, for he wept well,
Turned to mill-stones as they fell.

And the little children, who
Round his feet played to and fro,
Thinking every tear a gem,
Had their brains knocked out by them.

Clothed with the Bible, as with light,
And the shadows of the night,
Like Sidmouth, next, Hypocrisy
On a crocodile rode by.

And many more Destructions played
In this ghastly masquerade,
All disguised, even to the eyes,
Like Bishops, lawyers, peers or spies.

Last came Anarchy: he rode
On a white horse, splashed with blood;
He was pale even to the lips,
Like Death in the Apocalypse.

And he wore a kingly crown;
And in his grasp a sceptre shone;
On his brow this mark I saw—
'I AM GOD, AND KING, AND LAW!'

To........

One word is too often profaned
　For me to profane it;
One feeling too falsely disdained
　For thee to disdain it;
One hope is too like despair
　For prudence to smother;
And pity from thee more dear
　Than that from another.

I can give not what men call love:
　But wilt thou accept not
The worship the heart lifts above
　And the Heavens reject not,
The desire of the moth for the star,
　Of the night for the morrow,
The devotion to something afar
　From the sphere of our sorrow?

This, one of Shelley's most famous poems,
was written in Italy in 1821. It was published
in 1824, two years after his death.

Percy Bysshe Shelley

On 8th July, 1822, against the advice of the
local inhabitants, Shelley set out in his small
boat for a sail. The expected storm blew up,
the boat foundered, and Shelley, who could
not swim, was never seen alive again. Ten
days later his body was washed up on the
beach — he was identified by a book of
poetry in his pocket. His wife, Mary, died
in London almost 30 years later.

THE ENCHANTED

On the equator
lies the home of a
unique wild life

STRANGE hulks of volcanic mountain under a sullen sky . . . tortured rocks rising from the ocean . . . shores swarming with exotic wild life. . . .

These are the "Enchanted Islands," as Spaniards who discovered the Galapagos Isles in about 1535 nicknamed them on account of treacherous currents which seemed to have the power to draw or repel ships.

Until recently the mysterious isles, 650 miles west of South America and belonging to Ecuador, were

ISLANDS

uninhabited. As a result a unique animal and bird life flourished there. Today, in order to protect rare species from hunters, most of the islands have been made into sanctuaries.

Most outlandish of their creatures are the sea and land iguanas (1), which do not exist elsewhere. Five feet long, with saw-teeth and talons, they look like medieval dragons when, in the mating season, the black and grey of the males turns to flaring red and green. They are harmless, feeding on seaweed, while armies of red crabs (2) cleanse them of ticks.

Another shore dweller is the brown pelican (3), a migrant from the Americas, while the valuable fur seals (4) swim offshore. The hordes of penguins (5) include a special type called the Galapagos penguin, about which little is known.

The flightless cormorant (6), found on the two main islands of Narborough and Isabella, no longer needs to fly because it has few enemies in the Galapagos, and abundant food. Other creatures of the islands include the sea-lion and the blue heron. Only one predator mars the peace of the Galapagos—the snake.

THE AGE OF GREAT BEGINNINGS

The Victorian age saw no greater revolution than the coming of the railway, which the Queen used regularly on her travels. In the illustration above she arrives at the station with Albert Prince Consort to receive a red carpet welcome.

AT THE SEASIDE

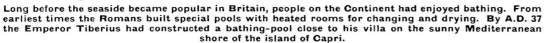

Long before the seaside became popular in Britain, people on the Continent had enjoyed bathing. From earliest times the Romans built special pools with heated rooms for changing and drying. By A.D. 37 the Emperor Tiberius had constructed a bathing-pool close to his villa on the sunny Mediterranean shore of the island of Capri.

Britons did not bathe until the eighteenth century, when a Sussex doctor recommended it. In 1732 men swam from hired boats, while ladies bathed from huts on the shore at Scarborough.

By 1785 bathing-machines had been invented, drawn by horses. From these the swimmer stepped unseen into the water beneath a canvas awning.

Fashionable people flocked to the seaside for cures. Sea-bathing received royal approval in 1789 when King George III was persuaded that sea-bathing was good for his health and took a dip at Weymouth, escorted by bathing-women.

Visits to the sea were becoming popular. In 1823 the first English promenade pier was built at Brighton so that people could walk nearly a mile across the waves.

Railways made the seaside more accessible. Victorian families spent whole days on the beach, where there were pony rides and sideshows for children.

By 1900 men and women bathed together. Costumes were less cumbersome, although still discreet. The bathing machines were disappearing, their place taken by huts. Minstrels entertained the bathers.

After the First World War people were no longer afraid of the sun. They romped on the beach in brief costumes, enjoying the sunshine and fresh air.

Holidays abroad, where sunshine was ensured, became popular. Beachwear was now designed by experts of fashion.

Today people from Britain go to France Italy, Spain and Yugoslavia in search of sunshine. Summer air-flights are booked months ahead.

Holidaymakers are not content with swimming, but want to explore below the waves. Equipped with masks, snorkel breathing equipment and fins they plunge down through the depths to the sea-bed itself, where they can spear fish or study sea-life.

185

WINDSOR CASTLE

Standing beside the River Thames in Berkshire, Windsor Castle is the largest inhabited castle in the world and has been a royal home for over eight hundred years. Though extensive alterations were made in the fourteenth century and early in the nineteenth century, much of the original stone structure remains as built on the thirteen-acre site in the twelfth century.

ROYAL FAMILY'S APARTMENTS BEGIN HERE

NORMAN GATE

The ROUND TOWER

ROYAL TOMB HOUSE

St. GEORGE'S CHAPEL

The HORSE CLOIST

The CURFEW TOWER

The Saxon kings had a palace close to Windsor before the days of William the Conqueror, who chose the present site, probably about the year 1078 (the year the Tower of London was begun). He built a fortress of wood surrounded by a stone wall to guard one of the approaches to London from the west.

The earliest architectural features in the castle date from the reign of Henry II, who began replacing the Conqueror's wooden stronghold with one of stone. King John, who succeeded Henry II, returned to Windsor after signing the Magna Carta in 1215 at Runnymede two miles away. Edward III, born at Windsor, rebuilt the stone castle on a more massive scale in 1344-54. Later additions were by George IV.

Geoffrey Chaucer, the poet, was Clerk of the Works for two years at a salary of two shillings a day. Although he was charged with the restoration of the chapel, the extent of his achievements appears to have been small. However, it is claimed that during this period he wrote some of his Canterbury Tales there.

Henry VIII loved Windsor and added much to its beauty. The story goes that having given Wolsey a chapel in which the Cardinal built a splendid tomb for himself, Henry confiscated both and left instructions for his own burial there. For some reason these instructions were ignored and the king was buried under a plain black slab in St. George's Chapel. For 300 years Wolsey's splendid sarcophagus lay unused, until taken to St. Paul's in 1806 to become the tomb of Admiral Lord Nelson.

The QUEEN'S TOWER

EDWARD III'S TOWER

HENRY III'S TOWER

HENRY VIII'S GATEWAY

The SALISBURY TOWER

Elizabeth I frequently resided at Windsor, and built the north terrace and gallery overlooking the beautiful countryside. Shakespeare presented his comedy "The Merry Wives of Windsor" there for the queen, who had asked him to write it.

Inspired by the magnificence of the Palace of Versailles, Charles the Second created the splendid state apartments at Windsor with their wealth of decoration, including the exquisite carvings of Grinling Gibbons. Charles also laid out the Great Park with the famous Long Walk, which runs for nearly three miles in a straight line.

During the Civil War, Windsor was a Roundhead stronghold, and Charles I was imprisoned in his own castle for a few days shortly before he was executed. And it was to Windsor that a handful of faithful followers made a final sad journey on a cold, snowy day in February 1649. They brought from the execution in London the dead body of their king for burial in the castle.

Queen Anne had a favourite window seat overlooking the north terrace, and it was here that she received the news of Marlborough's victory over the French at the Battle of Blenheim.

St. George's Chapel is a superb example of fifteenth century architecture. In the Royal Tomb House below it are buried sovereigns of every dynasty since Edward III. Above the stalls hang the banners of the Knights of the Garter. Samuel Pepys attended service here and says in his famous diaries ... "after prayers we to see the plate of the Chappell ... and a man to show us the banners of the Knights." He ends with the reflection that Windsor was "the most romantique castle that is in the world."

The Waterloo Chamber was created by George IV to commemorate the defeat of Napoleon. The walls are adorned with portraits by Lawrence of those who contributed to the victory. The immense table can seat 150 people and each year on June 18, the anniversary of the battle, the Waterloo banquet is held.

WINDSOR AND ETON

So much of England's history and so many great names are associated with Windsor that it is impossible to give more than the barest outline in this brief glimpse. Yet perhaps we might glance across the River Thames to Eton College, founded in 1440 by Henry IV, whose statue stands in the middle of School Yard. The tower at the end of School Yard, shown here, was built in 1517.

THE PIED PIPER OF HAMELIN

by ROBERT BROWNING

THERE is a German legend that in 1284 Hamelin town, near Hanover, was beset by a plague of rats.

Rats were everywhere. They ate the food, spoiled clothes, and the air was filled with their squeaking. The citizens of Hamelin demanded action from the harassed Mayor and Corporation.

Suddenly there appeared at the door of the council-chamber a strange figure, dressed in a long coat, half-red, half-yellow.

"Will you give me a thousand guilders if I get rid of the rats for you?" he asked. "*Fifty* thousand!" said the delighted Corporation.

Into the streets stepped the piper, playing his pipe until the rats poured forth in their thousands. They followed him down to the banks of the river, plunged into the water and were drowned.

The people of Hamelin were overjoyed. But the Mayor and Corporation refused to pay the piper the sum they had agreed.

Furious, the piper went out into the streets again, playing his pipe, and from the houses ran all the children, to follow the piper out of the town towards Koppelberg Hill.

Suddenly a huge door opened in the mountain, and piper and children passed through, never to be seen again.

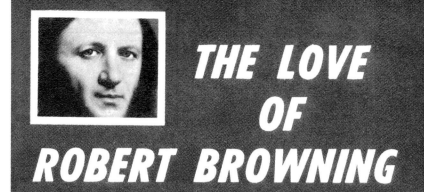

THE LOVE OF ROBERT BROWNING

THIRTY-TWO year old Robert Browning, traveller, playwright and poet, opened a new book of poems one day and began to read. He was enthralled.

Hastily taking up his pen, Browning wrote at once to the author of the book, Elizabeth Barrett, of Wimpole Street, London.

"I loved your poems," he wrote. "Please may I call on you?"

But Browning was soon to find that Elizabeth Barrett was an invalid, confined to the forbidding house in Wimpole Street and watched over by a harsh, eccentric father.

Browning begged to meet her, but for eighteen months Elizabeth refused to let him, for fear her father might forbid them meeting again. And for those eighteen months the two poets wrote to each other and became the greatest friends.

When at last Elizabeth and Robert met they fell in love.

But Robert Browning was a strong, outspoken man, and wanted none of this sickroom nonsense. With the help of friends, he eloped with Elizabeth, married her, and took her off to live in sunny Italy where her health vastly improved.

The two poets lived happily for fifteen years, and their marriage is one of the great love stories in the history of our literature. Then Elizabeth Barrett Browning died.

Elizabeth was, at first, the better-known poet.

But none of her work has any real dramatic power, and today it is regarded as unimportant. Browning, despite the vagueness and peculiarity of style in some of his longer works, is recognized as one of our greatest poets.

Browning's skill as a poet lay in his brilliant imagination. Very few of the situations he wrote about ever actually happened.

But poems like *How They Brought The Good News From Ghent to Aix, The Pied Piper of Hamelin* and *Evelyn Hope* not only lead us to think that the characters and events are real, but that Browning was there to see them.

Robert Browning was born in London on May 7, 1812. His father was a wealthy bank officer who encouraged Robert's lifelong ambition to become a poet.

For a long time Browning wrote poetry that was not understood, and consequently not popular. But rather than change his style he preferred to wait until people understood him.

After the death of his wife he wrote his greatest work—*The Ring and the Book*, a poem made up of a number of stories about people involved in a murder.

At the end of his life Browning went back to his beloved Italy and there, in Venice on December 12, 1889, he died. They brought him back to Westminster Abbey and buried him there: honoured resting place for a great poet.

HERE ARE EXTRACTS FROM THIS FAMOUS POEM

"If I can rid your town of rats
Will you give me a thousand guilders?"
"One? Fifty thousand!" was the exclamation
Of the astonished Mayor and Corporation.

Into the street the Piper stept,
Smiling first a little smile,
As if he knew what magic slept
In his quiet pipe the while . . .

And ere three shrill notes the pipe uttered,
You heard as if an army muttered;
And the muttering grew to a grumbling;
And the grumbling grew to a mighty rumbling;
And out of the houses the rats came tumbling.
Great rats, small rats, lean rats, brawny rats,
Brown rats, black rats, grey rats, tawny rats . . .
Until they came to the river Weser
Wherein all plunged and perished!

You should have heard the Hamelin people
Ringing the bells till they rocked the steeple.
. . . When suddenly, up the face

Of the Piper perked in the market-place,
With a, "First, if you please, my thousand
guilders!"

A thousand guilders! The Mayor looked blue;
So did the Corporation too . . .
"Beside," quoth the Mayor with a knowing wink,
"Our business was done at the river's brink;
We saw with our eyes the vermin sink,
And what's dead can't come to life, I think.
Beside, our losses have made us thrifty.
A thousand guilders! Come, take fifty!"
The Piper's face fell, and he cried,
"No trifling! I can't wait, beside!"
"How?" cried the Mayor, "d'ye think I'll brook
Being worse treated than a cook?
You threaten us, fellow? Do your worst,
Blow your pipe there till you burst!"

Once more he stept into the street;
And to his lips again
Laid his long pipe of smooth straight cane;
And ere he blew three notes . . .
There was a rustling, that seemed like a bustling

Of merry crowds justling and pitching and
hustling . . .
And, like fowls in a farm-yard when barley is
scattering,

Out came the children running.
All the little boys and girls,
With rosy cheeks and flaxen curls,
And sparkling eyes and teeth like pearls,
Tripping and skipping, ran merrily after
The wonderful music with shouting and
laughter . . .

And the wretched Council's bosoms beat,
As the Piper turned from the High Street . . .
And to Koppelberg Hill his steps addressed,
And after him the children pressed . . .

When, lo, as they reached the mountain's side,
A wondrous portal opened wide,
As if a cavern was suddenly hollowed;
And the Piper advanced and the children
followed,
And when all were in to the very last,
The door in the mountain-side shut fast.

THE POOR LITTLE RICH GIRLS OF BRITAIN

IN the spring of 1864 Jane Smith, aged twelve, lives with her father and mother, and a string of older and younger brothers and sisters, in a house in west London. Mr. Smith is a partner in a firm of importers in the City. He does not pretend to be a fine gentleman, of the kind who goes hunting and shooting; for he is in business, "something in the City" as the Victorians called it vaguely.

The Smiths are rather crowded in their little house, but it stands in a pleasant neighbourhood within easy reach of the City. Jane sleeps in her own bed in a room shared with her two sisters. The three boys have another bedroom, and there is a larger bedroom for their parents, with a little room off it for the baby.

Cook and the housemaid and the nurse sleep in the attics under the roof. On the first floor is a parlour and a nursery; on the ground floor a dining room and a hall. The kitchen is in the basement, so that all food must be carried upstairs on trays.

When Jane and her sisters get up they first wash in cold water drawn from the big jug on the washstand. Then they put on warm underwear and thick wool dresses. There are coal fires in the dining room and parlour, but the stairs and passages of the house are always very chilly.

The whole family assembles in the dining room. Breakfast is a substantial meal: tea, porridge, bacon and eggs. Mr. Smith and the boys are in a hurry.

Tom Smith, the eldest son, aged sixteen, has started work as a junior clerk. He and his father go off together to catch a horse-drawn bus for the City.

In fact, rich or just well-off, there was not much excitement for a girl in Victorian times. The only hope of future happiness was a good marriage—and every possible obstacle had to be overcome to achieve that

The other two boys walk off in the opposite direction, bound for a nearby private school. It is a school which takes boys of all ages and gives them a sound commercial education; plenty of arithmetic and geography, but no Latin or Greek. There is a gravelled playground, but no organized games.

Mr. Smith and all the boys wear top hats and black coats, like every other respectable man in London.

Wedding Bells

JANE has no idea of what father and brother Tom do when they reach the City; but then neither has her mother. No lady is expected to know how money is earned. Jane's duty, when she grows up, will be to marry some man and keep house for him, laying out to the best advantage what money he chooses to give her and never asking awkward questions about how much he keeps back for himself.

If no man in her own station in life asks her to marry him she will be an old maid, probably a maiden aunt; helping her sisters to look after their houses and children, with no independent life of her own.

She has no chance of a career except as a wife and mother. The professions are not open to women. A few years ago Miss Nightingale made nursing fashionable, but there are still very few lady nurses, and the bulk of the work in hospitals is still done by charwomen.

After breakfast Jane makes her own bed and helps to tidy her bedroom. That is the only housework she does, the only housework she knows how to do.

She enjoys visiting the kitchen and talking to the cook, an old friend who used to give her tit-bits when she was smaller. But mother disapproves. As a result she will never learn how to cook, and will depend all her life on hired professionals.

For a couple of hours Jane works in the parlour at the lessons set by her mother. She can write elegantly, and of course read. With the help of grammars and phrase-books she is learning to read French, though she might never speak it. Otherwise enough arithmetic to keep household books is all she will need.

In the middle of the morning the girls go shopping with mother, which is perhaps the most important part of their education.

All the food shops are within walking distance. They stock a wide range of goods, and prices seldom vary; but quality varies enormously, and must be judged by the buyer.

Nothing is tinned, nothing is in marked packets, nothing is guaranteed by the producer. If mother buys rancid butter, or tough mutton, or sugar adulterated with sand, no one will sympathize with her. Judging sound quality is an art, an art Mrs. Smith must teach to her daughters.

Walk in the Park

EVERYTHING they buy is put down on an account, so there is no need to carry money. Everything will be delivered at the back door, so that no lady ever carries a parcel. Presently they go home to lunch.

In the afternoon they all walk to the park, taking baby in his pram. It is quite a long walk, but they are used to walking.

Cabs, even the slow and clumsy fourwheeler, are too costly to be used every day; the elegant hansom is unsuitable for ladies; in a bus you may sit next to anybody. Ladies who cannot afford a private carriage must walk.

In the evening father and the boys come home for dinner. These people eat three square meals a day, where their ancestors ate one.

After dinner father reads aloud from a book of his choice, while his daughters listen over their embroidery.

It certainly seems a dull life to us—although Jane probably got as excited over pressing out some flower petals in a book as her counterpart today might get out of a new gramophone record!

But the worry was yet to come, the answer to the question "Will I marry?" Her mother would then be planning for her to meet all the eligible young men, for the "match-making mamma" was as much part of the Victorian scene as the great Queen herself.

Regent Street in the 1860s. Dainty parasols, crinolines and top hats were the fashion of the day.

The Victorian family at home. Note the heavy, ornate furnishings that characterized the era. Men and women in Queen Victoria's day may not always have been quite so "good" as they appeared to be, but at least they admired the standard of virtue set by the Queen herself

Real-Life Drama of the Brontë Sisters

EMILY BRONTË was a strange woman—one of the most mysterious writers in the history of our literature.

Born in August 1818, she was one of six children of an Irish parson, who had changed the family name from Brunty.

Their mother died, leaving the Reverend Patrick Brontë to rear his brood of five girls and one boy.

He persuaded his late wife's sister to do the housework at least temporarily—and succeeded so well in his pleas that she remained at their home, Haworth Parsonage, Yorkshire, for the rest of her life.

Emily loved her home, the dour parsonage, and left it only briefly—once to attend a school for the daughters of the clergy, and once to spend a year in Brussels with her sister, Charlotte.

Solitary Walks

ALTHOUGH there were servants in the parsonage, Emily was mistress of the kitchen, and her home-made bread was famous in the little town.

When occasionally her sisters realized that she was absent from the house, they knew where to find her.

She would be walking the wild, bleak moors which surrounded the town. There in the open countryside she seemed to find a quality which matched what was within her.

But for most of the time she was content to knead the family bread, sleeves rolled up and arms flour-whitened, at the same time studying a textbook.

Emily had loathed school, but not learning, and she spent much of her free time studying.

It was not until Charlotte found an accidentally-dropped notebook that anyone knew what Emily did with the rest of her time. The notebook, which Charlotte read in her own room, was filled with poetry which Emily had written.

When it turned out that Charlotte, Emily and Anne (the other sisters were dead) were all three engaged in writing poetry, they pooled their efforts.

The resulting book, called *Poems* by Currer, Ellis and Acton Bell was published at their own expense. Despite some good reviews, the book sold only a few copies.

The tragic novels of this talented trio reflect the sadness that hung over their own lives

CHARLOTTE

EMILY

ANNE

The three sisters, Emily, Charlotte and Anne. In the heart of the moors where they lived, very little happened. But in their imaginations were the stirring incidents and emotions which made their novels so vivid.

Within a year however, each of the sisters had completed a novel—Charlotte wrote *Jane Eyre*, Anne wrote *Agnes Grey* and Emily wrote *Wuthering Heights*.

The same publisher printed *Agnes Grey* and *Wuthering Heights* together, holding them back until *Jane Eyre* was a success. Even so, the combined volume lost money, and it was not until long after Emily's death that her work began to enjoy any real popularity. Apart from the poetry and a few essays, *Wuthering Heights* is all Emily wrote.

Perhaps she planned a second book. But if she did it is lost, and hints about it are part of the Brontë mystery.

Emily caught cold and succumbed rapidly to tuberculosis, which had already taken two of her sisters and her brother.

But she always declined to see a doctor, and threw away any medicines bought for her. Five minutes before she died she finally turned to Charlotte and said, "If you will send for a doctor, I will see him now."

It was the first, last, and only time she admitted defeat or allowed the thought of accepting help to enter her mind.

WAIF RESCUED FROM THE SLUMS

From the very first day that he was adopted by the kindly Mr. Earnshaw, the boy they named Heathcliff was the victim of jealousy. In revenge he fought a ruthless battle to become . . .

The Master of Wuthering Heights

NEVER did an act of kindness bring more unhappiness and tragedy than when the little gipsy-like boy was taken from the slums of Liverpool by Mr. Earnshaw to live with his family at Wuthering Heights.

They called the boy Heathcliff—the name of a son who had died in infancy—and it was the only name he ever had. The streak of wildness in him found understanding in Earnshaw's daughter Cathy, for that was her nature too.

Cathy and Heathcliff loved the freedom of the moors and would wander there for hours.

But Hindley, Cathy's brother, was jealous of the waif who had won his father's love and affection. Over the years his jealousy grew.

When Mr. Earnshaw died and Hindley

Heathcliff knew that Cathy, the girl he loved, was living in ease and luxury in the house of the Lintons.

brought his bride home to Wuthering Heights, she too disliked Heathcliff.

Through it all, Cathy's affection was the only thing that sustained him.

Hindley, embittered by the loss of his wife soon after the birth of his son Hareton, became even more harsh and unrelenting. One night he locked Heathcliff and Cathy out of the house.

They went to nearby Thrushcross Grange, comfortable home of the Linton family who took Cathy in, but not Heathcliff.

Cathy stayed five weeks at the Grange,

making friends with the Linton children, Edgar and Isabella.

When Edgar Linton asked her to marry him she was dazzled by the prospect, although she knew that she still loved Heathcliff.

Heathcliff went away, determined to better himself, but only as a means of revenge on Edgar Linton and Hindley Earnshaw. When he returned he had achieved some education and become a skilled gambler.

Now his revenge began. He won money from Hindley—and eloped with Edgar's sister Isabella. But it was a marriage of spite, and found no happiness.

Isabella left him, taking her son Linton with her.

Cathy, meanwhile, worn by the hatred and friction around her, became broken in spirit, and after the birth of her daughter, also named Catherine, she died.

Gambling and drinking brought about the death of Hindley Earnshaw—but not before he had gambled away Wuthering Heights to Heathcliff.

So Hareton Earnshaw was dependent on the man his father had hated.

But Heathcliff wanted the complete destruction of the Earnshaw family. That he did not achieve, for death struck again—and this time the victim was Heathcliff himself.

When finally Hareton Earnshaw married the young Catherine, Wuthering Heights found peace after years of torment.

THEY LIVE IN YOUR GARDEN

GARDENER'S FRIEND—THE LADYBIRD

IF you look carefully round your garden, you are more than likely to find a ladybird, especially if you have rose bushes.

The insect is certainly one of the gardener's best friends, for it feeds on green aphids, pests which do a great deal of damage to flowers and vegetables. (Inset.)

In Great Britain there are around 45 kinds of ladybird, and two of the most common are the "two-spot" and the "seven-spot," which can easily be identified by the number of black patches on their red wing-covers. Another kind of ladybird which you may see, although less common than the other two already mentioned, is the yellow "twenty-two spot" to the right of the picture.

The wings of the ladybird fold up like a fan beneath the highly-colourd wing-covers.

Like other insects with folding wings, ladybirds fly rather slowly over short distances.

The larva is blue in colour, marked with yellow dots, and when it is five or six weeks old the larva becomes a pupa. The ladybirds emerge from their pupae a week later.

There are over a thousand known types of ladybird beetle in the world. Some of them feed on plants, but in the main their food consists of insects. One Australian kind has been imported into many countries which grow citrus fruits, because it eats an insect which damages the fruit on the tree.

SUMMER EVENING MUSIC MAKER

ON a warm summer evening you may hear a curious high-pitched chirping sound, and wonder where it is coming from. If you look through the grass in the garden, the noise stops, but you may be lucky enough to see a small insect, green or brown, perched on a stem of grass.

This is a grasshopper, which is a relation of the locust. There are two kinds of grasshopper in the British Isles, known as the "short-horned" and the "long-horned" because of the length of their antennae.

The short-horned grasshopper (left) is a vegetarian, and it is his song that we hear in the summer. He is brown in colour, and produces his song by scraping his wing along his foreleg.

The long-horned grasshopper (right) is green, and often attacks other insects, hunting by night.

Both kinds of grasshopper, however, have one important feature in common—long, powerful legs which enable them to leap considerable distances. They hatch from eggs in May, and live until the September of the same year.

BUTTERFLY VISITORS TO BRITAIN

ONE of the most beautiful British butterflies is also one of the most common—the Red Admiral. It can be seen any time between June and October almost anywhere in the country, particularly around fruit orchards, where it is attracted by rotting fruit.

Some Red Admirals survive the British winter, and are reinforced in the following year by migrants from the Mediterranean which breed in this country.

The eggs are laid on nettle leaves, and change from green to greenish black as the caterpillar prepares to emerge. The colour of the caterpillar varies from black with yellow stripes to grey.

The chrysalis is grey, touched with gold, and can be found under the nettle leaves on which the caterpillar feeds.

Behind the Red Admiral in our picture are a Large (or Cabbage) White and a Small White. The Large White migrates each year to Britain, and lays its eggs on cabbage leaves. The caterpillars, when they hatch, feed on these leaves, to the annoyance of the cabbage grower.

The Small White is more common than its larger relation, and feeds on cabbages and nasturtiums.

Below (from left to right) are the caterpillars and pupae of the Red Admiral, and Large and Small White butterflies.

OH, TO BE IN ENGLAND!*

Have you seen a swallow this year? They are on their way
home again—and that's a sure sign that spring is coming

ONE certain sign that spring in Britain cannot be far away is the arrival of the swallows.

During late March and early April great flocks of these attractive little birds will be coming back to us after spending the winter in Africa and Southern Europe.

The swallows are, in fact, coming home. They were born here and they return to Britain for the summer to nest and breed. Many use the same nest year after year.

A swallow's nest consists of straw and small sticks stuck together with hundreds of neat little pellets which the birds make from mud collected on the edges of ponds and river banks.

The nest, which has an opening just big enough for the bird to enter, is often stuck with mud to the side of a wall.

Inside, the nest is lined with feathers. On this soft cushion the hen lays four or five white eggs with brown spots. Very often swallows raise two families during their stay.

The swallow is one of the most graceful and fast-flying of birds. Its long, narrow, pointed wings and forked tail enable it to dive and swoop at incredible speed.

The English name "swallow" comes from an ancient Anglo-Saxon word *swalewe*, meaning "backward and forward" which is just how the swallow flies when hunting the insects on which it feeds.

Swallows vary in length from seven to nine inches including tail feathers. They belong to a group of birds called *passeriformes*.

*Oh, to be in England now that April's there.—From the poem "Home-thoughts, from Abroad" by Robert Browning

The TRIGAN EMPIRE

A strange craft has landed on the planet Elekton, and the three occupants—visible only as luminous spheres—have taken over the minds and bodies of the Emperor Trigo, King Kassar of Hericon, and young Keren.

Young Janno—who alone knows the secret of the strange creatures—is a hunted fugitive.

Old Peric entered the royal apartments in search of his master, Trigo. He stared in alarm to see the emperor snarling orders to an officer.

The Trigan air fleet will take off at dawn tomorrow and bomb the country of Daveli! . . . Understood?

Yes, Imperial Majesty!

King Kassar of Hericon also gave his orders.

Admiral! . . . You will take the Hericon sea fleet to sea at sunset and bombard the cities on the southern coastline of Victris!

Peric met the wild eyes of the man he believed to be the Emperor of the Trigans.

Trigo . . . my emperor . . . old friend . . . what does this mean?

It means, Peric, that Kassar and I will be masters of the planet Elekton within a very few days!

The old man left the apartment, his mind in a whirl . . .

It can't be true . . . it can't . . . and yet . . .

Returning to his study, Peric found Janno raising himself, dizzily, to his feet.

That drink you gave me . . . it was . . . drugged . . .

Yes, my young friend . . .

I thought you were deranged in your mind . . . but now . . .

You mean . . . you believe me now . . . about Trigo and the other two?

Peric told Janno what he had seen and heard.

The man I saw was not Trigo! . . . Some alien and evil intelligence is directing his mind and his body.

I know it well enough . . . for a short while I was taken over by one of those fiends!

Peric crossed to a window which commanded a view of the harbour.

What are we going to do?

What can *we do? . . . It is already too late . . . look!*

In the glowing light of Elekton's setting suns, the vast sea fleet of Hericon was leaving harbour on its mission of destruction.

Where . . . where are they going?

To conquer Victris . . . and the Trigan air fleet takes off at dawn to destroy our friends of Daveli!

And then Peric and Janno heard the tramp of booted feet in the garden outside.

That's the door!

Janno felt a sudden shock of fear, which he instantly quenched.

They're looking for *me*! . . . Give me a sword, old friend . . . let me die fighting, like a Trigan!

But Peric had no sword . . . and it was with a heavy candlestick in his hand that young Janno faced the armed men.

Right! . . . Come and get me!

Next Episode: An exciting end to a painful 'invasion'

THE EDDYSTONE LIGHTHOUSE

1 To tell the story of the lighthouse we cannot do better than trace the history of the Eddystone. Fourteen miles S.W. of Plymouth jagged rocks rise from the sea-bed. At low tide they are visible to shipping, at high tide they are an invisible menace. On these rocks the first Eddystone was built, as seen on the right.

But the story of lighthouses began centuries ago. The first warning lights were beacons (left). It was not until Ptolemy built the Pharos light in 280 B.C. to guide ships into Alexandria that there was a structure to house the light.

THE PHAROS LIGHT

2 Later there were lighthouses built on the coast of Britain but to erect a light on a partly submerged reef, like the Eddystone, was not believed possible. Apart from gale force winds it would have to withstand the full fury of the sea itself. To get an idea of the power of those huge waves, imagine a force as great as three tons to the square foot! The Eddystone reef had wrecked many ships (below).

Then in 1686 a man came forward and undertook to build a lighthouse on the reef. He was Henry Winstanley, country gentleman and eccentric, who lived in Littlebury, Essex, in a manor house full of his inventions. The lighthouse was begun in 1695. Twelve iron bars were driven into the rock to hold the wooden superstructure. It was a long and arduous task, often hampered by the weather.

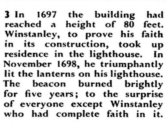

3 In 1697 the building had reached a height of 80 feet. Winstanley, to prove his faith in its construction, took up residence in the lighthouse. In November 1698, he triumphantly lit the lanterns on his lighthouse. The beacon burned brightly for five years; to the surprise of everyone except Winstanley who had complete faith in it.

4 Then in November Winstanley travelled his home to the house to carry out repairs. On 26 Nove a storm that was t the worst in En history sprang up. waves broke across rock and swept the house and its bu into the sea. All tha left were the iron

Soon afterwards a richly laden Virginia merchantman, The Winchelsea, was wrecked on the Eddystone rocks. Another lighthouse was needed. This time the task was given to John Rudyerd of London. His was begun in 1706 and finished in 1709. It was of timber on a granite base and stood 92 feet high.

RUDYERD'S LIGHTHOUSE

THE WRECK OF THE WINCHELSEA

In this early light illumination was provided by tallow candles or a coal fire, backed by a glass reflector.

6 It served for nearly 50 years, flashing its warning signal to ships. Then on 1 December, 1755, stores were landed as usual and the lighthousemen reported "all's well." On the 4th they could see flames, and rushed up the 70 feet of steps to find the lamphouse on fire. They had only a few buckets and many stairs to climb, which made fire-fighting impossible. The whole of the top of the lighthouse burst into flames like a huge candle raining down embers and molten lead.

7 The flames were seen from the mainland and in spite of heavy seas, fishing boats managed to rescue the keepers. Nothing of the lighthouse was left: the sea had swept away the wreckage.

JOHN SMEATON

8 Once again the Eddystone rocks stood bare, menacing shipping. John Smeaton was given the task of building another light. After having surveyed the rocks he drew up his plans. In August 1756 he began the construction. The foundation was of two-ton granite blocks cut so that they fitted together like a jig-saw puzzle. The stone had to be brought by boat and work could be done only at low tide.

Beside the present Eddystone stands the remains of Smeaton's light, which did over a century of faithful service.

An 8-sided revolving light 1873

9 It was finished in 1759 and stood for over 125 years. In 1870 there was a report that tremors had been felt in the lighthouse. A survey revealed that Smeaton's structure was good for another 100 years, but the rocks upon which it was built were being weakened by the sea. James Douglas began work on another lighthouse, just 40 yards from the old one, the stump of which still stands. It is this one that today protects shipping from the ever menacing Eddystone rocks.

THE STORY OF AUSTRALIA

GOLD!

RUMOURS that gold was to be found in Australia were rife! When two geologists found important deposits near Hartley, New South Wales in 1839 and 41, they only reinforced a suspicion which had been going around for some time, that the precious metal was available.

In fact, it had already been found, probably by James McBrien, a government surveyor, who had reported a find in the Fish River Valley, New South Wales, as early as 1823.

However, although all these three had found it, all of them had managed to keep it secret—with the advice of the authorities, of course.

But then two things happened which were to influence the course of events in Australia. In 1840, New South Wales ceased to be regarded as a penal colony and the number of free settlers started to outnumber the prisoners and emancipists. And then, during the late 1840s, gold was discovered in California and large numbers of people began to leave New South Wales to seek fortunes on the other side of the Pacific.

Among the Sydneysiders to make the voyage to California was Edward Hammond Hargraves. And it was he who was eventually to start the gold rush in Australia.

At the age of 33, attracted by stories of gold in the United States, he sailed for California in July, 1849. But, before long, he said that he knew of similar country back in Australia. Hargraves announced his intention to go home and find gold there.

Whether he could recognise gold-bearing areas by their geological formation or had merely heard stories of gold finds, Hargraves returned to Australia early in 1851, and made straight for the country he had described. Hiring a horse at Sydney, he set out across the Blue Mountains and eventually arrived at a place called Guyong.

There he met John Lister, the 23 year old son of a widow he had met earlier, a boy who had long been enthralled by tales of gold. Nothing could stop him from accompanying Hargraves, and in February, 1851, the two men set out for a place which Hargraves said would be rich in gold. There had been reports of gold in the area before, but no one, apart from Hargraves, really understood how to produce it from the earth.

In particular, the method of washing for alluvial gold from the river sands was quite unknown in Australia.

Before long, they discovered a water-hole in a creek-bed and Hargraves turned to Lister. "We are now walking over a goldfield," he is reported to have said, and Lister, though scarcely believing him, washed a pan of earth in the creek. Immediately they found traces of gold. Five times they panned, and only one of the five spadefuls of earth proved to be non-gold-bearing!

However, they did not make a great deal of money from their gold discoveries. They returned to Sydney, and Hargraves told the Government of his finds, asking only that they should give him £10,000 as a reward. The Government did as he asked, but also made him Commissioner of the goldfields.

And then the news was made widely known. Immediately gold fever struck Australia, and thousands of fortune-hunters made for the goldfields. Doctors, lawyers, bootblacks, butchers, bakers—thousands threw up their jobs in the towns and joined in the long trek across the Blue Mountains. Some parts of Sydney, such as Parramatta, were completely depopulated. It seemed Sir George Gipp's fears might be justified. It even seemed that life in Sydney would soon

Sir George Gipps was proud of the peaceful pastoral community he governed in New South Wales. It was a pleasant life, without problems, so that when a clergyman by the name of Clarke was shown into his office, he expected no more than the usual pleasantries which were passed at such meetings.

But instead, Clarke silently spread out a piece of cloth on the Governor's desk, and Gipps recoiled in horror at what he saw. Staring dully back at him were several pieces of gold.

Gold! It drove men mad. They turned their lives upside down in their quest for it. They turned towns upside down because of it. Even whole countries could be corrupted by the lust it created for easy fortunes.

"Keep it quiet!" he begged. He knew what temptations it could dangle before the most upright of men. And he could guess how it would affect some of the rough-and-tumble settlers in early Australia.

"Keep it quiet!" he begged the clergyman again. And Clarke did. But for how long could it be kept a secret?

grind to a halt.

That same year, gold was discovered in the Buninyong Ranges near Ballarat, and that was the start of the Victorian gold rush. This goldfield proved immensely rich, for during November of 1851 alone the gold carried from Ballarat to Melbourne by the Government escort weighed 2½ tons, about a third of the total amount raised in the goldfields as a whole.

Revolt

With the discovery of the goldfields, the population of Australia began to increase rapidly. From all over the world, excited prospectors arrived at the diggings, many of them from California, where, far from making their fortunes, they had lost all they had.

As in California, there were many unfortunate stories to be told. One in particular was enacted in Victoria and elsewhere. Diggers were so badly treated by officialdom, especially by the goldfield constables, that eventually the enraged miners rose in revolt.

It was the miner's dream to strike rich—to find just one big nugget of gold which would bring a fortune. But even small nuggets turned out to be few and far between at first. But

imagination was fired when the first big nugget was discovered in New South Wales in July, 1851. Known as the Kerr Hundredweight, this was a block of quartz and gold weighing 2,400 ounces and containing 1,272 ounces of gold.

The Holtermann nugget, also found in New South Wales, was the largest ever discovered, weighing 7,560 ounces and containing about 3,000 ounces of gold. Probably the most famous nugget of all was the *Welcome Stranger*, found near Ballarat in 1858. This was a lump of almost pure gold, weighing well over 2,000 ounces, and with the price of gold at the time between £3 and £4 an ounce, worth about £7,000.

The goldfields have long since dwindled, and now produce very little. The rough and ready, roistering days of the gold rush have gone forever, but a new prosperity based on the rich soil of Victoria has taken its place.

Today, Australia ranks fifth among the gold-producing nations of the world. This is because gold has also been discovered in other states of Australia, notably Queensland, but latterly in the newer goldfields in Western Australia. Here, in the aptly-named "Golden Mile" reef, between the towns of Kalgoorlie and Boulder, are some of the richest gold mines in the world.

Thousands of people had thrown up their town jobs and were trekking across the Blue Mountains in search of fortunes. All of them were in search of the same thing— gold!

Into The Valley Of Death

Six hundred men rode against the enemy at Balaclava in the Crimean War. Most perished before the Russian guns, but their exploit lives on in the immortal verses of Alfred Tennyson

THE soldier had survived the Charge of the Light Brigade, but now he lay ill in the hospital at Scutari, stunned from a kick by a horse. It seemed that nothing could rouse him from his torpor, but the doctor decided to make one last effort. He read him the poem which the Poet Laureate, Alfred Tennyson, had written about the immortal charge, those still famous verses, which include.

> *Their's not to make reply,*
> *Their's not to reason why,*
> *Their's but to do and die :*
> *Into the valley of Death*
> *Rode the six hundred.*

At once the soldier began to stir and, by the time the poem was over, was even sitting up. Soon, he was telling the doctor his account of the charge, and, within a few hours, he was well on the road to recovery. Else-where in the hospital other sur-vivors were asking for copies of the poem. Some were even singing it to their own tunes.

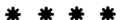

Very few poets in modern times have touched the hearts of ordinary people in this way, but Tennyson did, not in all his poems of course, for some of them were complicated and long, but in many of them. His *Ode on the Death of the Duke of Wellington* touched millions. It sounded like the tramp of marching men in a funeral pro-cession :

> *Bury the Great Duke*
> *With an empire's lamentation*
> *Let us bury the Great Duke*
> *To the noise of the mourning*
> *of a mighty nation.*

This magnificent poem has been called the greatest "poli-tical" or ceremonial poem in English. It can only be ap-preciated if it is realised that the Iron Duke, victor of Waterloo, meant to the Victorians as much as Winston Churchill meant to their grandchildren. "The last great Englishman is low," wrote Tennyson. And even now, who can resist his *The Revenge*, about how the historical Richard Grenville, commanding the ship, took on 53 Spanish vessels and wanted her scuttled rather than surren-dered :

> *Sink me the ship, Master Gunner — sink her, split her in twain!*
> *Fall into the hands of God, not into the hands of Spain!*

After his death in 1892, and after the death in 1901 of one of his warmest admirers, Queen Victoria, a reaction soon set in against Tennyson and, indeed, against all things Victorian. It reached its peak after the First World War, and the poet was accused of sentimentality, shal-low thinking and phoney pat-riotism, an absurd charge to bring against him, for he was simply reflecting the feelings of the people of his own day, which were his feelings also. Now the situation has com-pletely changed. Tennyson's reputation has soared once again, and most of the human

"My watch has stopped," said Tennyson. "What am I to do?" Then a guest arose from his seat and wound the watch up!

mice that tried to fell the mountain that was the poet and his work have already been forgotten.

Tennyson was born into a large Lincolnshire family in 1809 and his life was mainly uneventful. The worst blow he suffered was the loss of a great friend, Arthur Hallam, in 1833. Hallam was one of the most brilliant young men in Britain, and his friend later remembered him in his great poem, *In Memoriam*.

Unlike most poets, Tennyson really looked the part, for in his youth he was as handsome as a film star, in his old age, as striking and dignified as an institution should be. He was very strongly built and loved the country, sport and, above all, literature and poetry.

It took him many years to establish himself, for the critics of his day could be as venomous as vipers, but in 1850 he was Poet Laureate, famous in Britain and America alike.

He was made a baron in 1884. For many years he lived with his wife and family in the Isle of Wight, and it was there that an incident occurred which showed what a simple man he was and how a genius can be so wrapped up in himself that he cannot always cope with everyday life.

One day he came down to breakfast looking very serious indeed, and holding his watch out in front of him.

"My watch has stopped," he announced to all and sundry. "What am I to do?"

There was a deathly hush, then a guest rose solemnly from his seat, took the watch from him, wound it up, and gave it back.

Tennyson was a shy man, though not amongst his friends. He was everything the Victorians asked of a great man and, in the days before radio and televison, his every appearance was liable to cause a sensation.

In 1870, when his friend, Charles Dickens, died, he went to the funeral in Westminster Abbey, then found himself trapped in his seat. Mothers climbed on to seats all around him holding their children aloft so that they could later boast they had seen him; men jostled each other to gaze in awe at him. After the service he had to be rescued from the Abbey.

If Tennyson's place as the people's poet was due to his splendid, simple verse, his claim to greatness lay and lies in his marvellous choice of words. He

was a lord of imaginative language. This shows in long works like *Maud,* and *Idylls of the King* and in shorter pieces like *To Virgil* (the Roman poet). He could salute the great Latin writer in language which matched Virgil's:

Now thy Forum roars no longer,
fallen every purple Caesar's dome —
Though thine ocean-roll of rhythm
sound for ever of Imperial Rome —

And his masterly use of language shows in *Ulysses,* written when he was only 23. Ulysses had been a Greek leader at the siege of Troy and, in the poem, is home on the island of Ithaca again after many adventures on the voyage. He is bored with his life, his dutiful wife, his worthy son, whom he damns with faint praise as "blameless" and "decent." The quiet life is not for Ulysses, who has "drunk delight of battle with my peers

Far on the ringing plains of windy Troy." Shakespeare could not have bettered those last six words. What a picture they conjure up!

Ulysses decides to sail away again, feeling that "Some work of noble note may yet be done, Not unbecoming men that strove with Gods."

"Tis not too late to seek a newer world," he tells his friends. They will sail beyond the sunset, perhaps they will drown, but they may "touch the Happy Isles And see the great Achilles, whom we knew."

Many consider that last line one of the greatest ever written. Any other poet, perhaps even Tennyson, might have been tempted to dwell upon Achilles, the supreme Greek hero at Troy, to recall his deeds. But Tennyson/Ulysses merely says "whom we knew." Such economy is masterly, magical and more imaginative than hundreds of descriptive words.

The poem's last line had a

Survivors of the Charge of the Light Brigade felt their hearts stirring with pride as the doctor read Tennyson's poem about their immortal heroism.

particular appeal to Victorians, for it was a motto for them as well as Ulysses — "To strive, to seek, to find, and not to yield." It serves as well today.

It certainly serves for Tennyson, who died on October 6, 1892. One of the visitors to his bedside raised his hands and said: "Lord Tennyson, God has taken you, who made you a Prince of men." But he was also a man among men, which is why he was understood and loved by so many. No British poet of such stature has appeared since his day, and only Rudyard Kipling has appealed to a mass audience in the same way.

Only in our own day has a poet, Sir John Betjeman, been loved by a mass audience, but no successor has appeared to write about Tennyson as once he wrote about "Roman Virgil."

The DOVER ROAD

WRITTEN AND DRAWN BY
PETER JACKSON

DICKENS COUNTRY

The country between Gravesend and Rochester was loved by Dickens. Many incidents in his novels took place there.

CHALK Where the main road turns off to this village is a ruined cottage. It gave Dickens the idea for Joe Gargery's forge in *Great Expectations*.

In 1836 Dickens married Catherine Hogarth, and they spent their honeymoon in this cottage in the hamlet of Chalk.

Over the porch of Chalk Church is this quaint figure which always amused Dickens. He never went past without raising his hat to it in a friendly greeting.

From the moment when as a boy Dickens visited Gad's Hill Place with his father, he said he wanted to live there.

His father told him that if he worked hard, his wish would come true. And so it did. When he became a successful novelist, he bought it, dying there at the age of 58, in 1870.

BEFORE DICKENS' TIME, GAD'S HILL WAS NOTORIOUS AS A HAUNT OF HIGHWAYMEN AND ROBBERS

400 years before Dickens, another literary figure's work enthralled playhouse audiences. In Shakespeare's play "Henry IV" Part I, he chose Gad's Hill as the place where Prince Hal and Poins disguised themselves as highwaymen and scared the fat Falstaff. Later Falstaff described to them how brayely he had fought. It is said to be one of the funniest scenes in Shakespeare's plays.

In 1676, Nicks Nevison, a highwayman, robbed a gentleman at four o'clock in the morning at the bottom of Gad's Hill and galloped swiftly away.

He crossed the Thames at Gravesend Ferry and rode north at such a pace that by the late afternoon he had managed to reach the city of York.

Hurriedly changing into clean clothes, he made his way to the bowling green and there played a game with the Lord Mayor. Then he deliberately asked the time and was told that it was eight o'clock.

When he was later brought to trial for the robbery in Kent he was able to prove that he was in York playing bowls with the Lord Mayor on the day of the robbery. Nevison was acquitted of the charge.

Charles II suspected the truth and persuaded Nevison to confess to him. Charles was highly amused and gave him the nickname "Swift Nicks."

Years later the writer Harrison Ainsworth used the incident as Dick Turpin's ride to York on Black Bess in his novel "Rookwood."

Twilight of an Empire

As a last humiliation the Indian soldiers had fetters hammered on to their ankles.

THE POWDER KEG

THERE had been the Sikh wars, and now there was to be the Indian Mutiny. As usual, the British had only themselves to blame. Firstly, they had made enemies of the Brahmins, the most highly educated and influential class of Hindus, who had previously ruled the life of the Hindu. Education, law and religion and nearly every kind of business had been in their hands. But recently the influence of European education and a recently established British court of appeal which could rescind their decisions, were breaking down their privileges and power. Their hostility had increased when a new law was passed in 1856, which legalised the remarriage of Hindu widows. The law may have been passed in the spirit of purest benevolence, but to the Brahmins it merely meant that yet another attack had been made on one of their cherished institutions. Intent on causing as much trouble as possible, they began to spread rumours that the Government intended to abolish the caste system as a preliminary step to the forcible conversion of all natives to the Christian religion.

The native army, too, was becoming hostile to the British. A vast number of the more efficient British officers had been removed, and most of those who remained were either too old or had been worn out by the climate. The native army, too, had suddenly become conscious that they outnumbered their white comrades in arms in the ratio of six to one.

A fuse had been laid to a keg of gunpowder. All that was needed was the spark to set it off.

The spark was provided by the British themselves.

In 1857, the military authorities decided to introduce the Enfield rifle, which needed a greased cartridge with a top to it, which had to be bitten off by its user before loading. Rumours began to circulate that the cartridge grease was composed of beef fat and hog lard, the use of which would have defiled any Mohammedan and made a Hindu lose caste. More rumours followed. It was the intention, it was whispered in the bazaars, to reduce India's manhood to a common state of defilement by making him use the bullet. Then every Indian would be forced to turn Christian at the cannon's mouth. It was also rumoured that thousands of soldiers were on their way from England to enforce this conversion.

Although these rumours were obviously ridiculous, there was no doubt that many well meaning but ill-advised missionaries had indirectly contributed to the rumours by over zealously extolling their own religion, while violently condemning the Hindu and Mohammedan beliefs. Such fanatical behaviour must have seemed to an equally fanatical people, to be the prelude to a wholesale conversion to the Christian religion.

But it was the bullet which did the real damage.

Tide of fury

On 24th April, 85 soldiers of the 3rd Native Cavalry, while on parade at Meerut, refused to accept the greased bullet. A Court of Inquiry was convened which decreed that the troopers must be court-martialled for mutiny. The Court which finally sat in judgement saw no reason for leniency, and the troopers were given sentences from between five to ten years' hard labour. Incredible as it might seem, they could perhaps count themselves as lucky; two stiff necked officers of the court had asked for the death penalty.

But the army was not finished with them yet. At dawn on 9th May, the prisoners were brought out barefoot on parade to receive their sentences. After these had been read out, their buttons were ripped from their uniforms, and the uniforms themselves ripped up the back by bayonets. The final humiliation was yet to come. Standing there with their uniforms in shreds the prisoners had to suffer the degradation of having fetters hammered on to their ankles. It was too much for these poor troopers who had once been proud to serve the British. Frantically they began to call for help to their comrades, the sepoys (Indian troops) of the 20th Native Infantry, who could only stand there and weep silently for the prisoners.

Let us now move on to the evening of 10th May, that brief hour before sunset when the long shadows of the later afternoon made it possible for the British to venture out of their homes. Nothing could have been more peaceful that evening, as the ladies and their officers went out for their weekly Sunday promenade. There was a band playing, as it had always done, and as usual, the area around the bandstand was full of gallant officers anxiously looking after the wants of the eligible young spinsters, who sat listening to the current favourites of the time. In the native bazaar, things were somewhat different. In this stifling warren of alleyways, the sepoys were bitterly discussing the fate of the comrades languishing in jail. Suddenly, their anger, already close to boiling point, could no longer be contained. A party of troopers started off, shouting: "To horse, brothers. To the jail!" Within minutes, others had appeared as if from nowhere, to join the ever growing tide. By the time it had reached the jail, the band of rebels had reached 200. Freeing their 85 comrades, the mob moved on to the civil prison and freed a further 720 prisoners.

Orgy of murder

By then the army had been joined by all the criminal elements of the bazaars. Howling like demented dervishes, the mob went on its way, killing looting and burning, turning Meerut into a city of terror and horror for the 2,028 Europeans living there. In the orgy of murder and destruction that took place, no one was spared, from the Colonel of the Native Infantry, who fell from his horse under a hail of bullets, to innocent women and children who were dragged from their homes and butchered in the streets.

Then as quickly as it had flared up, the violence petered out. It was almost as if sanity had suddenly returned to a group of lunatics who had found themselves standing with bloodstained hands, amid scenes of hideous carnage of their own making. Aghast at what they had done, the sepoys began to flee from the city in small groups. All of them were heading for Delhi, where there lived the one man who might help them—Mohammed Bahadur Shah, last of the Moghul Emperors.

The mutineers and their supporters stormed the jail and freed 85 of their comrades.

Above: The band played and the gallant officers looked after the ladies.

Lines from the Rubáiyát of OMAR KHAYYÁM

translated by EDWARD FITZGERALD

Awake! for Morning in the Bowl of Night
Has flung the Stone that puts the Stars to flight;
And lo! the Hunter of the East has caught
The Sultan's Turret in a Noose of Light.

Here with a Loaf of Bread beneath the Bough,
A Flask of Wine, a Book of Verse—and Thou
Beside me singing in the Wilderness—
And Wilderness is Paradise enow.

The Worldly Hope men set their Hearts upon
Turns Ashes—or it prospers; and anon,
Like Snow upon the Desert's dusty Face
Lighting a little Hour or two—is gone.

The Moving Finger writes; and having writ,
Moves on: nor all thy Piety nor Wit
Shall lure it back to cancel half a Line,
Nor all thy Tears wash out a Word of it.

POEM in the PENNY BOX

It was written in the Persian sunshine eight hundred years ago—and a trick of fate preserved it for us to enjoy today

A HUNDRED years or so ago, it lay in a dusty bookshop, one of many volumes which had reached the saddest of fates, for the ticket above it said "All in this box, one penny."

And there it might have remained, lost and forgotten forever. But the man who picked it up was the famous poet and painter Dante Gabriel Rosetti. He read some of the pages and was greatly moved by them. And in that way, the Rubáiyát of Omar Khayyám was saved from oblivion.

Generations of people have since enjoyed the colourful romantic verses of this ancient Persian poet who asked so many questions about life.

Who was Omar Khayyám? Khayyám means "tent maker," and it is likely that this was the trade of his father. But for Omar, born towards the end of the eleventh century, there were much greater things in store.

He became a mathematician and an astronomer, and was eventually recognized by the Sultan as one of the country's greatest men.

But why a poet? It is said that Omar's studies of the heavens caused him to think very deeply about the universe around him, about life itself and the way in which it should be lived.

He expressed his thoughts in the *Rubáiyát*. This Persian word is the plural of *rubai*, meaning a verse of four lines in which the first two and the fourth lines rhyme. It is known in English as a *quatrain*.

Translator

THEN, across the years, we come to Edward FitzGerald, born in Woodbridge, Suffolk, in 1809. He became a friend of poets and a poet himself, but of no particular fame.

It was his poetic skill plus his knowledge of languages which led him to be a translator of poems—and one has to be a poet to achieve any success in that field; word-for-word translation is not enough if rhyme and rhythm are to be achieved.

So this quiet man came upon the writings of Omar Khayyám in Arabic, and managed to express in English—and in the self-same quatrains—the thoughts and philosophy of one who had mused on life in the Persian sunshine eight hundred years before.

The poems were published and, as we would say today, they flopped—until the moment when Rosetti paused in the bookshop at the notice which said, "All in this box, one penny."

Omar Khayyám was saved from obscurity, so far as the Western world was concerned. Before FitzGerald died in 1883 he had the satisfaction of seeing his work reprinted in four editions.

Now you, in your generation, can come under the spell of Omar.

Reasons for the Rhymes

THEY PLAYED THE FOOL AT GOTHAM

Three wise men of Gotham,
They went to sea in a bowl,
And if the bowl had been stronger
My song had been longer.

If the cuckoo stays, so does summer, said the men of Gotham, according to the legend. So they built a fence to keep it from flying away.

THE legend has been for centuries that the earlier inhabitants of Gotham, a village not far from Nottingham, were fools. But were they?

Did they, for example, once build a fence around the village to prevent the cuckoo from flying away, so that they could enjoy perpetual summer?

No, say those who deny the legend, what the villagers did was to prevent King John from passing through the village, because if he had done, his route would ever afterwards be a public highway, which they did not want.

The king was angry and decided to send his men to find out why they did it. The villagers knew that they were likely to suffer severe punishment, so they prepared for the arrival of the king's men, who were amazed to find them all behaving like idiots.

They reported back to the king that the men of Gotham could not be held responsible for their actions, so no punishment followed. So, as we would say today, the men of Gotham were not so dumb!

A manuscript of the middle fifteenth century gives the first known mention of "the folies of gotyam."

King John decided to ride through the village—but the inhabitants thought otherwise.

KNOW YOUR WORDS

RUNNER

Simple words often develop a wide range of meanings that is fascinating. One example is *runner*, derived from the basic English word run (from *rinnan* in the old Gothic languages).

Even when referring to a person, it has a variety of meanings. A runner can be someone taking part in a race, or a fugitive fleeing from pursuit; a messenger (particularly in olden times) or an errand boy. The early English police officers were known as *Bow Street Runners*, after their London headquarters. Yet in compounds the same word can mean a smuggler, e.g., *gun-runner*.

Botanically, a runner can be a slender stem of a plant like a strawberry, that grows along the ground putting out roots. On the other hand we have *runner beans*, with swift-growing stems that twine upwards.

A sledge has runners on which to slide over the snow, and a drawer has runners on which to slip in and out. A *table runner*, however, is an embroidered strip of cloth which extends the length of the table top.

A *runner-up* is the competitor who takes second place to the winner. This term came from dog-racing, and seems originally to have described those dogs which ran fast enough to take part in the final heat.

Hunter with a difference—a bull moose, with antlers in their full glory looks suspiciously at the crouching photographer and his cine-camera

Mr. MOOSE SEEKS PROTECTION

Hunters depleted these largest living members of the deer family to such an extent that they are now mostly found only in Alaska, safeguarded by the game laws there

IN Europe, we call it the elk, in North America it is the moose, but either way it is the largest living member of the deer family. Sometimes growing to a height of seven feet, and maybe weighing more than 1,000 lb., the male, or bull, moose has a set of antlers which is second to none.

The antlers are curious in that they branch out from the side of the head, and grow sideways rather than forwards. They do not reach full size until the moose is eight or nine years old; then they may be as much as five feet across from tip to tip. Each January the adult moose sheds its antlers, and the new pair are not fully grown until August.

Other points which make the moose easy to recognize are its long and thin-looking legs, a strange pouch of skin, called the "bell," which hangs from the throat, and a drooping muzzle which gives the moose the appearance of having a very Roman nose.

The female (cow) moose in winter has a lighter-coloured coat than the bull, whose long, coarse hair varies in shade from dark brown to a dirty grey. The coats of both the bull and the cow are finer during the summer months.

At one time moose were quite common anywhere between the north part of the United States and the north of Canada, but ruthless hunters killed them in such numbers that the herds decreased at an alarming rate. In New Brunswick alone it was said that on one shoot hundreds of moose were killed, stripped of their hides (for leather), and then left to rot.

Winter Yard

As a result, moose became scarce in many areas, and are now mostly found in Alaska, where they are protected by game laws. On the whole they tend to remain in the more deserted areas, in summer on marshy ground or near rivers and lakes, in winter among the forests on higher ground. Despite their size, moose can move swiftly and almost silently through these wooded areas.

During the snows of winter they make their homes in a "moose-yard." Each family of moose, normally a bull, a cow, and two seasons' fawns, trample down the deep snow to make the winter yard, in a part of the country where there is

enough food, in the form of trees like the birch, the maple and the fir.

In the summer, when they like to wade into rivers and lakes to feed on the water plants there, the fawns are born. The bulls fight fiercely for the cows in the mating season, and can be highly dangerous. Many hunters find targets for their guns by "moose-calling"; by imitating the sound of the cow's call they attract any bull moose in the area. Calves are born in May, in some very secluded spot, and the cow will turn savagely on any intruder, even attacking men if she thinks they are too near her fawns.

As soon as dawn appears, moose begin feeding, breaking off to rest when the sun is up, then feeding for an hour or so around midday. Another rest in the afternoon, a feed in the evening, and then they lie down for the night.

Moose generally lie facing away from the direction of the wind, so that the scent or sound of approaching danger is carried on the wind.

WHEN THE RED MAN RODE

written and illustrated by R. S. Embleton

◇◇

THE CHEYENNE

THEY have been called "the fiercest light cavalry in the world." To them war was the greatest game of all. No tribe fought more ferociously to retain its way of life—the Cheyenne way....

When the Spaniards colonised the south-west in the 16th century they introduced into North America an animal that was to change the way of life of the Indians of the Great Plains completely. For the first time the red man came into contact with the horse. At first it appeared to them as a monstrous beast, charging into battle carrying the iron-clad Conquistadors and trampling them underfoot. But in time the Indians realised the true value of the animal, and Comanche and Apache raiders drove off Spanish horses to trade with the Indians of the Great Plains. The horse became the most valuable of all currencies, to be traded, stolen or displayed as a symbol of courage and status. In time, as stray horses multiplied and roamed the prairies in their wild herds, man and horse became inseparable.

Long before the white man came to North America the Cheyenne lived in what is now Minnesota. They were farmers, and the only domesticated animal they knew was the dog. Each village had its pack of snarling mongrels that yapped and barked out a warning at the approach of strangers. In winter they were harnessed to sledges and in summer they hauled the belongings of the tribe on travois. For the most part they were left to forage for themselves and lived a pariah-like existence on the fringes of the camp.

At the end of the 17th century the Cheyenne crossed the Missouri River and wandered on to the Great Plains. There they came into contact with two influences that changed them from farmers and pottery makers into nomadic hunters. The first influence was the buffalo. Millions of these huge, shaggy beasts wandered the prairies, their herds blackening the landscape for miles. To the Plains Indians the buffalo was the very source of life. Weapons, food, clothing and shelter—all were provided by the buffalo. The second influence was the horse. With this animal, hunting the buffalo was made easy. By the beginning of the 19th century the Cheyenne had forgotten their old way of life and were famous both as warriors and horsemen. Their culture was totally dependent on the buffalo.

Life for the Cheyenne warrior was one of elaborate ceremony and ritual. Even warfare with his traditional enemies, the Crow and the Pawnee, was ritualised, and an elaborate set of rules governed behaviour in combat. Display of bravery was the most important activity in battle and scoring off the enemy was more important than killing him. The scoring was known as "counting coup"—touching or striking an enemy with hand or weapon. Killing and scalping the foe was considered a brave deed, but a man's rank as a warrior depended on his total score of coups, and a Cheyenne warrior would risk life and limb to charge into an enemy camp and touch his living enemy. Any warrior could lead a war party provided his courage in battle would induce other warriors to follow him,

and in this way the great War Chiefs of the Cheyenne won their reputations.

Eagle feathers were prized as decoration by the Cheyenne warriors and were extremely valuable. Thirty eagle feathers could be traded for a fine horse. The eagle had to be caught by hand and only a few warriors had the mystical powers and knowledge of the eagle-catching ritual. First a pit was dug and roofed with grass. The warrior then chanted the sacred eagle songs and purified himself in a sweat bath. He then anointed his body with eagle grease and climbed into the pit just before dawn. Across the top of the pit was a pole with meat wrapped around it for bait. The eagle catcher then began his vigil, waiting patiently for the bird to swoop out of the sky to take the bait. When the eagle alighted he slipped his hands through the grass and grabbed the eagle's feet above its terrible talons. The bird was then killed with a noose of rawhide. Afterwards the warrior made an offering to the dead eagle and again purified himself, basking in the admiration of his village.

Within the framework of the tribe the Cheyenne warriors were divided into five Military Societies, the Coyote, Elk, Shield, Dog and Bowstring. Each society had its own rituals and ceremonies and distinguishing dress. When a boy was ready

to go on the war path he first sought membership in one of the Societies. No Society was higher in official status than another, but their popularity and prestige depended upon their current achievements. If the Elk soldiers had won success in battle then their elk hoof rattles would be a much coveted status symbol for the young warrior. If the Coyote soldiers were favourites then their yellow and black war paint would be the desired badge of courage.

Until the 1850s the Cheyenne were entirely friendly toward the whites, and in September, 1851, they attended the Great Council at Fort Laramie where 10,000 Plains Indians signed an agreement with the United States Government and agreed to accept the territorial boundaries laid down in the treaties. But the United States was expanding fast. Settlers were pouring westwards. Pony Express Stations were established to link the Western frontier with the East and soldiers built forts to protect the wagon train routes. The confused Indians listened as glib negotiators altered treaties and made further promises and they watched as their lands were eaten away.

In 1859 gold was discovered in Colorado and miners began to pour into the territory. The Indians retaliated and mining camps and Pony

CONTINUED ON NEXT PAGE

Two Cheyenne warriors. For many centuries they fought on foot, until in the early 18th century they discovered the horse. Later they became superb cavalrymen.

Express Stations were attacked. Black Kettle, Chief of the Cheyenne, tried hard to preserve the peace. He brought his people into Sand Creek, north of Fort Lyon, and flew the Stars and Stripes over his tipi to show his loyalty. At dawn on 29th November, 1864, a band of Colorado Volunteers under Colonel J. M. Chivington attacked the Cheyenne camp.

Many reasons have been given for the attack, hatred of the Indians by the Colorado miners, a deliberate attempt to start an Indian war so that the Colorado Volunteers would not be drawn into the Civil War that was now tearing the Eastern United States apart. Whatever the reasons the attack was a cold-blooded massacre that brought condemnation from even the hardest frontiersmen. Cheyenne men, women and children were indiscriminately killed. Black Kettle managed to escape and the entire frontier erupted in warfare. Apache, Kiowa, Comanche, Sioux and Cheyenne took to the warpath and Colorado territory was entirely cut off from communication with the East. A campaign under General W. S. Hancock failed to defeat the Plains Indians and in 1868 young George Armstrong Custer took the field with the 7th Cavalry.

In November, 1868, Black Kettle was camped along the frozen Washita River. It was a hard winter and the snow lay inches thick across the prairie. As the sky began to lighten, the still air was shattered by the sound of bugles and Custer's 7th Cavalry came charging into the village, rifles crashing and sabres swinging. The Indians were taken completely by surprise. Black Kettle and over a hundred warriors were killed.

For the next 10 years the United States Army fought engagement after engagement to subdue

In the winter of 1868, Black Kettle's band was camped along the Washita River. One November dawn the camp was attacked by Custer's 7th Cavalry. The Indians were taken by surprise and many were killed, including women and children.

The buffalo gave food, shelter and clothing to the Cheyenne and the other Plains Indians; in fact, it was the very source of life for them. Hunting it became an easy sport when the Cheyenne acquired horses, but when the white man decimated the great herds almost to the point of extinction, the way of life of the Indians was doomed.

the wild Plains tribes. The Indian stood in the path of progress—there was no room for him any more.

In 1865 the construction gangs of the Union Pacific and the Kansas Pacific Railroads began to inch their way across the Great Plains. Thousands of Irish immigrants set out to lay a mile of track per working day and the steel rails began to eat their way into the prairies. The Iron Horse was sounding the death knell for the Cheyenne.

In 1870, leather factories in the East offered high prices for buffalo hides. Before this date there had been a steady demand for buffalo hides, but a dried bull hide weighed 40 or 50 pounds and was as stiff as a board. It was difficult to transport. The coming of the railways eliminated these difficulties and buffalo hides were at a premium. Buffalo hunters descended upon the herds and began to slaughter them in their thousands.

From 1872 to 1882 the buffalo hides were shipped eastwards at the rate of a million a year

until the prairies were littered with bleached bones and rotting carcasses. Enterprising white men discovered that the bones were worth five dollars a ton, and in 1874, the Santa Fe Railroad transported 3,500 tons of bones to the fertilizer factories in the East. The buffalo had been the life blood of the Indians. In one fateful decade the countless millions were reduced to a mere handful. Cheyenne Dog soldiers derailed the trains and attacked the buffalo hunters but now they were fighting for survival against hopeless odds.

In 1877, exhausted by the long years of war, bands of Cheyenne, who, with their allies the Sioux had defeated Custer the previous year at the Little Big Horn, began surrendering to the United States Army. General Crook held a Council with the Cheyenne and they agreed to give up their lands and remove to the reservations in Oklahoma. The new territory was far removed from their own hunting grounds. There were no buffalo, and game of any description was scarce. The Indians had to depend on the Indian Agency to supply Texas cattle for food.

Sickness and apathy overtook the Cheyenne and they began to yearn for their own lands and their old way of life. In July, 1878, 300 Cheyenne, men, women and children, under the leadership of Dull Knife, left the reservation to "go home." The gruelling march was one long, running fight.

For six months the little band outwitted the thousands of soldiers sent out to bring them in. Through blizzard and storm they struggled against overwhelming odds to reach their hunting grounds. On 18th January, 1879, less than half of them reached the Platte River and there surrendered to Lieutenant W. P. Clark. Thanks to the good offices of General Crook who petitioned the Government on their behalf they were given a reservation on the Tongue River and allowed to stay. There their descendants still live proudly as the Northern Cheyenne. They maintain close contact with the others of their tribe in Oklahoma, the equally proud Southern Cheyenne. In the days of their glory, no Indians were more respected by the whites than "the fighting Cheyennes."

HIAWATHA

by HENRY WADSWORTH LONGFELLOW

HIAWATHA, son of the West Wind, is sent by Gitche Manito, the Great Spirit, to teach and toil with the Red Indian tribes.

The boy is brought up by old Nokomis, his grandmother, a daughter of the Moon. He learns the language of the birds and animals.

When he reaches manhood, Hiawatha learns that his father, the West Wind, deserted his mother. Resolved to avenge her, he journeys to the kingdom of the West Wind.

For three days Hiawatha fights his father, but at last the West Wind explains he is immortal. For Hiawatha's valour the West Wind promises that when his son dies he can share his kingdom. Meanwhile, Hiawatha must go home and help his people.

For seven days Hiawatha fasts to get the blessing of Mondamin, the friend of man, for his people. Afterwards he wrestles with Mondamin, who dies. From his grave sprouts up maize.

Then Hiawatha builds the first canoe and clears the river. He kills the giant fish that terrorizes the lake.

His grandmother asks him to kill the magician, Pearl-Feather, sender of fog. Hiawatha shoots with arrows the serpents guarding the magician and finally kills Pearl-Feather with three more arrows.

Hiawatha marries Minnehaha, Laughing Water, beautiful daughter of the Arrowmaker. At night his bride walks round the maize fields, protecting the harvest with magic circles.

Hiawatha invents picture-writing for his people. But misfortunes fall upon him. The evil spirits kill both his friends. Ghosts visit his wigwam, and famine comes to the land.

Hiawatha calls upon Gitche Manito to help as Laughing Water lies dying of hunger, but in vain. His wife dies. Heartbroken, Hiawatha remains only to welcome those who bring the news of Jesus. Then he launches his birch canoe and sails into the sunset.

NOW READ BELOW EXTRACTS FROM THIS WONDERFUL POEM

By the shores of Gitche Gumee,
By the shining Big-Sea-Water,
Stood the wigwam of Nokomis,
Daughter of the Moon, Nokomis.

There the wrinkled, old Nokomis
Nursed the little Hiawatha,
Rocked him in his linden cradle,
Bedded soft in moss and rushes,
Safely bound with reindeer sinews.

Out of childhood into manhood
Now had grown my Hiawatha,
Skilled in all the craft of hunters,
Learned in all the lore of old men,
In all youthful sports and pastimes,
In all manly arts and labours.

"Wed a maiden of your people,"
Warning said the old Nokomis;
"Go not eastward, go not westward,
For a stranger whom we know not!"

Smiling answered Hiawatha:
"In the land of the Dacotahs
Lives the Arrow-maker's daughter,
Minnehaha, Laughing Water,
Handsomest of all the women.
I will bring her to your wigwam,
She shall run upon your errands,
Be your starlight, moonlight, firelight,
Be the sunlight of my people!"

*　　　　*

At the doorway of his wigwam
Sat the ancient Arrow-maker. . . .
At his side, in all her beauty,
Sat the lovely Minnehaha. . . .
Suddenly from out the woodlands
Hiawatha stood before them.

Straight the ancient Arrow-maker
Looked up gravely from his labour,
Laid aside the unfinished arrow,

Bade him enter at the doorway,
Saying, as he rose to meet him,
"Hiawatha, you are welcome!"

"After many years of warfare,
Many years of strife and bloodshed,
There is peace between the Ojibways
And the tribe of the Dacotahs."
Thus continued Hiawatha,
And then added, speaking slowly,
"That this peace may last for ever,
And our hands be clasped more closely,
And our hearts be more united,
Give me as my wife this maiden,
Minnehaha, Laughing Water,
Loveliest of Dacotah women!"

*　　　　*

This was Hiawatha's wooing!
Thus it was he won the daughter
Of the ancient Arrow-maker,
In the land of the Dacotahs!

Pleasant was the journey homeward,
Through interminable forests,
Over meadow, over mountain,
Over river, hill, and hollow.

Over wide and rushing rivers
In his arms he bore the maiden;
Light he thought her as a feather,
As the plume upon his head-gear.

Thus it was they journeyed homeward;
Thus it was that Hiawatha
To the lodge of old Nokomis
Brought the moonlight, starlight, firelight,
Brought the sunshine of his people,
Minnehaha, Laughing Water,
Handsomest of all the women
In the land of the Dacotahs,
In the land of handsome women.

POET FROM THE PINEWOODS

LONG after the Americans won their independence from Britain they remained dependent on this country for their cultural needs.

No one in Britain ever possibly imagined that there could be any such person as a *gentleman* in America. In Europe everyone was quite sure that all Americans were woodsmen and labourers—raw-boned, thick-skinned and not very well educated.

And as for a Yankee writing a book, or some verse—why, surely the fellows couldn't actually write, could they?

Gradually, however, some Americans began to get tired of always depending on Europe. They wanted to write, too, and they wanted to write about their own young country.

James Fenimore Cooper wrote novels about American wars and American Indians and about their wide open rolling country. And Henry Wadsworth Longfellow did the same as Cooper—but in sparkling rhythmic verse.

In his many poems Longfellow revealed himself as a writer of emotion and sentiment. Most of his poems tell wonderful stories for it was as a storyteller in rhyme that he really excelled.

Longfellow was born in Portland, Maine. By the time he was twenty-two he was a professor of modern languages.

A brilliant enough start to any young life, but tragedy was to come. For not long after he had married a childhood girl-friend she died suddenly.

Longfellow threw himself into his studies and his work of teaching languages at college. And wandering among the oaks and elms near his home he dreamed of the tales of past Americans and stopped only to write them down in verse.

When at last he published a volume of these verses he was famous at once. Then, realizing that the dreamings of a poet and the responsibilities of a college professor did not mix he made his choice—and resigned his professorship.

Unfettered now by academic matters, Longfellow captured the smell of pinewood and wigwam smoke and turned it into pulsating verse—*Hiawatha, Evangeline* and *The Courtship of Miles Standish* are three of his most famous poems.

Unhappiness never seemed far from this happy, brilliant poet. One day, when he was writing verse in his study, his second wife was badly burned in an accident before the fire of their sitting-room. Next day she died.

TAMING OF THE WEST

The West's worst years of crime were from 1867-1900. Murderous outlaws, thieves and unemployed cowboys lurked in the hills and plains between the Mississippi River and the Pacific Ocean. They were men who had been taught from youth to kill in self-defence against Indians and enemy armies, and who now used their guns for personal gain.
How did the peace officers of the West go about their stupendous task of bringing law to this vast territory?

1. At first street fights were common among quarrelsome cowboys in the small towns of North Texas and Kansas. Marshals dealt with these outbreaks the same way as they started—with blazing guns. Such fights generally meant the death of someone, even the marshal himself. But when, one day in 1875, "Big Clay" Allison from Colorado set out to tame the peace officers of Dodge City, Kansas, he found them ready and waiting. As Allison strode into Front Street he was confronted by Marshal Wyatt Earp, while from the doorways the guns of Deputy-Marshal Charlie Bassett and others covered him. Earp had his gun out and pressed into Allison's ribs before the big man could draw. Allison got out of town fast.

2. To prevent such fights, most marsh decided to forbid anyone to wear gun town. When Earp rounded a corner Dodge to find an army sergeant wearing his guns, the remedy was br With one hand he yanked away the gu with the other slapped the man's fa

6. Marshals and deputies of Dodge were paid 2.50 dollars an arrest by the town council, sharing the money out of a pool. When criminals fled a town, the sheriff of the county concerned would call together a posse of peace officers, deputies and willing, honest citizens who would ride in pursuit.

7. It was the sheriff's job to keep local jails in order and produce prisoners for court. Occasionally he might even have to guard his prisoners from the wrath of local people. In 1887 Bat Masterson sat all night with drawn guns in a Fort Worth cell to protect murderer Luke Short from the mob outside.

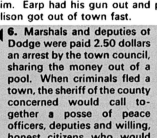

10. Bat Masterson always preferred to stop a quarrel before it started. He never arrested a man unless trouble was already under way. He managed to talk Jesse James, the cold-blooded young killer and robber, out of a row in the Long Branch saloon at Dodge. Jesse and his brother Frank had picked the quarrel when Bat coolly interfered.

Jesse, who had been terrorizing Clay County, Kentucky, since he was seventeen, actually listened to the Kansas peace officer and refrained from killing anyone on the spot.

One way of settling an argument without bullets was "buffaloing." The marshal simply struck the troublemaker over the head with a gun-butt or barrel, dazing him.

4. "Bat" Masterson, elegant deputy at Dodge and later sheriff of Ford County, "buffaloed" his prisoners with the cane he always carried. Later, citizens of Dodge presented Bat with a golden cane for his services to their town.

5. It was not only tough gunmen with whom the peace officers had to deal—there were law-breaking women, too, who had been taught to shoot as straight as any man. Gun-girl Calamity Jane (above), later wife of Marshal Bill Hickock of Abilene, liked nothing better in the way of fun than shooting out the mirrors and windows of saloon bars with her six-shooter. There was even a woman rustler, Belle Starr, who ran her own outfit in Indian territory, Oklahoma, and served six months' imprisonment for her crimes before she was finally murdered in 1889 by an unknown enemy as she rode along a lonely track.

8. Many cities had no proper courts, and their peace officers had to travel some distance to find a judge. Dodge did not get its own court until 1875. Even then the court was a very informal affair.

Judge Joe Frost of Dodge had to issue orders that anyone throwing "turnips, cigar stumps or old quids of chewing tobacco" in court would be thrown out. And when horse-thief James Martin went berserk in court and broke both windows and railings, the judge simply fined him ten dollars on the spot.

9. Not all matters were taken to court. Many lawmen administered their own rough justice. When Annie McDouglas, seventeen, and Jennie Stevens, sixteen, known as "Cattle Annie" and "Little Britches," ran away to join the Doolins outlaw gang in Oklahoma, it was Marshal Bill Tilghman's job to help bring them back. He caught up with Jennie and spanked her until, sobbing, she agreed to go home.

11. By 1877 crime was rising to such a peak that the peace officers of the West could no longer cope, whatever method they chose. Rustling and horse-stealing (above) were becoming too widespread for local lawmen to deal with alone. Frequent, well-organized train robberies by outlaw gangs like the James brothers or the Daltons lost the railroad companies thousands of dollars. These gangs were adept at flagging down a train at night (above left), leaping aboard and ransacking the mail-van and often killing the crew in the process. Bank hold-ups were carried out brazenly in broad daylight (left) and almost every day, somewhere, a stage-coach was robbed of its precious box of bullion by a gang of masked men (right), who left injured or dead guards and passengers behind them. And so gradually other help had to be brought in, to break the crime wave.

The Dream That Came True

So that his works could be performed on a grand scale, Richard Wagner had a burning ambition to build a theatre of his own

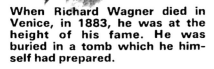

THE MAKE-BELIEVE WORLD OF LUDWIG II

When he was about to begin his studies at university, Ludwig, the eldest son of Maximillan II, found that he had become the new king of Bavaria. His reign was a troubled one and was not made any smoother by his patronage of the arts. His generosity to the composer Richard Wagner was almost limitless and this, together with his passion for building castles, like the one at Neuschwanstein, (pictured below) aroused the wrath of the government. Matters finally came to a head and Ludwig was declared insane. His uncle took over the regency on 10th June, 1886. Ludwig was taken to Berg, accompanied by his doctor. A few days later the two of them went for a walk from which they did not return. Ludwig had drowned in a lake and the doctor perished attempting to rescue him.

SOME composers have been brilliant pianists such as Mozart, Liszt and Rachmaninoff. Others have been average and some have been downright poor. Into the latter class we can put Richard Wagner. Perhaps it does not really matter for he wrote nothing for the piano, but it is interesting to think how somebody with so little practical skill at the keyboard could have achieved so much in the realm of music.

For Wagner was no minor composer. He was probably the most influential writer of operas (or music dramas as he liked to style them) there has ever been. His influence spread far wider than the musical world. It was felt in every other art during the nineteenth century.

Wagner was first and foremost a man of the theatre. His brother and sisters were opera singers, so the theatre was in his blood. Moreover music without drama seemed to mean little to him.

We must remember that in the first half of the nineteenth century Germany was a mass of independent kingdoms which were only loosely connected with each other.

Even the smallest of the states would have its own theatre complete with a staff of actors and musicians. It was therefore not too difficult for a man of talent to get work as a conductor in these theatres.

Although a poor pianist, Wagner was an excellent conductor and organiser and his ambitions were not limited to conducting in the theatres of provincial Germany. He wanted to be a composer and his compositions were far from ordinary.

Wagner conceived his operas on a large scale. Five hours is a common length for one of his works. They were certainly not the sort of entertainment that went down well with an audience who had done a hard day's work and wanted a little relaxation.

Another problem was that the forces he required were huge. The orchestra was vastly expanded and the operas required an immense amount of money to be spent on the production side.

In 1848 revolutions swept the whole of Germany. People with opinions which did not support the existing governments were suspect and Wagner, who had written arti-

When Richard Wagner died in Venice, in 1883, he was at the height of his fame. He was buried in a tomb which himself had prepared.

cles criticising the established rulers, was obliged to flee the country with a price on his head.

Although he was eventually allowed to return to Germany, in 1861, Wagner did not find the going easy. Even a simple opera is an extremely expensive art to mount for it requires singers, chorus and orchestra — not to mention scenery and costumes. Theatre managers were reluctant to take a chance on wildly extravagant new works of a man with a doubtful political background.

Strange Castles

But eventually Wagner's luck changed for he found a friend in Ludwig II who, at the age of eighteen, had just come to the throne of Bavaria. He was, if not exactly mad, as he was later alleged to have been, an odd person. He built a series of strange and wonderful castles, to his own ideas. One such castle, the Neuschwanstein, was perched on the edge of a cliff and was decorated inside with scenes from Wagner's operas.

His passion for Wagner's music seemed limitless. He called the composer to his capital, Munich, where there was a very good opera house which could stage his elaborate works without difficulty.

Wagner was now in the lucky position where no expense was spared in the performance of his operas. The king sometimes had performances of Wagner's works put on at which he was the sole audience.

But as with all fairy tales there had to be an end. The Bavarians were fond of their king despite his foibles but the great amount of money spent on Wagner and his operas naturally raised a great deal of opposition.

Also Wagner, who had opinions on everything as well as music, tried to interfere with the government. So once again he was driven out of Germany and made his home in Switzerland. But he still had the support and friendship of the king and this made possible the continued performance and publication of his works.

Eventually Ludwig raised enough money to enable Wagner to build an opera house to his own designs and exclusively for the performance of his own operas in a small town in Bavaria called Bayreuth. Here annual performances of Wagner's operas take place.

What happened to Ludwig? He was eventually declared mad and his uncle took over. He was taken to a country residence and he drowned himself in the nearby lake. But even today Ludwig II is still remembered by Bavarians with affection nearly one hundred years after his death.

Wagner's dream of having his operas performed in a theatre designed by the composer himself was finally realised when the opera house at Bayreuth was opened in 1876 with a production of *The Ring.* Although the opera was a great success it was also very costly to stage and it was not until six years later that the theatre was able to open its doors again. This time the opera performed was Wagner's *Parsifal.* Today, Bayreuth has become a mecca for all those who love Wagner's music and every year thousands of people flock to the town to hear performances of such operas as *Tristan and Isolde,* a scene from which is pictured below.

The Return of the Ring

Siegfried, whose memory of the past has been completely destroyed by a magic potion brewed by Hagen, the half brother of King Gunther, has just been warned by the Rhine maidens that he is doomed unless he returns to them the magic ring which is rightfully theirs. Siegfried refuses, and a few minutes later he is attacked by Hagen, who casts a spear which strikes Siegfried down.

Gloating, Hagen ran forward and snatched the spear from Siegfried's lifeless body. " All my plans have come about," he cried. " It was my magic potion which made him forget Brunhilde, my words that made Brunhilde agree to his death." Suddenly he heard a sound behind him, and turning he saw that Brunhilde and Gunther together with some of the court were standing there, their eyes filled with disbelieving horror.

" I understand all now," cried Brunhilde, rushing to Siegfried's side. " You knew not what you were doing when you renounced me. It was the curse of the ring, working through Hagen which has brought us both to this! " Gunther came forward then and gently aided Brunhilde to her feet. " I promise you that Hagen will pay dearly for this. But first we must give Siegfried a warrior's burial."

On Gunther's orders, Siegfried was placed on a warrior's shield, and then carried in procession to the banks of the river Rhine. There a funeral pyre was made and Siegfried's body was placed upon it. A torch was applied, and as the flames rose high into the sky, Brunhilde suddenly rode forward on her horse. " Siegfried, my beloved," she cried, " I come to join you." And with those words, she rode straight into the flames.

A few seconds later a great wave rose out of the river, carrying upon its crest the three Rhine Maidens. When the waters receded all those present saw that they had taken with them the bodies of Brunhilde and Siegfried.

Suddenly, one of the Rhine Maidens rose from the waters, triumphantly holding the ring in her hand. On seeing her, Hagen gave a fearful cry and plunged into the water where he attempted to snatch the ring from the hand of the Rhine Maiden. But the other two maidens twined their arms around him and pulled him down into the depths. In this manner the curse of the ring claimed its last victim. From thenceforth the ring was never seen again.

The legends surrounding British birds.

THE ROBIN

The robin is so beloved in Britain that it has almost become our "unofficial" national bird. Nobody would hurt one, and this custom of letting robins live unharmed goes back to very ancient days. The robin, like the wren, has always been a very special bird. In almost every county of England there are rhymes which foretell disaster for anyone who kills a robin, steals from his nest, or even cages the bird. Today many country folk still believe that should a robin fly into the house a death or other calamity will follow. It is even said that should you rob a nest, or even hold a robin, your hands will shake for ever after!

Robins, in all folklore, show a love and understanding of those who suffer. In the story of The Babes in the Wood it is the robins who cover the children with leaves to keep them warm. In his play Cymbeline Shakespeare writes of a robin "with charitable bill" who covers the dead with moss.

Like the wren, the robin helps mankind by bringing fire. His red breast is explained in a French legend telling of his eagerness in snatching the fire-brand from the wren and passing it to the lark who flies with it to earth. A Guernsey legend has the robin bringing fire to the island from across the sea. From Wales we have another legend of the robin not bringing fire, but trying to put out the fires of Hell. Daily he carried a drop of water in his bill for this purpose. His breast was scorched so he was called "Bronrhuddyn" (Breast Scorch) ever after.

Songs and nursery rhymes of the wedding of the robin and the wren have been sung and told through the ages, and many people even today really think that the wren is the hen-bird and the robin the cock-bird. They are, of course, quite different species. The true meaning of the "marriage" of these two birds stems from the mingling of two different cultures. One tribe worshipped the wren, the other the robin. This we know because the same legends are told of each bird. The "marriage" of the two birds was a happy symbol of the tribes settling down beside each other and they themselves intermarrying.

"Who Killed Cock Robin?" The first printed version of this ballad appeared in 1744, but it was clearly a song sung long before this date. A 15th century stained-glass window in Buckland Rectory shows a robin with an arrow through his breast. Little "Robin Redbreast" is, in fact, man's friend, warning of disasters and even foretelling the weather. In a rhyme from East Anglia it is said:

If a Robin sings in the bush,
Then the weather will be coarse;
If the Robin sings in the barn,
Then the weather will be warm.

It is only natural, then, that we humans, like all the birds, mourn the "Death of Poor Cock Robin."

"Who killed Cock Robin?"

"Who killed Cock Robin?"
"I" said the Sparrow,
"With my Bow and Arrow."

Robin Hood may have been a real man. But long before such a person robbed the rich to help the poor, and aided maidens in distress, calling himself Robin Hood, there were ballads sung of a folk hero with this name. One of the first mentions of this hero of the greenwoods comes in the second edition of "Piers Plowman" in the year 1377. Robin Hood, folk-hero of ballads, took his name from little Robin Redbreast, the friend of "Everyman".

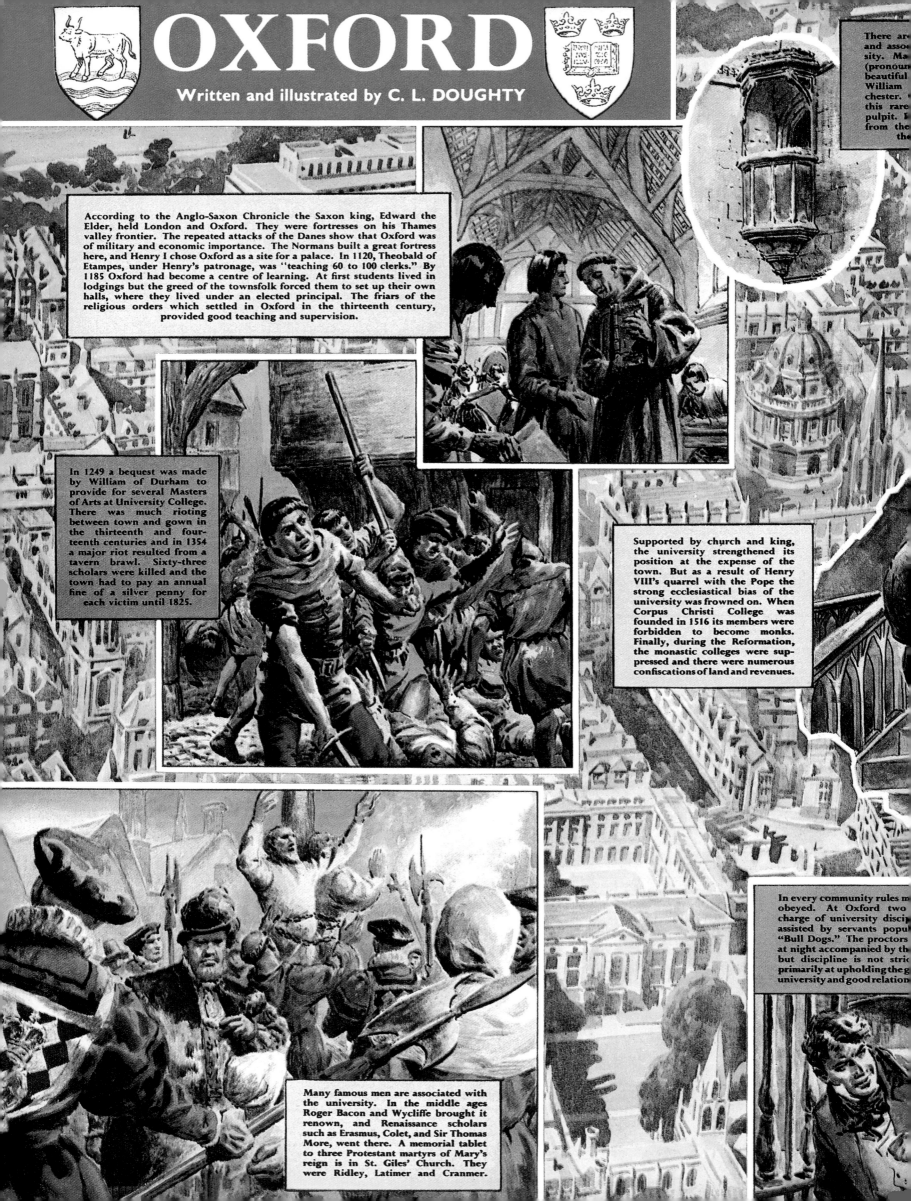

OXFORD

Written and illustrated by C. L. DOUGHTY

According to the Anglo-Saxon Chronicle the Saxon king, Edward the Elder, held London and Oxford. They were fortresses on his Thames valley frontier. The repeated attacks of the Danes show that Oxford was of military and economic importance. The Normans built a great fortress here, and Henry I chose Oxford as a site for a palace. In 1120, Theobald of Etampes, under Henry's patronage, was "teaching 60 to 100 clerks." By 1185 Oxford had become a centre of learning. At first students lived in lodgings but the greed of the townsfolk forced them to set up their own halls, where they lived under an elected principal. The friars of the religious orders which settled in Oxford in the thirteenth century, provided good teaching and supervision.

In 1249 a bequest was made by William of Durham to provide for several Masters of Arts at University College. There was much rioting between town and gown in the thirteenth and fourteenth centuries and in 1354 a major riot resulted from a tavern brawl. Sixty-three scholars were killed and the town had to pay an annual fine of a silver penny for each victim until 1825.

Supported by church and king, the university strengthened its position at the expense of the town. But as a result of Henry VIII's quarrel with the Pope the strong ecclesiastical bias of the university was frowned on. When Corpus Christi College was founded in 1516 its members were forbidden to become monks. Finally, during the Reformation, the monastic colleges were suppressed and there were numerous confiscations of land and revenues.

There ar[e]
and asso[...]
sity. Ma[...]
(pronoun[...]
beautiful [...]
William [...]
chester. [...]
this rare [...]
pulpit. [...]
from the [...]
the [...]

In every community rules m[...]
obeyed. At Oxford two [...]
charge of university discip[...]
assisted by servants popu[...]
"Bull Dogs." The proctors [...]
at night accompanied by th[...]
but discipline is not stric[...]
primarily at upholding the g[...]
university and good relation[...]

Many famous men are associated with the university. In the middle ages Roger Bacon and Wycliffe brought it renown, and Renaissance scholars such as Erasmus, Colet, and Sir Thomas More, went there. A memorial tablet to three Protestant martyrs of Mary's reign is in St. Giles' Church. They were Ridley, Latimer and Cranmer.

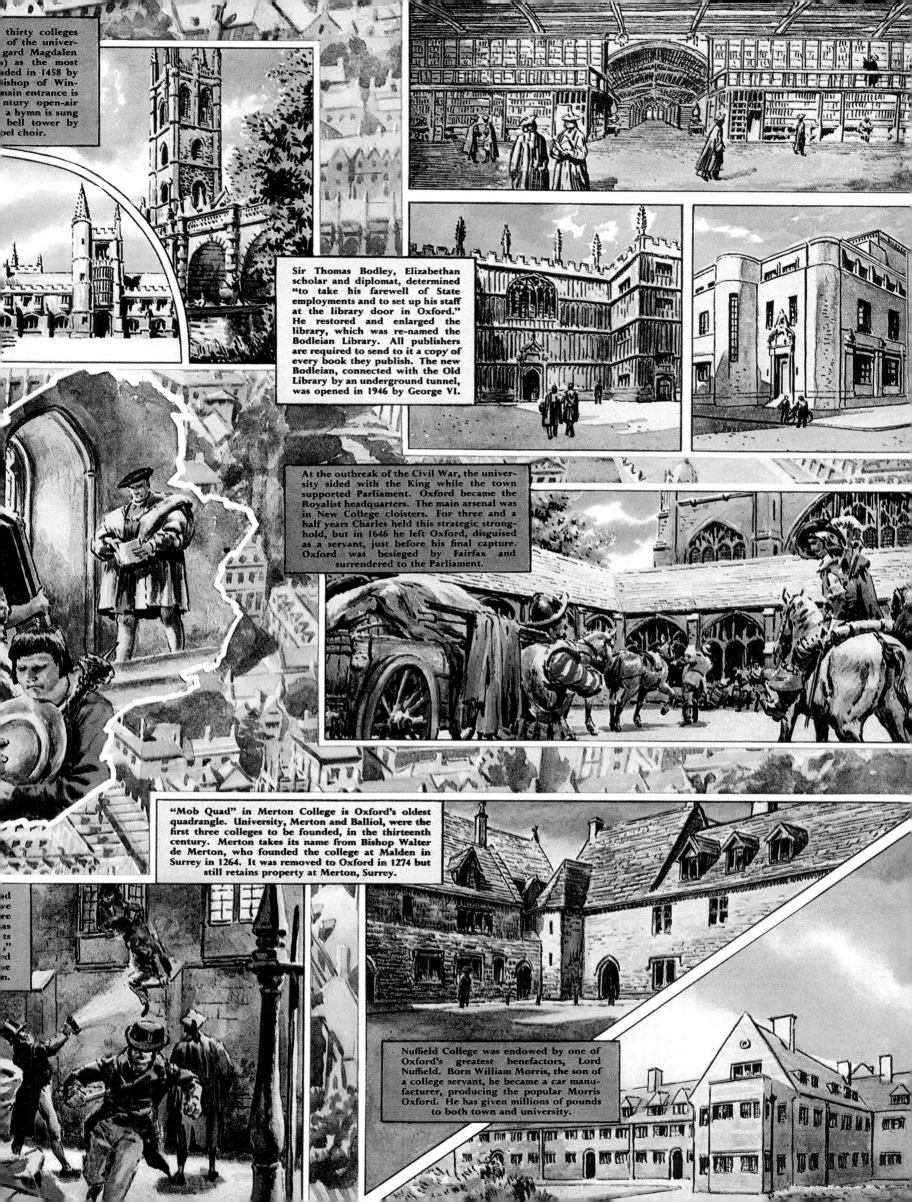

thirty colleges
of the univer-
gard Magdalen
×) as the most
ded in 1458 by
ishop of Win-
main entrance is
ntury open-air
a hymn is sung
bell tower by
pel choir.

Sir Thomas Bodley, Elizabethan scholar and diplomat, determined "to take his farewell of State employments and to set up his staff at the library door in Oxford." He restored and enlarged the library, which was re-named the Bodleian Library. All publishers are required to send to it a copy of every book they publish. The new Bodleian, connected with the Old Library by an underground tunnel, was opened in 1946 by George VI.

At the outbreak of the Civil War, the university sided with the King while the town supported Parliament. Oxford became the Royalist headquarters. The main arsenal was in New College cloisters. For three and a half years Charles held this strategic stronghold, but in 1646 he left Oxford, disguised as a servant, just before his final capture. Oxford was besieged by Fairfax and surrendered to the Parliament.

"Mob Quad" in Merton College is Oxford's oldest quadrangle. University, Merton and Balliol, were the first three colleges to be founded, in the thirteenth century. Merton takes its name from Bishop Walter de Merton, who founded the college at Malden in Surrey in 1264. It was removed to Oxford in 1274 but still retains property at Merton, Surrey.

Nuffield College was endowed by one of Oxford's greatest benefactors, Lord Nuffield. Born William Morris, the son of a college servant, he became a car manufacturer, producing the popular Morris Oxford. He has given millions of pounds to both town and university.

The WALRUS and the CARPENTER

by LEWIS CARROLL

The sun was shining on the sea,
   Shining with all his might:
He did his very best to make
   The billows smooth and bright—
And this was odd, because it was
   The middle of the night.

The Walrus and the Carpenter
   Were walking close at hand;
They wept like anything to see
   Such quantities of sand:
"If this were only cleared away,"
   They said, "it would be grand!"

"O Oysters, come and walk with us!"
   The Walrus did beseech.
"A pleasant walk, a pleasant talk,
   Along the briny beach:
We cannot do with more than four,
   To give a hand to each."

The Walrus and the Carpenter
   Walked on a mile or so,
And then they rested on a rock
   Conveniently low:
And all the little oysters stood
   And waited in a row.

"A loaf of bread," the Walrus said,
   "Is what we chiefly need:
Pepper and vinegar besides
   Are very good indeed—
Now if you're ready, Oysters dear,
   We can begin to feed."

"But not on us!" the Oysters cried,
   Turning a little blue.
"After such kindness, that would be
   A dismal thing to do!"
"The night is fine," the Walrus said.
   "Do you admire the view?"

"I weep for you," the Walrus said:
   "I deeply sympathize."
With sobs and tears he sorted out
   Those of the largest size,
Holding his pocket-handkerchief
   Before his streaming eyes.

"O Oysters," said the Carpenter,
   "You've had a pleasant run!
Shall we be trotting home again?"
   But answer came there none—
And this was scarcely odd, because
   They'd eaten every one.

****

ALICE WAS AN OXFORD GIRL

ONE hot summer afternoon Charles Lutwidge Dodgson, lecturer in mathematics at Oxford University, called on his friend, H. G. Liddell, Dean of Christ Church, Oxford, and asked permission to take out Liddell's three little daughters on the river.

Liddell readily agreed, and Dodgson and the three girls sailed off down the river. Because it was so hot they eventually landed at a meadow and sat under the shade of a haystack.

The girls grew bored and to keep them amused Dodgson began to tell them a story about a little girl, making it up as he went along. One of the Liddell children's names was Alice, so Dodgson called the girl in his story Alice, too.

Dodgson's story became more and more amazing as he went along—but it helped to pass the afternoon.

Some time after that summer day Dodgson decided to write down the story he had told. It was called *Alice's Adventures in Wonderland* and he sent it to Alice Liddell as a Christmas present.

Immediate Success

"A Christmas gift to a dear child in memory of a summer day," Dodgson wrote.

When, in 1865, *Alice's Adventures in Wonderland*, or *Alice in Wonderland* as the author and his readers preferred to call it, was published, Dodgson hid his identity under the pen-name "Lewis Carroll."

The story was an immediate success both with children and grown-ups. Everybody loved the White Rabbit, the Mad Hatter, the White Knight and the Red Queen, the Walrus and the Carpenter—part of the poem from the book is printed above—and all the other comical characters Lewis Carroll had invented.

And when, six years later, Dodgson followed up his great success with another story about Alice called *Through the Looking Glass*, his fame was assured.

Alice talks to the Red Queen, one of the many strange characters she encounters in *Through the Looking Glass*

Tenniel drawing from 'Through the Looking Glass'. Macmillan Co. Ltd.

But it was fame that Dodgson—or Lewis Carroll—really didn't seek. He would often deny that he—Charles Dodgson—had anything to do with the books published under the name of Lewis Carroll!

Indeed, Dodgson was a strange mixture. He had been ordained a deacon in the Church of England—but he never took the priesthood.

Instead, he preferred the world of mathematics at Oxford. And when he was not working on his Alice stories he was writing learned books on mathematics under his real name with titles like *A Syllabus of Plane Algebraical Geometry* and *Symbolic Logic.*

Dodgson never had any children of his own. He was a shy, nervous man whose stammer made him ill at ease with grown-ups.

But with children he was completely relaxed. He loved to play and talk with them, and to make up stories for them as he went along.

It is strange to think that one of those stories made up on the spur of the moment in a field near Oxford has become one of the best known and most frequently told tales in our language.

The TRIGAN EMPIRE

A strange craft has landed on the planet Elekton, and the three occupants—visible only as luminous spheres—have taken over the minds and bodies of the emperor Trigo, King Kassar of Hericon, and young Keren. And now they mean to conquer Elekton.

Janno—who knows the secret of the strange creatures—is a hunted fugitive at bay . . .

Janno faced the armed men fearlessly, but, to his astonishment, they made no attempt to attack him.

We mean you no harm, Janno . . . that is not our purpose for coming into the palace by a back entrance . . .

Well . . . what are you waiting for?

Three were Trigan officers whom Janno knew well, and three wore the trappings of the Hericon army.

We are making a desperate attempt to save the whole planet from disaster . . . by over-throwing the Emperor and the King!

Old Peric's eyes burned with hope.

Do you hear that, Janno? . . . we have allies against those evil creatures!

We must act swiftly, and ruthlessly. There's not much time!

They made their way to the royal apartments. There was a brief, but furious fight with the guards who tried to bar their way . . .

Aaaaaaah!

When they burst into the room where the sinister trio stood, the evil intelligence that directed the mind of Trigo saw Janno . . . and knew that something was amiss . . .

What does this mean? . . . Aaaaaah!

Yes, it is I! . . . Make a move and you are dead!

Orders were immediately sent to the Trigan and Hericon fleets, in the names of Trigo and Kassar, to return to their bases. Then the sinister trio were taken to a remote part of the palace gardens . . . to a cage which had once contained wild beasts . . .

In with you!

Janno aimed his pistol through the bars, and spoke with grim determination.

I give you the space of ten breaths . . . in that time you must agree to leave the minds and bodies you occupy, or I will kill Trigo, Kassar and my best friend Keren . . . and you fiends . . . I presume . . . will perish with them!

The alien intelligences panicked . . .

As luminous spheres, we are only able to survive for a few moments in the atmosphere of your planet!

We cannot leave these bodies!

We need to take over some other creature!

Then wise old Peric smiled grimly.

So you need to take over some other creature . . . well . . . I think that can be arranged!

Three gelfs were brought and tethered securely near to the cage.

There are your new hosts! . . . See that the change is made by dawn . . . or else!

In that lonely garden, during the dark hours of the night, when men and animals slept, three luminous spheres rose from the ears of Trigo, Kassar and Keren . . . and drifted away . . .

At dawn, Janno and his companions returned . . . and opened the cage . . .

Is it . . . really you . . . my uncle?

Yes, Janno! All Elekton is in your debt!

A Trigan officer raised his sword above the shrinking gelfs . . .

No! . . . Spare them! . . . They don't deserve it. but they shall live out their life span as gelfs!

The gelf is a long-lived creature, and the three in the cage became a target for sightseers from all over Elekton. They were well-treated . . .

. . . But no one ever dared to sleep anywhere near that fateful cage!

227

Lines from

A Shropshire Lad

Loveliest of trees, the cherry now
Is hung with bloom along the bough,
And stands about the woodland ride
Wearing white for Eastertide.

Now, of my three score years and ten,
Twenty will not come again,
And take from seventy springs a score,
It only leaves me fifty more.

And since to look at things in bloom
Fifty springs are little room,
About the woodlands I will go
To see the cherry hung with snow.

A. E. HOUSMAN

THE ARTS – Poetry

POET FROM THE AGE OF EIGHT

People were surprised when they read A. E. Housman's new book. This time the learned professor had not written about the classics—but instead, a beautiful volume of lyrics called "A Shropshire Lad."

ON a frosty March day in 1859, Alfred Edward Housman was born at Fockbury, in Worcestershire, the son of Edward Housman, a solicitor. Alfred, who was to become famous as a poet, was educated at Bromsgrove School and at Oxford, where he proved himself to be a brilliant scholar. When he left, he became a clerk in the Patent Office.

He lived an ordinary life, working diligently in the office by day and returning to his lodgings in Bayswater at night. It is probable that he would have remained relatively unknown for the rest of his life had he not written essays on the classics in his spare time. These essays were published in historical and literary journals, and established him as an authority on literature.

In those days, when the nineteenth century was drawing to its close, many people wrote books and articles on the Bible, and on the classics, which have remained unsurpassed to this day. Housman grew up in the England of Wordsworth, Byron, Shelley and Dickens. He, like them, made a great contribution to English literature.

His essays made such an impression that in 1892 he was appointed professor of Latin at University College, London. He could now devote all his time to the classics which he loved so much—but he startled everybody when, four years later, a new book appeared in the London bookshops.

The book bore Housman's name, but instead of finding an erudite study of the classics between the covers, people found his beautiful new work, *A Shropshire Lad*. This collection of lyrics entitled him to a place in the foremost ranks of English poets—and he later revealed that he had been writing poetry since he was eight years old.

In 1922 he published the second of his great works, *Last Poems*, which consists of forty-one lyrics. By now he was a famous man, yet he never gave up his simple and quiet way of life. He liked to walk in the countryside and watch the progress of the trees through the four seasons, for he was a great lover of nature, and he often went abroad for holidays. He loved good food, one of his favourite meals being lobster, with which he liked to drink a bottle of fine red burgundy.

Housman spent the last years of his life lecturing at Cambridge, but fell ill in 1932. He died at the age of seventy-seven on April 30, 1936, leaving behind him work that will always be remembered and loved.

WHAT WAS IN JACK HORNER'S PIE?

Nursery rhymes are often the first recitations we learn. Generations of children have known the words of such rhymes as "Humpty Dumpty," "Ride a Cock Horse," and "Mary, Mary, Quite Contrary," and we might easily imagine that these rhymes were written purely for the amusement of children.

But many of them have a story far deeper than the nursery version suggests, and in this series we are going back to the origins of the more famous rhymes. Sometimes it is difficult to separate truth from legend, but facts are there which cannot be ignored.

So, for a start, let us take the story of Jack Horner and the "plum" which he is said to have pulled out of the pie.

The legend has grown during the past hundred years that Jack Horner was steward to Richard Whiting, last of the abbots of Glastonbury, the first Christian Church in England and said to have been founded by St. Joseph of Arimathea.

When Henry the Eighth proclaimed that he was head of the Church in England it resulted in the dissolution of the Monasteries. The abbot of Glastonbury, hoping to gain special favour from Henry, sent his steward to London with a Christmas gift of a pie in which were hidden the title deeds of twelve manors.

The story is that Horner opened the pie during the journey and removed the deeds of the Manor of Mells. After the Dissolution, who should take up residence at Mells but a man named Thomas Horner! And when Abbot Whiting stood trial, the jury which condemned him included a King's man—Thomas Horner!

In the nursery rhyme Horner is referred to as "Jack." This term was applied to anybody regarded as a knave, and no doubt that is how the people saw him.

Records show that Abbot Whiting did indeed send several gifts to the king—and also that Glastonbury, although the richest abbey in the country, was the only monastery in Somerset left undamaged.

An early Somerset saying runs:

Hopton, Horner, Smythe and Thyme,
When abbots went out, they came in.

Yes, this happy little nursery rhyme of Jack Horner certainly has some dark deeds as its background:

Little Jack Horner
Sat in a corner,
Eating a Christmas pie;
He put in his thumb
And took out a plum
And said:
'What a good boy am I!'

THEY SAILED THE SEVEN SEAS

UNDER FIRE!

"GOODBYE, Dolly, I must leave you," sang the soldiers from the rails of Union Castle ships as they slipped out of Southampton en route for South Africa, and that most wretched of conflicts, the Boer War. The century had turned. Troops, munitions, guns, gun-carriages and wagons packed the liners to capacity. The docks at Cape Town were chaotic as Castle ship after Castle ship sailed in to off-load cargoes which were hopelessly mixed—wagons without wheels, gun-carriages whose guns could not be found, Government stores, and, of course, Her Majesty's Mail.

As the soldiers poured into South Africa, the Cornish miners, who had been working the up-country mines, poured out—all by Union Castle. A Boer prisoner-of-war camp at Simonstown was transferred in its entirety on board the *Kildonan Castle* anchored in the protection of Naval guns. There was no chance of escape now for the 2,500 prisoners who were so enchanted by the conditions of comfort and courtesy offered by Union Castle that any desire to escape was probably unthinkable! Ship's officers, crew and prisoners became one happy family. Three times a day there was fervent Dutch hymn-singing, and the Boers themselves begged leave to attend the English services. When news of the death of Queen Victoria was received on board, Captain Robinson of the *Kildonan* was offered the heartfelt sympathy of every prisoner on board. This, despite its many horrors, was the last of "The Gentlemen's Wars."

When, after six weeks, the *Kildonan's* prisoners were transferred to other ships they climbed into the rigging, cheered Union Castle to the echo and sang Dutch psalms.

The Boer War ended, and not very long after it came the end of a chapter in the Union Castle story. Two spanking new mail ships were ordered, one from the Clyde, the other from Belfast—the *Balmoral Castle* and the *Edinburgh* which were the last word in speed and comfort.

'Jewels' in war!

By now the on-the-dot punctuality of the Mail steamers had become something unique in the world. A ship which left Southampton at 5 p.m. on a Saturday, steamed in precisely 16½ days, into Table Bay. Years later, in the early '20s, one of the regularly dramatic sights in Cape Town was the passing, outside the breakwater at 11.30 a.m. precisely, of the great four-funnellers, *Windsor Castle* and *Arundel Castle*, one inward, the other outward bound. But before that ritual and peaceful passing of great ships there had been war.

When on 4th August, 1914, Great Britain found herself at war with Germany there were 41 ships of the Union Castle fleet sailing not only to South Africa but to South America as well.

By 4th September, 19 of these ships had been requisitioned. Out went the cushioned comfort of the passenger accommodation. In came the austerity of tier upon tier of close-packed bunks. Hospital berths and operating theatres appeared on some vessels: the decks of others bristled with guns. The Union Castle livery turned to a sombre grey, then to black, and finally in 1917, when the oceans of the world were filled with prowling German U-boats, to the dazzle-painting of camouflage.

The Castle boats "trooped" from India and to the disaster of Gallipoli. Alongside the bombarding Navy lay one-time liners. A wonderful picture is conjured up in the words of a Gallipoli soldier who wrote: "My chief memory is of those beautiful hospital ships, and their jewelled appearance among the dark hulls of the mighty Armada that lay like a city off Cape Helles and Gaba Tepe. I remember the *Dunluce Castle*, *Gloucester Castle*, *Braemar Castle* and others of the Union Castle Line whose names I have forgotten. . . ."

Spectacular convoy

One picture of Union Castle at war is followed by another which must have been memorable for all who saw it one morning in August, 1914, as the mists were rising from the top of Table Mountain. Six Castle ships were gathered together with steam up, laden with the last 4,000 Imperial troops ever to garrison South Africa, British troops bound for Europe and the Western Front. The Union of South Africa was by then a fact. Ever afterwards South Africa's soldiers were to be her own.

The battle-grey cruisers *Hyacinth* and *Astraea* joined their belching smoke with that of the Castle liners as the whole spectacular convoy steamed out of Table Bay and turned northwards to the Mother Country, and a grim way of seafaring life which was to last for four long years.

Through it all His Majesty's Mail got through to Cape Town, though when the Great War ended Union Castle had eight ships lost and 440 "Castle Men" had lost their lives.

Above: Sir Donald Currie, "father" of the Union Castle Line, lived to see the *Edinburgh Castle* being built. Dating from 1910, she and her sister ship, the *Balmoral Castle*, were fast and luxurious.

Above: A deck game in progress on the *Kinfauns Castle* (1900). Below: The four-funnel turbine mail steamer *Arundel Castle*, before being altered and redesigned in 1937 with two funnels.

Right: In World War I even hospital ships with their lights blazing were not safe. The *Llandovery Castle* was torpedoed by a German U-boat and then sunk by gunfire.

THE FLOWERS THAT BLOOM

SYMBOL OF PEACE

HOW could anything bright and beautiful enliven the muddy battlefields of Flanders at the end of the First World War? It seems incredible that loveliness could flourish where there had once been so much misery.

But there it was in the shape of hundreds of glowing red poppies (top) bringing life to a scene of slaughter. Because of this, the poppy became a symbol of peace. Britons have worn them in November on Remembrance Day ever since to recall to mind those who died in the two world wars.

Poppies are very old flowers. The ancient people thought that they were made by Somnus, the god of sleep, to ease the goddess Ceres of her cares and to cause her to sleep. Since, after her refreshing slumber, the crops revived, Ceres is usually shown (centre left) wearing a garland of corn mixed with poppies.

Farmers, however, dislike seeing poppies growing among their crops (bottom left) because they rob the soil of the nourishment the crops need. They are hard to get rid of, and seeds have been known to germinate after having been buried for 24 years.

This is not surprising, because the poppy is a very hardy plant which was probably introduced into Britain by the Romans. It is found wild in all the Mediterranean countries and in the Middle East.

By 1597, ornamental garden varieties began to appear in Britain. Elizabethan women thought that they looked nice but smelt nasty and called them, "John Silverpin, fair without and foul within."

Poppy capsules have been found on the sites of prehistoric dwellings, showing that the plant has been cultivated for centuries, partly for its edible seed.

This was eaten by the athletes in training for the early Olympic games, mixed with wine and honey. Bread glazed with the yolk of egg and sprinkled with poppy seed for ornament and flavour became popular.

Morphine, the pain killing drug used in medicine, is made from the juice obtained from the unripe head or seed capsule of the white poppy. When dried, this juice becomes opium, which the ancients used as a medicine.

THE STORY OF WORLD WAR ONE *by MICHAEL BUTTERWORTH Illustrations by FRANK BELLAMY*

ATTACK—and RETREAT at GALLIPOLI

THE long drawn-out and tragic affair that is known to history as the Gallipoli Campaign began on the morning of 19th February, 1915, with the combined British and French fleet opening fire on the shore defences lining the Dardanelles. It made a brave sight on that winter's day: the lines of tall grey ships, their funnels gushing coal-black smoke; the winking flashes of the big guns rippling their broadsides.

Forcing the Dardanelles looked an easy task—on paper. The Turkish defences comprised 11 forts strung along both shores, lines of sea mines laid in the narrows at the far end, and torpedo tubes fixed to fire upon any intruder. But most of the guns were of near-obsolete pattern, and numbered only about a hundred. Furthermore, the defenders were tragically short of ammunition—particularly of armour-piercing shells, the only type that could penetrate the armour plating of warships.

In the event, the initial bombardment was cut short by bad weather. In the days that followed, naval landing parties were put on shore, where they did great havoc among the battered enemy emplacements.

Then a strange rot set in. The civilian crews aboard the mine-sweepers failed in their task of clearing the passage for the big ships—a situation that was put right by the vision and energy of Commodore Roger Keyes (afterwards Admiral of the Fleet Lord Keyes), who called for volunteer seamen from the fleet, to man the sweepers.

It was not till 18th March that the full-scale attack was made. Admiral de Robeck, the commander-in-chief, led his fleet in three divisions, with Britain's four most powerful battleships in the van: *Queen Elizabeth*, *Agamemnon*, *Lord Nelson* and *Inflexible*; the French squadron of four battleships following, and the remainder of the fleet bringing up the rear.

By midday, the ships were engaging the forts in the Narrows, and de Robeck signalled the French Admiral Guépratte to close with the shore. This order was obeyed with great gallantry. At about 2 o'clock, the French *Bouvet* was hit in the magazine, and the great battleship blew up and sank in two minutes, taking over 600 men down with her. Shortly afterwards, the *Irresistible* was struck a heavy blow, followed by the *Inflexible*. The *Ocean* was shaken by

a violent explosion while manoeuvring to take the stricken *Irresistible* in tow.

Inflexible managed to limp away—but when night fell over the Dardanelles, the allies had lost three capital ships.

"We simply couldn't have failed..."

Admiral de Robek was a brave man, and a professional sailor of the old school; but it was an appalling thing to him to see fine ships and splendid crews being wiped out with such apparent ease. Despite the entreaties of his chief-of-staff, Roger Keyes, he did not order a follow-up attack on the next day—nor, indeed, on any other day. Instead, when the news of the losses caused doubt and consternation in London, he joined with others in accepting the view that the Dardanelles could not be forced without the aid of the Army.

Winston Churchill, the First Lord of the Admiralty and a prime mover of the whole scheme against Turkey, was all for pressing home the naval attacks—but opinion against it was too strong. Kitchener appointed General Ian Hamilton to command a

new army which was to be formed to land on the Gallipoli peninsula, and take the Straits by a military operation.

Meanwhile, no one in the Allied camp knew—and how could they?—what a devastating effect the bombardment of the 18th had had upon the Turkish army and people. That the British Fleet, with its long and unbeatable record, was knocking at the gates of the Dardanelles filled the teeming population of Constantinople with panic. Amid scenes of rioting, they began to flee the city, before the mighty shells rained down upon its narrow streets.

In the Narrows of the Straits, the Turkish and German gunners looked at their worn-out guns, and counted their dwindling ammunition supplies. They had fought well—the Turks with a religious frenzy that scorned death—but they knew that, within a few days when their guns fell silent, the Allied fleet would steam into the Sea of Marmara, and no power on earth could stop them.

It never happened. Other means were already afoot to force the Dardanelles.

CONTINUED ON NEXT PAGE

An armada of transports carried Allied troops to Gallipoli in April, 1915. Among them was the S.S. Clyde, shown here.

Ten years later, when he was in command of the peacetime Mediterranean Fleet, Roger Keyes took his ships through those self-same straits. He said at the time: ". . . it would have been even easier than I thought. We simply couldn't have failed. And because we didn't try, another million lives were thrown away and the war went on for another three years!"

The landings

When the Allies' new intentions became obvious, Enver put the German Liman von Sanders in command of the defences of Gallipoli. With six divisions at his disposal, he grouped them so as to be able to meet attacks from any quarter. One division he kept in reserve, near the Narrows, from whence they could be thrown at any point where reinforcements might be needed.

The commander of this division was Mustapha Kemal.

General Hamilton's force landed at Gallipoli on 25th April. In the armada of transports, protected by the Fleet, were 75,000 men: Britons, Australians and New Zealanders and French. Hamilton's plan of attack was to strike at Cape Hellas, at the southern tip of the peninsula; and also at a point about 13 miles up the western coast—with the intention of cutting off the defenders fighting at Cape Hellas. There were also to be diversionary attacks. It was a reasonably good plan—on paper.

The first to go in, at dawn on the 25th, were 1,500 Australians. Their objective was Gaba Tepe on the western coast. They approached the lowering cliffs under darkness, and jumped from their boats to wade ashore.

Instantly, they came under fire—but the Aussies fixed bayonets and charged. The enemy fled.

Then, instead of reaching level ground—as they had expected—the Australians came face to face with an unknown cliff. They were not at Gaba Tepe at all; in the darkness, a current had carried their boats nearly a mile north of their true objective.

Notwithstanding this setback, the Dominion troops managed to gain the heights, and put all opposition to flight. It was now daylight, and the horrors and doubts of the night assault were forgotten in a wild relief, and a determination to press on.

This they might have done—but for the personal intervention of Mustapha Kemal.

Kemal saw the general picture from a mountain crest of Chunuk Bair. He saw the warships and transports in the sea far below, and heard the firing from the assault points. A party of Turkish soldiers came bounding towards him in full retreat—and he saw the Australians coming after them. It was the turning point of his life—and a supreme moment of Turkey's history.

The story of Kemal's counter-attack has often been told: how he led his own battalion against the oncoming enemy, and afterwards ordered up his finest regiment, the 57th.

Fire from the shore forts struck the French battleship *Bouvet* **in the magazine, and the great vessel blew up and sank in two minutes with 600 men.**

Turkish troops, defending Gallipoli, opened fire (above) when the Australian soldiers approached the cliffs. Instantly, the Aussies fixed bayonets and charged (right) and the enemy fled.

"I don't order you to attack," he told the 57th. "I order you to die!" The 57th charged with bayonets—and were wiped out by massed small-arms fire.

The fanatical Turkish counter-attacks continued into the afternoon. By 4 p.m., the Dominion troops began to fall back and dig in.

This was the pattern of Gallipoli. In the Australian sector, as everywhere, the assaults ground to a halt, and the men began to dig shallow trenches to protect themselves.

So it was that the dream of a lightning conquest of Gallipoli—and a quick end to the war—collapsed into the reality of a bitter slogging match.

The peninsula became like the Western Front in miniature—and equally hideous.

A PICTURE HISTORY AND MAP OF IRELAND

Carried off by Irish raiders in the early part of the fifth century from his home in Roman Britain, St. Patrick was sold into slavery as a swineherd. After six years, he escaped and travelled by ship to Europe. He returned in A.D. 432 to Ireland, after fourteen years of training as a bishop.

The Irish Church flourished. Monasteries were set up by Irish monks all over Europe. When Brian Boru became High King of Ireland, he decided to expel the Norse invaders from Scandinavia. He defeated the Northmen at the Battle of Clontarf on April 23, 1014.

In 1169, Dermot, King of Leinster, asked Henry II, King of England, to help him in his feud with the King of Breiffne. When Henry went to Ireland in 1171, his supremacy as Lord of Ireland was acknowledged by the Irish bishops and by some of the Irish kings and chiefs.

As the years went by, the Norman settlers adopted Irish laws. The part of Ireland loyal to the English crown were the counties around Dublin. In 1494, the colony was in such danger of attacks from the Irish that orders were given to build a rampart known as the Pale.

In 1595, the Irish, led by O'Neill, Earl of Tyrone, revolted against the English, whom they defeated at Blackwater on August 14, 1598. Because of this and other rebellions, most of Ulster became vested in the English crown. James I divided the land among his English and Scottish protestant subjects.

The Royalists made a peace with the Irish and forces were joined to fight against the greater evil—Cromwell who landed in Ireland on August 15, 1649, and shortly afterwards stormed and sacked Drogheda and Wexford. The Irish were told to go "to hell or to Connaught"—the province with the poorest land in Ireland.

Shortly after Cromwell died James II, who was a Catholic, succeeded to the throne, but he lost it in 1662 to William of Orange. James fled to Ireland. He was followed by William, and the two armies met at the battle of the Boyne on July 1, 1690. The Irish were defeated and James fled to France.

Because the Irish were constantly rebelling, Parliament passed in 1800 the Act of Union between the Irish and English parliaments and so hoped to have greater control over the rebels. But three years later, Robert Emmett led a revolt in Dublin. He was captured, tried and hanged.

In 1845, the Irish potato crop was attacked by blight. The result was famine. Many of the Irish died of starvation or diseases which readily attacked their under-nourished bodies. Others left their homeland and went to America and England. In three years the population of Ireland was reduced by half.

One result of the famine was the reforming of land tenure in Ireland. The Land League, founded by Michael Davitt, refused to pay rents to landlords. They resisted eviction and boycotted the landlords and people who helped them. As a result, Parliament passed land reforming laws.

After the Easter Rebellion in 1916, the Irish Republican Army began fighting a guerrilla type of warfare with the English. This lasted until December 6, 1921, when a treaty was made giving independence to twenty-six counties of Ireland. Michael Collins formed the first Irish Government.

On April 18, 1949, legislation making the Irish Free State a republic came into effect, but Irish citizens still had most of the advantages of United Kingdom citizens. In 1956, the Republic of Ireland was admitted to membership of the United Nations.

The full Coat of Arms
of Northern Ireland.

ATLANTIC

OCEAN

Malin Hd.

*Giant's
Causeway*

Rathlin I.

Letterkenny

Londonderry

ANTRIM

Larne

DONEGAL

LONDONDERRY

TYRONE

Omagh

*Lough
NEAGH*

BELFAST

*Belfast
Loug.*

*Donegal
Bay*

Enniskillen

FERMANGH

ARMAGH

DOWN

Downpatrick

*Mourne
Mts.*

Sligo

SLIGO

LEITRIM

MONAGHAN

LOUTH

Dundalk

IRISH

Castlebar

ROSCOMMON

CAVAN

Kells

SEA

MAYO

LONGFORD

MEATH

*Croagh
Patrick*

Mullingar

Slyne Hd.

Connemara

GALWAY

W. MEATH

Athlone

Boyne R.

DUBLIN

Liffey R.

DUBLIN

Galway

OFFALY

KILDARE

Galway Bay

R. Shannon

Naas

The Curragh

*Aran
Islands*

LEIX

WICKLOW

Wicklow

CLARE

Ennis

CARLOW

*SHANNON
AIRPORT*

TIPPERARY

Killkenny

WEXFORD

R. Shannon

Limerick

KILKENNY

LIMERICK

Tipperary

Wexford

Rosslare

Tralee

WATERFORD

Waterford

KERRY

R. Blackwater

Killarney

Dingle Bay

CORK

Cork

Cobh

Glengarriff

CHANNEL

Mizen Hd.

ST. GEORGE'S

The Shield of Arms of
the Irish Republic.

237

"WE WANT THE VOTE!"

THE Independent Labour Party, the fore-runner of the present Labour Party, was formed in 1893. Its secretary and leader was a man called James Keir Hardie who was one of the first two Labour M.P.s. (John Burns was the other.)

The real beginning of the parliamentary Labour Party, however, did not come about until the establishment of the Labour representation committee in 1900.

For many years, the Independent Labour Party had been trying to convince the Trade Union Congress that a political party, independent of both the Conservatives and the Liberals, should be formed with T.U.C. backing.

The trade union movement had come a long way since the days of the Tolpuddle Martyrs but until 1900, its political efforts had been half-hearted.

During the second half of the 19th century, the Liberal Party had adopted some trade unionists as parliamentary candidates in industrial constituencies but these men had not belonged to any party of their own.

Another group which advocated the formation of a socialist or Labour Party was the Fabian Society, of which Bernard Shaw was perhaps the best-known member.

In 1900, the dream was realised. In the election of 1906, the Labour Party secured 26 seats.

The battle between the Labour Party and the two other political parties still continues today but the last battle in the fight between the Lords and the Commons for predominance in Parliament concerned the Budget of 1909. In the bid to

VOTES for WOMEN

EQUAL RIGHTS

GIVE US THE VOTE!

preserve their power, the Lords rejected a Finance Bill that struck at the very root of their influence —landed property.

Unfortunately for the Lords Lloyd George, Chancellor of the Exchequer at the time, determined that such interference from the Lords must end. In his speeches in London's East End district of Limehouse he attacked the Lords whenever possible, saying that they "toil not neither do they spin!"

The Commons passed a new Parliament Act which reduced the power of the Lords, while the King threatened to swamp the House of Lords with new Liberal peers.

The threat was enough and the Lords submitted to the removal of their power.

Cry for reform

This was an effective cry for reform but perhaps the loudest cry for election if not parliamentary reform came from a group of women.

The word "suffragette" was invented by the *Daily Mail* when Mrs. Emmeline Pankhurst founded the Women's Social and Political Union in 1903.

The fight for women's political rights had been going on quietly for many years. The first English society for female suffrage was formed in 1858. The first national society for women's suffrage was formed in 1867. A disadvantage, however, was that one of the points which they believed in very strongly was that a woman could demand a vote but she should also remain a lady.

This was altered with the coming of the Pankhursts. These women—a mother and her two daughters—decided that the time had come for aggressive action.

This action started in Manchester in October 1905. A meeting was being addressed by Sir Edward (later Lord) Grey. Two women appeared carrying small banners inscribed "Votes for Women". At question time they asked, "Will a Liberal government give votes to working women?" They were not answered but instead were thrown down the steps leading to the street. There they addressed the crowd until they were eventually arrested for obstruction.

More aggressive action followed. By chaining themselves to the railings and going on hunger strikes when in prison, the suffragettes caught the public attention. They used every normal political manoeuvre, but many that were not so "normal". They were fed forcibly and they were also released to recover their strength so that they could be imprisoned again. This was known as the "Cat and Mouse Act".

There was one martyr—Emily Davison. This supporter of women's suffrage threw herself in front of the King's horse at the Derby of 1913 and died from the injuries she received.

In 1914, the First World War put a stop to the activities of these women and they were given a chance to put their case in a more practical way.

Their magnificent work in keeping the factories operating and the transport services running, earned the respect of the men-folk of the entire nation.

Under the Representation of the People Act of 1918, women of 30 were given the right to vote. By proving themselves both capable and responsible, women won the right to a voice in the running of the country.

Another act of the same year allowed women to sit in the House of Commons and, ten years later, the voting age for women was reduced to 21, so giving women equal rights with men.

It had been a long hard struggle but the women had proved victorious in the end.

Nowadays, votes for women seem obvious and democratic but many things today seem obvious which at one time seemed quite revolutionary.

The idea that an opponent of the Government should be paid by the very Government that he opposes is singularly British and democratic. The concept of "Her Majesty's Loyal Opposition" is over a century old but in 1937 the Leader of the Opposition began to take a salary drawn from public funds. The late Lord Attlee was the first man to receive such a payment.

Now Parliament is a treasure-house of British tradition. This can be seen at every ceremonial or state occasion at the Houses of Parliament. It is also a unique and living institution of which every British citizen can be proud.

For a thousand years, Parliament has grown up side by side with the British nation. It is still growing. M.P.s are the first to admit that there is always room for improvement. As long as Parliament is not allowed to become merely a fossil, it will continue to be as strong, as enthusiastic and youthful as it has been throughout its long life.

The suffragettes used every normal political manoeuvre and many that were not so "normal" to achieve their end.

The DOVER ROAD

We stop to look at Dover Castle

WRITTEN AND DRAWN BY PETER JACKSON

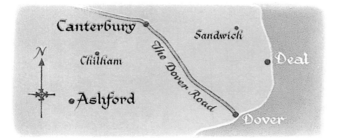

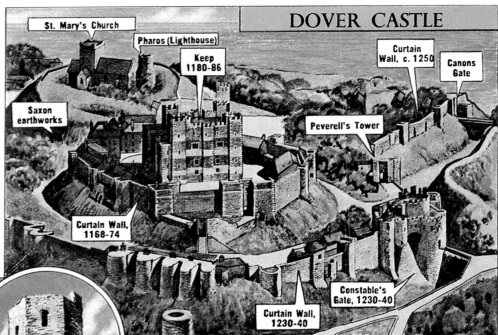

DOVER CASTLE

St. Mary's Church
Pharos (Lighthouse)
Keep 1180-86
Saxon earthworks
Curtain Wall, c. 1250
Canons Gate
Peverell's Tower
Constable's Gate, 1230-40
Curtain Wall 1230-40
Curtain Wall, 1168-74

The Pharos, or lighthouse, which the Romans erected about A.D. 50 is the oldest building still standing in England. Originally it was about 80 feet high and its beacon of fire guided the Roman galleys across the English Channel to Dover.

Throughout its long history, Dover Castle has been "the key and stronghold of all England," for it is the nearest castle to the continent of Europe. The first fortifications were erected before the Norman Conquest, but it was under Henry II that it began to take on its present shape. Henry II built the magnificent keep between 1180 and 1186 and the Curtain Wall which surrounds it. The stone outer walls of the castle stronghold were added in the thirteenth century.

In 1216 the barons grew tired of King John's cruel tyrannies and invited Louis, son of Philip of France, to be their king in John's stead. Louis was welcomed almost everywhere...but Dover Castle held out against him, and he laid siege to it. He had specially imported from France the latest and most formidable engines of war yet devised, and for months on end these huge catapults pounded the walls. But the castle stood firm as a rock and Louis finally withdrew his army in frustration.

When the Civil War began in 1642 the castle was captured by a few Dover merchants, led by one called Drake. He scaled the cliffs at a spot thought to be unclimbable and therefore not guarded strongly. He opened the gates to his comrades who took the castle in the name of Oliver Cromwell.

During Marlborough's campaigns, 1702-9, the keep housed French prisoners of war. When they were not gazing across the Channel at their native shore, which is easily seen on a clear day, they spent their time carving inscriptions, dozens of which can still be seen on their prison walls.

It still remains the important military garrison it has always been. During World War II "Operation Dynamo," which led to the rescue of the British army from the beaches of Dunkirk, was planned here. Its underground passages were used as shelters by the townsfolk against air-raids and shellfire from France.

Roger Payne

BIGGIN HILL CELEBRATES A BATTLE OF BRITAIN DAY

THE BATTLE OF BRITAIN

The first part of the battle was fought over the Channel. There were ten German squadrons to every one of ours, but the fast fighting Spitfires and Hurricanes, more than a match for Stuka and Dornier bombers, were helped by radar. Britain was the only country to have a radar system which was complete and highly reliable.

The chain of radar stations ▶ being erected along the coast had been rapidly completed when war was declared. It effectively guarded the South and East coasts and warned of the approach of enemy aircraft some minutes before they arrived. The British planes lay in wait for the enemy and took off to attack them as they came in over the coast.

The Germans were losing large numbers of bombers, in spite of the fact that the squadrons they sent over far outnumbered the planes the R.A.F. could send in to the attack. They shot down three hundred bombers during July and the beginning of August and in spite of all the damage to their airfields, the R.A.F. managed to keep their planes in the air.

Many people slept in the Tube stations while the destruction went on above them. Day and night attacks continued in a round-the-clock attempt to wipe out London. Thousands of people were killed and injured but the Germans did not possess the bombs to destroy so scattered a city.

The greatest battle came on September 15. A great fleet of German aircraft was assembled on the coast of France. They were attacked continually as they flew towards London. When they had dropped their bombs and turned for home sixty fighters of No. 11 group swept in to the attack, creating havoc among the enemy. This attack was led by Douglas Bader, the legless pilot. His success against the enemy and his courage in battle made his name a legend. He was later shot down over France and his many attempts to escape made him almost as great a legend to the Germans.

August 1940 Hitler ordered his air force commander, Marshal Goering, to launch the attack against British ports and cripple Britain. Winston Churchill told the nation: "The Battle of Britain is about to begin! The whole fury and might of the enemy must very soon be turned on us. Hitler knows that he will have to break us in this island or lose the war. If we can stand up to him, all Europe may be free. . . . Let us . . . so bear ourselves that, if the British Empire and the Commonwealth last for a thousand years, men will still say, this was their finest hour."

Biggin Hill, set in the picturesque South Weald countryside, became the R.A.F.'s centre of resistance to German bombers. The young pilots would sit on the grass verge of the runway, listening for the clang of the alarm bell. Then they would rush to their planes to continue the savage battle for mastery of the sky. The second phase of the Battle of Britain was an attempt to wipe out the airfields, including Biggin Hill. In this way Marshal Goering hoped that he would cripple the R.A.F., knock out British resistance, and win the battle of the air.

◄On August 15, Goering launched his mightiest assault. He called it the Eagle. Three great German airfleets were sent over in a combined attack. 1,800 aircraft flew over the Channel in five waves, and the battle lasted right through the day. The Germans lost 76 planes for an R.A.F. total of 34. The fighter pilots who beat them back were given the name, The Few, because their numbers were pitifully small, compared with their opponents. The failure of this assault made the Germans switch their attack to London.

Nine hundred aircraft bombed ▶ London's docks on September 7. They flew over in waves, each wave coming in to attack as the others turned for home. Soon most of the East End was blazing and the light from the huge fires guided the incoming planes to the target.

Bader's chief opponent was the German fighter ace, Adolf Galland, who shot down more than one hundred aircraft. Later in the war Galland became head of the German Fighter Command.

The Germans had to abandon their mass attacks in daylight, because of heavy losses and Hitler cancelled his invasion plans. The Battle of Britain had been won by a few R.A.F. fighter pilots. Winston Churchill said: "Never in the field of human conflict was so much owed by so many to so few . . ."

THE WOODEN WONDER!

SNOW covered the fields and houses as far as the eye could see. The sky was filled with yet more snow that drifted about and seemed to deaden all noise. It was February 18, 1944, and at Amiens jail in France, a little before midday, the guard had been changed and German soldiers just off duty stamped their feet to keep warm. One of them struck a match, lit his cigarette and was about to throw it away when he suddenly stopped, poised and listening intently. He shouted to his friends to be quiet, for somewhere in the blanket of silence came a low grumbling sound.

The noise grew louder, echoing off the forty-foot high outer walls of the jail and rising to a crescendo before anybody had time to move. Suddenly three grey shapes, with jutting engines and open bomb bays, flashed overhead and were gone. Seconds later the outer wall bulged and collapsed, blown in by the detonation of several delayed-action 500 lb. bombs. The echo of the explosions and the crash of falling stonework drowned the noise made by a second trio of Royal Air Force Mosquito aircraft that rushed over the prison, their bombs demolishing another part of the wall, wrecking the guards and Gestapo barracks and loosening the locked doors behind which hundreds of political prisoners, heroes of the French Resistance, were waiting.

Dazed by the explosions and covered in thick, choking dust, the prisoners prepared to make a break for freedom, for the word had been passed round the jail that R.A.F. bombers would try to blow the prison open at midday. That promise had been kept! Many of the political prisoners knew they were to be executed or transported to

FACTS ABOUT THE MOSQUITO...

Night fighter, bomber, pathfinder—the Mosquito was all of these

concentration camps, but what many of them did not realize was their sentences would have been carried out within the next forty-eight hours.

The raid was not a complete success. Many of the men and women who escaped were recaptured and a few were even killed by the very bombs that were meant to free them, for a stray one had ricocheted over the wall and hit a prison building. But two hundred of them stayed free, free to expose the Gestapo spies who had betrayed them, and free to prepare for the fighting that was going to take place on D-Day.

The noise of the explosions and aircraft engines brought people running from their houses near the prison. One Frenchman looked over the fields and saw a lone Mosquito, streaking low across the snow and being pursued by a German Focke-Wulf 190 with its nose and wings lit up by the flashes from its cannons and machine guns. Pieces flew off the Mosquito and suddenly it jerked and then nosed into the ground. So died Group Captain Charles Pickard, the leader of the daring raid, and with him Bill Broadley, the navigator who had refused promotion to continue flying with him.

The de Havilland Mosquito, one of the most beautiful aircraft ever to fly, was a potent weapon of the R.A.F. in the second World War, but it might never have flown if it had not been made of wood! The far-sighted design team received grudging permission to build the prototype only because it would not use up the precious metal needed to build aircraft already proven in battle.

Group Captain Charles Pickard, D.S.O. and two Bars, D.F.C.

The aircraft was fitted with two Rolls-Royce Merlin engines, the same engines used in the famous Spitfire fighter, and with these it was able to outstrip most enemy aircraft.

Initially designed as a bomber, the Mosquito was also used as a reconnaissance aircraft, as an intruder fighter and as a long-range night fighter which flew with the heavy bombers over Germany. It was also formed into special pathfinder squadrons that flew in at low-level and dropped flares to pin-point targets at night for the heavy bombers.

It was Mosquito aircraft that swept in at low-level to destroy the Gestapo headquarters in Oslo, Norway, and it was Mosquitoes that attacked Berlin deliberately to cause chaos and send running for shelter no less a person than Reichsmarschall Hermann Goering, Commander of the German air forces. Goering was furious and he ordered the immediate formation of a special squadron to hunt down Mosquitoes, but the most German pilots ever saw of the British aircraft was its tail rapidly disappearing into the distance!

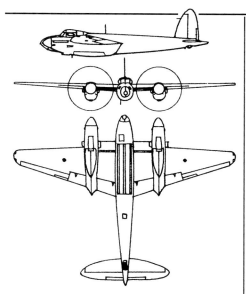

DE HAVILLAND MOSQUITO
(Bomber version)

ENGINES: Two Rolls-Royce Merlin, liquid cooled.
MAXIMUM SPEED: 400 miles per hour, approx.
WING SPAN: 54 feet 2 inches.
LENGTH: 40 feet 6 inches.
ARMAMENT: Maximum bomb load, 4,000 lbs.

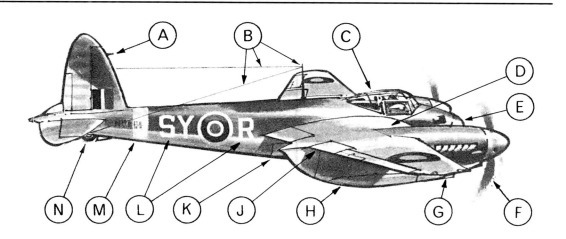

(A) Tail-mounted pitot head that operates the airspeed indicator. **(B)** Radio aerials and mast. **(C)** Pilot and navigator/bomb aimer sit side-by-side in the cockpit. Bomb aimer moves to the bomb sight in the perspex nose **(E)** during the attack. **(D)** Radiators for the engine-cooling liquid are buried in the leading edge of the wing. **(F)** Three-blade airscrew. **(G)** Air intake for oil-cooler. **(H)** Doors covering the retracting main undercarriage. **(J)** Landing flaps. **(K)** Bomb bay doors. Bombs or rockets were also carried under the wing. **(L)** Squadron and aircraft identifying letters. **(M)** Identification band and serial number of aircraft. **(N)** Retractable tail wheel.

SAINT PAUL'S
CATHEDRAL

Over thirteen centuries ago, on the site of the present St. Paul's Cathedral in London, Ethelbert, King of Kent, built a church dedicated to St. Paul. The first occupant of the Bishop's throne was Mellitus, who was consecrated by St. Augustine in the year 604. The Emperor Constantine had proclaimed Christianity as the State religion in the fourth century and it may be that there was a church (perhaps converted from a pagan temple) on this same site in Roman times.

For nearly seven hundred years this has been the Cathedral Seal of St. Paul's. It was made in silver in the year 1287 and is still in use today.

Bishop Erkenwald, whose tomb became a place of pilgrimage in the middle ages, rebuilt the Cathedral between 675 and 685. Throughout its history St. Paul's has often been destroyed or threatened with destruction by fire. In A.D. 962 it went up in flames when the whole of London was burned by the Viking raiders. Again in 1087, after the Norman conquest, the rebuilt Saxon church was destroyed by a great fire.

After a fire in 1087, Bishop Maurice decided to build a very great church indeed. Preparations alone took fifteen years. Much of the stone was shipped from Caen, in Normandy. Though delayed by another fire, the Choir section was completed by 1148. The spire was added in 1315 and the Chapter House in 1332. The total length of the Cathedral was 586 feet and the height of the spire 489 feet. This was eighty-five feet higher than Salisbury, completed in the year 1256.

On the north side of the present Cathedral, St. Paul's Cross marks the site of the old cross which was a great centre for open-air gatherings. Here, kings received homage, Papal Bulls were proclaimed, and amid a great crowd Cardinal Wolsey heard the Pope's condemnation of Luther. Here also many ecclesiastics preached sermons to the people of London.

From the fourteenth century the Nave, known as "Paul's Walk," was used for business purposes. The way between the North and South doors was used as a short cut even for those with mules and horses. After the Civil War the church became a cavalry barracks.

In 1561 the spire was struck by lightning and destroyed by fire. The efforts of five hundred citizens saved the Cathedral itself from destruction, but the spire was never rebuilt. During the reign of Charles II Christopher Wren produced plans for repairing the fabric, but in 1666 the Great Fire of London finally destroyed the whole of the Cathedral.

The Cathedral of today was not built to Wren's first design. Of the unused ones, the best is probably the one shown here. The original scale model of this design is kept in the Cathedral.

Perhaps the greatest feature of the Cathedral is the central Dome and Lantern. The heavy stone lantern is supported by an unseen brick cone beneath which is the internal painted dome. Outside the cone the exterior dome is built of lead on a timber framing. Wren strengthened his brick cone with iron chains, and in 1930 stainless steel chains were added and liquid concrete poured into the hollow piers supporting the inner dome.

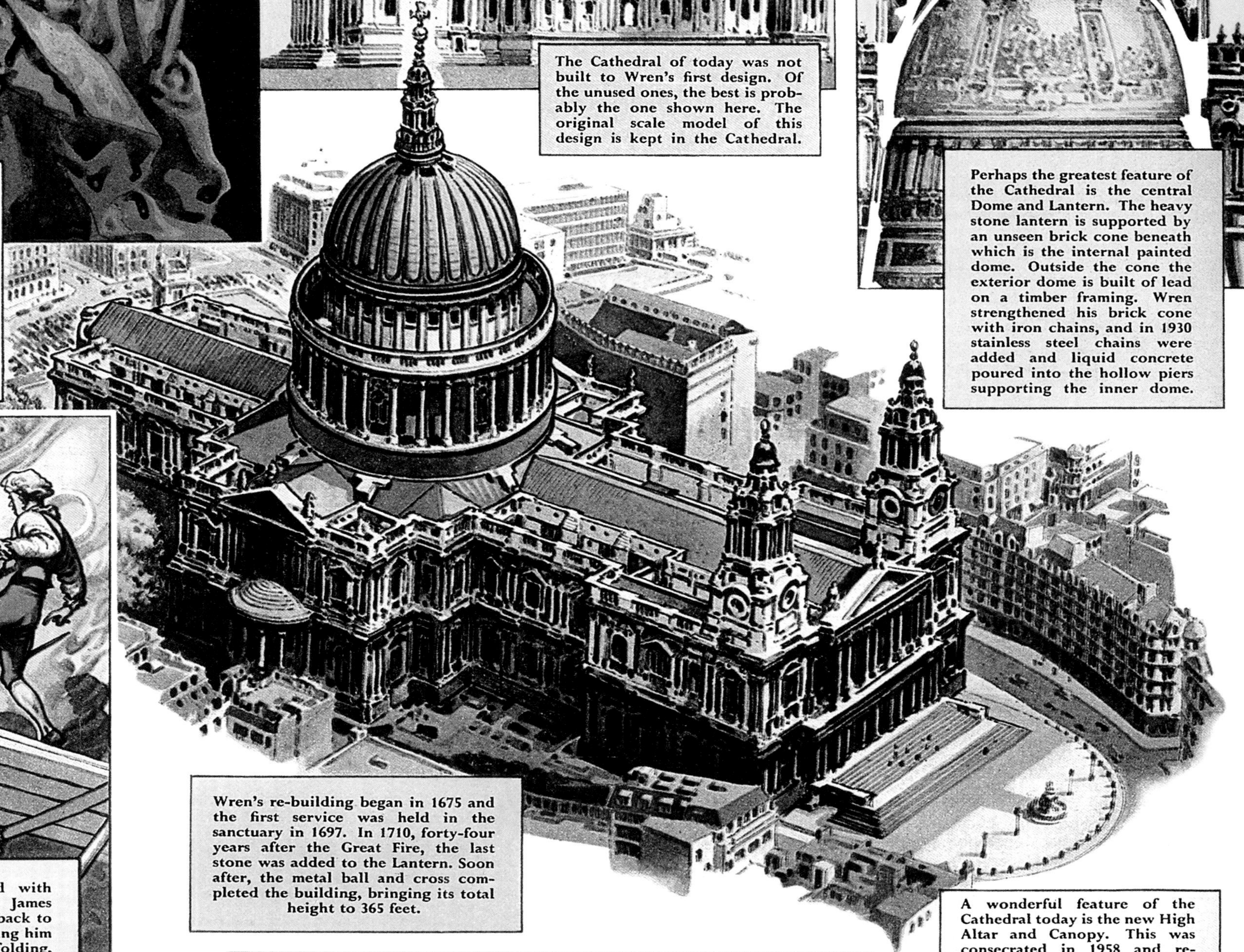

...ren was born ... of a Dean of ... designed the ..., as well as ... churches. In ... liked to sit ... the dome of ... uilding, but ... ese visits he ... nd died in a ... e at Hampton ... lived to the ... e, which was ... y rare

... dome is covered with ... paintings by Sir James ... e day he stepped back to ... His assistant, seeing him ... ling from the scaffolding, ... inting. Thornhill rushed ... nger, but the assistant ... ly saved his life.

Wren's re-building began in 1675 and the first service was held in the sanctuary in 1697. In 1710, forty-four years after the Great Fire, the last stone was added to the Lantern. Soon after, the metal ball and cross completed the building, bringing its total height to 365 feet.

A wonderful feature of the Cathedral today is the new High Altar and Canopy. This was consecrated in 1958 and replaced the marble altar and screen damaged by a bomb in 1941. Behind the Altar is the American Memorial Chapel.

...ed in his great church, and after him ...n were laid to rest there, including ...as buried in a casket (shown above), ... the body of Cardinal Wolsey. A ...t) to Wellington, the "Iron Duke," ...day in the body of the church.

This is one of the Cathedral's moments of glory and defiance. During a heavy incendiary raid on 29 December, 1940, the building was ringed by fire. It was damaged, and acres of buildings around were destroyed. But on the following morning the dome and twin towers, scarred and smoke begrimed, were seen still to be standing.

THE FARMER'S LIFE

NAPOLEON scathingly referred to the British as "A nation of shopkeepers"—he would have done better to say "a nation of farmers," for that is precisely what Britain has been for hundreds of years.

Today, despite the ever-decreasing numbers of people employed in agriculture, farming is still the nation's largest industry. On this page we show you how farmers have solved the labour problem by introducing more mechanization.

In contrast, the big picture on the right shows a typical farm of the eighteenth century. One of the first things to notice is the use of horses for all the heavy work: rolling, ploughing, harrowing and pulling the farm carts.

The men in the picture are doing jobs which today are the work of machines—hoeing (in the field behind the barn) and sowing (in the foreground).

The most complicated piece of machinery the farmer had was the mill (in the top right-hand corner of the picture) with which he ground his grain (and possibly that of his neighbours as well).

If the farmer of two hundred years ago visited a modern farm, what would he find? Great towers for storing grain or silage, cattle living in covered yards, poultry in rows of wire cages, young animals warmed by infra-red heaters—and the indispensable machinery, all colours, shapes and sizes, some of which are shown on this page.

Many modern ploughs are "mounted" on two arms on the tractor which are controlled hydraulically, so that the plough can be raised or lowered at will. A powerful wheeled tractor can pull a plough which turns four furrows at a time.

Scattering seed by hand is slow, wasteful and time-consuming. This seed drill can measure seed and place it directly in the furrows. Some drills also spread artificial fertilizer at the same time. The man on the back watches the seed in the drill.

The milk churn is out of date in a modern milking parlour. The milk goes straight into a measuring jar, and from there through pipes to a refrigerated bulk tank in the dairy for lorry collection.

Moving muck with a pitchfork is a long and tiring business. This foreloader is worked by the tractor's hydraulic system, and can also be used for earth-moving if a different bucket is fitted on the front.

This tanker combine harvests the grain, threshes it, and drops the straw at the back. The grain is stored in a tank and passed from there to a lorry or trailer through an auger, or grain lifter (on the right of the picture).

Straw or hay lying in a field is "parcelled" into bales by a pick-up baler, which compresses and separates it into equal blocks, ties these with twine, and tips the bales off the back for collection later.

Peas which are harvested for canning and deep-freezing must be processed as soon as possible. This experimental "pea-viner" sweeps up cut peas, shells them, and empties the peas into boxes.

Sugar-beet is harvested by means of this odd-looking machine which tops the green part, lifts the beet, and leaves the finished root crop to be picked up later. A tractor pulls the machine.

How to trim hedges without even stepping down from the tractor seat. This adjustable cutter-bar can cut the sides and tops of hedgerows with perfect ease. It is driven by power from the tractor.

After ploughing, fields are prepared for drilling. This set of discs, with a harrow behind, will "iron out" the furrows to make a seed-bed. Crawler tractors such as this one are used for very heavy work.

Space Probe

For centuries men have gazed at the mysterious objects in the night sky; now we have launched machines that will tell us more about our neighbours in space — the planets of the Solar System

THE Solar System is the Earth's home in space. Throughout history our ancestors have marvelled at the objects in the night sky, as many of us still do today. Back in the ancient past, the Sun and Moon, seemingly large and important, were worshipped as gods. The stars, appearing cold and remote, were less important, although many constellations (groups of stars) were given names suggested by their shapes — such as the Plough. And the starlike lights seen to move through the constellations were given the name *planets* — from the Greek for "wanderers" — and also worshipped as gods.

Today we know that the stars are other "suns", most incredibly remote from our planet Earth, at distances from which light rays travelling at almost 300,000 kilometres *each second* still take years, decades or centuries to reach Earthly eyes. The stars

CONTINUED ON NEXT PAGE

Man has been fascinated by the Sun, Moon and stars for thousands of years — we, the inhabitants of the "Space Age", no less than the early cavemen. We have used our celestial neighbours to help us tell the time, plant our crops, and find our way across the oceans. Now our machines have actually visited other planets in the Solar System, and may soon leave it to explore the endless realm of our Universe.

Pluto

Neptune

Uranus

Saturn

Our illustration shows the relative size of the planets that orbit the Sun in the Solar System, but is not to scale with regard to their distances apart. Jupiter is immense, with a mass nearly 2½ times that of all the other planets combined, and would house more than 1,300 Earths. But even this is completely outclassed by the Sun, which is roughly in the same proportion to Jupiter as Jupiter is to the Earth.

appear to be fixed in the sky only because they are so remote. All stars travel through space, but they have to move a long way over a long period of time before this becomes perceptible. In fact, we know that the constellations have distorted slightly since the time of Ancient Greece. And the planets — the wanderers — have continued to travel through the constellations because, as the Greeks suspected, they are not like the "fixed" stars.

Over a few nights we can observe the movement of several planets. They appear to shine, without the brightness of the Sun, but this is caused not by their own light but by the light they reflect from the Sun.

Our Moon also shines by reflected light. Actually very small in planetary terms, it looks so big and bright because it is very close to us, our nearest cosmic neighbour, at less than 400,000 kilometres from the Earth. The Moon orbits around our planet, tied by the pull of gravity, rather like a stone whirling round on a piece of string. Similarly, the Earth, or more accurately the combined Earth-Moon system, orbits around the Sun, like a runner treading endlessly round the same track.

The Sun is 150 million kilometres from the Earth, and the other eight planets within the Solar System track round it at different distances in their own orbits. But the planets are not all

alike; some are small and rocky, not unlike the Earth, while others are huge balls of gas. Several of the Solar System's planetary family have now been extensively studied, not only by astronomers using telescopes and other instruments, but also by space probes which have sent back dramatic and awe-inspiring pictures to Earth.

Astronomers believe that the Solar System was formed from a huge but localised cloud of gas in Space, which slowly collapsed under the pull of its own gravity. Most of the gas in the cloud was hydrogen — the simplest and most common element in the Universe — and much of this went into the central collapsing ball which was to become the Sun.

Only a little of the original material was left swirling around the young star. In these swirling rings, smaller bodies were formed as fragments of material collided and stuck together.

As the Sun became hotter and hotter, because of the nuclear reactions taking place at its core, the heat drove off lighter gases such as hydrogen and chemical compounds like methane and ammonia away from the inner region of the Solar System. Only balls of rock were left in comparative proximity of the Sun. *Mercury* is closest to it; it is a scorched, airless world only 4,880km in diameter, which travels once round the Sun every 88 days in an orbit ranging from

X marks the spot — the position of our Sun in the Galaxy. There are thought to be some 200,000 million stars in this disc-like system which is about 100,000 light years across and 10,000 light years thick. The Sun is about 30,000 light years off centre.

46 to 70 million km.

Venus is next, with a diameter of 12,104km, and a "year" that is 225 Earth-days long with an orbital distance of 108,210,000km from the Sun. Then comes our home in space, the planet *Earth*, just larger than Venus with a diameter of 12,742km, and an orbit that takes us round the Sun once every 365¼ days. The final member of the inner group of planets is *Mars*, with a diameter of 6,787km, and 227,941,000km from the Sun with an orbital period of 687 days.

Beyond Mars there is a belt of cosmic rubble — the asteroid belt — with pieces of rock ranging from the size of a grain of dust to that of a mountain. Some

astronomers now believe that this belt may represent the debris of a planet which failed to form. And beyond the asteroid belt lie four giant planets — where the heat from the Sun has never been enough to drive away all the gas that is their inheritance from the birth of the Solar System. *Jupiter*, containing over twice as much matter as all the other planets combined, is the giant of our Solar System and its volume is equal to over 1,300 Earths.

Next is *Saturn*, second only in size to Jupiter, with its famous ring system (but no longer unique, as the Voyager space probe discovered that Jupiter is also encircled by rings). Further out the cold worlds of *Uranus* and

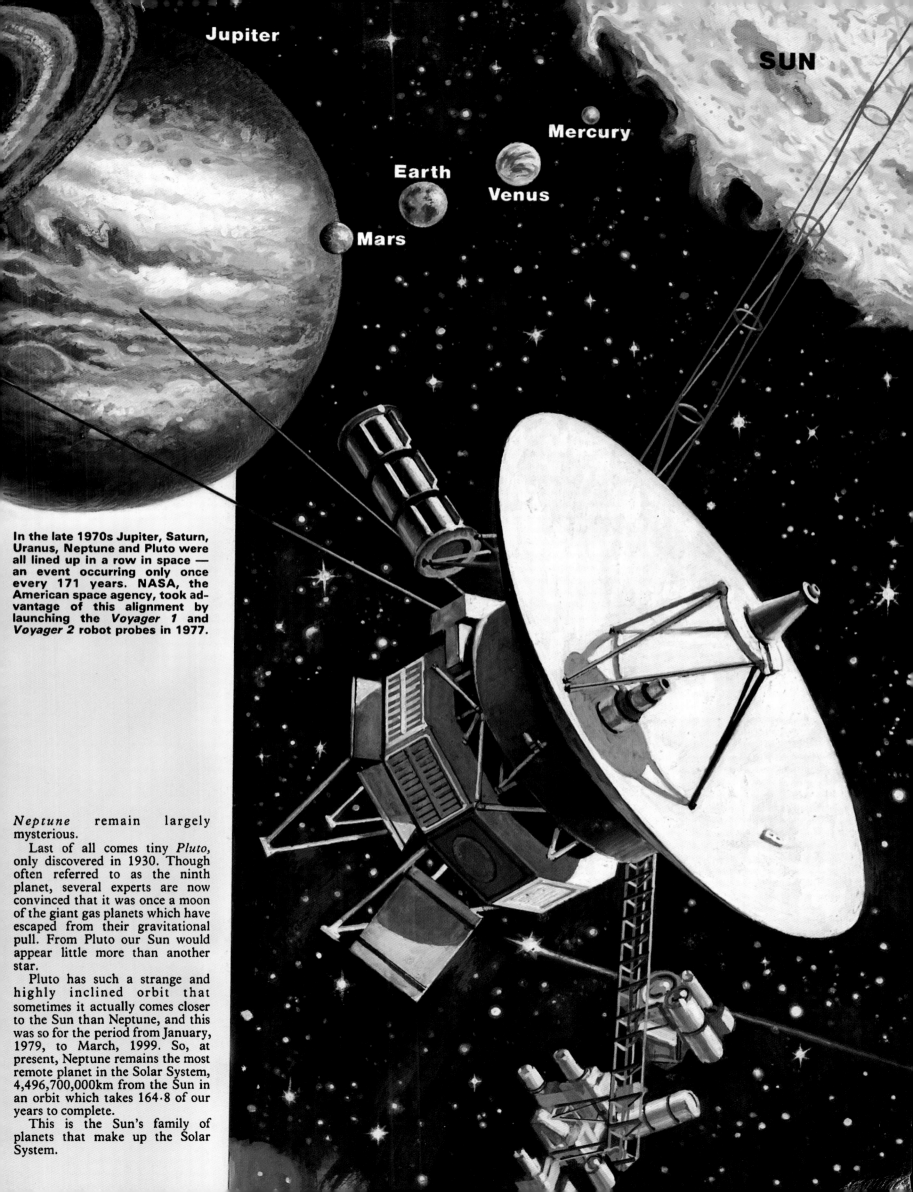

Jupiter

SUN

Mercury

Earth

Venus

Mars

In the late 1970s Jupiter, Saturn, Uranus, Neptune and Pluto were all lined up in a row in space — an event occurring only once every 171 years. NASA, the American space agency, took advantage of this alignment by launching the *Voyager 1* and *Voyager 2* robot probes in 1977.

Neptune remain largely mysterious.

Last of all comes tiny *Pluto*, only discovered in 1930. Though often referred to as the ninth planet, several experts are now convinced that it was once a moon of the giant gas planets which have escaped from their gravitational pull. From Pluto our Sun would appear little more than another star.

Pluto has such a strange and highly inclined orbit that sometimes it actually comes closer to the Sun than Neptune, and this was so for the period from January, 1979, to March, 1999. So, at present, Neptune remains the most remote planet in the Solar System, 4,496,700,000km from the Sun in an orbit which takes 164·8 of our years to complete.

This is the Sun's family of planets that make up the Solar System.

A PICTORIAL JOURNEY INTO THE FUTURE

1 Below Antarctica's snows technicians, kept warm within their walls of ice, gather weather data from space, from the polar winds and the surrounding seas and relay information to anywhere on earth. On the world map in front of them coloured lights trace the paths of weather reporting vehicles. Additional control consoles enable the operators to contact reporting stations throughout the world.

2 In an ice cavern on the sea bed drills probe for oil. In the background an atom-powered submarine-train passes and heads for the all-weather port on the shores of Antarctica. The submarine-train is equipped to tap a well, fill its tank cars, deliver the crude oil to a seashore refinery and return without surfacing, without being affected by storms or other surface disturbances.

3 The city of the future, over which looms the towers of the transport centre. Here is the terminus for passenger bus-trains, individual passenger vehicles and vertical take-off aircraft. From here, too, incoming motorists are directed by radio to areas where parking is available. A control system regulates all incoming traffic, reducing congestion to a minimum.

4 "Futurama" riders' view of the moon shows manned lunar crawlers making their way tortuously over the floors of canyons and up the sides of craters. Vehicles unlike anything seen on earth transport men and equipment on their exploratory travels. On the right is a control station for incoming spaceships, while the mountain range promises more adventures for the explorers.

1

2

3

4